Global Information Diffusion and Management in Contemporary Society

Zuopeng (Justin) Zhang
State University of New York at Plattsburgh, USA

A volume in the Advances in Knowledge Acquisition, Transfer, and Management (AKATM) Book Series

IGI Global
DISSEMINATOR OF KNOWLEDGE

Published in the United States of America by
IGI Global
Information Science Reference (an imprint of IGI Global)
701 E. Chocolate Avenue
Hershey PA, USA 17033
Tel: 717-533-8845
Fax: 717-533-8661
E-mail: cust@igi-global.com
Web site: http://www.igi-global.com

Library of Congress Cataloging-in-Publication Data

Names: Zhang, Zuopeng (Justin) 1973- editor.
Title: Global information diffusion and management in contemporary society / Zuopeng (Justin) Zhang, editor.
Description: Hershey, PA : Information Science Reference, [2018]
Identifiers: LCCN 2017042563| ISBN 9781522553939 (hardcover) | ISBN 9781522553946 (ebook)
Subjects: LCSH: Information technology--Management. | Knowledge management.
Classification: LCC HD30.2 G574 2018 | DDC 658.4/038--dc23 LC record available at https://lccn.loc.gov/2017042563

This book is published in the IGI Global book series Advances in Knowledge Acquisition, Transfer, and Management (AKATM) (ISSN: 2326-7607; eISSN: 2326-7615)

British Cataloguing in Publication Data
A Cataloguing in Publication record for this book is available from the British Library.

All work contributed to this book is new, previously-unpublished material.
The views expressed in this book are those of the authors, but not necessarily of the publisher.

For electronic access to this publication, please contact: eresources@igi-global.com.

Advances in Knowledge Acquisition, Transfer, and Management (AKATM) Book Series

ISSN:2326-7607
EISSN:2326-7615

Editor-in-Chief: Murray E. Jennex, San Diego State University, USA

MISSION

Organizations and businesses continue to utilize knowledge management practices in order to streamline processes and procedures. The emergence of web technologies has provided new methods of information usage and knowledge sharing.

The **Advances in Knowledge Acquisition, Transfer, and Management (AKATM) Book Series** brings together research on emerging technologies and their effect on information systems as well as the knowledge society. **AKATM** will provide researchers, students, practitioners, and industry leaders with research highlights surrounding the knowledge management discipline, including technology support issues and knowledge representation.

COVERAGE

- Cognitive Theories
- Cultural Impacts
- Information and Communication Systems
- Knowledge acquisition and transfer processes
- Knowledge management strategy
- Knowledge Sharing
- Organizational Learning
- Organizational Memory
- Small and Medium Enterprises
- Virtual communities

IGI Global is currently accepting manuscripts for publication within this series. To submit a proposal for a volume in this series, please contact our Acquisition Editors at Acquisitions@igi-global.com or visit: http://www.igi-global.com/publish/.

The Advances in Knowledge Acquisition, Transfer, and Management (AKATM) Book Series (ISSN 2326-7607) is published by IGI Global, 701 E. Chocolate Avenue, Hershey, PA 17033-1240, USA, www.igi-global.com. This series is composed of titles available for purchase individually; each title is edited to be contextually exclusive from any other title within the series. For pricing and ordering information please visit http://www.igi-global.com/book-series/advances-knowledge-acquisition-transfer-management/37159. Postmaster: Send all address changes to above address.

Titles in this Series

For a list of additional titles in this series, please visit:
https://www.igi-global.com/book-series/advances-knowledge-acquisition-transfer-management/37159

Contemporary Knowledge and Systems Science
W. B. Lee (Hong Kong Polytechnic University, China) and Farzad Sabetzadeh (Hong Kong Polytechnic University, China)
Information Science Reference • ©2018 • 340pp • H/C (ISBN: 9781522556558) • US $185.00

Enhancing Knowledge Discovery and Innovation in the Digital Era
Miltiadis D. Lytras (The American College of Greece, Greece) Linda Daniela (University of Latvia, Latvia) and Anna Visvizi (The American College of Greece, Greece)
Information Science Reference • ©2018 • 363pp • H/C (ISBN: 9781522541912) • US $215.00

N-ary Relations for Logical Analysis of Data and Knowledge
Boris Kulik (Russian Academy of Science, Russia) and Alexander Fridman (Russian Academy of Science, Russia)
Information Science Reference • ©2018 • 297pp • H/C (ISBN: 9781522527824) • US $225.00

Radical Reorganization of Existing Work Structures Through Digitalization
Punita Duhan (Meera Bai Institute of Technology, India) Komal Singh (Meera Bai Institute of Technology, India) and Rahul Verma (Bhai Parmanand Institute of Business Studies, India)
Business Science Reference • ©2018 • 287pp • H/C (ISBN: 9781522531913) • US $235.00

Maximizing Social Science Research Through Publicly Accessible Data Sets
S. Marshall Perry (Saint Mary's College of California, USA)
Information Science Reference • ©2018 • 328pp • H/C (ISBN: 9781522536161) • US $195.00

Promoting Interdisciplinarity in Knowledge Generation and Problem Solving
Mohammed Nasser Al-Suqri (Sultan Qaboos University, Oman) Abdullah Khamis Al-Kindi (Sultan Qaboos University, Oman) Salim Said AlKindi (Sultan Qaboos University, Oman) and Naifa Eid Saleem (Sultan Qaboos University, Oman)
Information Science Reference • ©2018 • 324pp • H/C (ISBN: 9781522538783) • US $195.00

For an entire list of titles in this series, please visit:
https://www.igi-global.com/book-series/advances-knowledge-acquisition-transfer-management/37159

IGI Global
DISSEMINATOR OF KNOWLEDGE

701 East Chocolate Avenue, Hershey, PA 17033, USA
Tel: 717-533-8845 x100 • Fax: 717-533-8661
E-Mail: cust@igi-global.com • www.igi-global.com

Table of Contents

Detailed Table of Contents

Information technologies have been deployed as a key competitive advantage by multinational and transnational businesses throughout the world. They have performed wonders for individuals, societies, and nations worldwide. Nevertheless, they have also generated numerous global issues. This chapter surveyed and discussed 10 of these issues: interruption of traditional business models, threats to privacy, cyberbullying, unethical behavior in the workplace in a digital world, undesirable impact of texting, new challenges of polling, online piracy, threats to national security, threats to human jobs, and obstacles to information technology innovations. Upon reading this chapter, the reader should be able to understand that every new technology has tradeoffs, and recognized issues lead to improvements and more innovations.

This chapter presents a glossary of business sustainability concepts. The business sustainability definitions have been subjected to an abstractive decomposition. The phrases and terms derived from the abstractive decomposition has been categorized into three types, and each answers the questions of why sustainability, how it could be achieved, and where it will lead the businesses. Concepts categorized under each of these questions are defined individually and described with contextual relevance and examples from literature or industry. The glossary has been presented with a logical order to supplement the table of phrases and concepts. This work is an extension of the work reported on defining business sustainability through an abstractive decomposition.

The extent to which a brand expresses and enhances one's identity is determined by the level of brand identification and this has a positive effect on word-of-mouth reports. Identification is often linked to the causes and aims of the organization; in instances where the organization is known to stand for a particular cause, consumers are likely to identify with the mission of the company and furthermore to demonstrate loyalty to its products. Drawing on the identity theory perspective, this chapter aims to examine the resistance to brand switching in the smartphone industry. The findings suggest that brand identifiers sometimes proactively generate negative word-of-mouth about brands that they do not identify with, especially after they are exposed to comparative advertising. Several insights regarding the literature on resistance to brand switching in the smartphones industry were identified, including conceptualizing social creativity. Suggestions are offered for future researchers, and implications for managerial practices on the study findings are provided.

This chapter is based on four case studies and the findings are based on three rounds of qualitative data coding. This study finds that the type of business benefits expected to be derived from an ERP upgrade project, and the similarities between a firm and a new ERP system business processes have a strong impact on an ERP upgrade decision. Strategic business benefit has a relatively high impact on the upgrade decision than the managerial and operational business benefits. In contrast, symbols attached to an ERP system and top management supports are not salient factors influencing the ERP upgrade decision. However, based on further analysis of the pattern-matching of cause-effect relationships tested in this study, this research suggests that top management supports are necessary but not a sufficient factor to justify for an ERP upgrade, when there are lack of strategic business benefit incentives and similarity between a firm and a new ERP system business processes. This also indicates that ERP upgrade decisions are made rationally rather than habitually and socially defined.

To support transformational business changes, IT must streamline the top-down process of new IT processes. In the ever-changing business world of today, no one knows what is around the corner, and to improve agility is the best way to organize to the test of the future. By defining IT maturity in your organization, you can map a route to successive levels of maturity and improved agility to reach a point where IT contributes to the execution, growth, and rapid transformation of the business. A successful IT service and asset management need to be efficient and agile to help transform from a traditional into a digital enterprise. In this chapter, the authors propose a global and practical strategic framework to improve ITSM service management processes with the additions of two drivers: agility control based on DevOps and security management based on SecOps.

Driven by the difficulty in achieving complete security with technical tools, business investigators are looking into organizational and behavioral issues that could help make systems more secure. This chapter looks at the security of systems from the organizational perspective. Specifically, this study attempts to identify if different organizations have different predisposition to particular type(s) of security threat sources. Using publicly available security breach data from a privacy rights clearinghouse to investigate which organizational characteristics predisposes an institution to an external or internal threat source, it was concluded that as size of organization and the number of its valuable documents increase by one unit, the organization's probability of suffering an internal attacks decrease. Furthermore, when executive members have a business degree rather than information-security-related degrees, the likelihood of suffering an internal attack increases. Also, the probability of an organization suffering an internal or external attack is not based on its industry type.

With the wide use of smartphones, mobile cyber has become an indispensable part of our lives. While smartphones are used almost every aspect of our lives, awareness of personal information protection is underdeveloped, and information leak has become one particular problem on mobile cyber. At the same time, personal information resources have become more valuable than ever. This chapter investigates users' attitudes toward cyber information leakage and methods to protect personal information. The software SPSS 19 was used to analysis the relationship among cyber environment, applicability and practicability of protection methods, economic cost, and overall evaluation (satisfaction). A suggestion that may promote personal information awareness and promote cyber security from technical, legal, and social aspects is also provided.

The rapid evolution of the communication technology started with the diffusion of information between connected computers to the present system in which voice, video, etc. are being exchange between systems. Driven by the global educational challenge in the twenty-first century, the Nigerian University Commission had stated that Nigerian university system will now go paperless as it has launched a portal called NUSMAP. The major set-back to the realization of the objectives of NUSMAP is that most Nigerian universities still handle their information system manually by using paper as a delivery vehicle. Some use the single management system. Other universities employ the LAN management model, where each department and/or unit has its own established management information system on the LAN. Very few universities use a campus network where departments/units can share information. In view of the above, the researchers propose a campus network that will be a modelled management information system for information diffusion and management in Nigerian universities.

The complexity of the environment and economical operation, tightly integrated with information and communication technologies, have challenged the management to adopt new paradigms and new approaches associated with new operating models. Internet of things, cloud computing, governance, and urbanism are some examples of new paradigms and new approaches in the area of information systems, which highlight the information as a basic resource for economic activity and justify the need to ensure appropriately the functions of production, storage, and distribution insofar as of its quality and availability depends on the effectiveness of corporate governance. This chapter, carried out by the European Club for Information Systems Governance in 2011 and 2012, provides evidence about the governance practices adopted in the area of information systems by large economic organizations in Portugal.

Preface

The world has been continuously evolving over the last decade. The fourth industrial revolution accompanied by the emerging paradigms of information technology (IT) and applications has resulted in the dramatic changes in many different industries, which has significantly transformed the ways for companies to reposition themselves to remain competitive in global markets. With the increasingly fierce global competition, there is an urgent need for companies to appropriately assess the value of their information and knowledge assets and use them effectively to achieve efficiency and competitiveness. Due to the importance of this subject, there is a growing demand for research on global information diffusion and management to provide insights on issues, challenges, and recommendations related to information resources management in the contemporary global society.

ORGANIZATION OF THE BOOK

This book presents 11 chapters submitted by contributors from nine different countries including Australia, China, India, Morocco, Nigeria, Portugal, Turkey, United Arab Emirates, United Kingdom, and United States of America, documenting their findings on the latest research and practice in global information diffusion and management in their countries. All contributors were invited to respond to two rounds of peer reviews. Emphasizing the importance of global information resources management in a different way, each chapter covers a broad range of topics related to information diffusions and management, such as data security, economics of information, enterprise systems, sustainability, marketing and word-of-mouth effect, mobile information leakage, IT agility, IT governance, social internet of vehicles (SIoV), and system implementation in higher education. Specifically, the book is organized as follows.

Chapter 1 reviews 10 contemporary global IT issues in terms of their issues, challenges, and opportunities.

Chapter 2 provides a glossary of business sustainability concepts from an information-management perspective.

Chapter 3 explores information diffusion problems by studying the negative word-of-mouth effect derived from consumers' resistance to brand switching in the smart-phone industry.

Chapter 4 analyzes decision-making for an ERP system upgrade.

Chapter 5 presents a strategic framework to improve the processes of IT service management and enable business transformations.

Chapter 6 investigates the vulnerabilities of different types of organizations to different sorts of data security threats.

Chapter 7 summarizes the latest challenges and trends of SIoV in countries of Gulf Cooperation Council.

Chapter 8 studies the information diffusion and management problems and their impact on a competitive labor market.

Chapter 9 examines issues of mobile information leakage and makes recommendations to promote people's awareness of mobile information protection.

Chapter 10 proposes a model of information systems to help address the challenges of information diffusions and management in the Nigerian University System.

Chapter 11 documents the IT governance practices of large organizations in Portugal.

CONTRIBUTIONS OF THE BOOK

In an era of technological explosion, innovations and information diffusions have been occurring in a faster speed than that can be embraced by people in the traditionally legal, social, or mental dimensions. While new technologies create many unprecedented opportunities, they have also posed many challenges for our societies; so, it is critically important for us to be aware of the issues resulted from new technologies so that our societies can move forward in harmony with them. The first chapter entitled "Global Issues of Information Technologies" surveys and discusses ten contemporary IT issues in the world including interruption of traditional business models, threats to privacy, cyber-bullying, unethical behavior in the workplace in a digital world, undesirable impact of texting, new challenges of polling, online piracy, threats to national security, threats to human jobs, and obstacles to information technology innovations. This chapter helps readers understand the tradeoffs of every new technology and recognize the issues and challenges that could lead to future improvements and innovations.

Although sustainability is a well-used and popular term, its use and interpretation often lack clarity. There is a considerable gap in the existing literature with respect to the definition of business sustainability in a holistic view. The chapter entitled "A Glossary of Business Sustainability Concepts" provides a glossary of business sustainability concepts from the perspective of information management. In particular, the chapter explores and derives various definitions of business sustainability through an abstractive decomposition methodology, and then classifies them into three types to address the following three fundamental questions: (1) why sustainability is important, (2) how sustainability could be achieved, and (3) where sustainability will lead businesses to. Based on examples from the existing literature and industrial practices, this chapter brings readers a comprehensive view of the landscape of business sustainability in different contexts.

Information diffusions play an important role in a global marketing context. Specifically, the word-of-mouth effect is closely related to the extent that a brand can express itself and establish its identify among all its stakeholders. From an identity theory perspective, the chapter entitled "Issues with the Importance of Branding, Brand Personality and Symbolic Meaning of Brands to the Consumer" investigates consumers' resistance to brand switching in the smart-phone industry and demonstrates that a negative word-of-mouth effect may be produced if the identifiers of a brand do not align with the brand itself, particularly when the brand is juxtaposed with others brands in advertisements. Contributing to the existing literature by providing insights on the resistance to brand switching in the smart-phones industry as well as the conceptualization of social creativity, this chapter lays a solid foundation for future researchers and provides valuable implications from managerial practices.

The success of system implementation and upgrade depends on many factors such as information flows, top management support, and users' participation. Based on four case studies and three rounds of qualitative data coding, the chapter entitled "Emergent Theory for Enterprise Resource Planning Upgrade Decision: A Multiple Case Study" explores the global information management issues in a system upgrade project. The chapter makes several significant findings to help decision-makers in need of an ERD system upgrade. For instance, the chapter identifies some crucial factors that may strongly influence an ERP system upgrade, such as the expected benefits and the new business processes that can be derived from the upgrade. In addition, strategic benefits influence more on the upgrade decisions than tactical and operational benefits. Overall, this chapter recommends that the support from top management is essential for an ERP system upgrade, but not the deciding factor, especially when there is no strategic benefit or new congruent business process that can be derived from the upgrade.

IT facilitates business transformation through streamlining top-down processes of implementing new technologies in organizations. To effectively deal with the challenges in today's volatile business world, organizations need to continuously improve their agility so as to adapt to the changing environments and remain competitive in a global market. Defining IT maturity allows an organization to develop a roadmap showing the levels of maturity and enhanced agility that the organization needs to reach successively at different points of its growth, where IT enables the entire process of business transformation through facilitating the assessment and adoption of new technologies. To help organizations transform from traditional to digital ones, the organizational IT service and asset management need to remain efficient and agile. Against this backdrop, the chapter entitled "Towards an Agile and Secure IT Service Management" develops a strategic framework to improve the processes of IT service management by incorporating two main drivers: Agility control based on DevOps and security management based on SecOps. The framework proposed by this chapter provides practical implications for global companies to facilitate their IT-enabled business transformations.

In the last decade, the increasingly complex nature of technologies has exacerbated the security problems of organizational systems. Companies are seeking innovative solutions using different robust methods to safeguard their cryptosystems. The chapter entitled "Data Security Threats Sources- An Empirical Examination of Institutional Characteristics" explores system security from an organizational perspective by studying if different types of organizations are vulnerable for different kinds of security threats. Analyzing publicly available security breach data, the chapter investigates some specific organizational characteristics that predispose an institution to an external or internal threat source and make some interesting findings. For instance, it was found that industry type is not a factor in deciding if an organization is more vulnerable for either internal or external threats. An organization is less vulnerable for internal threats when the organization's size and its number of valuable documents increase. However, an organization will be more likely to suffer from an internal attack if executive managers have business degrees rather than those related to information security.

The advent of Internet of Things (IoT) has further enhanced the ubiquity of the Internet, enabling the development of cutting-edge applications for connected objects. For instance, derived from both IoT and Intelligent Transportation Systems (ITS), the Internet of Vehicles (IoV) is an emerging paradigm that leverages the use of IoT applications for enabling the socialization among connected vehicles, which is commonly referred as the concept of Social Internet of Vehicles (SIoV). Examining SIoV from a GCC (Gulf Cooperation Council) perspective, the chapter entitled "Social Internet of Vehicles: A GCC (Gulf Cooperation Council) Perspective" summarizes the latest trends and challenges in GCC countries in the broader fields of IoT, IoV, and SIoV. This chapter provides some great insights about the opportunities that SIoV could bring to GCC countries, which sets a good example for other countries in the world.

In an increasingly globalized marketplace, information remains as one of the most important assets for organizations to be competitive. Studying the information problems in a global market, the chapter entitled "Information Problems in Competitive Markets and Their Impact on Labor Markets" indicates that a fully-informed economic agent can maximize her welfare through reducing the distortions of market information. Recent studies relax the assumption of an agent's full knowledge of market information in traditional economic literature and assume that market information is always distorted and asymmetric for individual players on the market. Furthermore, the problems of adverse selection and moral hazard cannot be completely eliminated due to information asymmetry. However, organizations can design, develop, and implement specific methods to better use their information and knowledge to reduce the effects from information asymmetry. The chapter discusses some useful approaches such as signaling and discrimination to help organizations achieve economic efficiency in a global market.

Due to the wide spread of smart-phones and other mobile devices, personal information resources on mobile cyberspace have become more valuable than over. However, personal information protection associated with mobile cyberspace has not received enough attentions. The chapter entitled "Mobile Cyber Information Leakage: Users' attitude and Information Protection Strategies" studies the attitudes of mobile users toward information leakage happening on mobile cyberspace in China and makes recommendations to protect people's mobile information resources. Specifically, the chapter analyzes mobile cyber environments in terms of the applicability and practicability of protection methods and their economic costs and then performs an overall evaluation of different methods. The chapter makes valuable suggestions to help promote the awareness of personal mobile information protection through exploring mobile cyber security from technical, legal, and social perspectives.

To effectively address the global educational challenges in the 21st century, the Nigerian University Commission states that Nigerian University System will take an initiative to become paperless through its recently launched portal called NUSMAP. To accomplish this primary objective of NUSMAP requires the Nigerian University System to overcome several major hurdles. For instance, most Nigerian universities still manually operate their information systems with paper as the only delivery mode. Although some universities have implemented a centralized management system, many others still employ the LAN management model in which each individual departments or units have their own specialized management information system on the LAN. Considering the needs of the Nigerian University System, the chapter entitled "A Modeled Management Information System for Information Diffusion and Management in Nigerian Universities" proposes a campus network serving as a modeled information system that can be used for all campuses in the Nigerian University System for effective information diffusions and management in the universities.

To ensure successful operations in global marketplaces, managers are constantly searching for viable approaches to innovatively utilizing information and communication technologies. The emerging paradigms such as IoT, Smart City, and Blockchains further highlight the importance of information as a crucial asset for ensuring the sustainable functions of organizations encompassing all the primary and supporting activities in a value chain. From the perspective of IT governance, the chapter entitled "Information Systems Governance: The Case of the Largest Companies in Portugal" documents the analysis carried out by the European Club for Information Systems Governance in 2011 and 2012. The chapter provides insightful evidence about the IT governance practices adopted by large economic organizations in Portugal.

Zuopeng (Justin) Zhang
State University of New York at Plattsburgh, USA

Acknowledgment

On behalf of all the contributors of this book, I am delighted to share this sampling of the latest research on global information diffusions and management with our readers and hope that this book will serve our readers as an avenue to gain a perspective on the recent challenges and development of global information recourse management research. Specially, I would like to thank the Director of Intellectual Property and Contracts, Ms. Jan Travers, and Assistant Development Editor, Ms. Jordan Tepper, for their encouragement and guidance throughout this endeavor. I am also deeply grateful to the individual reviewers who diligently worked with us. Without their time and efforts, this book would never have come to be.

Chapter 1
Global Issues of Information Technologies

Taowen Le
Weber State University, USA

ABSTRACT

Information technologies have been deployed as a key competitive advantage by multinational and transnational businesses throughout the world. They have performed wonders for individuals, societies, and nations worldwide. Nevertheless, they have also generated numerous global issues. This chapter surveyed and discussed 10 of these issues: interruption of traditional business models, threats to privacy, cyberbullying, unethical behavior in the workplace in a digital world, undesirable impact of texting, new challenges of polling, online piracy, threats to national security, threats to human jobs, and obstacles to information technology innovations. Upon reading this chapter, the reader should be able to understand that every new technology has tradeoffs, and recognized issues lead to improvements and more innovations.

INTRODUCTION

Information technology innovations and their widespread applications since 1980s have forever changed human lives and societies. Internet aided by more recent technological advancements such as mobile telecommunication, cloud computing, and big data mining have connected people throughout the world digitally and instantly. Information technology diffusions have brought enormous changes to public domains such as business, education, medicine, and government. More importantly, combined with new discoveries in various fields such as material science, healthcare,

DOI: 10.4018/978-1-5225-5393-9.ch001

and biology, information technology is bringing forth new realities at a pace never before experienced in human history.

As information technologies continue their diffusions throughout the world, people everywhere begin to enjoy and recognize the great convenience and benefits they bring, of which the following is but a small sample:

Business

Information technologies in the form of computer hardware and software were utilized in business organizations as early as in 1960s. Since then, nearly all business organizations in developed countries and many business organizations in developing countries have used some information technologies in their daily operations. They have been used not only for business and financial record keeping, but also for product design, process automation, market analysis, payment handling, supply chain management, organization management, and general decision support (Cron & Sobol, 1983; Stephens, 1999; Zuckerman, 2004; Attaran, 2004; Lu & Ramamurthy, 2011; Luftman et al, 2017).

Education

TV networks made government-managed TV universities possible in countries such as China in the 1980s. Non-interactive courses were broadcasted through TV networks to designated locations. With the design of EdNet (Education Networks), Internet-based distant education first became available in countries such as the United States in the 1990s. Interactive courses taught on one campus could be attended by students at various satellite campuses. Today, online education programs have benefited students of every level throughout the world. The seemingly unlimited information resources are often a few clicks away. The great wealth of knowledge is presented in many different ways and made available not only to students, but also to everyone else, making learning possible and relatively easy for all in the world (Greenhow et al, 2009).

Healthcare

Like in other fields, information technologies have brought innumerable advances in healthcare, which have enabled medical personnel to provide patients with more accurate diagnoses and more effective treatments. Some of the best known include Computerized Axial Tomography (CAT), special X-ray tests that produce cross-sectional images of the body using X-rays and a computer (Davis 2016), Magnetic Resonance Imaging (MRI), a noninvasive medical test that uses a powerful magnetic field, radio frequency pulses, and a computer to produce detailed pictures of organs, soft tissues, bone, and virtually all other internal body structures (RadiologyInfo.org, 2017), and heart bypass surgery which creates a new route, called a bypass, for blood and oxygen to reach the heart, without opening the chest or stopping the heart. More recent technologies include 3D visualization and augmented reality for surgery, interoperability solutions for exchanging patient information across care settings, robotic nurse assistant, remote patient monitoring, and anti-aging drugs, tooth regeneration (Coutre, 2016; Govette, 2016).

Government

E-government has enabled governments throughout the world to provide more convenient and effective services to citizens and residents. Hundreds of services which traditionally require physical presence of people are now available to people without geographical or time constraints. Big data technologies have enabled governments to more accurately analyze problems and implement more effective measures or procedures to tackle them. Public benefits include and certainly are not limited to more effective traffic control, poverty relief, public security system, and natural disaster prevention (Welch et al, 2004; Klamo et al, 2006; Sneada & Wright, 2014).

Communication and Socialization

Modern telecommunication technologies have made communication and socialization not only easier and cheaper, but also more instant. Video conferencing has provided a very convenient platform for people across the global to meet "face-to-face." Popular social networking sites such as Facebook, Twitter, WeChat, LinkedIn, Google+, YouTube, Instagram, Pinterest, Tumblr, Snapchat, Reddit, Flickr, Swarm by Foursquare, Kik, and Shots have enabled families, communities, and people throughout the world to stay connected (Boyd & Ellison, 2007; Bolton et at, 2013; Greenhow & Askari, 2017).

Indeed, information technologies have impacted just about everyone in the world; they create problems at the same time as they bless lives. While it was impractical to discuss in one chapter all issues pertaining to information technologies, this chapter will sample ten of them. There has been neither a book nor a journal article that has specifically discussed all these issues. While some of the problems discussed in this chapter might seem obvious to IT professionals, they are not always so apparent to the general public. It is important that the general public be educated about the pros and cons of new information technologies so that they could look at the new technologies from the proper perspectives and strive to maximize the benefits while minimizing the associated consequences.

Discussions of this chapter will be organized around important dimensions of society rather than of computing. Economy, community, politics, and culture will be considered broadly. Specifically, this chapter will examine the following global issues of information technologies:

- Interruption of Traditional Business Models
- Threats to Privacy in a Digital World
- Cyberbullying
- Unethical Behavior in the Workplace in a Digital World
- Undesirable Impact of Texting
- New Challenges of Polling
- Online Piracy
- Threats to National Security
- Threats to Human Jobs
- Obstacles to Information Technology Innovations

INTERRUPTION OF TRADITIONAL BUSINESS MODELS

The disruptive nature of information technologies has been long recognized. In a study published in 2003, Lyytinen and Rose conclude that the adoption of Internet computing in firms has radically impacted their IT innovation both in development processes and services (Lyytinen & Rose, 2003).

A company's business model, simply put, is a framework for revenue generations. It is defined by its revenue source, products or services to offer, pricing strategies, and targeted customer groups. Prior to the diffusion of Internet technologies to the commercial sector, businesses throughout the world basically followed the model of direct sales of products or services. Although there were many variations in practice, revenues were typically generated from these products or services, and business competitions were usually more recognizable and manageable because they were typically local.

The diffusion of Internet technologies, especially the availability of faster Internet connectivity and various online tools, brought forth the era of E-commerce. E-commerce offers many great advantages to businesses and customers. Businesses enjoy lower operational costs and a virtually-unlimited customer base. Physical company set-ups are no longer mandatory, and it is much easier to start and manage a business. Customers could now easily locate, compare, and acquire products without having to travel from store to store. They are no longer constrained by geographical or time limitations.

However, there are serious trade-offs with E-commerce. Businesses now face much wider and greater competitions. Competitions are no longer local or within the country, but global. The greater availability of similar products or services combined with limited face-to-face interactions between businesses and customers result in lesser customer loyalty. Moreover, many hackers target at businesses, and information security becomes a serious challenge for many businesses. For customers, there is little guarantee of product quality, and since it is easier to start a business, many not-so-great businesses have emerged to mislead customers and swallowed up customers' savings. Online registration and online payment processes present equally-challenging security risks for customers.

Aside from these disadvantages of E-commerce which have been globally recognized and accepted, information technologies have also interrupted the traditional business models by fostering new competing models. While numerous such models have emerged, this chapter will examine two unique and major models, the Google model and the Amazon model, as illustrations of interruptions to traditional business models:

The Google Model: Making Money by Giving Away Service for Free

In the minds of most people, Google is a search site or search engine whose primary service is web searching. Users need no registration to use Google, and the information search service from Google is free. However, Google seems to be doing very well financially. So where do Google's financial profits come from, and how does Google generate its revenues?

The need for knowledge and information exists everywhere and in everyone. However, Google does not really create the needed knowledge and information; instead it directs or redirects the user to sources or websites where the needed information is presented. Using an advanced ranking algorithm known as PageRank, Google directs users to relevant information sources or websites instantly.

For Google, the merchandise of the information economy is not information; it is attention. These commodities have an inverse relationship. When information is cheap, attention becomes expensive. Attention is what users give to Google and what Google sells to advertisers. Google's business is not searching but advertising. More than 96 percent of its $29 billion in revenue in 2010 came directly from advertising, and most of the rest came from advertising-related services. Google makes more from advertising than all the nation's newspapers combined. As Google sees it, positive user feedback in the form of user clicks, comments, and purchases help advertisers make more effective ads and provide users greater satisfaction in clicking the ads, while punishing noise and spam. Therefore, Google believes that advertising should not be a binary transaction between publisher and advertiser, but a three-way relationship that also includes the user (Gleick, 2011).

Few users have realized that as they use Google, Google captures, records, and analyses their clicks, their opening of each webpage, the length of time each page staying open, the ads they click, and any additional links they follow. Such information collectively formulates users' attention or preferences. Therefore, users "pay" to use Google through the sale of their attention or preferences.

Google's unique business model or revenue generation mechanism along with its impressive financial successes has caused many traditional businesses to seek new ways to stay profitable.

The Amazon Model: Online Total Retail

One of the earliest E-commerce companies is Amazon. It was founded in 1994 and brought online in 1995 as Amazon.com. The company began as an online bookstore and sold to all 50 states and over 45 countries in the first two months of business (Hartmans, 2017). While the largest brick and mortar bookstores and mail order catalogs might offer 200,000 titles, Amazon could "carry" several times more, since it would have a practically unlimited virtual warehouse: those of the actual product makers or suppliers (Erb & James, 2017, p265). Today, Amazon has diversified to sell music, videos, software, video games, electronics, apparel, furniture, food, toys, and jewelry. During the past 22 years, Amazon has moved into one adjacent area after another and then built them into thriving franchises. It was regarded as the most innovative company in 2017 (Robischon, 2017).

Amazon has also utilized new information technologies such as lines of robots in their fulfillment centers to provide customers with speedy order fulfillments and deliveries. Amazon's increasing dominance is now less about what it sells than how it sells. And that portends a second wave of change that will further devastate competitors and transform retail again. Amazon programs such as AmazonFresh are viewed by some as Amazon's last mile quest for total retail domination (McConvey, 2013).

The Amazon business model of online total retail is another technology-intensive successful model. It has greatly challenged retailers throughout the world. While numerous smaller retailers have already been forced out of business, many larger retailers are also pressured to rethink the sustainability of their bricks-and-mortar business models.

THREATS TO PRIVACY IN A DIGITAL WORLD

To many people, security and privacy seem to go hand in hand. Better-protected privacy means greater personal security. However, security and privacy could also become a paradox. As the world becomes more turbulent and chaotic, citizens and residents desire greater protection or security from their governments. To provide greater public security, governments collect more private and sensitive data from citizens and residents. In a digital world where information security is constantly threatened, government databases that stores vast amounts of citizen and resident information remain popular targets for hackers throughout the world.

In addition to government organizations, business organizations such as utility companies and healthcare providers also collect and maintain great volumes of information about their customers. Prior to the digital age, the physical nature of customer information files and the limited potential for information spreading did not cause too many people to worry. However, diffusions of modern information technologies are eliminating barriers that used to protect customers' information and privacy. With the availability of modern database and network technologies, customer data now exists in digital format, and any security leakage could lead to immediate and unlimited information spreading.

Of particular concerns are the many information service providers such as Google, Baidu, and Youtube. They provide seemingly free services to Customers such as website searching or video uploading and downloading, yet they not only electronically track and record every action users perform while using their services, but also install software such as cookies to user devices to track user behaviors on the network. As people walk on a dirt road leaving footsteps, their online activities including searching, purchases, reading, watching, writing, and communication leave digital traces which are targets of collection, storage, analyses, and manipulation by these companies.

Social media websites such as Facebook have also caused privacy concerns. As described by Tom Simonite, Facebook has implemented numerous technologies to capture everyone's every relationship with objects, organizations, and each other. Facebook not only gathers data from user profiles which contain age, gender, e-mail address, relationship status, mobile telephone numbers, historical information such as places users have lived and worked, but also collect user photos shared on the site as they are often tagged with a precise location. Facebook also tracks user activity elsewhere on the Internet, using the "Like" button. The button appears on apps and websites outside Facebook and allures people to reveal their interests in brands, products, or digital contents with a simple click. Moreover, Facebook also automatically collects data on users' online lives outside Facebook's borders: in certain apps or websites, when users listen to a song or read an article, the information is passed along to Facebook, even though the user does not click "Like." Combining such information with a map of social connections users make on Facebook website, Facebook has an incredibly rich record of users' lives and interactions (Simonite, 2012).

Concerned customers and users naturally turn to the government for remedies. They pressure their governments to enact more and tighter laws and regulations to protect their privacy. However, two potential problems exist.

First, the world consists of many countries, and each country is deeply influenced by a unique set of cultures and beliefs. Government regulations in one country might not be applicable to others. Take Google for example, Google is a U.S.-based company whose primary service to the public is free website searching. In the United States, freedom of speech is so highly valued that it seems to surpass both rights to privacy and societal harmony. Thus, no filtering or censorship exists with Google in the U.S. However, Google faced difficulties both in China and Europe a few years ago. China, with a recorded history of five thousand years, highly values societal harmony. In the Chinese culture, people value societal harmony more than personal freedom, and they are willing to sacrifice certain personal freedom for the greater good of societal peace and harmony. Therefore, when China's national government demanded Google in China to place certain filters against search results that would likely cause social disturbances or challenge moral standards in China, people in China supported the government with great understanding.

In Europe, people seem to value privacy more than freedom of speech. For Europeans, privacy is a fundamental right to all residents. They believe that everyone has the right to respect for his private and family life, his home and his correspondence. In January 2011, the European Commission made a legislative proposal on the right to be forgotten, empowering every European resident the right to force Web companies as well as offline firms to delete or remove their data to preserve their privacy (Whittaker, 2013).

Secondly, even in one single country, government regulations might not be the ultimate solution. In the U.S., for example, many people feel that the Congress has been less than effective in enacting appropriate laws. While laws tend to pass slowly, technology moves quickly (Thompson, 2012).

Realistically, the best privacy protection governments could provide for citizens and residents might be (1) educating users about the risks of the digital world, (2) encouraging users to exercise self-control in the digital world, and (3) requiring service providers to provide explanation of how they utilize user information.

Regardless of what governments throughout the world would do, privacy will remain a vital concern.

CYBERBULLYING

Modern information technologies have fundamentally changed the way people interact or relate with each other. Along with this change emerges the unfortunate issue of cyberbullying. While bullying has never been extinct from the world, the virtual digital space afforded by modern information technologies seems to have added an additional dimension to bullying, which may be referred to as cyberbullying. As more and more younger people become users of modern mobile devices such as iPhones or smart phones, cyberbullying is becoming an increasingly serious challenge for nations worldwide.

For the purpose of this discussion, *cyberbullying* refers to bullying behavior carried out through Internet service such as e-mails, chat rooms, discussion groups, online social networking, instant messaging, or web pages. Cyberbullying behaviors include but are not limited to sending malicious emails and texts, spreading rumors via email or social media sites, posting defamatory comments, photos, or videos online, setting up fake profiles to launch cyberattacks on others, and other harassment offenses (NoBullying.com, 2017).

The following statistics about cyberbullying in the U.S. as reported by the National Crime Prevention Center, i-SAFE inc., the Cyberbullying Research Center, knowthenet.org.uk, the Hartford County Examiner, Cyberbulling.us, the American Osteopathic Association, Ipsos (the global research association for Reuters) News, Bitdefender and Covenant Eyes help portray the seriousness of cyberbullying in the world today (GuardChild.com, 2017):

- Over 50% of adolescents and teens have been cyberbullied; about the same percentage have engaged in cyberbullying acts
- Over 25% of adolescents and teens have been cyberbullied repeatedly through their cell phones or the Internet
- 88% of teens using social media have seen others cyberbullied on a social media site
- The most common type of cyberbullying is mean, hurtful comments and rumor spreading
- Of those cyberbullied, 87% reported occurrence on Facebook, 19% on Twitter, and 13% on BlackBerry messenger
- The most frequent locations where cyberbullying occurs are chat rooms, social media sites, email, and instant messaging
- All races are impacted by cyberbullying

Damages from cyberbullying are more real and profound than many might realize. The vicious nature of cyberbullying and its extensive reach make it much more treacherous than bullying in person. While seasoned adults are more capable of withstanding cyberbullying, younger people are particularly vulnerable and susceptible to psychological and physical damages of cyberbullying. These damages include not only embarrassments and depression, but also losses of interest in school, changes of life course, and even suicides.

It is possible that cyberbullying might occur more frequently in the U.S. than in some other countries because the U.S. culture deeply roots itself in freedom of speech, and some might mistake such freedom as saying whatever they want. However, cyberbullying is a wide-spread problem throughout the world and is causing damages worldwide. How might such damages be minimized if not altogether eliminated? While different people might suggest different preventive measures, two are particularly attention-worthy: (1) timely reporting to proper authorities or sharing with family members or friends, and (2) timely giving appropriate guidance to students, children, or friends who have experienced cyberbullying.

It has been reported that the in the U.S., only a small percentage of cyberbullying victims would reveal to proper authorities or share with others, and considering that over 50% of adolescents and teens have experienced cyberbullying, a much smaller percentage of parents are aware that their children have been cyberbullied (GuardChild.com, 2017):

- Only 16% parents know their child has been cyberbullied
- Only 12% parents say their child has experienced cyberbullying
- Over 50% of young people do not tell their parents about their being cyberbullied
- Only 10% of cyberbullied kids tell parents about the incident
- 60% of teens never reported the problem to relevant social media website
- Less than 20% of cyberbullying incidents were reported to law enforcement
- Only 1% of teenagers would consider telling a teacher as their first response to cyberbullying

It is not difficult to imagine that if people are not reporting cyberbullying sufficiently in the U.S. where people are generally outspoken, the percentage of incident reporting would be even lower in countries where people are generally more conservative and timid.

While prevention and management efforts might be necessary at multiple levels involving adolescents, parents, teachers, and health care professionals, parents play a particularly important role. Experts believe that parents should not only monitor their children's activities online and on social media, but also ask pressing questions about how things are going at school and with friends (Dotinga, 2015).

Equally important is proper education. Parents and teachers need to communicate to young people that they genuinely care about them and stand ready to support them. To encourage victim reporting, Internet service providers should not only implement and enforce rules governing the use of their services, but should also provide easy, friendly, and encouraging reporting mechanisms for potential victims to report their incidents.

Upon learning about cyberbullying incidents, parents and teachers should offer victims timely and appropriate counsel and guidance on how to cope with the incidents. Internet service providers could also offer easy-to-notice and easy-to-access counsel and guidance to potential victims of cyberbullying.

UNETHICAL BEHAVIOR IN THE WORKPLACE IN A DIGITAL WORLD

Unethical behaviors in the workplace have always existed. Some scholars regard them as deviant workplace behaviors and suggest that they vary along two dimensions: minor versus serious, and interpersonal versus organizational. On the basis of these two dimensions, they classify unethical workplace behaviors into four categories: production deviance, property deviance, political deviance, and personal aggression (Robinson & Bennett, 1995). A more recent study classifies unethical workplace behaviors in relevance to financiers, customers, employees, suppliers, and society (Kaptein, 2008).

According to a recent report by the Ethics Resource Center (ERC) in the U.S., each day roughly 120 million people walk into a workplace somewhere in the United States, and almost half of them personally witnessed some form of ethical misconduct during a one-year time period. The five types of most frequently observed unethical behaviors in the U.S. workplace are (1) misusing company time, (2) abusive behavior, (3) employee theft, (4) lying to employees, and (5) violating company Internet policies (Schwartz, 2015).

Although the first four types are nothing new, the diffusion of information technologies or a digital world has made them more complicated and more difficult to control. The fifth type is a direct byproduct of the digital world.

Misusing Company Time

Companies pay employees to do companies' work. Typical traditional violations might include lengthy work-irrelevant conversations with fellow employees, making personal phone calls during work hours, and running personal errands on company time. Such violations are generally noticeable and easy to catch and control. However, in the digital world, personal messaging (email or instant messaging) could be easily covered, surfing the web for personal reasons could be easily disguised, and personal errands could be easily conducted online during work hours.

Abusive Behavior

Traditionally, certain employees might abuse their position and power to mistreat others through unkind or improper words or deeds. However, the abused employees would know who the abusers are, and the abusers might feel the pressure of potential lawsuits. In a digital world, however, certain abuses could be easily committed anonymously. Some people might argue that the awareness that all digital behaviors leave traces may cause abusers to think twice before committing abuses, the fact that few have been actually caught encourages abusive behavior in the workplace as well.

Employee Theft

Traditionally, employee thefts would occur in the form of shoplifting, check tampering, hiding sales in order to skim, or manipulating expense reimbursements. Although the problems might be serious, the good-and-old practice of segregation of duties (with duty to authorize, duty to keep physical goods, and duty to keep records respectively resting on different individuals) makes employee thefts relatively easy to detect. However, in a digital world, any employee who obtains certain "inside" information could invade the company's information systems and "exercise" the power of all three duties, authorizing the transferring of company goods or resources and forging transaction records difficult to track.

Lying to Employees

Traditionally, employers might lie to employees about earning expectations, personnel changes, competitions, salaries, or certain transactions. However, most of such lies could be discovered by employees afterwards. In a digital world, employers could easily gather enough "supporting" evidences from the practically unlimited resources of data and information available from the Internet and patch up "truthful" lies. Employers could also easily manipulate or mislead public opinions about certain issues, products, or policies.

Violating Company Internet Policies

Nearly all companies in the U.S. and many companies worldwide provide Internet access in the workplace. However, Internet access is provided for the benefit of company work, not personal enjoyment or fulfillment. Yet the digital world is a tempting place; it is full of websites to browse, movies to watch, and games to play. Many employees fail to withstand these temptations and engage themselves in Internet activities unrelated to company work.

In addition to the above five types of unethical workplace behaviors, the following types of unethical workplace behaviors are also intensified by the digital world:

Disclosing Confidential Information

Keeping business secretes such as funding strategies, pricing models, design specifications, or product formulas is extremely important for companies as they strive to survive and thrive in a world of competition. It is unethical for employees to disadvantage their companies by disclosing their companies' confidential information. However, the modern communication platforms and channels of the digital world make it extremely easy to disclose confidential information anonymously and make such disclosures very difficult to track or prosecute.

Stealing Others' Work

The World Wide Web is a giant sea of knowledge and carries the work of millions of authors, scientists, engineers, and other intellectual contributors. Search engines such as Google and Bing empower Internet users with the capability to find and tap into such tremendous resources in a matter of seconds; however, together with word processing and imaging tools, they also make it extremely easy for people to steal others' ideas, thoughts, and work.

UNDESIRABLE IMPACT OF TEXTING

Texting has significantly changed the way of communication, especially among those of the younger generations. While teenagers were the first to embrace texting, texting has also established popularity among adults and elementary school children, who are texting much more frequently than before. No doubt texting offers numerous advantages compared with traditional ways of communication.

More Concise Communication

Although texting allows lengthy paragraphs, it is designed to encourage shorter messages. Therefore, one or two-sentence ideas and thoughts are more common.

Minimum Disturbance to People Around

Meetings or event proceedings could be annoyingly disturbed by ringing phones and by people making or answering phone calls. However, text messages could enter or leave the room quietly and quickly, minimizing interruptions to others around.

Quicker Turnarounds

Texting is immediate, and recipients do not expect formality with texting, making exchanges of messages or ideas more immediate.

Higher Response Rate

Texting enjoys a higher response rate than telephone calls and email messages. People hesitate to take telephone calls not only because of inconvenience but also because of not knowing what to expect. Responding to email messages takes greater efforts, and many email messages easily get buried in junk mail. With texting, however, recipients know what to expect, and texting takes little effort.

Better Decisions

Telephone calls carry surprises. Some of these surprises require people to make important real-time decisions, such as one from an automobile shop that is repairing someone's only car. In such situations, people usually must make immediate decisions in the absence of sufficient information or knowledge. Texting, however, allows people the opportunity to make off-line decisions, and during the off-line time, people could do needed research or investigation which would enable them to make better-informed and wiser decisions.

Excellent Icebreakers

People of timid personalities might not likely engage in face-to-face communications. Even when they speak, their participation would be brief. However, texting help lesson any embarrassment they might feel and will likely engage them through longer conversations.

Easier Records

Most people do not take notes or record conversations during telephone calls. Therefore, it is easy to forget content of conversations, especially details such as numbers, dates, and locations. However, with texting, everything is in record form as long as it is not deleted.

Cleaner Communication

Because messages in texting can be kept by recipients as proofs and because it takes little effort to formulate decent messages because of their briefness, people generally use cleaner wording or language while texting.

Despite the many advantages texting offers, its undesirable impact should not be ignored. The following are just a few identifications of such impact:

Development of Discomfort With Face-to-Face Communication

Longtime users who depend on texting as primary means of communication may become uncomfortable with face-to-face communication. This could be particularly true for younger people since they have not established or solidified their face-to-face communication skills. The reason that young people are often found texting to each other in the same room may very well be that they are uncomfortable with face-to-face communication.

Easy Misunderstanding

Unlike in-person communication, texting does not offer the benefit of facial expressions, speech tongues, voice volumes, and body gestures. Even though there are smiley faces to aid the texting process, the accuracy of communication in texting is not comparable to that in face-to-face communication, and texting could easily result in misunderstanding.

Increased Distraction From Work

Texting seems so brief and harmless that people send to each other without much consideration of where the recipients might be or what they might be doing. As a result, people receive more text messages than they used to receive telephone calls. Driven by a natural urge to read and respond, people at work and students in the classroom become more easily and more frequently distracted from work on hand.

Difficult In-Depth Communication

Texting can be ineffective or awkward when complex or technical issues are discussed or when discussion requires high-frequencies of interactive diagnoses or analyses.

Short bursts of phrases common in texting encourage superficial conversations, but are insufficient for in-depth communication.

Limited Message Size

Texting programs typically impose a size limit on messages, and longer messages usually result in confirmation procedures which require senders to approve the splitting of the message into multiple smaller messages. Consequently, most texting users choose writing shorter and less descriptive messages instead of longer and more expressive messages.

Deterioration of Proper Language Usages

Most people do not follow proper grammar or practice proper language usage while texting. Longtime texting will likely develop and fortify incorrect language usage habits. Some people might argue that language is a means of communication; just as language usages of one hundred years ago replaced certain language usages of one thousand years ago, why should not popular language usages today replace some languages usages of yesterday?

Development of Impatience

People might be slow to respond to a telephone call or email message, but they seem more responsive to text messages. Overtime, such immediate texting turnarounds could develop greater impatience in people and promote people's expectation of immediate gratification of their requests or desires. This could result in serious challenges for societies and for the world, as impulsive and impatient members of the world are causing increasingly greater damages to societies and the world already.

Uninterrupted Intrusion

With traditional means of communication, there is a possible hideout for people. In the absence of emergency, telephone callers usually restrain from telephoning after certain hours, and people traveling could setup message systems to handle incoming phone calls. However, texting can be so brief and quiet that people feel no geographical or time constraints sending texts.

Disastrous Driving

Numberless tragedies involving texting while driving have been reported by television stations, newspapers, news websites, or Internet in general. Drivers might think reading or sending a text message takes only a brief moment; however, too many variables and unknowns exist on the road to allow distractions from the road, even just a brief moment.

With its advantages and disadvantages, texting is becoming widely adopted as a new way of communication in business, education, and government organizations. For example, a growing number of HR departments are using it for talent searches. However, while texting can improve the candidate experience and speed up the process when handled properly, many firms do not have the infrastructure or resources to implement a centralized texting platform, integrated solution, or structured texting campaigns. In many cases, without a thoughtful strategy, texting for talent can become a major detriment to an organization's recruitment brand (Raphael, 2014).

Whether texting will replace telephone calls and email messages in business, education, or government environments or continue as their supplement remains a question to be answered.

NEW CHALLENGES OF POLLING

Polling started in the 19th century, as newspapers tried to gauge popular sentiment by sending reporters into the streets, armed with questionnaires and tasked with collecting opinions. By the 1930s, George Gallup, Elmo Roper, and others had improved upon these primitive practices. They pioneered new approaches that relied on sampling and probability. Even so, they suffered a few remarkable failures. Yet they learned from their failures and took advantage of the rise of the telephone, which made it possible for researchers to call just about anybody and produce almost completely random samples of the population.

Their work began to look scientific, and polling entered a kind of golden era in the 1970s that mixed relatively low costs with reliable conclusions. Ever since, most political polls have gotten the right result the vast majority of the time (Miller, 2015).

The invention and diffusion of wireless telecommunication technologies since early 1990s, however, have presented new challenges to pollsters. Although the wide use of cellphones enables pollsters to reach people more easily, most households have dropped their landlines. While area codes of traditional landline telephone numbers accurately represent geographical locations, an important factor in successful polling, area codes of cellphone numbers do not necessarily indicate the actual residency of the cellphone users. In addition, the built-in contacts and display functions of cellphones enable cellphone users to recognize instantly whether phone calls come from recognized sources. Most cellphone users decline phone calls from unfamiliar sources. These new challenges often lead to inaccuracies of telephone polling. Moreover, in countries such as the United States, pollsters are disallowed from auto-dialing cellphones, which raises polling costs in most situations.

More recently, various web-based survey programs such as SurveyMonkey have been designed and implemented. Their popularity has grown not only among academic researchers and business marketers, but also with pollsters. Advantages of online polling include:

Lower Polling Costs

As fewer real-time administrators are needed, online polling saves on labor costs and overhead expenses.

Greater Convenience for Pollsters and Respondents

Pollsters are no longer constrained by time. Once a poll is designed and posted online, pollsters only need to monitor the online process, and they may do that at their convenience. Respondents are no longer required to respond real-time. Responses could be made at a time most convenient for the respondents, and they may even be allowed to save partial responses and continue the process at a later time.

More Immediate Analyses and Results

As respondents submit new responses, these responses are not only automatically recorded, but also automatically included in electronic and automated analyses. Results are dynamically updated and immediately provided.

Shorter Turnaround Time

In comparison with traditional telephone polling, online polls can be more rapidly deployed. Once posted online, all targeted respondents could participate at the same time, which would be impractical with telephone polling. Therefore, online polling typically enjoys shorter turnaround time.

Less Intimidating and More Effective Polls

With online polling, through programming, certain questions may or may not be displayed depending on user responses to earlier questions, making polls seemingly shorter and less intimidating. In addition, single-choice questions can be programmed to allow only one choice, minimizing user response errors.

Greater Likelihood of Truth Disclosures

Respondents no longer speak with pollsters directly; therefore, there is a greater likelihood that they would truthfully share personal opinions or preferences.

As with other technological advancements, there are also tradeoffs with online polling. Disadvantages of online polling include:

Lesser Respondent Availability for Sampling

Certain populations may not have Internet access. This is particularly true in developing countries. Effective probability samples may be difficult to construct. In such cases, alternative polling methods should be considered.

More Difficult Representation Assurance

Many online polls today are grossly unrepresentative. Anyone who sees the survey link could jump in. Possible remedies include forming large panels of survey participants whose information, when analyzed or processed properly, provides true reflections of public opinion. However, that "proper" way remains to be discovered.

Greater Likelihood of No Response

As online surveys become increasingly employed, Internet users are becoming increasingly annoyed by the seemingly endless online survey or voting requests. More and more online polls are being ignored or deleted without response. Pollsters may need to consider incentive offerings to encourage participation.

Greater Likelihood of Proxy Responses

People rarely pick up a telephone call pretending to be someone else. However, with online polling, a family member or friend can easily fill in and respond to a poll. It is difficult to prove the identity of the person who responds online. A possible remedy might be including an affirmative question at the beginning of the poll such as "I am the person whom this survey is intended for: Yes No."

Less Reliable Data

In the absence of experienced pollsters providing timely clarification as during telephone polling, certain online respondents constrained by education or social backgrounds, might misunderstand certain questions and provide unintended responses, thus lowering data reliability. Possible remedies might include using simple wording in survey questions and providing visible online help tips on any terms or names that could use clarification.

Greater Risk of Poll Tampering

Online polling is as venerable to hacking and virus attacks as any other Internet application program. Experienced hackers could interfere with online poling by tampering with the way responses are submitted or counted or by submitting responses for people who did not actually respond. While difficult to prevent or discover such interferences, heavy penalties should be imposed on all known hacking practices.

Despite these new challenges, polling will continue to be conducted throughout the world. As new technologies are often ecological, it will be no surprise for online polling to replace traditional survey methods.

ONLINE PIRACY

Online piracy refers to any unauthorized reproduction or use via Internet technologies of copyrighted books, recordings, television programs, patented invention, trademarked product, or other forms of protected intellectual property.

Piracy existed long before digital media became prominent; however, it had relatively limited impact for several reasons: (1) the associated risk was high compared to the financial benefits, (2) pirating goods was often difficult and required technical expertise, (3) the quality of pirated products were usually inferior compared to the originals. However, in the digital world, these limiting factors quickly disappeared. For example, an identical quality copy can be easily manufactured and costs very little. A digital download or copy can be made instantly and costs nothing financially. Consequently, online piracy has become a very serious global issue worldwide, and developers and distributors of various types of media are increasingly focused on combating piracy and the loss of potential profits it represents (Harenber, 2011).

Many developers and distributors seek solutions from technology itself. They place various digital controls such as registration procedures or authorization mechanisms over downloading, copying, or using of digital materials. However, technical measures alone have proven insufficient.

Relevant industries have placed great pressures on legislative bodies throughout the world to establish and enforce more up-to-date and more effective laws to safeguard their interests. However, because of the many potential parties and interest groups involved, law making remains a lengthy process in almost all countries while technologies continue emerging at high speed and change cultures and societies along the way. Laws and regulations simply cannot keep up with technologies.

Many Americans probably remember SOPA, the Stop Online Piracy Act, a controversial United States bill introduced in 2011 to expand the ability of U.S. law enforcement to combat online copyright infringement and online trafficking in counterfeit goods. Provisions included the requesting of court orders to bar advertising networks and payment facilities from conducting business with infringing websites, and web search engines from linking to the websites, and court orders requiring Internet service providers to block access to the websites. The proposed law would have expanded existing criminal laws to include unauthorized streaming of copyrighted content, imposing a maximum penalty of five years in prison. While the bill received much support nationwide, major internet companies and many others opposed the bill. Wikipedia and Reddit, along with other popular websites, even coordinated a service blackout in protest against SOPA. Finally, SOPA was put on hold. If it will ever be enacted as law, it will very unlikely be as originally proposed (Downes, 2012; Pepitone, 2012; Samuelson, 2012).

If one single nation can be so divided regarding a proposed anti-online-piracy bill, an effective worldwide anti-online-piracy agreement or legal measure would be even more difficult to achieve. However, anything less than a unified global system of protection would be ineffective in combating online piracy. No doubt online piracy will remain a challenging global issue for years to come.

THREATS TO NATIONAL SECURITY

National securities are of primary concerns to all countries, and new major technologies have typically found their first deployment in the arena of national security including military service. Information technologies are no exceptions. During the 1990 Gulf War against Iraq, the United States Military surprised the world with its eye-opening power gained through deployment of information technologies. Since then, military applications of digital networks aided by satellite systems have been attached great importance by countries throughout the world.

The collapse of the Berlin Wall in 1989 and the dissolution of the Soviet Union in 1990-1991 ended the Cold War of the world. However, regional military conflicts have never stopped, and military competition continued among major countries of the world, only that information technology innovations have equipped national security forces throughout the world with newer and more impactful weapons.

In 2010, Stuxnet, a malicious computer worm, was launched against Iran. It was specifically designed to destroy Iran's nuclear enrichment facility at Natanz. It tampered with the code of the programmable logic controller used to control the centrifuges at Natanz, destroyed about a thousand centrifuges, and disrupted Iran's nuclear program (Denning, 2012). In 2012, Flame, known also as SKyWIper and Flamer, another weapon entirely made of code, was launched against cyber espionage in Middle Eastern countries. With a size of 20 MB (40 times the size of Stuxnet), it was said to be one of the largest malware ever engineered. It was a computer malware of about 20 modules that attacked computers running the Microsoft Windows operating system. The malware had worm-like capabilities and spread through local networks by exploiting different vulnerabilities (Wangen, 2015). Since then, "code weapon" and "code war" have become widely-known military terms.

Fighting on unfair ground and maintaining technological superiority is a goal and a challenge for the military. According to Patrick Tucker, despite some $63.5 billion in research and development funding allocated to the U.S. Defense Department in fiscal year 2015, the proliferation of cheap computers, cheap Internet and cheap drones is changing geopolitical realities faster than Washington can keep up (Tucker, 2014).

To maximize competitive advantages, weaponized drone technologies have been under heavy development in major countries throughout the world. Countless other new weapons are also in the making.

In the midst of information technology-based military competition, the U.S., Russia, China, England, Japan, Israel, and other technology-literate countries seem to have benefited the most and therefore become the largest winners. Small and technologically-disadvantaged countries seem to have lagged further behind and become the largest losers. Indeed, some have become victims of competition among major powers, and some have become virtually tributary subordinates to superpowers such the U.S. and Russia.

Unfortunately, even superpowers such as the U.S. are not necessarily safe. Terrorism has remained a major threat to Americans. In fact, terrorism has become an important threat to countries throughout the world, especially to countries that seem to possess greater military powers. Terrorism occurs in many different ways, and unfortunately, the diffusion of information technologies such as Internet and telecommunication technologies have supplied potential terrorists with increasingly greater convenience and more knowledge in planning, organizing, and executing attacks.

To combat terrorism, technological mechanisms such as metal detectors, explosive detection devices, and other screening equipment have been widely deployed at airports, train stations, government buildings, and other important locations throughout the world. More recently, lie detectors have been piloted at U.S. borders.

However, although information technologies have brought forth countless new weapons and new defense systems, national securities remain threatened globally, and no country or people feel safer than before the first computer network of ARPANET was invented in 1969.

THREATS TO HUMAN JOBS

Academic debates over whether technology is destroying human jobs have long existed. Some believe that as information technology continues to develop at accelerated speeds, many existing human jobs will inevitably be replaced by technologies. Others argue that although new technologies might cause certain jobs to be obsolete, they also create many previously nonexistent job opportunities.

Among those who believe that technologies have hindered human employment are Professor Erik Brynjolfsson of the MIT Sloan School of Management and his collaborator and coauthor Andrew McAfee, associate director of the MIT Center for Digital Business at the Sloan School of Management. They believe that advances in computer technology such as industrial robotics and automated translation services destroy jobs faster than creating them and have resulted in the sluggish employment growth in the United States since the turn of the century. They speculate that many types of human jobs will be threatened as powerful new technologies are increasingly adopted not only in manufacturing, clerical, and retail work but also in professions such as law, financial services, education, and medicine (Rotman, 2013).

Many labor economists disagree. Among them is Richard Freeman at Harvard University. He argues that it is very difficult to extricate the effects of technology from other macroeconomic effects and he doubts that technology should be held responsible for the sluggish employment growth in the United States earlier in the century. David Autor, another MIT economist who has extensively studied the connections between jobs and technology, also doubts that technology could account for such an abrupt change in total employment (Rotman, 2013).

Economists and other academicians are not the sole parties concerned about potential threats of modern technologies to human employment. Current and future employees everywhere also worry about their job prospects tomorrow. Horses have been referenced frequently as a type for humans. When tractors replaced horses in farming, automobiles replaced horses in transportation, and armed vehicles replaced horses in the battlefield, needs for horses quickly diminished. Although horses are still maintained for sports or recreation purposes, the number of horses employed today is ignorable comparing to before.

The situation, however, is different for humans. First, technologies are discoveries and inventions of humans, and any sufficiently advanced technology is based on human knowledge or algorithms. Although algorithms perform wonders such as crones and driverless vehicles, they have boundaries. Technologies are capable only within their human-defined boundaries. Therefore, it is simply unlikely that technologies would replace humans altogether.

Secondly, when new technologies emerge, they indeed create new employment opportunities. Constrained by inherent limitations, horses cannot adapt to new situations, and they simply become unemployable. Humans, on the other hand, could learn and obtain the education and training needed and update their employability for the newly created employment opportunities.

Needless to say, with the diffusion of every new technology, there will be new winners and new losers. Some will need to upgrade knowledge and skills, some may find themselves in different locations and with lower salaries, and some will lose positions and status previously enjoyed.

Interruptive technologies have occurred many times previously, but they are emerging at accelerated speeds today, with tens of millions of workers potentially affected globally. There are no simple solutions, because increased efficiency rewards everyone with lower prices for higher-quality goods and services. Workers must constantly improve their productivity to increase their value. They need to update knowledge and upgrade skills to stay competitive in the economy of tomorrow (Crichton, 2015).

Although continued diffusion of new information technologies such as robotics, crones, and driverless cars potentially threatens millions of existing jobs, through active and adequate preparation, humans will continue to survive and thrive just as they survived and thrived through all previous revolutions and automations

OBSTACLES TO INFORMATION TECHNOLOGY INNOVATIONS

Most economists today would agree that technology innovations have become the primary driving factor for the world's economy today. They not only spark new interests in investors, create new markets, force existing companies to improve their market competitiveness through business process reengineering, but also motivate governments throughout the world to reexamine and realign economic policies to foster greater economy growth.

As important as they are, technology innovations are a tricky business. While some believe that information technologies could fuel innovations (Dibrell, et al., 2008), the diffusion of information technologies has created a number of obstacles to hinder technology innovations.

First, no effective protection mechanism exists to safeguard technology innovations. Although most countries have patent laws in place, they are less than effective in the digital world. A *patent* is "property right granted by a national government that gives the patentee the exclusive right to use, manufacture, or sell an invention for a prescribed period of time" (Latimer, 2004, p1). Thus, patent laws do not actually protect secretes, but reveal them. As discussed earlier, factors that made traditional protection measures effective disappeared in the digital age, and online piracy remains a serious concern not only for technology innovators but also for potential investors.

Secondly, existing patents and the existence of patent trolls hinder technology innovations. Patent laws are enacted to encourage technology innovations in two ways: (1) protecting inventors for a certain period of time thus allowing them a significant lead in competition so as to help them recover the research and development costs associated with their innovations; (2) requiring technology innovators to reveal publicly details of their inventions so as to promote more innovations. During the protected period, any unauthorized reproduction or use of the technologies would be prosecutable by law. It seems wonderfully great, but there is one problem: too many patents exist in the field of information technology making new innovations extremely difficult and risky.

According to Lindsey Gilroy and Tammy D'Amato of the U.S. Patent Board, "the iPhone, even with its 200 patents, is still a simple product with few components. A telecommunications network, like the 4G wireless network new and ongoing development, has so many moving parts that it depends on tens of thousands of individual patents to keep the entire machine running. As of 2008, there were 18,300 patents and 16,254 pending applications particular to the development of a 4G network. While 4G offers innovation, it hasn't reinvented the wheel and still relies on the over 80,000 patents that form the backbone of telecommunications connectivity" (Gilroy & D'Amato, 2011, p3). It is practically impossible for new innovators to be fully aware of all existing patents prior to setting out for new inventions. Consequently, patent trolls have emerged.

Although no universal agreement has been achieved regarding the definition of patent trolls, the term "patent troll" has quickly become one of the most threatening terms to the technology industry. Simply put, a patent troll is a person or company who acquires patents from others for the sole purpose of suing accused infringers far beyond the patent's actual value or contribution to the prior art. Countless potential innovators have become innocent captives of patent trolls (Mayergoyz, 2009).

Thirdly, the perceived threats of technology innovations to human jobs cause concerns and hesitation in countries that do not possess capabilities to absorb massive unemployment, resulting in reduced budgets for technology research and development. Societal stability is important to all countries, especially to countries of large populations. Fast and excessive technology innovations could lead to massive unemployment for a period of time. In populous countries, massive unemployment could easily transform into social instability, threatening societal harmony and national securities of these countries.

CONCLUSION

The Postman Framework

In his address to the New Tech '98 Conference, Neil Postman shared five ideas about new technologies: (1) All technological change is a trade-off; there are pros and cons with every new technology. (2) The advantages and disadvantages of new technologies are never distributed evenly among the population. (3) Embedded in every technology there is a powerful idea, sometimes two or three powerful ideas. (4) Technological change is not additive but ecological. New technologies are not simple additions to what is already there; they change the world. (5) People often become mythic about diffused technologies; they tend to think of technological creations as a part of the natural order of things instead of thinking of them as strange intruders whose capacity for good or evil rests on human awareness of what they do for us and to us (Postman, 1998).

As discussed in this chapter, information technologies have been deployed as a key competitive advantage by multinational and transnational businesses throughout the world. They have performed wonders for individuals, societies, and nations worldwide. Nevertheless, they have also generated numerous global issues. This chapter briefly sampled and discussed ten of these issues.

Each issue results from the diffusion of certain specific technologies. Postman's framework could help us better understand the related technologies. We could ask ourselves: What tradeoffs do the technologies present? Who are the winners and losers as these technologies are diffused into regular use? What countries are most likely positively impacted and what countries most likely negatively impacted by these technology? What grand idea(s) underlines these new technologies and how the idea(s) might impact the economic, social, cultural, and political institutions? How might the diffusion of these technologies changing structures, patterns, or norms in the world?

Asking and answering these questions would help us better understand and appreciate new technologies.

The Technology Acceptance Model

Some thirty years ago when business organizations other than financial institutions just began embracing computer technologies, a research was conducted proposing what was widely known later as the Technology Acceptance Model (TAM). The research proposed that system features and capabilities result in user motivation which drives users to use a certain system (Davis, 1986). Although many models have been proposed to explain and predict the use of a system, the Technology Acceptance Model seems to have been accepted most widely in the field. In later research, Davis and research partners noted that the TAM models system usage intentions and behavior as a function of perceived usefulness and perceived ease of use. The original scales for measuring the TAM constructs have been confirmed to be reliable and valid in several replications and applications spanning a range of technologies and user populations (Davis & Venkatesh, 1996).

Humans desire productivity, efficiency, comfort, convenience, freedom, good health, peace, safety, and happiness. Theses desires will never end and will continue to drive discoveries and inventions of new technologies. According to TAM, as long as these new technologies possess the right capabilities and are easy to use, they will find their acceptance.

Of course, as new technologies emerge, there will be new issues to face and new problems to overcome. However, to humans, issues and problems are opportunities for enhancements and improvements. They motivate people to search for better solutions, and they drive newer technology innovations. So has human history evolved, and so will it continue to move forward.

Future Directions of Technology Development

We live in a time of technology explosion. Technology innovations and diffusions seem to occur faster than we are legally, socially, or mentally prepared. While new technologies are blessing people's lives in many ways, it is also critically important that our societies and our world move forward in harmony.

Therefore, the planning and implementation of future technologies will need to better consider their potential impact on individuals, communities, societies, countries, and the world as a whole. First, relevant government policies and guidelines need to be developed and more government initiatives need to be implemented to neutralize or minimize potentially undesirable impact of new technology applications. Secondly, as most issues discussed are global challenges, there needs to be better-coordinated joint efforts from different levels of governments and different parts of the world. Thirdly, of particular importance would be a global education program that helps put things in the correct perspectives for technology users worldwide.

In many ways, the future directions of technology development lie in the collective wisdom of governments, technology researchers and innovators, technology commercialization companies, and technology user communities.

REFERENCES

Attaran, M. (2004). Exploring the relationship between information technology and business process reengineering. *Journal of International Management*, *41*(5), 585–596.

Bolton, R. N., Parasuraman, A., Hoefnagels, A., Migchels, N., Kabadayi, S., Gruber, T., ... Solnet, D. (2013). Understanding Generation Y and Their Use of Social Media: A Review and Research Agenda. *Journal of Service Management*, *24*(3), 245–267. doi:10.1108/09564231311326987

Boyd, D. M., & Ellison, N. B. (2007). Social Network Sites: Definition, History, and Scholarship. *Journal of Computer-Mediated Communication*, *13*(1), 210–230. doi:10.1111/j.1083-6101.2007.00393.x

Coutre, L. (2016). *Cleveland Clinic announces top 10 medical innovations for 2017*. Retrieved July 24, 2017, from http://www.modernhealthcare.com/article/20161027/news/161029924

Crichton, D. (2015). Fear Not the Robot: Automation Will Continue to Raise Our Quality of Life. *National Review*. Retrieved on August 1, 2017, from https://www.nationalreview.com/nrd/articles/417033/fear-not-robot

Cron, W. L., & Sobol, M. G. (1983). The relationship between computerization and performance: A strategy for maximizing the economic benefits of computerization. *Journal of International Management*, *6*(3), 171–181.

Davis, F. (1986). *A Technology Acceptance Model for Empirically Testing New End-User Information Systems: Theory and Results* (Unpublished Doctoral Dissertation). MIT Sloan School of Management, Cambridge, MA.

Davis, F., & Venkatesh, V. (1996). A Critical Assessment of Potential Measurement Biases in the Technology Acceptance Model: Three Experiments. *International Journal of Human-Computer Studies*, *45*(1), 19–45. doi:10.1006/ijhc.1996.0040

Davis, L. M. (2016). *CT Scan (CAT Scan, Computerized Axial Tomography)*. Retrieved July 24, 2017, from http://www.emedicinehealth.com/ct_scan/article_em.htm

Denning, D. E. (2012). Stuxnet: What Has Changed? *Future Internet*, *4*(3), 672–687. doi:10.3390/fi4030672

Dibrell, C., Davis, P., & Craig, J. (2008). Fueling Innovation through Information Technology in SMEs. *Journal of Small Business Management*, *46*(2), 203–218. doi:10.1111/j.1540-627X.2008.00240.x

Dotinga, R. (2015). One in Five Teens May Be Bullied on Social Media. *HealthDay News*. Retrieved July 28, 2017, from http://health.usnews.com/health-news/articles/2015/06/22/1-in-5-teens-may-be-bullied-on-social-media

Downes, L. (2012). Who Really Stopped SOPA, and Why? *Forbes*. Retrieved from https://www.forbes.com/sites/larrydownes/2012/01/25/who-really-stopped-sopa-and-why/#2f883dfc7b76

Erb, J. J., & James, S. R. (2017). *Global Logistics for Dummies*. Chichester, UK: John Wiley & Sons, Ltd.

Gilroy, L., & D'Amato, T. (2011). *How many patents does it take to build an iPhone?* Retrieved August 1, 2017, from https://inovorg2011-2.wikispaces.com/file/view/2.1-How+many+patents+does+it+take+to+build+an+iPhone.pdf

Gleick, J. (2011). How Google Dominates Us. *The New York Review of Books*. Retrieved July 26, 2017, from http://www.nybooks.com/articles/2011/08/18/how-google-dominates-us/

Govette, J. (2016). 15 Amazing Healthcare Technology. *Innovations*. Retrieved from https://getreferralmd.com/2016/01/healthcare-technology-2016/

Greenhow, C., & Askari, E. (2017). Learning and Teaching with Social Network Sites: A Decade of Research in K-12 Related Education. *Education and Information Technologies*, *22*(2), 623–645. doi:10.100710639-015-9446-9

Greenhow, C., Robelia, B., & Hughes, J. E. (2009). Learning, Teaching, and Scholarship in a Digital Age: Web 2.0 and Classroom Research: What Path Should We Take Now? *Educational Researcher*, *38*(4), 246–259. doi:10.3102/0013189X09336671

GuardChild.com. (2017). *Cyber Bullying Statistics*. Retried July 28, 2017, from http://www.guardchild.com/cyber-bullying-statistics/

Harenber. (2011). *Online Piracy*. Retrieved on July 31, 2017, from http://piracy.web.unc.edu/brief-history-of-online-piracy/

Hartmans, A. (2017). 15 Fascinating Facts You Probably Didn't Know about Amazon. *Business Insider*. Retrieved November 28, 2017, from http://www.businessinsider.com/jeff-bezos-amazon-history-facts-2017-4/#amazon-wasnt-the-companys-original-name-1

Kaptein, M. (2008). Developing a Measure of Unethical Behavior in the Workplace: A Stakeholder Perspective. *Journal of Management*, *34*(5), 978–1008. doi:10.1177/0149206308318614

Klamo, L., Wang, K. L., Le, T., & Huang, W. (2006). Successfully Implementing e-Government: Fundamental Issues and a Case Study in USA. *Electronic Government: An International Journal*, *3*(2), 158–173. doi:10.1504/EG.2006.009216

Latimer, M. T. (2004). Patenting Inventions Arising from Biological Research. *Genome Biology, 6*(1). *Article*, *203*, 1–9.

Lu, Y., & Ramamurthy, K. (2011). Understanding the Link between Information Technology Capability and Organizational Agility: An Empirical Examination. *Management Information Systems Quarterly*, *35*(4), 931–954. doi:10.2307/41409967

Luftman, J., Lyytinen, K., & Zvi, T. (2017). Enhancing the Measurement of Information Technology (IT) Business Alignment and Its Influence on Company Performance. *Journal of Information Technology*, *32*(1), 26–46. doi:10.1057/jit.2015.23

Lyytinen, K., & Rose, G. M. (2003). The Disruptive Nature of Information Technology Innovations: The Case of Internet Computing in Systems Development Organizations. *Management Information Systems Quarterly*, *27*(4), 557–596. doi:10.2307/30036549

Mayergoyz, A. (2009). Lessons from Europe on How to Tame U.S. Patent Trolls. *Cornell International Law Journal, 42*(2), 241-270.

McCorvey, J. J. (2013). Amazon Fresh is Jeff Bezos' Last Mile Quest for Total Retail Domination. *Fast Company*. Retrieved July 26, 2017, from https://www.fastcompany.com/3014817/amazon-jeff-bezos

Miller, J. J. (2015). Modern Pollster: The Profession Must Adapt to Cell Phones and the Internet. *National Review*. Retrieved July 31, 2017, from https://www.nationalreview.com/nrd/articles/415667/modern-pollster

NoBullying.com. (2017). *A Comprehensive View of Cyberbullying in the USA*. Retrieved July 28, 2017, from https://nobullying.com/cyberbullying-in-usa/

Pepitone, J. (2012). SOPA Explained: What It Is and Why It Matters. *CNN Money*. Retrieved November 28, 2017, from http://money.cnn.com/2012/01/17/technology/sopa_explained/index.htm

Postman, N. (1998, March). *Five Things We Need to Know About Technological Change*. Address to New Tech '98 Conference, Denver, CO.

RadiologyInfo.com. (2017). *Magnetic Resonance Imaging (MRI) – Body*. Retrieved July 24, 2017, from https://www.radiologyinfo.org/en/info.cfm?pg=bodymr

Raphael, T. (2014). The Pros and Cons of Texting for Talent. *ERE*. Retrieved July 29, 2017, from https://www.eremedia.com/ere/the-pros-and-cons-of-texting-for-talent/

Robinson, S. L., & Bennett, R. J. (1995). A Typology of Deviant Workplace Behaviors: A Multidimensional Scaling Study. *Academy of Management Journal*, *38*(2), 555–572. doi:10.2307/256693

Robischon, N. (2017, February 13). Why Amazon Is The World's Most Innovative Company Of 2017. *Fast Company*.

Rotman, D. (2013). How Technology Is Destroying Jobs. *MIT Technology Review*. Retrieved August 1, 2017, from https://www.technologyreview.com/s/515926/how-technology-is-destroying-jobs/

Samuelson, P. (2012). Can Online Piracy Be Stopped By Law? *Communications of the ACM*, *55*(7), 25–27. doi:10.1145/2209249.2209260

Schwartz, A. (2015). *The 5 Most Common Unethical Behaviors in the Workplace*. Retrieved July 28, 2017, from https://www.bizjournals.com/philadelphia/blog/guest-comment/2015/01/most-common-unethical-behaviors-in-the.html

Sneada, J. T., & Wright, E. (2014). E-government research in the United States. *Government Information Quarterly*, *31*(1), 129–136. doi:10.1016/j.giq.2013.07.005

Somonite, T. (2012). What Facebook Knows. *Technology Review*. Retrieved from https://www.technologyreview.com/s/428150/what-facebook-knows/

Stephens, D. O. (1999). The Globalization of Information Technology in Multinational Corporations. *The Information Management Journal*, *33*(3), 66–71.

Thompson, N. (2012). How to Get Privacy Right. *New Yorker Magazine*. Retrieved July 28, 2017, from http://www.newyorker.com/culture/culture-desk/how-to-get-privacy-right

Tucker, P. (2014, July). How Technology Is Transforming the Future of National Security. *Defense One*, 1-8.

Wangen, G. (2015). The Role of Malware in Reported Cyber Espionage: A Review of the Impact and Mechanism. *Information*, *6*(2), 183–211. doi:10.3390/info6020183

Welch, E. W., Hinnant, C. C., & Moon, M. J. (2004). Linking Citizen Satisfaction with E-Government and Trust in Government. *Journal of Public Administration: Research and Theory*, *15*(3), 371–391. doi:10.1093/jopart/mui021

Whittaker, Z. (2013). *Google's European Conundrum: When Does Privacy Mean Censorship?* Retrieved July 28, 2017, from https://www.cnet.com/news/googles-european-conundrum-when-does-privacy-mean-censorship/

Zuckerman, A. (2004). The Non-Techie CEO's Guide to Global Supply Chain Technology. *World Trade*, *18*(2), 30–34.

KEY TERMS AND DEFINITIONS

Computerized Axial Tomography (CAT): Special x-ray tests that produce cross-sectional images of the body using x-rays and a computer.

Cyberbullying: Bullying behavior carried out through internet service such as e-mails, chat rooms, discussion groups, online social networking, instant messaging, or web pages.

Flame: A modular computer malware that attacks computers running the Microsoft Windows operating system, known also as Flamer, sKyWIper, and Skywiper.

Magnetic Resonance Imaging (MRI): A noninvasive medical test that uses a powerful magnetic field, radio frequency pulses, and a computer to produce detailed pictures of organs, soft tissues, bone, and virtually all other internal body structures.

Online Piracy: Any unauthorized reproduction or use via Internet technologies of copyrighted books, recordings, television programs, patented invention, trademarked product, or other forms of protected intellectual property.

Patent: Property right granted by a national government that gives the patentee the exclusive right to use, manufacture, or sell an invention for a prescribed period of time.

Patent Troll: A person or company who acquires patents from others for the sole purpose of suing accused infringers far beyond the patent's actual value or contribution to the prior art.

SOPA: Stop Online Piracy Act, a controversial United States bill introduced on October 26, 2011 by U.S. Representative Lamar S. Smith and a bipartisan group of 12 initial co-sponsors to expand the ability of U.S. law enforcement to combat online copyright infringement and online trafficking in counterfeit goods.

Stuxnet: A malicious computer worm that was launched against the nuclear enrichment facility at Natanz in Iran.

Chapter 2
A Glossary of Business Sustainability Concepts

Arunasalam Sambhanthan
Curtin University, Australia

ABSTRACT

This chapter presents a glossary of business sustainability concepts. The business sustainability definitions have been subjected to an abstractive decomposition. The phrases and terms derived from the abstractive decomposition has been categorized into three types, and each answers the questions of why sustainability, how it could be achieved, and where it will lead the businesses. Concepts categorized under each of these questions are defined individually and described with contextual relevance and examples from literature or industry. The glossary has been presented with a logical order to supplement the table of phrases and concepts. This work is an extension of the work reported on defining business sustainability through an abstractive decomposition.

1. INTRODUCTION

Sustainability is a well-used and popular term, but its use lacks in clarity. There are a number of terms, such as sustainable development and triple bottom line, which are interchangeably used with the term 'sustainability' (McKenzie, 2004). At the business level, sustainability is often equated with eco-efficiency (Dyllick & Hockerts, 2002). Documented research exists on the review of sustainability terms and their definitions (Glavič & Lukman, 2007). These authors give prominence to terms like cleaner production, pollution prevention, pollution control, minimization of resource usage, eco-design and other similar terms. However, there is a considerable gap in

DOI: 10.4018/978-1-5225-5393-9.ch002

the research literature in terms of defining business sustainability with a holistic view. Being a branch of the Sustainability discipline, business sustainability has quite a number of perspectives and angles that have been researched. Investigations of the business sustainability concept include consumer behavior, climate change, stakeholder management, innovation and strategy. In the context of consumer behavior and sustainability, there are studies on measuring the gaps between customers' expectations and their perceptions on green products (Tseng & Hung, 2013); investigation of factors influencing the sustainable consumption behaviors of rural residents (Wang, Liu, & Qi, 2014); the role of moral leadership for sustainable production and consumption (Vinkhuyzen & Karlsson-Vinkhuyzen, 2014); survey and analysis of consumer behavior on waste mobile phone recycling (Yin, Gao, & Xu, 2014) and the empirical investigation of green purchase behavior among the younger generation (Kanchanapibul, Lacka, Wang, & Chan, 2014). Definition of climate strategies for business (Pesonen & Horn, 2014) and the influence of stakeholders' power and corporate characteristics and social and environmental disclosure (Lu & Abeysekera, 2014) are studies that document the relation of climate change and sustainability. The climate change related studies take more of an environmental sustainability angle when looking at sustainability. In terms of innovation, the link between eco-innovation and business performance (Cheng, Yang, & Sheu, 2014) and sustainability oriented innovation in small and medium enterprises (Klewitz & Hansen, 2014) are some notable studies that have been recently published. These studies look at the economic dimension of sustainability in the context of small and medium businesses. From a management perspective, there are studies on, for example, keeping track of corporate social responsibility as a business and management discipline with particular reference to Pakistan (Memon, Wei, Robson, & Khattak, 2014); a study related to the strategic niche management of cleaner vehicle technologies from prototype to series production (Sushandoyo & Magnusson, 2014); and the critical importance of strategic competencies for sustainable development (Mulder, 2014). The management related studies have been primarily focused on the strategic and sustainable development angles of the subject. However, there is still a lack of research in terms of integrating these disciplinary perspectives in sustainability related research.

Business sustainability definitions are manifold in the published literature. Due to the complexity involved in terms of semantics and conceptualizations, it is quite challenging to find meanings for some of the terms pertaining to sustainability even in dictionaries (Glavič & Lukman, 2007). Forty-one selected terms from environmental engineering domain including cleaner production, pollution prevention, pollution control, minimization of resource usage and eco design have received prominence in the aforementioned review article. By the mid-1990s there were over hundred definitions of sustainability that have been constructed by different organizations for theorizing and measuring sustainability in their context (Marshall & Toffel, 2005). The main reason for this variability relies on the incompatibility of the sustainability definition crafted by the World Commission on Environment and Development to a variety of organizational settings. In fact, this definition has practical limitations pertaining to operationalization and implementation in organizational settings. Therefore, the practice of contextualizing sustainability definitions according the organizational requirements has been a longstanding dilemma. On the other hand, there is an observable vacuum in the current academic literature with regard to a holistic definition of business sustainability concept. Aiming to address the above vacuum, a recent documented research conceptualizes business sustainability using abstractive decomposition (Sambhanthan, Potdar, & Chang, 2017). The authors have constructed a new definition of business sustainability through analyzing and restructuring a number of existing definitions of business sustainability from the documented literature. Yet, the process level detailed view of all the building blocks of the new definition of business sustainability could be a possible extension to the aforementioned research. For example, the definition crafted by the authors includes the term stakeholder which has around a number of different classifications ranging from involvement based classification (i.e. direct, indirect) to environment based classification (i.e. internal, external). Thus, it is confusing to the readers as to what the actual term stakeholder means for the sustainability of businesses. In fact, grasping the underlying infrastructure is essential for the comprehension of the core definition in any domain. Thus, this chapter aims at clearly outlining the conceptual boundaries of business sustainability terminologies outlined in the business sustainability conceptualization documented by (Sambhanthan, Potdar, & Chang, 2017).

Software development industry is experiencing an exponential growth in the recent times with the increase of software exports to developed nations. Yet, sustainability related investigations related to software development industry are limited in the published literature except few works documented in the recent years (Sambhanthan & Potdar, 2016c); (Sambhanthan & Potdar, 2015); (Sambhanthan & Potdar, 2016b); (Sambhanthan & Potdar, 2017); (Sambhanthan et al., 2017); (Sambhanthan & Potdar, 2016a). This entails the need for an effort towards more contextualized research focused on software domain.

The next section briefly reviews and summarizes the contemporary issues related to business sustainability theorization and application.

2. THEORETICAL UNDERPINNINGS

Sustainability conceptualizations date back to 1980s when the first definition of sustainability has been propounded by the World Commission on Environment and Development (WCED) (Costanza & Patten, 1995). This definition has been crafted from a system perspective considering the economic, societal and ecological systems to remain in balance. There has been over hundred definitions of business sustainability out there in the published literature by mid 1990s according to some documented sources (Marshall & Toffel, 2005). The latest of this kind is the holistic conceptualization of business sustainability covering all four bottom lines (Sambhanthan et al., 2017). Besides this exponential growth in the definitional paradox of business sustainability research, a recent study alarms that the concept of sustainability is heavily influenced by the time factor. For example, short-termism has been highlighted to be one of the most recent trends in business sustainability research by the authors of this claim (Bansal & DesJardine, 2014).

By logic, a straightforward definition of business sustainability could be derived from the definition proposed by the WCED. This definition could likely to be as "the ability of firms to respond to their shot-term financial needs without compromising their ability to meet their future needs" (Bansal & DesJardine, 2014). However, it is questionable whether this definition covers a holistic picture of business sustainability. It is inevitable for a definition of this kind to serve the purpose of theorizing business sustainability with a multi-industry viewpoint. Hence, the following definition has been documented with a holistic perspective covering all four bottom lines of sustainability.

Business Sustainability could be achieved through efforts that are concentrated on;

1. Core competencies,
2. Effective production,
3. Embracing opportunities,
4. Exploring suitable and sustainable revenue models,
5. Focusing on economic performance,
6. Managing risks,
7. Pursuing right customer groups,
8. Supporting ecological viability in the existing infrastructure processes and systems,
9. Resource conservation using technology,
10. Growth in business,
11. Improved health and safety,

12. Reduction of environmental impact,
13. Increased production value,
14. Rewarding employees for their performance, and
15. Maintaining long-term support for organizational performance. (Sambhanthan et al., 2017)

The key issues associated with the successful usage and application of this definition relies on the clarity and comprehensibility of the definitional elements. For example, embracing opportunities is a critical part of sustainability according to the new definition. The opportunities has been highlighted as an essential part of sustainability conceptualization in a past documented research (Pojasek, 2007). A clear description and context to the conceptual element 'opportunities' could benefit the understanding and comprehensibility of business sustainability concept. Likewise, there are a variety of conceptual elements which are directly or indirectly associated with the business sustainability definition presented by (Sambhanthan et al., 2017) has been described in this research (see Table 1).

The concept clustering adapted in this article follows the work reported by (Costanza & Patten, 1995). The above research asks questions such as what? when? And how long to assess the persistency of a sustainable system. Similarly, this article asks the questions as to why? how? and where? to cluster the sustainability concepts stuffed inside the definition crafted and documented by (Sambhanthan et al., 2017). In fact, the above definition aims to be a holistic definition encompassing the maximum possible conceptual and theoretical elements of business sustainability. Anchored on the approach documented by (Costanza & Patten, 1995) the typical questions asked on classifying the sustainability concepts includes key questions such as why business sustainability is essential?, how business sustainability could be achieved? and where it will lead the businesses?. The reason for adapting this approach for classification includes that the constructs of sustainability definitions could be better represented through this kind of a classification. In fact, the clear representation and categorization of concept themes is essential to position any new concept in the context.

Anecdotal evidences suggest that there is no universally accepted definition for business sustainability exists in the published literature (Montiel & Delgado-Ceballos, 2014); (Sambhanthan & Potdar, 2016b). A survey conducted among senior managers asking them to define business sustainability highlights a substantial part of responses including all three bottom lines of sustainability (i.e. economic, social and environmental) while a few definitions emphasized exclusively the planet dimension of sustainability. The results also highlighted that only a tiny fraction of respondents mentioning about the long-term component of Corporate Sustainability (Montiel & Delgado-Ceballos, 2014). Indeed, a concurrent documented study suggests that short-termism is an essential part of corporate sustainability (Bansal & DesJardine, 2014). Hence, the standardize-ability of business sustainability definitions to differing practical contexts is a definite challenge for theoretical sustainability researchers.

In overall, sustainability conceptualizations are varying in the practice based literature. While substantially sharing major characteristics with the original definition drawn by WCED, many definitions are quite more specific to the context of certain organizations. Yet, there is an observable vacuum in terms of sustainability definitions focusing on industries and clusters. Thus, this article re-specifies the holistic definition crafted by the authors for assessing and benchmarking sustainability in organizations. This article clearly outlines the conceptual elements of business sustainability from a practical point of view.

3. SOFT SYSTEMS METHODOLOGY (SSM)

An abstractive decomposition of business sustainability definitions has been the primary method used in this article. Abstractive decomposition is an approach in systems thinking literature that has been propounded by management scientist Peter Checkland for modelling complex human activity systems and being used even after more than four decades of application and development (Checkland, 2000). Primarily, soft systems methodology has been well used in differing domains for modelling complex human activity systems (Lester, n.d.); (Richardson, 2016); (Mingers, 2000); (Holwell, 2000). The method of abstractive decomposition has been applied for analyzing the literature definitions on business sustainability (Sambhanthan et al., 2017). The definitions abstracted from the literature on the above perspectives were subjected to text analysis and phrase level categorization of concept themes from the derived pool of concept pieces. The above iterative process of categorization and re-categorization has yielded a new definition of business sustainability covering three main thematic classifications of business sustainability namely efforts, utilization and outcome. These three main thematic classifications are then tweaked into questions asking why business sustainability is important in organizations? how business sustainability could be achieved in organizations? and where the efforts directed on business sustainability will lead the businesses? These questions were asked to categorize the concept themes that are focused on areas which are relevant to these questions. The concept themes were encapsulated and clustered into these thematic concepts which are then transferred into three questions as depicted in table 1. This presentation has been done to ease the comprehensibility of the concept themes and to highlight the synergetic nature of the idea of business sustainability when approached through an abstractive decomposition.

The rationale and justifications for asking these questions as part of the categorization process is listed below.

1. **Why Business Sustainability?:** The reason for the criticality of having businesses sustained. This question answers the need of business sustainability in organization and include concepts which are focusing on the reasons for sustainable business practices in the organizations.
2. **How Business Sustainability Could Be Achieved?:** The know how or the process through which the sustainability of the businesses could be achieved. This question answers the ways in which business sustainability could be achieved including the processes and methods used for ensuring organizational sustainability.
3. **Where It Will Lead Businesses?:** The destination where businesses will be heading through implementing sustainability measures. This question answers the ultimate outcome of sustainability measures taken in the organizations.

4. GLOSSARY

This section covers the glossary of terms. The Table 1 depicts the three questions and the initial concept themes derived from the abstractive decomposition of definition. This section covers the most substantive concepts from Table 1 that are categorized under three questions that includes; why business sustainability? (Covering the reasons for the need for sustainability initiatives in organizations), how business sustainability could be achieved? (The know-how of achieving sustainability in organizations), Where sustainability will lead the businesses? (The outcome of sustainability initiatives in businesses). Each category of these questions is covered with the contextual description of relevant terms, examples from past research or industry and reasoning.

4.1 Why Business Sustainability?

This section covers the purpose of business sustainability. Concepts related to the relevance and criticality of sustainability in businesses has been defined in this section. The key concepts that are defined under this section includes concepts such as responsibilities, needs and stakeholders.

Table 1. Questions and initial concept themes derived from abstractive decomposition

Why Business Sustainability?	How Business Sustainability Could be Achieved?	Where it will lead the Businesses?
Results from => **Responsibilities** **Responsibilities can be** (i.e. Economic, Environmental, Social) (Pojasek, 2007) **To meet => Needs** **Needs of** (Customers, Firms, Stakeholders*) **Needs can be** (i.e. Present, Past, Future) (Laine, 2014) ***Stakeholders can be** (Direct, Indirect, Past, Present, Future, Internal, External) (Dyllick & Hockerts, 2002)	**Architectural Strategy** **Business Approach** (Galbreath, 2009) **Concentrate on Core-Competencies** **Co-ordination of** (Product Design, Manufacturing, Delivery, Distribution, Disposal) (Hong, Kwon, & Jungbae Roh, 2009) **Decision Making** (Cagnin, Loveridge, & Butler, 2013) **Design Appropriate Products** **Effort on =>** (Demand, Supply) (Hong et al., 2009); (H. Breitner, 2005) **Embrace Opportunities** (Pojasek, 2007) **Find Suitable Revenue Models** (H. Breitner, 2005) **Focus Economic Performance** (Benn & Dunphy, 2014) **Focus on Infrastructure** **Focus on Production** (Hong et al., 2009) **Methodology** **Manage Risks** (i.e. Economic, Environmental, Social) (Galbreath, 2009) **Production of** (Goods, Services) (H. Breitner, 2005) **Pursue Right Target Groups** **Support Ecological Viability of** (Planet, Species) (Benn & Dunphy, 2014) **Technological Factors** **Usage of =>** {Processes (i.e. operational), Systems} (Cagnin et al., 2013)	**Conservation of =>** (Energy, Natural Resources) (Laine, 2014) **Development of =>** (Social, Cultural, Business) (Cagnin, Loveridge, & Butler, 1999) **Ecological Viability of** (Planet, Species) (Benn & Dunphy, 2014) **Economic Viability** (Benn & Dunphy, 2014) **Equitable Democratic Practices** **Health & Safety** (Community, Consumer, Worker) (Benn & Dunphy, 2014) **Impact Reduction of =>** (Earth Life, Ecosystem) (Benn & Dunphy, 2014) **Institutional-Political** **Rewarding** for Working People (Socially, Creatively) (Benn & Dunphy, 2014) **Social Justice** (Benn & Dunphy, 2014) **Spatial** (Cagnin et al., 2013) **Value** to Stakeholders **(Added, Increased)** * **Value** can be (Short term, Long term, Social, Environmental) (Galbreath, 2009)

Responsibilities

Responsibilities is defined as the obligations (both legal and moral) and commitment of the organization towards its economic growth, the environment in which it exists and the society in which it operates in both tangible and intangible forms. (i.e.: it is a responsibility of an IT organization to have a proper training program to manage the growth of their employees within their organization). Organizational attitudes and provision for training has a positive relationship with employee satisfaction and eventually results on employee retention (Acton & Golden, 2003). These responsibilities could be economic, environmental or social in nature. All sorts of tangible and intangible activities and resources which involve a monetary value in the business could be considered as *economic* responsibilities. For example, the core revenue generating projects in a software business. All sorts of activities and entities which could have an effect on the tangible and intangible space in which the business exist could be considered as *environmental* responsibilities. For example, emission rate in a factory and the scarp materials of an engine are two forms of aspects which could cause an effect on the environment. Anything related to the society in which the business exists could be considered as *social* responsibilities. For example, pressure groups in the society which could cause considerable challenge to the management in terms of environmental friendliness of the business operations.

Needs

Needs is defined as the emerging psychological drive of the consumers related to the core business specialization of the organization. A need for more updated version of a subscription based software product could be a possible need of the clients of a software company. There is a shift in software building practices being driven by supply side issues to demand side issues (Bennett et al., 2000). {Note: The client need has been noted to be of paramount concern when building the software product}

Stakeholders

Anyone who is interested in the business directly or indirectly would be defined as stakeholder. For example, customers who are interested on the product quality of the company, shareholders who are interested on the dividends of the company. Stakeholders have been categorized to be in different types: *direct* stakeholders {a term which denotes the outcomes generated straightway from something. i.e.: direct outcome of changes in policy regulations}, *indirect* stakeholders {a term which is used to denote the non-straight impacts on something. i.e.: any non-straight impact}, *internal* stakeholders {a term which is used to denote something inside the organization. i.e.: staff working in the company is internal stakeholders of the organization}, *external* stakeholders {a term which is used to denote something outside the organization. i.e.: customers of the company are external stakeholders}.

4.2 How Business Sustainability Could Be Achieved?

This section covers the know-how of business sustainability. Concepts related to the methods of achieving sustainability in businesses has been defined in this section. The key concepts that are defined under this section includes concepts such as architectural strategy, business approach, core competencies, co-ordination of production functions, decision making, efforts on sustainability, embracing opportunities, find suitable revenue models, economic performance, focus on infrastructure, production methodology, materials production, pursue target groups, supporting ecological viability, technological factors, usage of processes and systems.

Architectural Strategy

Architectural Strategy is defined as the core strategy applied by the organization in architecting / producing the core product / service offering in a more cost effective and lean manner that could contribute towards the total quality management and sustainable practices of the organization at large. For example, the strategy employed for developing software architectures needs to be reconsidered and evolved over the time. The architectural strategy of complex engineered systems evolves over the time. Therefore, architectural strategy could have a major impact on ensuring the sustainability of the software businesses (Woodard Charles Jason, 2006).

Business Approach

Business Approach is defined as the approach implied by the organization in enhancing the business value and marketability of its product / service offerings. Examples include internationalization of software firms, push / pull marketing strategies, growth strategies and competitive strategies. The internationalization of software firms using network relationships would have an impact on the foreign market selection and mode of entry as well as product development and market diversification activities (Coviello & Munro, 1997).

Core-Competencies

Core-competencies is defined as the total accumulation of skills, methods, know-how and capabilities a company possess in order to produce its intended products or services. Examples include Skill level of the software engineers in a software business. An investigation about identifying technical competencies of software engineers based on a case study from Spanish software development companies has documented a pyramid model which comprises of skills and competencies of software professionals from junior programmer to IT director (Colomo-Palacios, 2012).

Co-Ordination of Production Functions

The activities related to the overall organization, arrangement and direction of business activities within a specified scope boundary and responsibility level. Examples include Organization of project resource requirements for a short-term software development project. A research by (Faraj & Sproull, 2000) investigated about coordinating expertise in software development teams. The findings report a strong relationship between the expertise coordination and team performance that remains significant over and above team input characteristics, presence of expertise, and administrative coordination. The activities that are reported as production functions includes product design, manufacturing, delivery, distribution and disposal. *Product design* is the process through which the core product is built could be defined as product design. For example, internal process mechanism of a company in building its software product. *Manufacturing* is the process through which the product is manufactured could be defined as manufacturing. For example, process adapted for building, assembly and fitting of components in a car manufacturing company. *Delivery* is the completion and handing over phase of any project based organization could be defined as delivery. For example, completion, deployment and user training of the final software product. *Distribution* is the process of handing over the finished goods to the end customer. For example, the process involved in handing over a software product to the client company such as dispatching, contacting and sign off. *Disposal* is the process of destroying the scrap product at the end of its lifecycle. For example, the disposal of a used car into steel, rubber and other related materials which could be made easily recyclable or degradable.

Decision Making

The process of evaluating the options, establishing alternatives and selecting the best possible option against a certain set of standards and procedures which governs the scope boundaries of the functioning of a project / organization. Examples include Selecting the best possible vendor for outsourcing the accounting function of a multinational software company. A study by (Hersh, 1999) reports that the decision support systems are playing a major role in facilitating sustainable decision making.

Efforts on Sustainability

The activities which are undertaken by the organizations in order to initiate, expedite and successfully conclude the sustainability related endeavors which could result in favorable outcomes to the organization. Examples include making a code green policy in a software company and making the e-wastes of the company sustainable ("Virtusa Environment Day," 2010). For example, designing with current technology in mind and greening the software development as well as virtualization and consolidation are identified as two measures the companies could take in terms of ensuring the software sustainability (Hanselman & Pegah, 2007). The efforts on sustainability includes maintaining a balance between demand and supply. *Demand* is the emerging requirement for a certain product from the customer end which could also be considered as the opening through which the products could be made available to the end users. For example, the demand for higher education courses in business discipline. *Supply* is the availability of certain product / service to address the demand which could also be considered as the capability of the provider to address the demands of the customer for a certain product / service. For example, Availability of degree programs with an Information Systems major to address the emerging need for information systems business consulting professionals in software industry.

Embracing Opportunities

The activity which aims at tapping any possible opportunity in terms of being and becoming a sustainable business. For example, utilizing the opportunity created by a legislative change to better promote off the shelves software. Another example would be to leverage the upcoming technological pervasiveness to forge e-opportunities arising in the market (Fenny, 2001). The *opportunities* are defined as the avenues through which the business could develop its horizons could be considered as opportunities. For example, an IT organization could possibly utilize the opportunities opened by a positive legislative change in the country in which operate in terms of hiring foreign nationals for job. Another example would be the grabbing of a market boom created by the macro environmental political changes in the global market for software products (i.e. the market for developing cloud applications for security problems generated by the increasing data recovery issues).

Find Suitable Revenue Models

The structure and approach through which the return on investments could be leveraged. For example, advertising revenue model for a social media based business initiative.

Economic Performance

The metrics used to assess the degree of greatness between the driver and outcome of a production / service creation process. For example, measurement of overall project team between the projects initiations to delivery. For example, (Paul & Anantharaman, 2004) documented a comprehensive study on the influence of HRM practices on Organizational commitment based on a study conducted among software professionals in India. The study further suggests that HRD practitioners and researchers should further develop commitment-oriented organization policies.

Focus on Infrastructure

The overall mechanism through which the production related activities are managed, overseen and controlled. For example, IT infrastructure for managing the software development process of a company.

Production Methodology

The know-how of producing the core business outcomes (products / services) compliance with global standards on aspects such as quality, accessibility and sustainability. For example, ISO 9001 standards on product quality, W3C Accessibility Standards on design quality, Global Reporting Initiative compliance for accounting excellence. Another example would be the agile software development methods which are used in developing software products by ICT organizations. A research by (Highsmith & Cockburn, 2001) highlights that the agile development combines creative teamwork with an intense focus on effectiveness and maneuverability. Tropos is another example for Agent-Oriented Software development methods which is used in the industry (Bresciani, Perini, Giorgini, Giunchiglia, & Mylopoulos, 2004). The goods and services delivered by the organizations are processed through this production methodology. Goods are defined as the end products or things which are supplied to the customers. For example, a piece of software and the associated goods such as the user manual, implementation guide and the operation instructions which are packaged together for a software deliver could be considered as goods of a software development business. Services are defined as the services which are provided to the end users as the outcome of the business activity. For example, Software as a Service provided to the stock brokerage firms.

Pursue Target Groups

Target groups are defined as the actual beneficiaries of a certain business activity which is intended to deliver value for end users. For example, the target group for stock rating engine software could be stock brokerage firms which provide consultancy services to its clients on stock market fluctuation behaviors.

Materials Production

The process of creating the core business outcome using the methods, technologies and infrastructure present in the company, e.g. Software development in a software business. The spiral model of software development and enhancement which covers a number of process steps involved in software development such as progress through steps, evaluate alternatives, develop and verify next level product, planning for the next phase and determining objectives, alternatives and constraints (Boehm, 1988).

Supporting Ecological Viability

The total possibility of the reduction of business's impact on the environment on which it exists. For example, utilizing e-waste for further recycling to reduce environmental impact caused through the used CRT monitors. Four conceptual elements which look at corporate ecological sustainability are total quality environmental management, ecologically sustainable competitive strategies, technology transfer thorough technology-for nature- swaps and reducing the impact of populations on ecosystem (Shrivastava, 1995). These conceptual elements highlight the importance of looking at the businesses' impact on earth. In fact, all these four conceptual elements have a link to the ecological element of the business.

Technological Factors

The factors pertaining to the technological resources, infrastructure and waste. Example: e-waste. The Greening of IT including the infrastructure and e-waste is of importance to make sure the technological waste is optimized in an IT organization (Murugesan, 2008).

Usage of Processes and Systems

The utilization of processes and systems is defined as the overall utilization of all sorts of available, resources, infrastructure and facilities of the company to achieve its optimum value. Example could include the usage of unutilized solar power for producing more energy in a software firm. *Processes* are the step by step activities which direct the overall know how of the entire business happenings from strategic directions to day to day activities. For example, Recruitment process in an ICT company. *Systems* are the overall interrelationship between people, processes and business entities which make the whole of a business. For example, student management system in a university.

4.3 Where These Measures Will Lead the Businesses?

This section covers the outcome of business sustainability endeavors of the organizations. Concepts related to the outcome of sustainability related efforts in businesses has been defined in this section. The key concepts that are defined under this section includes concepts such as conservation of resources, social-cultural and business development, equitable democratic practices, health and safety, social justice and value.

Conservation of Resources

The retention and long-life usage of energy and other scarce resources to achieve the maximum outcome of energy resources. For example, utilization of low latency energy consumers in production process in a factory environment. Energy is defined as the core power generating source in any business which could be derived or transformed from any natural, man-made or alternative sources such as electricity and gas. For example, electricity could be an energy which could be created from natural sources like water, solar power or any other man-made settings like atomic energy generation practices. Natural Resources are defined to be the resources which could be harnessed from the nature itself. For example, oil and gas.

Socio-Cultural and Business Development

The development of the total accumulation of values, norms, practices and morals of a society in a more organized and targeted manner. For example, organizing cultural events to contribute towards the cultural richness of the country in which the company operates. The development of business is defined to be the total accumulation of deeds, activities, revenues, resources, infrastructures and people which are used in the creation of new goods and services to deliver value to the customers with a personalized focus. For example, software company delivering software products to its client companies.

Equitable Democratic Practices

The practices of the company which are in compliance with the equality and considerable contribution of company's wealth for the society in which operates in the form of co-operate social responsibility. For example, a software business could sponsor the cost of establishing a computer laboratory in a rural village closer to which the company is located in.

Health and Safety

The physical and mental wellbeing of the employees working for the company and any other measures taken by the organization to make the employees feel safe and comfortable to work in an environment. Examples include, ergonomically designed work environment and chair arrangements in a software company, better HR practices to govern harassment free work place in an IT company, Secure IT practices to make the journalists work independently in a publishing house. The health and safety of community, consumer and worker are mentioned here. A *community* is defined as the collective gathering of people with shared interests, norms, values and beliefs. A typical example could be a virtual community which functions as a meeting place for software developers and other software related professionals to discuss about the technical and professional issues about their respective areas of specialization. These communities are facilitated by the professional bodies such as the IEEE / ACM as well as could be open communities where anyone could create a free account to share information and knowledge about these issues. The *consumer* is defined as the people who use a certain product to satisfy a sort of need they have. For example, soap users. A *worker* is defined as the person who perform a certain sort of activity to produce a certain outcome as part of his duty. For example, software engineer.

Social Justice

The consciousness about the society and its betterment in all sorts of actions taken by the organization in regards to fulfilling its day to day operations. For example, being social responsible and committed through contributing to the social wellbeing projects which could result in better social recognition for the organization.

Value

Value is defined to be the transferable qualities added to a product or service during the process of creation or delivery. Value could be added or increased with short term or long-term focus. *Addition* is the injection of something which could be quantified in monetary terms. *Increase* is the act of scaling up in something which could be quantified in monetary terms. *Short term* is a period which is relatively smaller that could have an impact on the sustainability of the organization. For example, short term accounting reporting practices of the organization. *Long term* is a period which is relatively larger that could have an impact on the sustainability of the organizations. For example, the strategic manpower sourcing practices of the organization.

5. SUMMARY

This article covers the key terms and concepts in business sustainability according to the definition derived through abstractive decomposition. The three main categories of concepts that are defined in this article includes the questions such as why business sustainability? How to achieve business sustainability? Where it will lead the businesses? Each concept has been defined, described and related to examples from the published literature or industry to give context to the concepts. The main concentration of the article has been focused on individually defining the glossaries associated with sustainability and contextualizing those concepts to the context of software development businesses.

REFERENCES

Acton, T., & Golden, W. (2003). Training the knowledge worker: a descriptive study of training practices in Irish software companies. *Journal of European Industrial Training, 27*(2/3/4), 137–146. 10.1108/03090590310468958

Bansal, P., & DesJardine, M. R. (2014). Business sustainability: It is about time. *Strategic Organization*, *12*(1), 70–78. doi:10.1177/1476127013520265

Benn, S., & Dunphy, D. (2014). *Can democracy handle corporate sustainability? Constructing a path forward.* Retrieved from http://www.tandfonline.com/doi/abs/10.5172/impp.2004.6.2.141#.VT8jsiGqqko

Bennett, K., Layzell, P., Budgen, D., Brereton, P., Macaulay, L., & Munro, M. (2000). Service-based software: the future for flexible software. In *Proceedings Seventh Asia-Pacific Software Engeering Conference. APSEC 2000* (pp. 214–221). IEEE Comput. Soc. 10.1109/APSEC.2000.896702

Boehm, B. W. (1988). A spiral model of software development and enhancement. *Computer*, *21*(5), 61–72. doi:10.1109/2.59

Breitner, H. G. H. (2005). E-Learning (M. H. Breitner & G. Hoppe, Eds.). Heidelberg, Germany: Physica-Verlag HD. doi:10.1007/3-7908-1655-8

Bresciani, P., Perini, A., Giorgini, P., Giunchiglia, F., & Mylopoulos, J. (2004). Tropos: An Agent-Oriented Software Development Methodology. *Autonomous Agents and Multi-Agent Systems*, *8*(3), 203–236. doi:10.1023/B:AGNT.0000018806.20944.ef

Cagnin, C. H., Loveridge, D., & Butler, J. (1999). *An Information Architecture to Enable Business Sustainability*. Academic Press.

Cagnin, C. H., Loveridge, D., & Butler, J. (2013). Business Sustainability Maturity Model. *Computer Communication Review*, 1–15.

Checkland, P. (2000). Soft systems methodology: A thirty year retrospective. *Systems Research and Behavioral Science*, 17.

Cheng, C. C. J., Yang, C., & Sheu, C. (2014). The link between eco-innovation and business performance: A Taiwanese industry context. *Journal of Cleaner Production*, *64*, 81–90. doi:10.1016/j.jclepro.2013.09.050

Colomo-Palacios, R. (2012). *Professional Advancements and Management Trends in the IT Sector*. IGI Global. Retrieved from https://books.google.com/books?hl=en&lr=&id=8qSeBQAAQBAJ&pgis=1

Costanza, R., & Patten, B. C. (1995). Defining and predicting sustainability. *Ecological Economics*, *15*(3), 193–196. doi:10.1016/0921-8009(95)00048-8

Coviello, N., & Munro, H. (1997). Network relationships and the internationalisation process of small software firms. *International Business Review*, *6*(4), 361–386. doi:10.1016/S0969-5931(97)00010-3

Dyllick, T., & Hockerts, K. (2002). Beyond the business case for corporate sustainability. *Business Strategy and the Environment*, *11*(2), 130–141. doi:10.1002/bse.323

Faraj, S., & Sproull, L. (2000). Coordinating Expertise in Software Development Teams. *Management Science*. Retrieved from http://pubsonline.informs.org/doi/abs/10.1287/mnsc.46.12.1554.12072

Fenny, D. (2001). *Making Business Sense of the E-Opportunity*. Retrieved April 28, 2015, from http://sloanreview.mit.edu/article/making-business-sense-of-the-eopportunity/

Galbreath, J. (2009). Addressing sustainability: A strategy development framework. *Int. J. of Sustainable Strategic Management*, *1*(3), 303–319. doi:10.1504/IJSSM.2009.026284

Glavič, P., & Lukman, R. (2007). Review of sustainability terms and their definitions. *Journal of Cleaner Production*, *15*(18), 1875–1885. doi:10.1016/j.jclepro.2006.12.006

Hanselman, S. E., & Pegah, M. (2007). The wild wild waste. In *Proceedings of the 35th annual ACM SIGUCCS conference on User services - SIGUCCS '07* (pp. 157–162). New York: ACM Press. 10.1145/1294046.1294083

Hersh, M. A. (1999). Sustainable decision making: The role of decision support systems. *IEEE Transactions on Systems, Man and Cybernetics. Part C, Applications and Reviews*, *29*(3), 395–408. doi:10.1109/5326.777075

Highsmith, J., & Cockburn, A. (2001). Agile software development: The business of innovation. *Computer*, *34*(9), 120–127. doi:10.1109/2.947100

Holwell, S. (2000). Soft Systems Methodology: Other Voices. *Systemic Practice and Action Research*, *13*(6), 773–797. doi:10.1023/A:1026479529130

Hong, P., Kwon, H., & Jungbae Roh, J. (2009). Implementation of strategic green orientation in supply chain. *European Journal of Innovation Management*, *12*(4), 512–532. doi:10.1108/14601060910996945

Kanchanapibul, M., Lacka, E., Wang, X., & Chan, H. K. (2014). An empirical investigation of green purchase behaviour among the young generation. *Journal of Cleaner Production*, *66*, 528–536. doi:10.1016/j.jclepro.2013.10.062

Klewitz, J., & Hansen, E. G. (2014). Sustainability-oriented innovation of SMEs: A systematic review. *Journal of Cleaner Production*, *65*, 57–75. doi:10.1016/j.jclepro.2013.07.017

Laine, M. (2014). Defining and Measuring Corporate Sustainability: Are We There Yet? *Social and Environmental Accountability Journal*, *34*(3), 187–188. doi:10.1080/0969160X.2014.967956

Lester, S. (n.d.). *Soft systems methodology*. Retrieved from https://www.umsl.edu/~sauterv/analysis/F2015/Soft Systems Methodology.html.htm

Lu, Y., & Abeysekera, I. (2014). Stakeholders' power, corporate characteristics, and social and environmental disclosure: Evidence from China. *Journal of Cleaner Production*, *64*, 426–436. doi:10.1016/j.jclepro.2013.10.005

Marshall, J. D., & Toffel, M. W. (2005). Framing the elusive concept of sustainability: A sustainability hierarchy. *Environmental Science & Technology*, *39*(3), 673–682. doi:10.1021/es040394k PMID:15757326

McKenzie, S. (2004). *Social Sustainability - Towards Some Definitions*. Retrieved April 28, 2015, from https://atn.edu.au/Documents/EASS/HRI/working-papers/wp27.pdf

Memon, Z. A., Wei, Y.-M., Robson, M. G., & Khattak, M. A. O. (2014). Keeping track of "corporate social responsibility" as a business and management discipline: Case of Pakistan. *Journal of Cleaner Production*, *74*, 27–34. doi:10.1016/j.jclepro.2014.03.057

Mingers, J. (2000). An Idea Ahead of Its Time: The History and Development of Soft Systems Methodology. *Systemic Practice and Action Research*, *13*(6), 733–755. doi:10.1023/A:1026475428221

Montiel, I., & Delgado-Ceballos, J. (2014). Defining and Measuring Corporate Sustainability: Are We There Yet? *Organization & Environment*, *27*(2), 113–139. doi:10.1177/1086026614526413

Mulder, K. (2014). Strategic competencies, critically important for Sustainable Development. *Journal of Cleaner Production*, *78*, 243–248. doi:10.1016/j.jclepro.2014.03.098

Murugesan, S. (2008). Harnessing Green IT: Principles and Practices. *IT Professional*, *10*(1), 24–33. doi:10.1109/MITP.2008.10

Paul, A. K., & Anantharaman, R. N. (2004). Influence of HRM practices on organizational commitment: A study among software professionals in India. *Human Resource Development Quarterly*, *15*(1), 77–88. doi:10.1002/hrdq.1088

Pesonen, H.-L., & Horn, S. (2014). Evaluating the climate SWOT as a tool for defining climate strategies for business. *Journal of Cleaner Production*, *64*, 562–571. doi:10.1016/j.jclepro.2013.10.013

Pojasek, R. B. (2007). A framework for business sustainability. *Environmental Quality Management*, *17*(2), 81–88. doi:10.1002/tqem.20168

Richardson, N. (2016). Review of Soft Systems Methodology in Action. *Philosophy of Management*, *15*(3), 1–4. doi:10.100740926-015-0023-5

Sambhanthan, A., & Potdar, V. (2015). Green Business Practices for Software Development Companies. *International Journal of Enterprise Information Systems*, *11*(3), 13–26. doi:10.4018/IJEIS.2015070102

Sambhanthan, A., & Potdar, V. (2016a). Business sustainability frameworks a survey. In *2016 IEEE/ACIS 14th International Conference on Software Engineering Research, Management and Applications, SERA 2016* (pp. 171–177). IEEE. 10.1109/SERA.2016.7516143

Sambhanthan, A., & Potdar, V. (2016b). Organisations' Responsibilities towards Corporate Sustinability. *International Journal of Strategic Information Technology and Applications*, *7*(2), 44–58. doi:10.4018/IJSITA.2016040104

Sambhanthan, A., & Potdar, V. (2016c). Waste management strategies for Software Development companies: An explorative text analysis of business sustainability reports. In *2016 IEEE 14th International Conference on Software Engineering Research, Management and Applications (SERA)* (pp. 179–184). IEEE. 10.1109/SERA.2016.7516144

Sambhanthan, A., & Potdar, V. (2017). A Study of the Parameters Impacting Sustainability in Information Technology Organizations. *International Journal of Knowledge Based Organizations*. Retrieved from https://www.igi-global.com/article/a-study-of-the-parameters-impacting-sustainability-in-information-technology-organizations/182275

Sambhanthan, A., Potdar, V., & Chang, E. (2017). *Business Sustainability Conceptualization*. Springer International Publishing; doi:10.1007/978-3-319-51472-7_1

Shrivastava, P. (1995). The role of corporations in achieving ecological sustainability. *Academy of Management Review*, *20*(4), 936–960. doi:10.5465/AMR.1995.9512280026

Sushandoyo, D., & Magnusson, T. (2014). Strategic niche management from a business perspective: Taking cleaner vehicle technologies from prototype to series production. *Journal of Cleaner Production*, *74*, 17–26. doi:10.1016/j.jclepro.2014.02.059

Tseng, S.-C., & Hung, S.-W. (2013). A framework identifying the gaps between customers' expectations and their perceptions in green products. *Journal of Cleaner Production*, *59*, 174–184. doi:10.1016/j.jclepro.2013.06.050

Vinkhuyzen, O. M., & Karlsson-Vinkhuyzen, S. I. (2014). The role of moral leadership for sustainable production and consumption. *Journal of Cleaner Production*, *63*, 102–113. doi:10.1016/j.jclepro.2013.06.045

Virtusa Environment Day. (2010). Retrieved May 18, 2015, from http://www.csrwire.com/press_releases/29830--2010-Virtusa-Environment-Day

Wang, P., Liu, Q., & Qi, Y. (2014). Factors influencing sustainable consumption behaviors: A survey of the rural residents in China. *Journal of Cleaner Production*, *63*, 152–165. doi:10.1016/j.jclepro.2013.05.007

Woodard Charles Jason. (2006). *Architectural Strategy and Design Evolution in Complex Engineered Systems*. Retrieved from http://citeseerx.ist.psu.edu/viewdoc/download?doi=10.1.1.109.3608&rep=rep1&type=pdf

Yin, J., Gao, Y., & Xu, H. (2014). Survey and analysis of consumers' behaviour of waste mobile phone recycling in China. *Journal of Cleaner Production*, *65*, 517–525. doi:10.1016/j.jclepro.2013.10.006

Chapter 3
Issues With the Importance of Branding, Brand Personality and Symbolic Meaning of Brands in the Smartphone Industry

Dominic Appiah
University of Plymouth, UK

Wilson Ozuem
University of Gloucestershire, UK

ABSTRACT

The extent to which a brand expresses and enhances one's identity is determined by the level of brand identification and this has a positive effect on word-of-mouth reports. Identification is often linked to the causes and aims of the organization; in instances where the organization is known to stand for a particular cause, consumers are likely to identify with the mission of the company and furthermore to demonstrate loyalty to its products. Drawing on the identity theory perspective, this chapter aims to examine the resistance to brand switching in the smartphone industry. The findings suggest that brand identifiers sometimes proactively generate negative word-of-mouth about brands that they do not identify with, especially after they are exposed to comparative advertising. Several insights regarding the literature on resistance to brand switching in the smartphones industry were identified, including conceptualizing social creativity. Suggestions are offered for future researchers, and implications for managerial practices on the study findings are provided.

DOI: 10.4018/978-1-5225-5393-9.ch003

INTRODUCTION AND RATIONALE

Marketing research based on identity theory focuses on how individual consumers behave in agreement with the most salient identity (i.e. the highest in the hierarchy), because it provides the most meaning for the self (Arnett, German & Hunt, 2003; Reed, 2002; Farhana, 2014). This stream of research also frames the customer–brand relationship in the light of what is 'me' and what is 'not me' (Kleine, Kleine & Allen, 1995). Drawing on Bhattacharya, Rao and Glynn's (1995) research, this study posits that customers who identify with a brand are likely to be loyal to the brand, but all brand-loyal customers need not identify with the brand. This view necessitates a detailed analysis of two main aspects of brand loyalty literature to ascertain which perspective is preferred in a competitive market in order to establish and consolidate consumer loyalty.

The chapter examines two major limitations in brand loyalty. The first is that the sustainability of brand loyalty predictors refers to resisting both time and market disruptions (Lam, Arheane & Schillewaert, 2010). However, the brand loyalty literature has mainly focused on how brands perform under normal market conditions (Keller & Lehmann, 2006; Ozuem, Thomas, & Lancaster, 2016). Yet as the business environment grows more complex, globalised and innovative, market disruptions become more prevalent. The second limitation in brand loyalty is that the perceived value of a brand is conceptualised and operationalised as a functional utilitarian value. As is prevalent in the brand loyalty literature, this does not capture other non-utilitarian factors, such as socio-psychological benefits, that might motivate customers to continue buying what they buy (e.g. Bagozzi, 1975; Gardner & Levy, 1955; Holbrook & Corfman, 1985; Richins, 1994; Sheth, Newman & Gross, 1991; Solomon, 1983; Sweeney & Soutar, 2001; Hsu & Liou, 2017). Taking a cognition-based approach, this study proposes that customers identify with brands to satisfy one or more self-definitional needs (Lam et al., 2013; Ahearne, Bhattacharya & Gruen, 2005; Bagozzi & Utpal, 2006; Bhattacharya & Sanker, 2003).

This chapter seeks to examine consumer identification with brands in the Smartphone industry. Specifically, the Smartphone industry was chosen as the product category for this study because it represents a context in which brand switching is most likely to occur due to multiple alternatives and short inter-purchase frequencies (Campo, Gijsbrechts & Nisol, 2000; Goldsmith, 2000). Notably, the market for Smartphones is probably the most dynamic of any in the world, considering the degree and rate of change in technology (Azize, Hakan & Cemal, 2013; Cecere, Corroche & Battaglia, 2015).

OVERVIEW OF THE SMARTPHONE INDUSTRY

There has been a huge increase in the number of Smartphone users recently. The Smartphone is a multi-functional device which apart from its telephone functionalities has a wide range of applications such as e-mail, Internet, calendar, notepads and in-built cameras (Norazah, 2013; Wang, Park & Fesenmaier 2012). The Smartphone is a significant shift from the traditional mobile phone and a major difference between the two is that various applications can be added after the purchase of the Smartphone device, whereas they cannot to the mobile phone. Hence Smartphones are considered radically innovative products due their additional features which are similar to miniature computers.

The evolution of the Smartphone has impacted significantly on consumer behaviour and choice. Mobile phone technology was initially used only for communication purposes but has recently advanced to include additional features that have created a greater market and altered the purchase behaviour of the consumers (Slawsby et al., 2003; Dwivedi, 2015). In this modern era of technological advancement, users of mobile phones expect other features such as media support, Internet connectivity and special applications (Jones, 2002; Hansen, 2003 and Norazah, 2013). There is the need to emphasise that recently, Smartphones have attracted the attention of all age groups from teenagers to the older generation, and special features in terms of both hardware and software have largely contributed to the impact on customer choice and purchase intentions, enabling manufacturers to innovate new services that have created a competitive environment.

The dramatic growth in the usage of Smartphones has attracted researchers and academics (Massoud & Gupta, 2003; Barnes & Scornavacca, 2004; Park & Yang, 2006), and special features in Smartphones have created greater perception and expectations (Edell & Burke, 1987; Aaker, 1997; Dickinson, Ghali, Cherret, Speed, Davis & Norgate, 2014; Wang et al., 2012). The significant component of the Smartphone that drives demand and helps manufacturers maintain a strong influence in the Smartphone market is the operating system (OS). There are many software operating systems such as iOS (Apple), Android (Google), Windows (Microsoft), Symbian (Nokia), and RIM (Blackberry). Innovations in hardware and software have triggered enormous growth in the Smartphone market, since the multi-functional operations in these devices generate the trust in technology that consumers expect. Trust in Smartphone devices and their features ultimately adds brand recognition and this is the primary factor that affects intentions to purchase (Nah et al., 2003).

SMARTPHONE MARKET STRUCTURE

The Smartphone market has experienced strong growth in recent years mainly due to technological advancement in the industry. A MarketLine (2017) report confirmed an impressive volume of 1,349.6 million sales of Smartphone units in 2016, which according to the report represents 92.7 per cent of the market's overall volume in the mobile phone industry as compared to ordinary mobile devices with a sales volume of 106.3 million units, which constituted 7.3 per cent of the market total in the same year.

The current global Smartphone market continues to be dominated by a small number of large technology firms such as Apple, Samsung and Huawei. Apple's Smartphone market share continues to grow across the globe, after consumers increasingly turn their backs on competing Android devices. It realised $215,639 million in revenue 2016. Samsung, in particular, has seen its market share dropping across the world, retaining revenues of $172,840 million in the year 2015, a decrease of 2.7 per cent compared to fiscal 2014. Huawei's consumer business segment develops, manufactures and sells a range of Smartphone devices, with the company recording $59,453 million revenue in 2015 (MarketLine, 2017).

In spite of the significant growth in the industry, the Smartphone market is changing with severe threats facing the industry (Felix, 2015). Manufacturers in high demand leverage their competitive advantage to enable them to maintain their position in the market and a positive brand image, to explore new revenue streams and most importantly achieve a sustainable product differentiation to drive sales (Gartner, 2016).

THEORETICAL AND CONCEPTUAL FOUNDATIONS

Although brands themselves are not new and have operated as a force in the organisation of production since the mid to late nineteenth century (Lury, 2004); the term 'brand' has only come to prominence in the last ten three decades (Quinton, 2013; Mitchell, Hutchinson, Quinn & Gilmore, 2015). It was during the 1990s when a previously diffused set of practices – product design, retail design, point-of-purchase marketing, among other things – became consolidated into an integral approach to marketing and business strategy known as branding. Branding has evolved from marking property and ownership, and identifying the origin and content of goods, to connoting different types of values, meanings and reputations. Davies and Ward (2005) posit that there is little that remains unbranded in some respect, and even those that seek to create goods devoid of the obvious visual trappings of 'brand' do so by constructing a specific and clear set of values around their products. Hence they insist that branding has become one of the most important aspects of business practice regardless of sector or product. Branding is also increasingly used as a marketing strategy for non-commercial organisations such as political parties, sports organisations, charities and celebrities (Moor, 2007). Gardner and Levy (1955, p. 35) have conceptualised brand in their early work as *'the complex symbols representing a variety of ideas and attributes that surround a product'.*

These ideas include subjective perceptions based on imagery, symbolism, reputation and other extrinsic attributes. The ideas are said to embody and communicate many things about a brand to consumers. Such attributes are held together by a particular brand name. The brand names may communicate unique functional attributes, subjective virtues surrounding the brand and other information that consumers may have accumulated over a period of time. These accumulated ideas are said to influence consumers' perception of brands and the reality of what brands mean to them (Arnold, 1992).

Gardner and Levy (1955) and Levy (1959) expressed the more profound view that the consumer realities which influence and stimulate individual purchase decisions are mainly based on individual subjective ideas of brand and perceived realities, rather than objective realities or specific products or services. Such perceived reality is not based on the functional attributes of a brand alone (Farhana, 2014). Indeed, brand attributes are selected based on a consideration of their utilitarian functions (see, for example, Carpenter, Glazer & Nakamoto, 1997) and this is beyond the 'technical' skills of consumers. Rather, everything people associate with a brand, both intrinsic and extrinsic, contributes to what consumers purchase. In the same vein, Penrose (1995, p. 83), referred to a package of psychological promises bundled with a product or service on offer to the consumer.

King (1973) gave a more in-depth analysis of brands as the epitome of the marketing process. He explained that a product or service is what a firm manufactures or offers, whilst a brand is what the consumer buys and what makes the company succeed. While the product is the intrinsic element of the brand, it represents the basic element in a whole article to which the consumer attaches value. This subjective belief held by customers represents the essence at the heart of a brand.

This is exemplified in terms of the 'psychological values' brought to bear on enhancing the functional benefit of a brand beyond its utility capacity (Levy, 1999). Such psychological value is embodied in the complex variety of 'soft' attributes and other associations that determine the desirability of purchasing a particular brand instead of its alternatives. These subjective attributes embody the values over and above the basic product that a brand provides to consumers.

Brands are sometimes seen in terms of their identities and brand names along with their long-term communication elements. They are also regarded as 'added value' that can enhance the intrinsic value of products (Farquhar, 1989). De Chernatony and

McDonald (1992) opined that the added value that a brand provides differentiates it from a commodity. In the same vein, Doyle (1994) defines a brand as a successful integration of an effective product, distinctive identity and added value. The definition of brand as added value has its origin in economics where added value refers to the difference between the cost of an offering and the actual price it can attract in sales.

In a marketing context, it refers to subjective attributes such as those built around names, symbols, colours, slogans, tag lines and other devices created to link a product to the market. For instance, in the definition of brand offered by the American Marketing Association (AMA), the professional body of marketers in the United States of America, Kotler and Armstrong defined brand as 'a name, term, sign, symbol, design or a combination of these, which is used to identify the goods and services of one seller or group of sellers and to differentiate them from those of competitors' (Kotler & Armstrong, 1994, p. 285).

The above definition resonates with the historical role of branding as an identification of ownership. What seems implicit in the ownership is that it fits very well with production-era marketing for which the above definition is perfectly suited. It also provides a simple definition that aggregates the various elements that make up a branded item. However, it is important to look deeper into the meaning of a brand as the basis for creating continual value for the consumer. Reviews are therefore centred on analyses of brand meanings, rather than the descriptive categorisation of brands.

Murphy (1992) used Gestalt theory to explain the complex nature of the brand. According to Murphy (ibid.), while a brand is made up of different constituents of both tangible and intangible elements, it is not simply the sum of its individual parts that makes it distinct. Therefore, 'any attempt to analyse the whole by breaking it down to its molecular components' (Murphy, 1992, p. 2) will not adequately capture the concept. A brand thus acts as a gestalt in that it is a concept that is more than the sum of its parts; parts that may have developed out of numerous scraps of information that it has established in the minds of consumers.

In order to establish a different pattern of beliefs and values that consumers internalise as a gestalt (Solomon, 2002), a brand needs to offer credible, coherent and attractive value propositions over time. To Murphy, a brand represents a relational pact that is effectively a 'pact between the owner and consumer to shop with confidence in an increasingly complex world, and it provides the owner with higher volume, often higher margins and greater certainty as to future demand' (Murphy, 1992, p. 3).

In keeping with the notion that a brand embodies many parts, Keller (1998, p. 4) defines the brand as 'a product, then, but one that adds other dimensions to differentiate it in some way from other products designed to satisfy the same needs'. In terms of the gestalt analogy made by Murphy (1992), one can argue that these differentiation and satisfaction dimensions are also part of what makes a brand. Yet this does not explain the whole concept, because the uniqueness of physical composition (product) and presentation are not sufficient to offer as a strong concept of brand.

Keller (1998) went on to observe that brands tend to create uniqueness through perceptions in the mind of the consumer, and that there is no other brand quite like a successful brand. If the differentiation of a physical product does not represent the whole brand, what explanations can one have for the concept of brand? Brand has been rightly defined as a product or service that a particular firm is offering to customers in the marketplace which is differentiated by its name, presentation and the uniqueness of its compositions. However, it is erroneous to assume that is sufficient alone to explain the essence of a brand.

With increasing technological and manufacturing sophistication, many brands competing in the same product category can be produced to a virtually identical specification. Furthermore, they can be produced at exactly the same cost. This in turn can create parity among brands in the same product category. With the possibility of such conditions, one cannot assume that uniqueness of composition and presentation makes a brand. This by itself suggests that there are many other factors that come together to explain a brand.

The multifaceted explanation of what a brand connotes is also apparent in practice. Indeed, empirical research on the concept of brand has reported the multifaceted meaning of the concept to many people involved with it. For instance, empirical research by de Chernatony and McWilliam (1990) and de Chernatony and Dall'Olmo Riley (1998) found that in practice, managers variously viewed and typified a brand on the basis of its corresponding role within the individual functional department to which their professional orientation exposed them. They identified twelve representations of brands as: i) a legal Instrument; ii) a logo; iii) a company; iv) a shorthand; v) a risk reducer; vi) an identity system; vii) an image in consumers' minds; viii) a value system; ix) a personality; x) a relationship; xi) adding value, and xii) an evolving entity. Despite these numerous manifestations, consumers are always prepared to 'impart to the brand as authority and unity, a cohesion, which functions as a gestalt prompting recognition, confidence and easy familiarity' (Murphy, 1990, p. 3).

Following from the above discussion, it can be said that many people know what a brand is because they can immediately come up with an example of a typical brand. However, an objective definition remains elusive. No single definition can satisfactorily explain the concept of brand. Kapferer (2001) observed that the inability to come up with a singular definition reflects the complexity that is inherent in any attempt to define a concept, which in reality may mean different things to many people. Kapferer (2001, p. 3) explains further that:

It is as if any definition that came to mind would not be complete. Some people talk about the name by which a product is known, others about added value, image, expectation, values, still others about the differentiating mark of the product and consumer badge. In fact they are all right in their own way; a brand is all of these things simultaneously.

In light of the complexity of this discussion, one could agree with Kapferer that the reality of the modern brand makes it impossible to assert that a singular definition can capture all types of brands in their guises. One may not be able to reduce all of a brand's parts to only one encompassing definition. Building on the issues discussed above, a specific definition of brand is offered to reflect the particular approach of the research reported in this study. Hence, a brand is defined in terms of its perceptual, intangible elements, as much as its tangible aspects. This chapter takes orientation from Murphy's (1990, p. 4) definition of brand as:

a blend of attributes, both tangible and intangible, which are relevant and appealing, and which meaningfully and appropriately distinguish one brand's uniqueness from another.

In light of the above discussion, there is no singular acceptable conceptual definition of a brand. It is worth noting that this definitional problem is not peculiar to brand. Conclusions could be drawn to the effect that definitions adopted by researchers, particularly in the social sciences, are generally more often than not controversial in nature (Kerlinger & Lee, 2000). Therefore, an examination of the meaning of brand in this chapter will be based upon its ability to be many things to many people. However, for the purposes of the current study, a brand must convey authority, cohesion and confidence and it must prompt recognition in the mind of the consumer.

Following de Chernatony and Dall'Olmo Riley's (1998) work, this chapter discusses the concept of brand in terms of four distinctive themes, which are: i) the brand as a conveyor of information to the consumer; ii) the brand as symbolism (Levy, 1959); iii) brand as relationship; and iv) brand as a risk reducer (Roselius, 1971).

BRAND AS SHORTHAND: A CONVEYOR OF INFORMATION AND MEANINGS

Brands have personal and social meanings. As the social meaning of brands becomes more important than their functional usage, the experiences that consumers have with brands become more mediated rather than formed based on the direct effect of the functional meaning of the brand. This implies that brand is understood to mean not only what it is functionally used for, but also some other ideas or feelings as its symbolic nature becomes more important than its functional impact (Levy, 1959, 1999). A symbol is something (a word, an image or an object) that stands for or signifies something else (Peter, Paul, Olsen & Grunert, 1999, p. 274). A brand therefore is also a symbol.

The symbolic nature of a brand is more apparent as the consumer uses the purchase of a brand to enhance their sense of self. Consumers are also increasingly making non-purchases of brands a significant gesture for expressing their belief about issues. For instance, the boycotting of brands such as Nike and Gap by anti-globalisation campaigners represents an attempt to symbolically express beliefs about the appropriateness of the global intention of these brands and their manufacturing process. This implies that consumers are 'able to gauge grossly and subtly the symbolic language of brands and then translate them into meanings themselves' (Levy, 1999, p. 207).

Consumers draw the meanings they associate with brands from several sources of association. The specific stimulus of celebrity endorsers such as Michael Jordan for Nike and various Hollywood makeup artists for Revlon are well-known sources of brand communication. Other extrinsic cues such as packaging, colours, smells and shapes represent important sources of marketing stimuli about brands that consumers store in their memory.

Marketing mixes, such as elaborately staged television commercials and price and product design, represent another source of symbolism. Deliberate media communications such as product placement, journalists' and opinion leaders' comments are other sources of ideas and knowledge about brands. When making sense of a marketing stimulus, consumers interpret the meaning of these stimuli in relation to previous associations from various sources that are linked with these images. These associations influence the meaning derived from marketing stimuli and the inferences drawn from them. Solomon (2001) observed that the meaning which consumers derive from this process is influenced by their perception of signs that are related to brands through either conventional or agreed upon associations. One can therefore say that symbolic meanings represent the psychological and social meanings of brands for consumers. Consequently, the non-functional meaning of a brand becomes more relevant than its physical attributes or its functional consequences. A brand is more symbolic in nature and its essence depends on its psychological and social value more than its functional attributes (Carpenter et al., 1997). However, its symbolic aspects cannot be said to represent the whole brand, because there can never be a brand without a product, service, process or experience that serves as the core concept around which psychological and social meanings are associated, and from which symbolic interpretations are derived.

It can therefore be concluded that defining a brand solely in terms of symbolic meaning is too artificial. Moreover, total reliance on a brand's functional meaning will be too mechanical in orientation. The functional side of a brand represents the object to which a specific sign is attached. Both object and sign inform meaningful consumer interpretations of a brand. Therefore, symbols constitute an important facet of brand meaning upon which consumer purchase decisions are based.

BENEFITS OF BRANDS

Brand associations are based on the functions or benefits that the consumer derives from the brand, which are the personal values consumers attach to brand attributes, i.e. what consumers think the brand can do for them (Del Rio, Vazquez & Iglesias, 2001; Keller, 1993; Bharadwaj, Tuli & Bonfrer, 2011; Moon & Sprott, 2016). A major distinction is often made between the categories of benefits provided by a brand. Brands possess functional, symbolic and experiential meaning and a single brand may offer a mixture of benefits. (Park, Jaworski & Maclnnis, 1986; Keller, 1993; Bharadwaj et al., 2011; Moon & Sprott, 2016). Some researchers suggest that a distinction lies between functional, symbolic and experiential beliefs, thus evoking differing behaviours such as purchase intentions by consumers according to belief categories (Orth & De Marchi, 2007; Park et al., 1986; Park, Eisingerich & Park, 2013).

A functional concept is a firm-derived brand meaning which is designed to solve consumption needs generated outside the organisation. A symbolic concept, on the other hand, is designed in such a way as to provide the consumer with associations with a particular group, role or self-image. An experiential concept is internally generated and sates appetite for stimulation and variety (Park et al., 2013). Expanding on the earlier work of Park et al. (1986), Keller (1993) specifies functional benefits are those that provide a solution to a specific and practical problem. Symbolic benefits on the other hand fulfil needs generated internally, such as self-enhancement. They allow the consumer to signal to others their self-image or their association with a desired group or role.

Experiential benefits are those providing 'sensory pleasure and cognitive stimulation' (Park et al., 2013; Richins, 1994). Benefits from brands may exist in a mixture of the forms described, providing all benefits at once. This idea is further supported by Bhat and Srinivas' (1998) empirical work, which suggests that a brand's value to consumers may be concurrently symbolic and/or functional. When brands meet the functional, symbolic and experiential needs of consumers, benefits are created which deliver value to the consumer. Sheth et al. (1991) propose that there is a wider range of different types of value, specifically functional value, social value, emotional value, epistemic value and conditional value. As one would expect, functional value provides functional benefits, social value provides symbolic benefits, and emotional value provides experiential benefits. In a similar manner, Del Rio et al. (2001) refer to the nature of brand utilities for the consumer. More specifically, the authors suggest that brand utilities may be classified based on two basic dimensions: their functional and symbolic values. The delimitation of what is understood as a functional or a symbolic utility is defined by the needs to be satisfied by the brand. The significance of brand associations for consumers is recognised in that they have an influence on consumer behaviour. Consumers have choice, an intention to purchase, a willingness to pay a price premium for the brand, and preparedness to recommend the brand to others (Park & Srinivasan, 1994; Cobb-Walgreen, Ruble & Donthu, 1995; Aggarwal & Rao, 1996; Hutton, 1997; Yoo, Donthu & Lee, 2000). In particular, consumers are more inclined to recommend a brand when they associate it with relevant emotional experiences (Westbrook, 1987).

Functional Benefits of Brands

The functional benefits of brands are often product-oriented and satisfy immediate and practical needs. Such benefits are often associated with solving or avoiding problems (Keller, 1993; Bharadwaj et al., 2011). Functional benefits, particularly those based on attributes linked directly to consumer decisions, are not without their limitations since they can fail to be differentiated and moreover are easily replicated (Aaker, 1996). Functional congruity in consumers is led by utilitarian motives, and expresses the extent to which the functional attributes of a brand match the expectations of the consumer in terms of how the product should perform to accomplish its main goal (Kressman, Sirgy, Hermman, Hubber, Hubber & Lee, 2006). The greater the functional congruity, as perceived by the consumer, the more likely they are to identify with the brand.

Brand loyalty is also an outcome of the functional utility of a brand as derived by the consumer (Bhattacharya, Rao & Ann, 1995; Mitchell et al., 2015). The widely studied concept of utilitarian value is described as instrumental (i.e. functional, task-related) and primarily related to cognitive evaluation on the part of the consumer. Utilitarian value is linked with the notion of product performance and usefulness (Mano & Oliver, 1993). For example, savings, convenience and product quality are classified amongst utilitarian values or benefits (Chaudhuri & Holbrook, 2001; Ailawadi, Scott & Karen, 2001).

Experiential Benefits of Brands

How consumers experience brands and the benefits derived from brand experience (experiential benefits) has gained much attention in marketing practice (Brakus, Bernd & Zarantonello, 2009; Ebrahim, Ghoneim, Irani & Fan, 2016). Consumers' 'experiences' occur when they search for products, shop for them and receive service, and when they consume them. When they go through this process they are exposed to the utilitarian benefits of the product. At the same time, they are also exposed to brand-related stimuli which prompt subjective, internal responses that constitute 'brand experience'. Such brand-related stimuli include design, logo, identity and packaging and the environment in which the products are sold. Brand experiences include particular sensations, feelings, cognitions and behaviours on the part of consumers which occur in response to particular brand-related stimuli. Such stimuli are the source of 'subjective, internal consumer responses' such as sensations, feelings and cognitions which are referred to collectively as the 'brand experience' (Brakus, et al., 2009). Brand experience is not necessarily motivationally based. Indeed, experiences occur even when the consumer has no particular connection to the brand.

Research on experiential consumption highlights the important role of particular experiential needs in consumption. Adopting a hedonic perspective to consumption, Hirschman and Holbrook (1982) suggest that products evoke an emotive response amongst consumers. A brand designed with an experiential concept seeks to fulfil the needs of stimulation and/or variety on the part of the consumer. Empirical work conducted by Brakus et al. (2009) suggests four dimensions of brand experience: sensory, affective (including emotional and social relationships and belonging), behavioural and intellectual. In other words, brands variously evoke four types of experiences. The authors also demonstrated how brand experience directly affects consumer satisfaction and loyalty, and such a relationship is indirectly mediated by brand personality. Consumer experiences with the brand are more than the fulfilment of their functional needs (Underwood, Kliene & Burke, 2001; Ebrahim et al., 2016). However, brand experiences provide the consumer with value in a similar way to utilitarian benefits (Brakus et al., 2008).

Experiential needs are internally generated and include the need for pleasure and cognitive stimulation (Park et al., 1986). Holbrook and Hirschman (1982) have similarly suggested that fun and enjoyment are amongst the experiential benefits of consumption. Brand experiences may be short-lived or long-lived and it is those that are long-lasting which consumers store in their memories. These ultimately impact upon customer satisfaction and loyalty (Oliver, 1980; Reicheld, 1996). Since the experiential nature of the brand evokes feelings in consumers, different types of feelings emerge. Keller (2001) described brand feelings as emotional responses and reactions with respect to the brand, identifying six significant types of brand-building feelings as follows:

- ***Warmth:*** *Warmth is the extent to which the brand makes consumers feel a sense of 'calm or peacefulness'. Consumers may consequently feel sentimental or affectionate towards the brand.*
- ***Fun:*** *Feelings of fun are upbeat. Consumers may feel amused, joyful and cheerful.*
- ***Excitement:*** *Excitement relates to the extent to which the brand makes consumers feel that they are energised and are experiencing something special. Brands which evoke the feeling of excitement may result in a feeling of elation or the described feeling of 'being alive'.*
- ***Security:*** *Feelings of security occur when the brand induces the feeling of safety, comfort and self-assurance in the customer.*
- ***Social Approval:*** *Feelings of social approval occur when the brand results in consumers feeling positively about the way others perceive them.*
- ***Self-Respect:*** *Self-respect occurs when the brand makes consumers feel better about themselves through a sense of pride, accomplishment or fulfilment.*

'Brand experience' is also used in the inference of the brand personality. The consumer draws upon his/her specific experience to extract information to form a judgment about the brand's personality (Brakus et al., 2009; Dion & Arnould, 2016). Brand experience is also key to the self-brand connection process, since consumers use their experiences with the brand to infer meaning. The impact of a brand is dependent upon the quality of consumers' experiences with that brand and the extent to which such experiences create vivid linkages in the mind of the consumer (Fournier, 1998). Some consumers form meaningful and personal connections between themselves and a brand to the extent that the brand is closely associated with the individual's self-concept (Escalas & Bettman, 2003; Dion & Arnould, 2016).

For consumers, meaning associated with the brand may be derived from the image or 'personality' of the brand (Dion & Arnould, 2016) that develops with time from advertising and the 'dynamics of popular culture in society' (Keller, 2008). These are also derived from the individual's own personal experiences with the brand (Escalas, 2004). The underlying notion of the self-brand connection construct is that when brand associations (meanings) are used to construct one's self or to communicate one's self to others, a strong connection is formed between the brand and the consumer's self-identity (Escalas, 2004).

Emotional Connections

Experiential benefits create emotional benefits which enable emotional brand connections in consumers. According to Aaker (2009), 'it makes sense for marketers to consider emotional, self-expressive and social benefits' as a source of value. The author describes emotional benefits as 'the ability of the brand to make the buyer or user of a brand feel something during the purchase process or user experience'. Thomson, Hamilton and Rust (2005) and Park et al. (2009) emphasise the role of emotional reactions to the brand in forming consumer–brand connections.

On a similar note, brand affect is defined as 'a brand's potential to elicit a positive emotional response in the average consumer as a result of its use' (Sung & Kim, 2010). Customers are known to form affect-laden (emotion-based) relationships with brands that match their personality. These provide a means to self-expression, self-definition and self-enhancement. Brand value is subsequently co-created through the affective relationships that customers form with brands, and this may be determined through both direct (i.e. usage or consumption) or indirect (i.e. pure perception) contact with the brand (Merz, Yi & Vargo, 2009). It is widely accepted in the literature that brands are built through a combination of rational and emotional elements and that emotions evoked by brands may enhance buying and consumption processes (Hirschman & Holbrook, 1982).

Research suggests that consumers can become emotionally attached to consumption objects such as brands and these subsequently predict their commitment to the brand (brand loyalty), and their willingness to pay a price premium for it (Thomson et al., 2005). Such attachment reflects an emotional bond with the brand (Shimp & Madden, 1988). Researchers and practitioners have recognised the importance of creating emotional connections between consumers and brands. Berry (2000) suggests that any great brand makes an emotional connection with the intended audience. He further argues that such a brand reaches beyond the purely rational and purely economic level to spark feelings of closeness, affection and trust, since consumers live in an emotional world and their emotions influence their decisions. The author suggests an even deeper connection by stating that 'brands that connect with customers' emotions are those that reflect customers' core values'. For consumers, advertising often connects brands to the emotional benefits associated with product use. Emotional benefit information is thought to provide data about affect-based experiences such as excitement and joy associated with the brand (Ruth, 2001). A key driver in emotional brand connection is the concept of self-congruence, which is the fit between the consumer's self and the brand's personality or image (Aaker, 1991; Sirgy, 1982; Malär, Krohmer, Hoyer & Nyfenneger, 2011). The consumer's self-concept is involved in emotional brand attachment (Chapin & Roedder, 2005;

Park, MacInnis & Priester, 2009). Consumers purchase brands with a specific personality to use in the expression of their self-concept (Aaker, 1991; Belk, 1988). The self-congruity literature is reviewed in depth later on in this chapter.

SYMBOLIC NATURE OF BRANDS

Brands serve as symbolic resources which users may employ to construct meaning to themselves and, further, to signal meaning for others to assign social identities to them (Elliott & Wattanasuwan, 1998; McCracken, 1988). The more 'symbolic' the brand, the more likely the brand is to enable the user to communicate their self-concept (Escalas & Bettman, 2005). The symbolic nature of brands, specifically the range of distinctive images they reflect (Chaplin & Roedder, 2005; O'Keeffe, Ozuem & Lancaster, 2016) has meant that they are particularly useful as a means for satisfying the self-definitional needs of consumers (Bhattacharya & Sanker, 2003; Fournier, 1998). In some cases, consumers derive symbolic meaning from the association they make between the brand and the typical user of the brand (Muniz & O'Guinn, 2001).

The symbolic benefits of brands allow consumers to construct their self-identity and to signal this to others. Individuals select brands that bear unique personalities and images, which they use to express a self-image or an idealised self-image which can serve a self-enhancing or self-consistency role (Aaker, 1997; Sirgy, 1982). The idea of the signalling component of the brand resonates with Ligas and Cotte's (1999) holistic framework in which the process of brand-meaning negotiation is explained using symbolic interactionism. The authors suggest that consumers do not always necessarily act independently when interpreting marketer-induced brand meaning in the cultural system since social forces also exert their influence. It is within the social environment that the consumer most often attempts to signal his/her own intended meaning to others.

Earlier work from Belk (1988) suggests that consumers possess symbolic meanings of brands which they then use to 'extend and bolster a consumer's self-concept'. More specifically, by owning brands which they perceive to possess symbolic images that are congruent with certain elements of their own self-concept, consumers maintain or strengthen their self-concept (Dolich, 1969). As an extension of this ownership, consumers are also able to express their own identities, in that the brands they choose project images similar to their own self-image (Aaker, 1991; Sirgy, 1982). This view has been supported by other researchers who suggest that symbolic benefits correspond with the need for social approval, self-expression and outer-directed self-esteem.

Consumers may value the exclusive nature of a brand because of the way in which it relates to their self-concept (Solomon, 1983; Orth & De Marchi, 2007). Self-congruity is driven by self-consistency motives such that the greater the similarity between the brand image or brand personality and the consumer's self-concept, the higher the self-congruity. Since self-consistency is a means of self-expression, the greater the self-congruity, the more likely consumers are to identify with the brand to uphold their self-consistency (Kressman et al., 2006). Symbolic needs are internally generated and are motivated by social meaning (Solomon, 1983). For example, self-enhancement, group membership and ego-identification are defined as symbolic needs (Park et al., 1986). A symbolic need helps the consumer to be defined as a member of a specific group (Hoyer & MacInnis, 1997).

The branding literature exploring the role of brands in consumers' lives reveals that brands can provide self-definitional benefits beyond utilitarian benefits (Aaker, 1991; Escalas & Bettman, 2005; Fournier, 1998; Keller, 1993; Keller & Lehmann, 2006; Bharadwaj et al., 2011). The idea of brands as a means for self-expression has come to the fore because brand consumption allows consumers to express their identities by choosing brands whose images are perceived to be similar to their own self-images (Aaker, 1991). Since consumers by nature seek to reaffirm their self-image, brands allow consumers to not only express their identities, but also to reaffirm their principles or beliefs (Kleine III et al., 1993; Levy, 1959; Solomon, 1983; Chernev, Hamilton & Gal 2011). As implied earlier by Hoyer and MacInnis (1997), consumers may choose brands to allow them the particular association with other stereotypical brand users (Escalas & Bettman, 2003, 2005).

Consumer choices about brands may be used to send social signals to other consumers about themselves, as is particularly the case with luxury brands (Han, Joseph & Dreze, 2010). In some instances, consumers extract meaning from the brand by assessing its personality, such that the signalling effect may be based not only on a stereotypical user of the brand but also on the brand's personality (Lee, 2009). The symbolic values of brands extend deeper than their role as a signalling device in that they help consumers to retain a sense of the past, to categorise themselves in society, and to communicate cultural meanings such as social status and group identity (Belk, 1988). Consistent with this view, it is apparent that the symbolic consumption of brands enables consumers to communicate some of their cultural categories such as age, gender, social status and other cultural values such as family and tradition (McCracken, 1986).

In an attempt to explain the symbolic nature of the brand, Menneaghan (1995) suggests that the brand is separate from the product. The product performs the function and the brand is 'grafted on by advertising'. Since products are easy to replicate, the emergent symbolic meanings form a basis for the positioning and differentiation of brands. According to some researchers, consumer purchasing behaviour is influenced by the symbolic meaning of the brand in the form of shared values (Sirgy, 2000). According to Zhang and Bloemer (2008), consumer–brand value congruence describes the similarity between a consumer's own personal values and his or her perceptions of the brand's values. Further, the authors provide empirical evidence for consumer–brand value congruence as having a significant and positive effect on satisfaction, trust, affective commitment and loyalty.

The Symbolic Nature of Brands and Brand Personality

Two streams of literature are applied to understand the symbolic benefits of brands: self-congruity research (Sirgy, Johar, Samli & Claiborne, 1991) and brand personality research (Aaker, 1997). Self-congruity refers to how much a consumer's self-concept is congruent with the personality of a typical user of the brand. Brand personality is the set of human characteristics associated with a brand (Aaker, 1997). Consumers tend towards those brands with similar personality traits to themselves. Noteworthy is the symbolic interactionist perspective study of brand personality which proffers that brand personality is negotiated not only in the social environment but also within the individual environment.

The unique personality dimensions of the brand tailors its intended meaning beyond the aggregate perspective to an individual level (Aaker, 1997; Ligas & Cotte, 1999). For consumers, the symbolism and meanings that constitute brand personality are not necessarily inherent in brands but are usually intentionally and sometimes unintentionally included with corporate communications and customer reactions (Wee, 2004). A traditional view of brand personality is that its traits become associated with a brand via the people who represent it; for example, a typical user of the brand, the company's employees or Chief Operating Officer (CEO) and the endorsers of the brand (McCracken, 1989). Batra, Lehmann and Singh (1993), on the other hand, suggest that a brand's personality is indirectly created over time by the entire marketing mix. The personality of the brand may be considered a non-functional benefit (Plummer, 1984) and is of importance in building competitive advantage and brand loyalty amongst consumers (Plummer, 1984; Aaker, 1996, 1997). Why and how brand personalities affect consumer brand loyalty is explained by Kim, Han and Park (2001). Their study suggests that it is the self-expressive value and distinctiveness of the brand that influences the attractiveness of the brand's personality and thus loyalty towards the brand. Brand personality enables a consumer to articulate his/her self (Belk, 1988), whether an ideal self or exact aspects of the self (Kleine III et al., 1993). It is thus an important determinant of consumer preference and usage (Biel, 1993).

Later research supports this idea by articulating that consumers incline towards brands with particularly salient personality characteristics that enable them to highlight their own personalities, in particular situational contexts (Aaker, 1999; Helgeson & Supphellen, 2004). In other words, consumers exhibit a strong desire to build relationships with brands that project a personality that they are comfortable with, in the same way as interacting with someone they like (Aaker, 1996; Phau & Kong, 2001). To enhance their connections with brands, consumers view brands anthropomorphically and assign various characteristics and personalities to specific brands. They therefore form connections between certain brands and their own identities (Escalas & Bettman, 2003). Once products and brands are associated with 'human' qualities, people may interact with them in ways that parallel social relationships, and their interactions are guided by the norms that govern these relationships (Aggarwal, 2004). This mechanism further reinforces the consumers' self-concept through self-worth and self-esteem enhancement (Aron, Aron & Smollan, 1995).

The concept of brand personality is considered to be a subset of brand image and thus the two constructs are very closely associated (Aaker, 1996; Biel, 1992; Keller, 1993). Personality expression is a key dimension representing the image of symbolic brands (Bhat & Srinivas, 1998; Keller, 1993). Not only do people use objects and brands to remind themselves of who they are, but they also often imbue brands with human characteristics that define distinct brand personalities (Aaker, 1997), leading to the formation of relationships with brands that reinforce self-concept through mechanisms of self-worth and self-esteem (Fournier, 1998). Krohmer et al. (2007) suggest that a match between a consumer's personality and the brand personality has important brand performance implications in that consumers are more likely to positively evaluate a brand which they perceive to have similar personality characteristics to themselves. It appears, therefore, that self-congruence affects brand performance. The authors argue that since brand personality specifies personality traits, this may have more influence on consumers than brand image which focuses more closely on the functional attributes and benefits of the brand.

PREVAILING PERSPECTIVES ON BRAND LOYALTY

It is important that companies build strong brands. A strong and healthy brand is instrumental in creating a sustainable competitive advantage (Aaker, 1995; Bhattacharya & Lordish, 2000). The transition to a relationship marketing paradigm places brand loyalty as a central indicator of customer relational strength (Oliver, 1999). Brand loyalty has traditionally been conceived of as a behavioural construct relating to intentions towards repeat purchases (Nam, Ekinci & Whyatt, 2011).

Brand loyalty is a 'deeply held commitment to rebuy or re-patronise a preferred product or service consistently in the future, causing repetitive same-brand or same-brand-set purchasing, despite situational influence and marketing efforts having the potential to cause switching behaviour' (Oliver, 1999, p. 34).

Dimitriades (2006) shares this view and suggests it is widely accepted that satisfied consumers are less sensitive to price change, less influenced by competitor attacks, and more loyal to the firm for longer than dissatisfied customers.

In line with all the above definitions, loyalty to a brand is expressed due to a positive attitude, which makes a consumer repeatedly demand goods or services of a particular brand, or a limited number of brands within a suitably defined period of time (Dwivedi, 2015). Consistent with this view, Copeland (1923) shares the opinion that consumers may possess a strong attitude, which may have a strong effect on their behaviour towards a particular brand. He refers to this phenomenon as brand insistence. He further describes brand insistence in terms of recognition, preference and insistence.

Behavioural and Attitudinal Loyalty

Despite the large number of studies on brand loyalty, much of the research over the past three decades investigates consumer loyalty from two perspectives and so, broadly, there are two schools of thought underlining the definition of brand loyalty. These are behavioural loyalty and attitudinal loyalty (see, for example, Bandyopadhyay & Martell, 2007; Dick & Basu, 1994; Ozuem, Patel, Howell & Lancaster, 2017)

The first marketing studies perceived customer loyalty in a behavioural way, measuring the concept as a behaviour involving repeat purchases of a particular product or service. This behaviour was evaluated either by the sequence in which goods and services are purchased, as a proportion of purchases, as an act of recommendation, as the scale of the relationship, its scope, or as a measure of several of these criteria combined (Hallowell, 1996; Homburg & Giering, 2001; Yi, 1990). Nam et al. (2011) confirmed the above-mentioned perception by stating that loyalty has traditionally been conceived of as a behavioural construct relating to intentions towards repeat purchase. Put simply, Nam et al. (2011) refer to behavioural loyalty as the frequency of repeat purchases, and repeat purchases may to a certain degree capture a consumer's loyalty towards his or her brand of interest.

Kuusik and Varblane (2009) identify three sub-segmented reasons for behaviourally loyal customers: those that are (i) forced to be loyal (e.g. by monopoly or high exit costs), (ii) loyal due to inertia, and (iii) functionally loyal. Oliver (1999) attaches the concept of inert loyalty to routine purchases, so a sense of satisfaction is not experienced and it becomes a task. From a marketing perspective, this would suggest that as long as there are no specific 'triggers' to compel behaviourally loyal customers to change providers, they will remain passively loyal (Roos, 1999). According to Liu, Wu and Hung (2007), even when presented with more attractive alternatives, consumers who have high inertia will be reluctant to change and this behaviour can be linked to a consumer's familiarity and a perception that frequenting a familiar service vendor requires less effort. They state that consumer inertia has greater influence on repeat purchase intentions, and they recommend that managers make efforts to develop consumer consumption inertia.

Day (1969) criticised this one-dimensional view as behaviourally centred, and therefore not particularly useful to distinguish true loyalty from 'spurious loyalty'. Since then, many researchers have recognised the need to add an attitudinal component to the behavioural one (Berné, Mu'gica & Yague, 2001; Dick, Mu'gica & Basu, 1994; Jacoby & Kyner, 1973; Oliver, 1997). Similarly, Day's criticism above was embraced by Uncles and Laurent (1997) who argued that by classifying these behavioural observations as a form of loyalty, there is a tendency to overlook customers who are emotionally attached to products and services. This can lead to overestimations of loyalty customer bases and the stability of portfolios (Crouch, Perdue, Timmermans & Uysal, 2004). Significantly, Dick and Basu (1994) contend that a favourable attitude and repeat purchase was ideal to define loyalty, by viewing loyalty as an attitude-behaviour relationship in their framework.

Attitudinal loyalty on the other hand can be defined as capturing the emotional and cognitive components of brand loyalty (Kumar & Shah, 2004; Ozuem, Thomas & Lancaster, 2016). Oliver (1999) aligns his description with this belief by defining loyalty as a deeply held commitment to rebuy or re-patronise preferred products or services consistently in future, despite situational influences and marketing efforts having the potential to cause switching behaviour. Brand commitment, therefore, is the pledging or binding of a person to his or her brand choice within a product class (Lastovicka & Gardner, 1977; Leckie, Munyaradzi & Johnson, 2016). Chaudhuri and Holbrook (2001) treat brand commitment as synonymous with attitudinal loyalty. The issue of commitment is discussed in more detail in the next chapter.

Attitudinal loyalty represents a more long-term and emotional commitment to an organisation or brand (Bennett & Rundle-Thiele, 2002; Shankar et al., 2003), which is why attitudinal loyalty is referred to as 'emotional loyalty' and is regarded as being 'much stronger and longer lasting' (Hofmeyr & Rice, 2000). The idea has been compared with marriage (Albert & Merunka, 2013; Dwyer et al., 1987).

Consistent with the above, attitudinal loyalty refers to the psychological commitment that a consumer makes in the purchase act, such as intentions to purchase and recommend without necessarily taking repeat purchase behaviour into account (Jacoby, 1971; Ozuem et al., 2017). Jacoby and Kyner (1973) defended Jacoby's (1971) definition of brand loyalty. Their definition was expressed as a set of six necessary and collectively sufficient conditions. According to these authors, brand loyalty is: (1) biased (i.e. non-random), (2) a behavioural response (i.e. purchase), (3) expressed over time, (4) undertaken by some decision-making unit, (5) fulfilled with respect to one or more alternative brands out of a set of such brands, and (6) a function of psychological (decision-making, evaluative) processes. They stated that it is the evaluation process (the sixth condition) that makes an individual develop a commitment towards a brand. It is this notion of commitment, they argued, that provides an essential basis for differentiating brand loyalty from other forms of repeat purchasing behaviour.

Attitudinal loyalty is preferred to behavioural loyalty (Day, 1969; Dick & Basu, 1994) for the following reasons. A behaviourally loyal customer may be spuriously loyal, that is, they might stay loyal to a brand, organisation or service provider until a better alternative in the marketplace is available (Dick & Basu, 1994). An attitudinally loyal customer, on the other hand, has some attachment or commitment to an organisation, service or brand, and is not easily swayed by a slightly more attractive alternative. Attitudinal loyalty not only indicates higher repurchase intent, but also resistance to counter-persuasion and adverse expert opinion. It is an indicator of a willingness to pay a price premium and to recommend the service provider or brand to others.

From the reasons established above, this study adopts the idea of attitudinal loyalty towards a brand or service provider and defines brand loyalty as the consumer's intention to visit or willingness to recommend a particular brand regardless of price change. The choice of attitudinal loyalty is emphasised by Shankar et al. (2003) who viewed attitudinal loyalty as similar to the type of affective or cognitive loyalty proposed by Oliver (1999). This represents a higher order or a long-term commitment of a customer to an organisation or brand, which cannot be inferred by merely observing customer repeat purchase behaviour.

BRAND SWITCHING AND RESISTANCE

Switching occurs when a customer is motivated to review available alternatives in a marketplace due to a change in competitive activity in the marketplace (Seiders & Tigert, 1997; Appiah, Ozuem & Howell, 2017). Similarly, Hogan and Armstrong (2001) posited that brand switching is about replacing an incumbent resource with a more valuable one to achieve competitive advantage. Sathish, Kumar, Naveen and Jeevanantham (2011) indicated that brand switching is a consumer behaviour that sees the behaviour of consumers differ based on the satisfaction level of consumers with providers or companies. Hence brand switching can be defined as the process of being loyal to one product or service, and switching to another, due to dissatisfaction or any other problems. They further argue that even if a consumer is loyal to a particular brand, if the brand does not satisfy his/her needs the consumer may switch to a competing brand. Therefore, management needs to constantly evaluate and redirect its resources and capabilities in order to maintain a strong position relative to competitors (Itami & Roehl, 1987).

Consumer loyalty is defined as the degree to which a consumer exhibits repeat purchasing behaviour from a service provider, possesses a positive attitudinal disposition toward the provider, and considers using only this provider when a need for this service arises (Gremler & Brown, 1996). Losing a consumer is a serious setback for a firm in terms of its present and future earnings. In addition to losing the benefits discussed above, the firm needs to invest resources in attracting new consumers to replace the ones it has lost and this incurs expenditure on advertising, promotions and initial discounts. Peters (1987) shows that it can cost five times more to acquire a new consumer than to retain an old one. Consequently, retaining an established current consumer base is much more attractive and viable than searching for new consumers.

Product characteristics are likely to affect exploratory tendencies such as brand switching proponents (BSPs) and innovation in product contexts with a large number of available alternatives and a short inter-purchase frequency (Hoyer & Ridgway, 1984). These characteristics include product involvement, perceived risk, brand loyalty, perceived brand differentiation/similarity, hedonism (or pleasure) and strength of preference (Hoyer & Ridgway, 1984; Van Trijp, Hoyer & Inman, 1996). When individuals are highly involved with a product and loyal to a brand, their propensity to switch is likely to be lower (Hoyer & Ridgway, 1984; Sloot, Verhoef & Franses, 2005).

Individuals who are involved with a product have 'a narrow latitude acceptance' (Sherif & Sherif, 1967); thus, they are unlikely to be persuaded to switch. Similarly, according to Sloot et al. (2005), loyal consumers are less likely to switch to another brand. Persuasion to switch may be manifested in the form of sales promotions such as offers and discounts, which have been found to encourage switching across various product contexts (Kahn & Louie, 1990).

Further, high perceived risk indicates that individuals are concerned with losses resulting from their purchases (Mitchell, 1999). High perceived risk leads to avoidance tendencies and behaviours (e.g. commitment to a brand, repeat purchase behaviour) as consumers are 'more often motivated to avoid mistakes than to maximise utility in purchasing' (Mitchell, 1999, p. 163). Further, perceived similarity between brands within a product class indicates that individuals are likely to exhibit switching tendencies, such as alternating among familiar brands within a product class (Hoyer & Ridgway, 1984).

Hedonism may also encourage switching within specific categories of products (Hoyer & Ridgway, 1984; Van Trijp et al., 1996). Hedonism is associated with enjoyment or pleasure that an individual derives from specific products (Griffin,

Babin & Modianos, 2000). Consumers are more intrinsically motivated with products that are associated with affective (hedonic) sensations (Hirschman & Holbrook, 1982); thus the repeated consumption of such products is likely to elicit switching tendencies (Van Trijp et al., 1996).

Market disruptions are the major cause of brand switching. Market disruptions are major events occurring in a market that threaten customer–brand relationships (Fournier, 1998; Stern, Thompson & Arnould, 1998; Appiah, Ozuem & Howell, 2016). Disruption is defined as a situation where markets cease to function in a regular manner, typically characterised by rapid and large market declines. For instance, disruptions in the financial markets are caused by a glut of sellers willing to trade at any price, combined with the near or total absence of buyers at a particular time. In these circumstances, prices can decline precipitously (Shapiro, 2010).

In the financial market, disruptions can result from both physical threats to the stock exchange or unusual trading. According to a report by Shapiro (2010), concerns over the financial situation in Greece and uncertainty concerning elections in the United Kingdom, among other things, constrained the financial market of that time with implications for trading.

However, this research focuses on disruptions that occur within product markets. As noted by McGrath (2011), the concept of 'market disruption' that occurs in a product market immediately harkens to research in two areas that have enjoyed significant development over the years: technology and innovation. Disruptions literally uproot and change how we think, behave, do business, learn and go about our day-to-day activities. According to Christensen (1997), disruptions displace existing markets, industries and technology and can produce something new, more efficient and more worthwhile.

The theory of disruptive innovation introduced by Christensen (1997) offers an explanation for the displacement of industry by smaller competitors, which are almost always new entrants (Bower & Christensen, 1995; Christensen, 1997). Disruptive innovation is an innovation that helps create a new market and eventually goes on to disrupt an existing market (Ozuem, Howell & Lancaster, 2008). The term is used in business and technology literature to describe innovations that improve products or services in ways that markets do not expect; first by designing for a different set of consumers in the new market, and later by lowering prices in the existing market.

According to McGrath (2011), the theory's explanatory power comes from the notion that industry incumbents and new entrants follow different technology trajectories. Industry leaders tend to focus on sustaining innovations that continuously improve their flagship products and increase their overall performance in attributes that are perceived as being important for their existing customer base. Over time, the performance increase achieved through sustaining innovations begins to overshoot the needs of the best customers who pay the most, whereas the new entrants' disruptive products become good enough to meet the needs of the dominant incumbents' customers.

Christensen identified a number of industries in which the pattern of disruption closely fits with his theory. These include retail, computers, hospitals, automobiles and others. Typical instances of market disruptions include:

1. Aggressive competitors' sales promotions
2. Industry crisis (for example, salmonella found in peanut butter)
3. Product recalls (e.g. Samsung 2016 Note 7 recall and Toyota's 2010 recall)
4. Negative publicity (e.g. rumours)
5. Technology and Innovation (Apple's iPhone launch)

All the above events and others have had a profound effect on the relative position of brands in the eyes of consumers, but there has been little research into how these disruptions impact upon and affect the perceived value of brands in disruptive times.

As discussed above, there are different factors and determinants which affect consumers in switching from one product to another. The next section looks at two main switching behaviours for the purpose of this study.

Brand Switching as Functional Utility Maximisation

Switching occurs when a customer is motivated to review their available alternatives in the marketplace due to a change in competitive activities in the market (Seiders & Tigerts, 1997). Economists view consumer choices as a means to achieve maximisation of functional utility (McFadden, 1986). In addition, a common practice among marketing researchers is to model consumer brand switching as choices based on product attributes and the marketing mix (Guadagni & Little, 1983).

However, according to the original text on multi-attribute utility theory (Lancaster, 1966), consumer utility includes not only a brand's functional, but also its socio-psychological, attributes. Furthermore, McFadden (1986, p. 284), contends that it is necessary to incorporate psychometric data in choice models because these factors also shape the utility function. Surprisingly, it was only recently that research on choice models revived the need to incorporate softer, non-product related attributes, such as customers' attitudes and perceptions, into models of brand choice and brand switching (Ashok, Dillon & Yuan, 2002; Swait & Erdem, 2007). These researchers posit that such softer attributes also play an important role in predicting brand choice and brand preference.

Following existing models of brand choice, 'relative perceived value' is defined as the extent to which the utilitarian value of the functional benefits of a branded offering exceeds those of another alternative in the same product category (Lam et al., 2010). When customers experience difficulty in generating positive information about their choice, they may infer that the amount of positive information is rather limited and may reverse their attitude towards the chosen brand (Wänke, Bohner & Jurkowitsch., 1997). With its relevance to functional utility, relative perceived value influences switching behaviour as functional utility maximisation. In line with recent developments in choice modelling, social identity theory suggests that brand switching also serves socio-psychological purposes besides functional utility maximisation (Rao et al., 2000; Tajfel & Turner, 1979). This theory posits that people derive their identity from affiliations with social groups. They value such membership and distinguish themselves from those who do not share such affiliations, forming the in-group and the out-group. According to Lam et al. (2010), when a social identity is threatened, that is, negatively perceived, in-group members will likely respond by resorting to three basic strategies: social mobility, social creativity, and social change. Social mobility refers to a person's attempt to leave or dissociate him/herself from the group, and moving from a lower-status group to a higher status one is an example (ibid.). Social creativity describes a person's attempt to 'seek positive distinctiveness for the in-group by redefining or altering the elements of the comparative situation' (Tajfel & Turner, 1979, p. 43). For example, a business school that does not compare favourably with other schools in overall evaluation may seek out specific dimensions of comparison that grant it superiority over these other schools (Elsbach & Kramer, 1996).

Finally, social change refers to direct competition with the out-group to retrieve higher status. In the marketing context, social change can be initiated either by competitors or by customers who identify with a brand. Market disruptions that are externally caused by competitors (e.g. radically innovative brands) can be viewed as attempts to initiate social change between competitors to vie for favour amongst customers. When a radically new brand is introduced, some customers may perceive it as having a more attractive identity than the incumbent's identity.

From the customer's point of view, brand identifiers sometimes proactively generate negative word-of-mouth about brands that they do not identify with, especially after they are exposed to comparative advertising. From the identity theory perspective, the researcher proposes that customers may switch to a new brand for self-enhancement purposes to maximise socio-psychological utility (e.g. symbolic benefits) rather than functional utility (e.g. functional benefits). In support of the social mobility argument, Rao, Davis and Ward (2000) insist that firms migrate from the National Association of Securities Dealers Automated Quotations (NASDAQ) stock market to the New York Stock Exchange (NYSE) to preserve a positive identity.

CONCLUSION AND MANAGERIAL IMPLICATIONS

In the marketing context, the narrative analysis by Stern, Thomson and Arnold, (1998) of marketing relationships implies that customers may switch to a brand they used to dislike by revising their view of the brand's identity and reference group. Research into cultural assimilation also reports that immigrants swap their cultural identities in consumption as they assimilate into the mainstream culture (Oswald, 1999). Similarly, Chaplin and Roedder (2005) suggest that as children mature into adolescents, their self-concept becomes more sophisticated and so do their connections with brands. When the boundary between the in-group and the out-group is impermeable and changing group membership is not realistic, social mobility is not a viable strategy to cope with identity threats. For example, people rarely change their political affiliation, as social identity theory suggests that under such circumstances people will engage in social creativity (Tajfel & Turner, 1979). Tajfel and Turner (1979, p. 43) posit that social creativity can take multiple forms, such as (1) comparing the in-group with the out-group based on some new dimensions, (2) changing the values assigned to the attributes of the group such that previously negative comparisons are now cast in a positive light, and (3) avoiding using the high-status out-group as a comparative frame of reference. In other words, social creativity is a form of identity-based comparison that is based on in-group biases, and defined as a strong belief in the superiority of the group with which a person identifies. It is a form of prejudice against the non-identified group. Brewer (1979) posits that such in-group biases are both cognitive and motivational because these biases motivate in-group members (e.g. brand identifiers) to attend only to elements that the in-group will evaluate more positively than the out-group.

REFERENCES

Aaker, D. A. (1991). *Managing Brand Equity*. New York: The Free Press.

Aaker, D. A. (1995). *Building Strong Brands*. New York: The Free Press.

Aaker, D. A. (1996). Measuring Brand Equity across Products and Markets. *California Management Review*, *38*(3), 102–120. doi:10.2307/41165845

Aaker, D. A. (1996). *Building Strong Brands*. New York: The Free Press.

Aaker, D. A. (2009). *Managing Brand Equity*. Simon and Schuster.

Aaker, J. (1997). Dimensions of Brand Personality. *JMR, Journal of Marketing Research*, *34*(3), 347–356. doi:10.2307/3151897

Agarwal, M. K., & Rao, V. R. (1996). An empirical comparison of consumer-based measures of brand equity. *Marketing Letters*, *7*(3), 237–247. doi:10.1007/BF00435740

Aggarwal, P. (2004). The Effects of Brand Relationship Norms on Consumer Attitudes and Behaviour. *The Journal of Consumer Research*, *31*(1), 87–101. doi:10.1086/383426

Ahearne, M., Bhattacharya, C. B., & Gruen, T. (2005). Antecedents and Consequences of Customer–Company identification: Expanding the Role of Relationship Marketing. *The Journal of Applied Psychology*, *90*(3), 574–585. doi:10.1037/0021-9010.90.3.574 PMID:15910151

Ailawadi, K. L., Scott, A. N., & Karen, G. (2001). Pursuing the Value Conscious Consumer: Store Brands Versus National Brand Promotions. *Journal of Marketing*, *65*(1), 71–89. doi:10.1509/jmkg.65.1.71.18132

Albert, N., & Merunka, D. (2013). The Role of Brand Love in Consumer-Brand Relationships. *Journal of Consumer Marketing*, *30*(3), 258–266. doi:10.1108/07363761311328928

Appiah, D., Ozuem, W., & Howell, E. K. (2016). Towards a Sustainable Brand Loyalty*: Attitudinal Loyalty Perspective. Eighteenth Annual International Conference*. Global Business and Technology Association.

Appiah, D., Ozuem, W., & Howell, K. E. (2017). Brand Switching in the Smartphone Industry: A Preliminary Study. *Global Business and Technology Association Conference*, Vienna, Austria.

Arnett, D. B., German, S. D., & Hunt, S. D. (2003). The Identity salience Model of Relationship Marketing success: The case of Non-profit Marketing. *Journal of Marketing*, *67*(4), 89–105. doi:10.1509/jmkg.67.2.89.18614

Arnold, D. (1992). *The handbook of brand management*. Century Business. The Economist Books.

Aron, A., Aron, E. N., & Smollan, D. (1992). Inclusion of Other in the Self–Scale and the Structure of Interpersonal Closeness. *Journal of Personality and Social Psychology*, *63*(4), 596–61. doi:10.1037/0022-3514.63.4.596

Ashok, K., Dillon, W. R., & Yuan, S. (2002). Extending Discrete Choice Models to Incorporate Attitudinal and Other Latent Variables. *JMR, Journal of Marketing Research*, *39*(2), 31–46. doi:10.1509/jmkr.39.1.31.18937

Azize, S., Hakan, K., & Cemal, Z. (2013). Creating Commitment, Trust and Satisfaction for a Brand: What is the Role of Switching Costs in Mobile Phone Market? *Procedia: Social and Behavioral Sciences*, *99*, 496–502. doi:10.1016/j.sbspro.2013.10.518

Bagozzi, R. P. (1975). Marketing as Exchange. *Journal of Marketing*, *39*(10), 32–39. doi:10.2307/1250593

Bagozzi, R. P., & Utpal, M. D. (2006). Antecedents and Purchase Consequences of Customer Participation in Small Group Brand Communities. *International Journal of Research in Marketing*, *23*(1), 45–61. doi:10.1016/j.ijresmar.2006.01.005

Bandyopadhyay, S., & Martell, M. (2007). Does Attitudinal Loyalty Influence Behavioural Loyalty? A Theoretical and Empirical Study. *Journal of Retailing and Consumer Services*, *14*(1), 35–44. doi:10.1016/j.jretconser.2006.03.002

Barnes, S. J., & Scornavacca, E. (2004). Mobile Marketing: The Role of Permission and Acceptance. *International Journal of Mobile Communications*, *2*(2), 128–139. doi:10.1504/IJMC.2004.004663

Batra, R., Lehmann, D. R., & Singh, D. (1993). The Brand Personality Component of Brand Goodwill: Some Antecedents and Consequences. In Brand Equity and Advertising. Hillsdale, NJ: Lawrence Erlbaum Associates.

Belk, R. W. (1988). Possessions and the Extended Self. *The Journal of Consumer Research*, *15*(9), 139–168. doi:10.1086/209154

Berne´, C., Mu'gica, J. M., & Yague, M. J. (2001). The Effect of Variety-Seeking on Customer Retention in Services. *Journal of Retailing and Consumer Services*, *8*(6), 335–345. doi:10.1016/S0969-6989(01)00002-9

Berry, L. L. (2000). Cultivating Service Brand Equity. *Journal of the Academy of Marketing Science*, *28*(1), 128–137. doi:10.1177/0092070300281012

Bharadwaj, G. B., Tuli, R. K., & Bonfrer, A. (2011). The Impact of Brand Equity on Shareholder Wealth. *Journal of Marketing*, *75*(9), 88–104. doi:10.1509/jmkg.75.5.88

Bhat, S., & Srinivas, K. R. (1998). Symbolic And Functional Positioning Of Brands. *Journal of Consumer Marketing*, *15*(1), 32–43. doi:10.1108/07363769810202664

Bhattacharya, C. B., & Lordish, L. (2000). *Towards a System for Monitoring Brand Health from Store Scanner Data*. MSI working Paper, Report No. 00-111.

Bhattacharya, C. B., Rao, H., & Glynn, M. A. (1995). Understanding the bond of identification: An investigation of its correlates among art museum. *Journal of Marketing*, *59*(4), 46. doi:10.2307/1252327

Bhattacharya, C. B., & Sanker, S. (2003). Consumer-Company Identification: A Framework for Understanding Consumers' Relationship with Companies. *Journal of Marketing*, *67*(4), 76–88. doi:10.1509/jmkg.67.2.76.18609

Biel A. L, (1993). Converting Image into Equity. In *Brand Equity and Advertising: Advertising's Role in Building Strong Brands*. Hillsdale, NJ: Lawrence Erlbaum Associates.

Bower, J. L., & Christensen, C. M. (1995). Disruptive Technologies: Catching the Wave. *Harvard Business Review*, (2-3), 43-53.

Brakus, J. J., Bernd, H. S., & Shi, Z. (2008). Experiential Attribute and Consumer Judgments. In *Handbook on Brand and Experience Management*. Cheltenham, UK: Edward Elgar Publisher. doi:10.4337/9781848446151.00022

Brakus, J. J., Bernd, H. S., & Zarantonello, L. (2009). Brand Experience: What Is It? How Is It Measured? Does It Affect Loyalty? *Journal of Marketing*, *73*(3), 52–68. doi:10.1509/jmkg.73.3.52

Brewer, M. B. (1979). Ingroup Bias in the Minimal Intergroup Situation: A Cognitive–Motivational Analysis. *Psychological Bulletin*, *86*(2), 307–324. doi:10.1037/0033-2909.86.2.307

Campo, K., Gijsbrechts, E., & Nisol, P. (2000). Towards understanding consumer Response to Stock outs. *Journal of Retailing*, *76*(2), 219–242. doi:10.1016/S0022-4359(00)00026-9

Carpenter, G. S., Glazer, R., & Nakamoto, K. (1997). *Reading on Market-Driving Strategies: Towards a New Theory of Competitive Advantage*. Addison Wesley.

Cecere, G., Corrocher, N., & Battaglia, R. D. (2015). Innovation and Competition in the Smartphone Industry: Is there a Dominant Design? *Journal ofTelecommunications Policy,* (39), 162-175.

Chaplin, L. N., & Roedder, D. J. (2005). The Development of Self-Brand Connections in Children and Adolescents. *The Journal of Consumer Research*, *32*(1), 119–129. doi:10.1086/426622

Chaudhuri, A., & Holbrook, M. B. (2001). The Chain of Effects From Brand Trust And Brand Affect To Brand Performance: The Role Of Brand Loyalty. *Journal of Marketing*, *65*(2), 81–93. doi:10.1509/jmkg.65.2.81.18255

Chernev, A., Hamilton, R., & Gal, D. (2011). Competing for Consumer Identity: Limits to Self-Expression and the Perils of Lifestyle Branding. *Journal of Marketing*, *75*(3), 66–82. doi:10.1509/jmkg.75.3.66

Christensen, C. M. (1997). *The Innovators Dilema: When New Technologies Cause Great Firms to Fail*. Boston: Harvard Business School Press.

Cobb-Walgren, C. J., Ruble, C. A., & Donthu, N. (1995). Brand Equity, Brand Preference, and Purchase Intent. *Journal of Advertising*, *24*(3), 2540. doi:10.1080/00913367.1995.10673481

Copeland, M. T. (1923). Relation of Consumer's Buying Habits to Marketing Methods. *Harvard Business Review*, *1*, 282–289.

Crouch, G. I., Perdue, R. R., Timmermans, H. J. P., & Uysal, M. (2004). *Consumer Psychology of Tourism, Hospitality and Leisure*. Oxon, UK: CABI. doi:10.1079/9780851997490.0000

Davies, J. B., & Ward, P. (2005). Exploring the Connections between Visual Merchandising and Retail Branding. An Application of Facet Theory. *International Journal of Retail & Distribution Management*, *33*(7), 505–513. doi:10.1108/09590550510605578

Day, G. S. (1969). A Two-Dimensional Concept of Brand Loyalty. *Journal of Advertising Research*, *9*, 29–35.

de Chernatony, L., & Dall'Olmo Riley, F. (1998). Defining Brand: Beyond the Literature with Expert Opinion. *Journal of Marketing Management*, *14*(5), 417–443. doi:10.1362/026725798784867798

de Chernatony, L., & MacDonnald, M. (1992). *Creating Powerful Brands*. Oxford, UK: Heinermann and Butterworth.

de Chernatony, L., & McWilliam, G. (1990). Appreciating Brands as Assets through using a Two-Dimensional Model. *International Journal of Advertising*, *9*(2), 111–119. doi:10.1080/02650487.1990.11107137

Dell Rio, A. B., Vazquez, R., & Iglesias, V. (2001). The Effects of Brand Associations on Consumer Response. *Journal of Consumer Marketing*, *18*(5), 410–425. doi:10.1108/07363760110398808

Dick, A., & Basu, K. (1994). Customer Loyalty: Towards an Integrated Conceptual Framework. *Journal of the Academy of Marketing Science*, *22*(2), 99–113. doi:10.1177/0092070394222001

Dickinson, J. E., Ghali, K., Cherrett, T., Speed, C., Davies, N., & Norgate, S. (2014). Tourism and the smartphone app: Capabilities, emerging practice and scope in the travel domain. *Current Issues in Tourism, 17*(1), 84–101. doi:10.1080/13683500.2012.718323

Dimitriades, Z. S. (2006). Customer Satisfaction, Loyalty and commitment in service organisations: Some evidence from Greece. *Management Research News, 29*(12), 782–800. doi:10.1108/01409170610717817

Dion, D., & Arnould, E. (2016). Persona-fied Brands: Managing Branded Persons through Persona. *Journal of Marketing Management, 32*(1-2), 121–148. doi:10.1080/0267257X.2015.1096818

Dolich, I. J. (1969). Congruence Relationships between Self Images and Product Brands. *JMR, Journal of Marketing Research, 6*(1), 80–84. doi:10.2307/3150001

Doyle, P. (1994). *Marketing Management and Strategy*. Englewood Cliffs, NJ: Prentice-Hall.

Dwivedi, A. (2015). A higher-order model of consumer brand engagement and its impact on loyalty intentions. *Journal of Retailing and Consumer Services, 24*, 100–109. doi:10.1016/j.jretconser.2015.02.007

Dwyer, F. R., Schurr, P. H., & Oh, S. (1987). Developing buyer-seller relationships. *Journal of Marketing, 51*(2), 11–27. doi:10.2307/1251126

Ebrahim, R., Ghoneim, A., Irani, Z., & Fan, Y. (2016). A Brand Preference and Repurchase Intention Model: The Role of Consumer Experience. *Journal of Marketing Management, 32*(13-14), 13–14, 1230–1259. doi:10.1080/0267257X.2016.1150322

Edell, J. A., & Burke, M. C. (1987). The power of feelings in understanding advertising effects. *The Journal of Consumer Research, 14*(3), 421–433. doi:10.1086/209124

Elliott, R., & Wattanasuwan, K. (1998). Brand as Symbolic Resources for the Construction of Identity. *International Journal of Advertising, 17*(2), 131–144. doi:10.1080/02650487.1998.11104712

Elsbach, K. D., & Kramer, M. K. (1996). Members' Responses to Organizational Identity Threats: Encountering and Countering the Business Week Rankings. *Administrative Science Quarterly, 41*(3), 442–76.

Escalas, J. E. (2004). Narrative Processing: Building Consumer Connections to Brands. *Journal of Consumer Psychology, 14*(1-2), 168–180. doi:10.1207153276 63jcp1401&2_19

Escalas, J. E., & Bettman, J. R. (2003). You Are What You Eat: The Influence of Reference Groups on Consumers' Connections to Brands. *Journal of Consumer Psychology*, *13*(3), 339–348. doi:10.1207/S15327663JCP1303_14

Escalas, J. E., & Bettman, J. R. (2005). SelfConstrual, Reference Groups, and Brand Meaning. *The Journal of Consumer Research*, *32*(12), 378–389. doi:10.1086/497549

Farhana, M. (2014). Implication of Brand Identity Facets on Marketing Communication of Lifestyle Magazine: Case Study of a Swedish Brand. *Journal of Applied Economics and Business Research.*, *4*(1), 23–24.

Farquhar, P. H. (1989). Managing brand equity. *Marketing Research.*, *1*(3), 24–33.

Felix, R. (2015). *The state of the Global Smartphone Market. Statista Infographics*. Retrieved from: https://www.statista.com/charts/2512/smartphone-market-share

Fournier, S. (1998). Consumers and Their Brands: Developing Relationship Theory in Consumer Research. *The Journal of Consumer Research*, *24*(3), 343–373. doi:10.1086/209515

Gardner, B. B., & Levy, J. S. (1955). The Product and the Brand. *Harvard Business Review*, *33*(3-4), 33–39.

Gartner. (2016). *Worldwide Smartphone grew 9.7 percent in Fourth Quarter of 2015*. Retrieved from: http://www.Gartner.com/newsroom

Goldsmith, R. E. (2000). Characteristics of the Heavy User of Fashionable Clothing. *Journal of Marketing Theory and Practice*, *8*(4), 21–28. doi:10.1080/10696679.2000.11501877

Gremler, D. D., & Brown, S. W. (1996). Service Loyalty; its Nature, Importance and Implications. In B. Edvardsson, S. W. Brown, R. Johnston, & E. Scheuing (Eds.), *QUIS V: Advancing Service Quality: A Global Perspective*. New York, NY: ISQA.

Griffin, M., Babin, B. J., & Modianos, D. (2000). Shopping Values of Russian Consumers: The Impact of Habituation in a Developing Economy. *Journal of Retailing*, *76*(1), 33–52. doi:10.1016/S0022-4359(99)00025-1

Guadagni, P. M., & Little, J. D. C. (1983). A Logit Model of Brand Choice Calibrated on Scanner Data: A Logit Model of Brand Choice Calibrated on Scanner Data. *Journal of Marine Science*, *2*(3), 203–238. doi:10.1287/mksc.2.3.203

Hallowell, R. (1996). The Relationships of Customer Satisfaction, Customer Loyalty, and Profitability: An Empirical Study. *International Journal of Service Industry Management*, *7*(4), 27–42. doi:10.1108/09564239610129931

Han, Y. J., Joseph, C. N., & Drèze, X. (2010). Signaling Status with Luxury Goods: The Role of Brand Prominence. *Journal of Marketing*, *74*(4), 15–30. doi:10.1509/jmkg.74.4.15

Hansen, L. (2003). Service Layer Essential for Future Success. *Ericsson Mobility World*. Available at: http://www.ericsson.com

Helgeson, J. G., & Supphellen, M. (2004). A Conceptual and Measurement Comparison of Self-Congruity and Brand Personality. *International Journal of Market Research*, *46*(2), 205–233. doi:10.1177/147078530404600201

Hirschman, E. C., & Holbrook, M. B. (1982). Hedonic consumption: Emerging Concepts, Methods and Propositions. *Journal of Marketing*, *46*(3), 92–101. doi:10.2307/1251707

Hofmeyr, J., & Rice, B. (2000). *Commitment-Led Marketing*. Chichester, UK: Wiley.

Hogan, E. J., & Armstrong, G. (2001). Toward a Resource Based Theory of Business Exchange Relationships: The Role of Relational Asset Value. *Journal of Business-To-Business Marketing*, *8*(4), 3–28. doi:10.1300/J033v08n04_02

Holbrook, M. B., & Corfman, K. P. (1985). Quality and Value in the Consumption Experience: Phaedrus Rides Again. In C. V. S. How, J. J. Merchandise, & J. C. Olson (Eds.), *Perceived Quality*. Lanham, MD: Lexington Books.

Holbrook, M. B., & Hirschman, E. C. (1982). The Experiential Aspects of Consumption: Consumer Fantasies, Feelings, and Fun. *The Journal of Consumer Research*, *9*(2), 132–140. doi:10.1086/208906

Homburg, C., & Giering, A. (2001). Personal Characteristics as Moderators of the Relationship between Customer Satisfaction and Loyalty— an Empirical Analysis. *Journal of Psychology and Marketing*, *18*(1), 43–66. doi:

Hoyer, W. D., & MacInnis, D. J. (1997). *Consumer Behaviour*. Boston: Houghton Mifflin Publishers.

Hoyer, W. D., & Ridgway, N. M. (1984). Variety seeking as an explanation for exploratory behaviour: A theoretical model. In T. C. Kinnear (Ed.), *Advances in Consumer Research* (Vol. 11, pp. 114–119). Provo, UT: Association for Consumer Research.

Hsu, L. C., & Liou, D. K. (2017). Maintaining Customer-Brand Relationships in the Mobile Industry: The Mediation Effects of Brand Relationship Benefits and Quality. *International Journal of Mobile Communications*, *15*(4), 388. doi:10.1504/IJMC.2017.084861

Hutton, J. G. (1997). A Study of Brand Equity in an Organisational-Buying Context. *Journal of Product and Brand Management*, *6*(6), 428–439. doi:10.1108/10610429710190478

Itami, H., & Roehl, W. T. (1987). Mobilizing Invisible Assets. Harvard University Press.

Jacoby, J. (1971). A Model of Multi-Brand Loyalty. *Journal of Advertising Research*, *11*(3), 25–31.

Jacoby, J., & Kyner, D. B. (1973). Brand Loyalty vs. Repeat Purchasing Behaviour. *JMR, Journal of Marketing Research*, *10*(1), 1–9. doi:10.2307/3149402

Jones, S. (2002). *3G Launch Strategies, Early Adopters, Why & How to make them yours.* Tarifica Report.

Kahn, B. E., & Louie, T. A. (1990). Effects of Retraction of Price Promotions on Brand Choice Behaviour for Variety-Seeking and Last-purchase Loyal Consumers. *JMR, Journal of Marketing Research*, *27*(3), 279–289. doi:10.2307/3172586

Kapferer, J. N. (2001). *Reinventing the Brand: Can Top Brands Survive the New Market Realitie?* London: Kogan Page.

Keller, K. L. (1993). Conceptualizing, Measuring and Managing Customer-based Brand Equity. *Journal of Marketing*, *57*(1), 1–22. doi:10.2307/1252054

Keller, K. L. (1993). Conceptualizing, Measuring and Managing Customer-based Brand Equiy. *Journal of Marketing*, *57*(1), 1–22. doi:10.2307/1252054

Keller, K. L. (2001). Building Customer-Based Brand Equity. *Journal of Marketing Management, 10*(2), 16–26.

Keller, K. L. (2008). *Strategic Brand Management: Building, Measuring, and Managing Brand Equity* (3rd ed.). Upper Saddle River, NJ: Pearson Education, Inc.

Keller, K. L., & Lehmann, D. R. (2006). Brands and Branding: Research Findings and Future Priorities. *Journal of Marine Science*, *25*(6), 740–759. doi:10.1287/mksc.1050.0153

Kerlinger, F. N., & Lee, H. B. (2000). Foundations of Behavioural Research (4th ed.). Holt, NY: Harcourt College Publishers.

Kim, C. K., Han, D. C., & Park, S. B. (2001). The Effect of Brand Personality and Brand Identification on Brand Loyalty: Applying the Theory of Social Identification. *The Japanese Psychological Research*, *43*(4), 195–206. doi:10.1111/1468-5884.00177

King, S. (1973). *Developing New Brands*. Bath, UK: Pitman Publishing.

Kleine, S. S., Kleine, R. E. III, & Allen, C. T. (1995). How is a Possession 'Me' or 'Not Me'? Characterizing Types and Antecedents of Material Possession Attachment. *The Journal of Consumer Research*, *22*(12), 327–343. doi:10.1086/209454

Kottler, P., & Amtrong, G. (1994). *Principles of Marketing*. Prentice Hall.

Kressman, F., Sirgy, M. J., Hermmann, A., Hubber, F., Hubber, S., & Lee, D. J. (2006). Direct and Indirect Effects of Self-Image Congruence on Brand Loyalty. *Journal of Business Research*, *59*(9), 955–964. doi:10.1016/j.jbusres.2006.06.001

Krohmer, H., Malär, L., & Nyffenegger, B. (2007). The Fit between Brand Personality and Consumer's Self: The Importance of Self-Congruence for Brand Performance. *AMA Winter Educators' Conference Proceedings*.

Kumar, V., & Shah, D. (2004). Building and Sustaining Profitable Customer Loyalty for 21st century. *Journal of Retailing*, *80*(4), 317–330. doi:10.1016/j.jretai.2004.10.007

Kuusik, A., & Varblane, U. (2009). How to Avoid Customers Leaving: The Case of the Estonian Telecommunication Industry. *Baltic Journal of Management*, *4*(1), 66–79. doi:10.1108/17465260910930458

Lam, S. K., Ahearn, M., Hu, Y., & Schillewaert, N. (2010). Resistance to Brand Switching When a Radically New Brand Is Introduced: A Social Identity Theory Perspective. *Journal of Marketing*, *74*(6), 128–146. doi:10.1509/jmkg.74.6.128

Lam, S. K., Ahearne, M., Mullins, R., Hayati, B., & Schillewaert, N. (2013). Exploring the Dynamics of Antecedents to Consumer–Brand Identification with a New Brand. *Journal of the Academy of Marketing Science*, *41*(2), 243–252. doi:10.100711747-012-0301-x

Lancaster, K. J. (1966). A New Approach to Consumer Theory. *Journal of Political Economy*, *74*(2), 132–157. doi:10.1086/259131

Leckie, C., Munyaradzi, W. N., & Johnson, L. W. (2016). Antecedents of Consumer Brand Engagement and Brand Loyalty. *Journal of Marketing Management*, *32*(5-6), 5–6, 558–578. doi:10.1080/0267257X.2015.1131735

Lee, J. W. (2009). Relationship between Consumer Personality and Brand Personality as Self-Concept: From the Case of Korean Automobile Brands. *Academy of Marketing Studies Journal*, *13*(1), 25–44.

Levy, S. J. (1959). Symbols for Sale. *Harvard Business Review*, *37*(7/8), 117–124.

Levy, S. J. (1999). Symbols for Sale. In *Brand Consumers Symbols and Research*. London: Sage Publications. doi:10.4135/9781452231372.n18

Ligas, M., & Cotte, J. (1999). The Process of Negotiating Brand Meaning: A Symbolic Interactionist Perspective. *Advances in Consumer Research. Association for Consumer Research (U. S.)*, *26*(1), 609–614.

Liu, T. C., Wu, L. W., & Hung, C. T. (2007). The Effects of Inertia and Switching Barriers on Satisfaction-Retention Relationship: A Case of Financial Service Industries. *Journal of Management*, *24*, 671–687.

Liz, M. (2007). *The Rise of Brands*. Oxford, UK: Berg Publishers.

Lury, C. (2004). *Brands: The Logos of the Global Economy*. London: Routledge.

Malär, L., Krohmer, H., Hoyer, W. D., & Nyffenegger, B. (2011). Emotional Brand Attachment and Brand Personality: The Relative Importance of the Actual and the Ideal Self. *Journal of Marketing*, *75*(4), 35–52. doi:10.1509/jmkg.75.4.35

Mano, H., & Oliver, R. L. (1993). Assessing the Dimensionality and Structure of the Consumption Experience: Evaluation, Feeling, and Satisfaction. *The Journal of Consumer Research*, *20*(3), 451–466. doi:10.1086/209361

Massoud, S., & Gupta, O. K. (2003). Consumer perception and attitude toward mobile communication. *International Journal of Mobile Communications*, *1*(4), 390–408. doi:10.1504/IJMC.2003.003993

McCracken, G. (1988). *The Long Interview*. London: Sage. doi:10.4135/9781412986229

McFadden, D. (1986). The Choice Theory Approach to Market Research. *Journal of Marine Science*, *5*(4), 275–297. doi:10.1287/mksc.5.4.275

McGrath, R. G. (2011, January). When your Business Model is in Trouble. *Harvard Business Review*, 96–98.

Meenaghan, T. (1995). The Role of Advertising in Brand Image Development. *Journal of Product and Brand Management*, *4*(4), 23–34. doi:10.1108/10610429510097672

Merz, M. A., Yi, H., & Vargo, S. L. (2009). The Evolving Brand Logic: A Service-Dominant Logic Perspective. *Journal of the Academy of Marketing Science*, *37*(3), 328–344. doi:10.100711747-009-0143-3

Mintel Group. (2017). *Smartphone Purchasing Process*. London: Author.

Mitchell, R., Hutchinson, K., Quinn, B., & Gilmore, A. (2015). A framework for SME retail branding. *Journal of Marketing Management*, *31*, 17-18, 1818-1850.

Mitchell, V.-W. (1999). Consumer Perceived Risk: Conceptualisations and Models. *European Journal of Marketing*, *33*(1/2), 163–195. doi:10.1108/03090569910249229

Mollerup, P. (1997). *Marks of Excellence: The History and Taxonomy of Trademarks*. London: Phaidon.

Moon, H., & Sprott, E. D. (2016). Ingredient Branding for a Luxury Brand: The Role of Brand and Product Fit. *Journal of Business Research*, *69*(4), 5768–5774. doi:10.1016/j.jbusres.2016.04.173

Muniz, A. M. Jr, & O'Guinn, T. C. (2001). Brand Community. *The Journal of Consumer Research*, *27*(4), 412–432. doi:10.1086/319618

Murphy, J. (1990). *Brand Strategy*. Cambridge: Director Books.

Murphy, J. (1992). What is Branding? In J. Murphy (Ed.), *Branding, a key marketing tool* (pp. 1–12). London: Macmillan. doi:10.1007/978-1-349-12628-6_1

Nah, F. F.-H., Zhao, F., & Zhu, W. (2003). Factors influencing Users' Adoption of Mobile Computing. In J. Mariga (Ed.), *Managing E-commerce and Mobile Computing Technologies Book*. Hershey, PA: Idea Group Inc.

Nam, J., Ekinci, Y., & Whyatt, G. (2011). Brand Equity, Brand Loyalty and Consumer Satisfaction. *Annals of Tourism Research*, *38*(3), 1009–1030. doi:10.1016/j.annals.2011.01.015

Norazah, M. S. (2013). Students' dependence on smart phones: The influence of social needs, social influences and convenience. *Campus-Wide Information Systems*, *30*(2), 124–134. doi:10.1108/10650741311306309

O'Keeffe, A., Ozuem, W., & Lancaster, G. (2016). Leadership Marketing: An Exploratory Study. *Journal of Strategic Marketing*, *24*(5), 418–443. doi:10.1080/0965254X.2014.1001867

Oliver, R. (1980). A cognitive Model of The Antecedents and Consequences of Satisfaction Decisions. *JMR, Journal of Marketing Research*, *17*(4), 460–469. doi:10.2307/3150499

Oliver, R. L. (1997). *Satisfaction: A Behavioural Perspective on the Consumer*. New York: Irwin/McGraw-Hill.

Oliver, R. L. (1999). Whence Consumer Loyalty? *Journal of Marketing*, *63*(10), 33–44. doi:10.2307/1252099

Orth, U. R., & De Marchi, R. (2007). Understanding The Relationships Between Functional, Symbolic, And Experiential Brand Beliefs, Product Experiential Attributes, And Product Schema Advertising-Trial Interactions Revisited. *Journal of Marketing Theory and Practice*, *15*(3), 219–233. doi:10.2753/MTP1069-6679150303

Oswald, L. R. (1999). Culture Swapping: Consumption and the Ethnogenesis of Middle-Class Haitan Immigrants. *The Journal of Consumer Research*, *25*(3), 303–318. doi:10.1086/209541

Ozuem, W., Howell, K. E., & Lancaster, G. (2008). Communicating in the New Interactive Marketplace. *European Journal of Marketing*, *42*(9/10), 1059–1083. doi:10.1108/03090560810891145

Ozuem, W., Patel, A., Howell, K., & Lancaster, G. (2017). An exploration of consumers' response to online service recovery initiatives. *International Journal of Market Research*, *54*(1).

Ozuem, W., Thomas, T., & Lancaster, G. (2016). The Influence of Customer Loyalty on Small Island Economies: An empirical and Exploratory Study. *Journal of Strategic Marketing*, *24*(6), 447–469. doi:10.1080/0965254X.2015.1011205

Park, C. S., & Srinivasan, V. (1994). A Survey-Based Method for Measuring and Understanding Brand Equity and Its Extendibility. *JMR, Journal of Marketing Research*, *31*(2), 271–288. doi:10.2307/3152199

Park, C. W., Eisingerich, A. B., & Park, J. W. (2013). Attachment– Aversion (AA) Model of Customer–Brand Relationships. *Journal of Consumer Psychology*, *23*(2), 229–248. doi:10.1016/j.jcps.2013.01.002

Park, C. W., MacInnis, D. J., & Priester, J. R. (2009). Research Directions on Strong Brand Relationships. In D. J. MacInnis, C. W. Park, & J. R. Priester (Eds.), *Handbook of Brand Relationships*. Armonk, NY: M.E. Sharpe.

Park, C. W. B., Jaworski, J., & MacInnis, D. J. (1986). Strategic Brand Concept-Image Management. *Journal of Marketing*, *50*(4), 135–145. doi:10.2307/1251291

Park, J. K., & Yang, S. (2006). The Moderating Role of Consumer Trust and Experiences: Value Driven Usage of Mobile Technology. *International Journal of Mobile Marketing*, *1*(2), 24–32.

Park, R. E. (1959). Race and Culture. Glencoe, IL: The Free Press.

Penrose, E. T. (1995). *The Theory of the Growth of the Firm* (3rd ed.). Oxford University Press. doi:10.1093/0198289774.001.0001

Peter, J., Paul, J., Olson, C., & Grunert, K. G. (1999). *Consumer Behaviour and Marketing Strategy* (European Edition). London: McGraw Hill.

Peters, T. (1987). *Thriving on Chaos*. New York: Alfred A. Knopf.

Phau, I., & Kong, C. L. (2001). Brand Personality and Consumer Self Expression: Single or Dual Carriageway? *Journal of Brand Management*, *8*(6), 428–444. doi:10.1057/palgrave.bm.2540042

Plummer, J. T. (1984). How Personality Makes a Difference. *Journal of Advertising Research*, *24*(6), 27–31.

Quinton, S. (2013). The Community Brand Paradigm: A Response to Brand Management's Bilemma in the Digital Era. *Journal of Marketing Management*, *29*(7-8), 7–8, 912–932. doi:10.1080/0267257X.2012.729072

Rao, H., Davis, F. G., & Ward, A. (2000). Embeddedness, Social Identity and Mobility: Why Firms Leave the NASDAQ and Join the New York Stock Exchange. *Administrative Science Quarterly*, *45*(2), 268–292. doi:10.2307/2667072

Reed, A. I. I. (2002). Social Identity as a Useful Perspective for Self-Concept Based Consumer Research. *Journal of Psychology and Marketing*, *19*(3), 235–266. doi:10.1002/mar.10011

Reicheld, F. (1996). *The Loyalty Effect: The Hidden Force behind Growth, Profits, and Lasting Value*. Boston: Harvard Business School Press.

Richins, M. L. (1994). Valuing Things: The Public and Private Meanings of Possessions. *The Journal of Consumer Research*, *21*(10), 504–521. doi:10.1086/209414

Roos, I. (1999). Switching processes in customer relationships. *Journal of Service Research*, *2*(1), 376–393. doi:10.1177/109467059921006

Roselius, T. (1971). Consumer Rankings of Risk Reduction Method. *Journal of Marketing*, *35*(1), 55–61. doi:10.2307/1250565

Ruth, J. A. (2001). Promoting a Brand's Emotion Benefits: The Influence of Emotion Categorization Processes on Consumer Evaluations. *Journal of Consumer Psychology*, *11*(2), 99–113. doi:10.1207/S15327663JCP1102_03

Sathish, M., Kumar, K. S., Naveen, K. J., & Jeevanantham, V. (2011). A Study on Consumer Switching Behaviour in Cellular Service Provider: A Study with reference to Chennai. *Far East Journal of Psychology and Business*, *2*(2), 72.

Seiders, K., & Tigert, D. J. (1997). Impact of Market Entry and Competitive Structure on Store Switching/Store Loyalty. *International Review of Retail, Distribution and Consumer Research, 7*(3), 227–247. doi:10.1080/095939697343003

Shankar, V., Smith, A. K., & Rangaswamy, A. (2003). Customer Satisfaction and Loyalty in Online and Offline Environments. *International Journal of Research in Marketing, 20*(2), 153–175. doi:10.1016/S0167-8116(03)00016-8

Shapiro, L. M. (2010). *Severe Market Dissruption on 6th May, 2010: Congressional Testimony*. Collingdale, PA: Diane Publishing Co.

Sherif, C. W., & Sherif, M. (1967). *Attitude, Ego-involvement, and Change*. Westport, CT: Green Wood Press.

Sheth, J. N., Newman, B. I., & Gross, B. L. (1991). Why We Buy What We Buy: A Theory of Consumption Values. *Journal of Business Research, 22*(2), 159–170. doi:10.1016/0148-2963(91)90050-8

Shimp, T. A., & Madden, T. J. (1988). Consumer-Object Relations: A Conceptual Framework Based Analogously on Sternberg's Triangular Theory of Love. *Advances in Consumer Research. Association for Consumer Research (U. S.), 15*(1), 163–168.

Sirgy, J. M. (1982). Self-Concept in Consumer Behaviour: A Critical Review. *The Journal of Consumer Research, 9*(12), 287–300. doi:10.1086/208924

Sirgy, M. J., Grewal, D., & Mangleburg, T. (2000). Retail Environment, Self-Congruity, and Retail Patronage: An Integrative Model and a Research Agenda. *Journal of Business Research, 49*(2), 127–138. doi:10.1016/S0148-2963(99)00009-0

Slawsby, A., Leibovitch, A. M., & Giusto, R. (2003). *Worldwide Mobile Phone Forecast and Analysis, 2003-2007.* IDC Report, No. 29586.

Sloot, L. M., Verhoef, P. C., & Franses, P. H. (2005). The Impact of Brand Equity and the Hedonic Level of Products on Consumer Stock-Out Reactions. *Journal of Retailing, 81*(1), 15–34. doi:10.1016/j.jretai.2005.01.001

Solomon, M. R. (1983). The Role of Products as Social Stimuli: A Symbolic Interactionism Perspective. *The Journal of Consumer Research, 10*(10), 319–329. doi:10.1086/208971

Stern, B. B., Thompson, J. C., & Arnould, E. J. (1998). Narrative Analysis of a Marketing Relationship: The Consumer's Perspective. *Journal of Psychology and Marketing, 15*(3), 195–214. doi:

Sung, Y., & Kim, J. (2010). Effects of Brand Personality on Brand Trust and Brand Affect. *Journal of Psychology and Marketing*, *27*(7), 639–661. doi:10.1002/mar.20349

Swait, J., & Erdem, T. (2007). Brand Effects on Choice and Choice Set Formation under Uncertainty. *Journal of Marine Science*, *26*(5), 679–697. doi:10.1287/mksc.1060.0260

Sweeney, J. C., & Soutar, G. N. (2001). Consumer Perceived Value: The Development of a Multiple Item Scale. *Journal of Retailing*, *77*(2), 203–220. doi:10.1016/S0022-4359(01)00041-0

Tajfel, H., & Turner, J. C. (1979). *The Social Identity Theory of Inter-Group Behaviour, in Psychology of Intergroup Relations*. Chicago: Nelson-Hall.

Thompson, D. V., Hamilton, R. W., & Rust, R. T. (2005). Feature Fatigue: When Product Capabilities become too much of a Good Thing. *JMR, Journal of Marketing Research*, *42*(4), 431–442. doi:10.1509/jmkr.2005.42.4.431

Uncles, M., & Laurent, G. (1997). Editorial, Special Issue on Loyalty. *International Journal of Research in Marketing*, *14*(5), 399–404. doi:10.1016/S0167-8116(97)80224-8

Underwood, R. L., Klein, N. M., & Burke, R. R. (2001). Packaging Communication: Attentional Effects of Product Imagery. *Journal of Product and Brand Management*, *10*(7), 403–422. doi:10.1108/10610420110410531

Van Trijp, H. C. M., Hoyer, W. D., & Inman, J. J. (1996). Why Switch? Product Category-Level Explanations for True Variety-Seeking Behaviour. *JMR, Journal of Marketing Research*, *33*(3), 281–292. doi:10.2307/3152125

Wang, D., Park, S., & Fesenmaier, D. R. (2012). The Role of Smartphones in Mediating the Touristic Experience. *Journal of Travel Research*, *51*(4), 371–387. doi:10.1177/0047287511426341

Wanke, M., Bohner, G., & Jurkowitsch, A. (1997). There Are Many Reasons to Drive a BMW: Does Imagined Ease of Argument Generation Influence Attitudes? *The Journal of Consumer Research*, *24*(9), 170–177. doi:10.1086/209502

Wee, T. T. T. (2004). Extending Human Personality to Brands: The Stability Factor. *Journal of Brand Management*, *11*(4), 317–330. doi:10.1057/palgrave.bm.2540176

Westbrook, R. A. (1987). Product/Consumption Based Affective Responses and Post Purchase Processes. *JMR, Journal of Marketing Research*, *24*(3), 258–270. doi:10.2307/3151636

Yi, Y. (1990). A Critical Review of Consumer Satisfaction. In V. Zeithaml (Ed.), American Marketing Association (pp. 68–123). Chicago: Academic Press.

Yoo, B., Donthu, N., & Lee, S. (2000). An Examination of Selected Marketing Mix Elements and Brand Equity. *Journal of the Academy of Marketing Science*, *28*(2), 195–211. doi:10.1177/0092070300282002

Zhang, J., & Bloemer, J. M. M. (2008). The Impact of Value Congruence on Consumer-Service Brand Relationships. *Journal of Service Research*, *11*(8), 161–178. doi:10.1177/1094670508322561

KEY TERMS AND DEFINITIONS

AMA: American Marketing Association.
BSP: Brand switching proponents.
CEO: Chief operating officer.
NASDAQ: National Association of Securities Dealers Automated Quotations.
NYSE: New York Stock Exchange.
OS: Operating system.

Chapter 4
Emergent Theory for Enterprise Resource Planning Upgrade Decision:
A Multiple Case Study

Celeste See-Pui Ng
Yuan Ze University, Taiwan

ABSTRACT

This chapter is based on four case studies and the findings are based on three rounds of qualitative data coding. This study finds that the type of business benefits expected to be derived from an ERP upgrade project, and the similarities between a firm and a new ERP system business processes have a strong impact on an ERP upgrade decision. Strategic business benefit has a relatively high impact on the upgrade decision than the managerial and operational business benefits. In contrast, symbols attached to an ERP system and top management supports are not salient factors influencing the ERP upgrade decision. However, based on further analysis of the pattern-matching of cause-effect relationships tested in this study, this research suggests that top management supports are necessary but not a sufficient factor to justify for an ERP upgrade, when there are lack of strategic business benefit incentives and similarity between a firm and a new ERP system business processes. This also indicates that ERP upgrade decisions are made rationally rather than habitually and socially defined.

DOI: 10.4018/978-1-5225-5393-9.ch004

INTRODUCTION[1]

Enterprise Resource Planning (ERP) upgrade is one of the major activities in ERP maintenance 'iceberg' (Ng, 2011). ERP upgrade, from the ERP-clients' perspectives, requires extensive attentions and efforts. But, on-going business improvement and benefit-realization are necessary for this kind of enterprise system (Seddon, Calvert, & Yang, 2010). This is in-line with the initial reason, for organizations to embark on lengthy, expensive and stressful ERP projects in the first place (Panorama, 2017). However, according to the latest Panorama's 2017 ERP market survey, 37% of ERP client-organizations realize less than half of the anticipated business benefits and only 45% of them recoup their ERP software investment costs within three years (Panorama, 2017).

ERP market is reaching maturity, therefore the vast majority of the installed base are typically in ERP upgrade cycles (Jimenez & Lee, 2011). Even though a typical ERP upgrade cycle is between five to seven years (Acumatica, 2010), some organizations will put off their ERP upgrade project in order to wait for the return on investment from previous investment (Paul, 2008). This issue gets worsen considering the fact that conducting an ERP upgrade project is risky as it has a higher total cost of ownership and uncertainty with unproven fresh solutions, such as SAP S/4 Hana, Oracle Cloud and Microsoft Dynamics 365 (Kimberling, 2017).

Prior researches in ERP upgrade can be broadly divided into practice-oriented and theory-oriented research outcomes. Practice-oriented studies, typically meant to prescribe what to do, focus on issues such as critical success factors (Nah & Delgado, 2006; Olson & Zhao, 2006) and best practices (Beaty & Williams, 2006; Herschberg, 2004; Paul, 2009). On the other hand, theory-oriented output studies, i.e. theory-building in particular, are focussing on explaining why an ERP upgrade phenomenon happened, (Khoo & Robey, 2007; Ng, 2006, 2011). However, most of these theory-testing papers merely propose theoretical frameworks useful to understand this phenomenon but they have not provided sufficient empirical findings to support or refute the proposed research frameworks.

As a result, we know very little about ERP upgrade decision, and there is a paucity of empirical evidence and theory in the field of ERP upgrade decision (Dempsey, Vance, & Sheehan, 2013; Law, Chen, & Wu, 2010). An ERP upgrade decision is defined as "a decision made which results in the installed old ERP version (partly or as a whole) being replaced by a newer version either from the same or different vendor's product," (Ng, 2011). Thus, this study is meant to provide some empirical data: (1) to support (or refute) the suitability of previously proposed concepts for ERP upgrade decision, and (2) to offer more generalizability power and enhance prior ERP upgrade decision concepts developed from case studies. The research questions addressed here are: what is the nature of ERP upgrade decision, and how do firms justify their upgrade decisions in a competitive and dynamic business environment.

ERP UPGRADE THEORETICAL BACKGROUND

Khoo & Robey (2007) describe ERP upgrade decision as contingent upon or dependent on a set of criteria. The set of criteria given by the authors includes internal organization requirements such as business needs, IT needs and the type of risk mitigation policy adopted (e.g., being an IT exploiter, early adopter or efficient follower – see (Maier, Rainer Jr., & Snyder, 1997)); external dependence on vendor's ERP software functionality and technical support; and an organization's internal resource availability for conducting an ERP software upgrade. The findings are consistent with the logic and reasoning in the contingency theory. This means that there is no one best way or best set of indicators for making an ERP upgrade decision. However, we believe that this is a common set of criteria that companies, in general, use in making ERP upgrade decision rationally.

On the other hand, Dempsey, Vance and Sheehan (2013) propose that ERP upgrade decision is mainly based on the weighting between prohibiting factors and motivation factors. The prohibiting factors are found to be the extent of customization, risk of business disruption, lack of confidence in new version, and cost of upgrade. In contrast, the motivating factors are competitive advantage, benefit realization, consolidation of resources, soaring cost/level of maintenance, and withdrawal of vendor support.

Similar to an ERP implementation project, an ERP upgrade decision has to be justified by its value, usefulness, and contribution to the business of client-organizations (Ng, 2011). Based on the critical review of trade press reports and academia research studies, Ng (2011) proposes an ERP upgrade decision conceptual model consisting of four basic concepts that have high impacts on the ERP upgrade decision. They are incentives or benefits for doing an upgrade (the extrinsic motivating factor), prior experiences and perceptions of an ERP system (the symbols attached to an ERP system), the fit (or similarity) between an ERP system and a firm's business processes, and the organizational issue of top management supports.

Both Khoo & Robey (2007) and Dempsey, Vance & Sheehan (2013) ERP software upgrade decision criteria are mainly based on rational (or economic) factors. On the contrary, Ng (2011) ERP software upgrade decision criteria covers both rational (such as incentives for doing an upgrade, the fit between a new ERP software and a firm's business processes, and the top management supports) and emotional (i.e. prior experiences, perceptions or the symbols attached to an ERP system) factors. A comparison among the three studies abovementioned is given in Table 1.

Table 1. A Comparison of prior studies of factors influencing an ERP upgrade decision

Previous Studies	Research Method & Number of Cases Adopted	Business Needs	IT Needs	Risk Mitigation Policy Adopted	Dependency on Vendor	Resource Availability	Extent of Customization	Symbols Attached	Top Management Supports
Khoo & Robey (2007)	Case study method – based on ONE Fortune 500 company	✓	✓	✓	✓	✓			
Dempsey, Vance and Sheehan (2013)	Case study method – based on ONE multinational company	✓ (competitive advantage, benefit realization)	✓ (consolidation of resources, soaring cost/ level of maintenance)	✓ (risk of business disruption)	✓ (with-drawal of vendor support)	✓ (cost of upgrade)	✓	✓ (confi-dence in new version)	
Ng (2011)	Literature review	✓ (incentive or benefit)	✓ (incentive or benefit)	✓ (symbols attached)	✓ (incentive or benefit)	✓ (symbols attached – costly)	✓ (degree of fit or similarity)	✓	✓

This research is based on Ng (2011), which covers the four key ERP upgrade concepts of incentive, similarity between a new software and an existing system, top management supports and symbols attached to an existing ERP software. The detail descriptions of the four concepts are as follows.

Incentives – Research conducted by marketing research groups such as Aberdeen Group (Aberdeen Group, 2010) and AMR Research (Swanton, Samaraweera, & Klein, 2004) show that one of the top factors to consider in an ERP upgrade decision is whether there is any apparent value and immediate returns from an ERP upgrade. This is the motivating forces that drive an ERP upgrade decision (Khoo & Robey, 2007). In general, the incentives or benefits that can be obtained from an ERP system can be grouped into two perspectives, i.e., the technology and business needs (Ng, 2006; Rahim, Shanks, & Johnston, 2011). The incentives possibly derived from an ERP upgrade, from the technology perspective, can be conformity to government regulation (such as financial and environmental compliance), the information technologies adopted by the supply chain and best practices (such as internal control and risk management) (Kumar, 2008), better IT platform such as service-oriented architecture and better integration with other systems (Bjorlin, 2008), and fewer hardware & software costs and maintenance costs (Jimenez & Lee, 2011). From the business perspective, the incentives for upgrading an ERP system for strategic and managerial business benefits may include enhancing competitiveness (Dempsey et al., 2013), creating a foundation for other business initiatives such as business intelligence and customer relationship management (Beaumont, 2004), better business processes and decision-making (Seddon et al., 2010), new and enhanced functionality in the new release (Columbus, 2013; Jimenez & Lee, 2011). For operational business benefits, this will include business transactions cycle time reduction and operational cost reduction (Ng & Chang, 2009), and process optimization and improved access to information (Seddon et al., 2010).

The presence of incentives for doing an ERP upgrade is considered as an important element for convincing and persuading top management to keep their ERP systems up to date. However, in the absence of incentives for doing an ERP upgrade, there will be difficult to justify the decision and obtain buy-ins to take up on this effort.

Symbols attached – according some researchers, information systems are used and introduced primarily for their symbolic value (Feldman & March, 1981). However, this initial symbolic value(s) may change after it has been used and interacted with other people who use the system or have prior upgrade experience. This is because not all users experience positive impacts from the system use or software upgrade (Khoo, Robey, & Rao, 2011). Empirical findings by Ng and Tan (2004) suggest that symbolism attached to an ERP system is another important component to be considered in examining ERP upgrade decision. Some of the symbols found to be attached to an ERP system are extravagance costs of an ERP upgrade project, the sense of uncontrollability with the new changes of a new ERP upgrade software system and reliance on vendor for supports (Ng & Tan, 2004). Some companies perceive ERP upgrade as expensive and risky to business (Swanton, 2004), and a painful cxperience (Wailgum, 2010). Others find frequent upgrade can be costly and disruptive (Kimberling, 2010).

Positive symbols associated with an ERP system increase one's willingness to upgrade the system for continued use as it is perceived as a worthwhile effort. On the other hand, negative symbols attached to an ERP system will make one feels doubtful and unwilling to accept the challenges to upgrade the system.

Similarity with a firm's internal business processes – Some ERP client-organizations prefer to delay an ERP upgrade because of the new version does not conform to their ways of doing business (Swanton et al., 2004). This is especially the case for some ERP client-organizations, which might have done a lot of customizations to the ERP software during their initial implementation projects. According to Columbus (2013), misfits in business processes will result in customizing an upgrade system, which costs tenfold in services to every dollar spent on the software upgrade itself. This is similar to the initial ERP implementation project, whereby business process fit between an ERP system and the implementing-firm has impacts on the upgrade decision as it can increase the risks and uncertainties involved in an upgrade project (Ng, 2013; Wang, Klein, & Jiang, 2006). As a result, some ERP client-organizations may delay their ERP upgrades and keep an outdated or unsupported version of an ERP system until they can justify the risks and costs of an ERP upgrade with its values. In this situation, their systems are not up to the vendor's standard of state-of-the-art software or business processes. Thus, the similarity between a firm's existing business process and a new ERP software business processes is a practical factor that has an impact on an ERP upgrade decision. The more similarities in the two systems' business processes the more buy-ins and lesser resistances will be for the upgrade decision.

Top management supports – Some organizations find that ERP upgrade project is a good opportunity to consolidate various ERP software instances to obtain a better business process efficiency (Bjorlin, 2008). In contrast, other companies perceive that as long as the existing business operation is functioning properly then they do not have the urgent need to do upgrade (Aberdeen Group, 2010). In this case, there will be low management supports for the upgrade decision. In overall, different organizations have different top management perceptions for when the right time for conducting an ERP upgrade project is. Prior literature on ERP implementation has proven that top management supports are critical for the success of the implementation project (Wang, Shih, Jiang, & Klein, 2008). Likewise, getting the supports and commitments from the top management are crucial as upgrade causes changes in an organization and these require strong leaderships for change management (Jimenez & Lee, 2011). Having top management supports for an ERP upgrade suggests that, from the management perspectives regardless operationally, tactically or strategically, there is a need and benefit for doing so. As a result, there will be fewer obstacles and more supports for making this decision.

Based on the above professional trade press and academic literature, related empirical evidences and theoretical assumptions associated with making an ERP upgrade decision, this study composes four initial theoretical propositions to be tested in this research. They are as shown in Table 2. The key concepts or independent variables considered are the incentives factor (Khoo & Robey, 2007), symbols attached to an ERP system (Khoo et al., 2011; Ng & Tan, 2004), similarity between a firm and a new ERP system business processes (Ng, 2013; Wang et al., 2006), and supports from top management (Wang et al., 2008); and the dependent variable is the ERP upgrade decision, i.e. upgraded willingly versus unwillingly, a.k.a. forced upgrade. This study focusses on the perspective of the decision makers, i.e. the top management.

RESEARCH METHODOLOGY

Case study research method is applied in this study as it allows multiple forms of inquiry that is useful to understand and provide detailed explanations of the phenomenon studied here. Positivist case study typology is adopted as we intend to provide detailed empirical evidence to validate existing untested propositions for ERP upgrade decision (Paré & Elam, 1997). According to Yin (2003), this type of case study is suitable for illustrating support or challenging theoretical assumptions held prior to the data collection.

The criteria, i.e. the control variables used in this study, set for choosing the right case study are that: (1) all companies come from the same industry, i.e. IT-related manufacturing industry, and (2) are located in Taiwan. For literal replication, two

Table 2. Initial theoretical propositions tested in this study, adapted from Ng (2011)

	Description
Proposition-1:	Incentives have strong positive impacts on making an ERP upgrade decision willingly.
Proposition-2:	Positive symbols attached to an ERP system have strong positive impacts on making an ERP upgrade decision willingly.
Proposition-3:	The similarity between a firm and a new ERP system business processes has strong positive impacts on making an ERP upgrade decision willingly.
Proposition-4:	Supports from top management have strong positive impacts on making an ERP upgrade decision willingly.

ERP client-organizations are required and they have previously made their ERP upgrade decisions willingly. On the other hand, for theoretical replication, two ERP client-organizations are chosen such that they have done their ERP upgrade unwillingly or by force. Case study protocol (with interview questions around the theories) is developed and used as a guide during the data collection process.

The targets of respondents in this study are the top executives (such as vice-president, CIO, and CFO) and different functional area key users, who involve in making ERP upgrade decision, are familiar with their ERP systems and are well informed about the characteristics of their ERP systems. Information is gathered with the intent of analyzing and interpreting about the phenomenon. Data collection methods applied here are (1) structured and semi-structured interviews; (2) documentations such as reports, procedure and manuals; and (3) participant observations. Participant observers in this study function as key informants, identify unknown individuals and data sources, and organize meetings in the organizations. They also serve to ensure construct validity in this study by reviewing the interview transcripts.

Prior to each interview, the interview questions are sent to the interviewees a week earlier in order to allow them to prepare or write down their responses for each question related to their prior and/or recent ERP upgrade decision. Whenever necessary, the researchers transcribe the interviews immediately after each interview. Then, the transcribed text is sent back to the interviewees to review the interview data to ensure the interpreted data is authentic and the same as its original intent and meaning, to ensure construct validity. In addition, chain of evidence, i.e. survey reports and multiple interviewees, are applied to ensure construct validity of variables considered in this study. For each case, a case study database is developed for ease of future data references and management, and to enforce reliability of this study. To achieve the internal validity of the findings, causal relationship and quotes from the interviews are used.

For data analysis, three rounds of coding are employed. (1) The first round involves using the In Vivo coding method. In this first round of coding, In Vivo coding – is used to identify the specific text segments, in all interview transcripts, those are relevant to and cause an ERP upgrade decision, i.e. the dependent variable. (2) The second round of coding makes use of the descriptive coding method (Miles, Huberman, & Saldaña, 2014). In this round, (i) descriptive code or interpretive code is assigned to the In Vivo codes, identified in the first round; and (ii) common descriptive codes belong to the same theme are grouped together. (3) The third round, hypothesis coding is adopted (Miles et al., 2014). In this round, (i) common themes of the causes of an ERP upgrade decision, found in the second round, are then mapped onto a set of codes, derived from deductive coding based on the predetermined independent variables in our propositions in Table 2; and (ii) frequency counts of each cause are conducted.

In order to test the propositions in this study, (1) case comparison analysis (Flick, 2006; Yin, 2003) is conducted to confirm and identify how the incentives factor, symbols attached to an ERP system, similarity between a firm and an ERP system business processes and supports from top management differ between ERP client-organizations that are willingly and unwillingly decided to implement their ERP upgrade projects; (2) pattern-matching (Eisenhardt, 1989; Yin, 2003) is adopted to determine if the predicted key cause-effect patterns between independent and dependent variables defined before and after data collection are being matched; and (3) tabular displays and graphs (Leonard-Barton & Deschamps, 1988) are used to visualize the key cause-effect patterns and core themes represented by each case.

FINDINGS AND DISCUSSIONS

Four case studies were conducted and the characteristics of each case study were illustrated in Table 3 below. These case companies are located in Taiwan and belong to the manufacturing industry. As shown, two of the cases (labelled as Company W and Company R, for anonymous purpose) had willingly upgraded their ERP systems, whereas the other two cases (named Company S and Company T) were forced to upgrade their ERP systems. The latter two cases were forced to upgrade meant that they would delay or would not have upgraded their systems if they had the choices. They upgraded their ERP systems unwilling because of vendor supports termination for their software version, conformity to the international financial reporting standard (IFRS), lack of the understandings of the needs for an upgrade and lack of budget for it. The data collection was started in late 2011 and completed in 2012. A total of 25 interview transcripts were produced from the four case studies.

Proposition 1: Incentives Have Strong Positive Impacts on Making an ERP Upgrade Decision Willingly

Based on the results of the coding done in the interview transcripts, case-by-case, specific to the concept of "ERP upgrade incentive," 39 In Vivo codes are obtained. From this, we find that business benefit incentives can be broadly divided into three common theme categories, i.e. strategic, managerial and operational incentives. These three categories of coding scheme are consistent with the prior empirical evidence, see (Shang & Seddon, 2003). Examples of the descriptive codes for each incentive category are shown in Table 4. The illustrations of the direct quotes are as follows.

Table 3. Case studies characteristics

	Company W	Company S	Company T	Company R
Industry	Manufacturing industry (a leading global supplier of liquid crystal display)	Manufacturing industry (capacitors, transformers, consumer electronic products)	Manufacturing industry (optical storage media and CD packaging box, public listed company)	Manufacturing industry (top five Micro UPS manufacturers in the world, public listed company)
Number of employees	14,000	180	3,000	7,000
Enterprise size	Large (more than 200 employees)	SME (less than 200 employees)	Large (more than 200 employees)	Large (more than 200 employees)
Annual revenue	NTD$2.18 billion	NTD$600 million	NTD$28.4 billion	NTD$20 billion
Initial ERP system	In year 2005 – WorkflowERP	In year 2002 – WorkflowERP (Local ERP)	In year 2000 – SAP 4.6C	In year 1996 – MFG/PRO ERP system, QAD
Reasons for ERP implementation	(1) Business expansion (2) More effective working environment (3) Improving efficiency in internal administrative operations (4) Synchronizing all data coming from various plants	(1) Transforming its 20 years old company (2) Re-shuffling workforce (3) Improving company's productivity quality (4) Changing old and relatively poor ways of doing business (business reengineering)	(1) Integrating ERP information and optimizing workflow (2) Better understanding of the conditions and status of current business operations (3) Integration with foreign customers (4) Improving customer satisfaction (5) Meeting the needs of company's future rapid growth	(1) Centralized and integrated databases. (2) Supporting inter-company process (3) New business requirements (product cost and period-end cost allocation requirement)
Current ERP system	SAP ECC 6.0	Workflow ERP GP (Local ERP)	SAP ECC 6.0	SAP ECC 6.0
Frequency of upgrade	Twice	Once – delay and forced upgrade	Once – delay and forced upgrade	Once
Number of interviewees	Seven (vice-president, IT director/CIO, IT manager, financial director, IT personnel, SD key user, FICO key user)	Five (vice-president, IT manager, financial manager, production manager, ABAB member)	Seven (vice-president, ERP team manager, Purchasing vice manager, accounting vice manager, ABAB member, production key user, MRP key user)	Six (vice-president, sales key user, SAP team leader, SAP Basis member, MRP manager, finance key user)

Table 4. Case comparisons of different types of incentive perceived in an ERP upgrade decision – for proposition-1

	Incentive Or Business Benefit Categories*		
	Strategic (e.g., attract investor, future business expansion/growth, business profit, IT business strategies)	**Managerial** (e.g., better budgeting, planning, controlling, decision-making, unify business operations, compliance, maintenance supports)	**Operational** (e.g., bug-free, operational efficiency, data integration, operational control, unsatisfied users, working efficiency)
Company W	4/10 (40%)	2/10 (20%)	4/10 (40%)
Company S (forced upgrade)	0/4 (0%)	1/4 (25%)	3/4 (75%)
Company T (forced upgrade)	1/10 (10%)	7/10 (70%)	2/10 (20%)
Company R	6/15 (40%)	7/15 (47%)	2/15 (13%)

*Note: x/y represents the ratio and (%) represents the percentage of number of codes for a particular category of incentive over the total number of codes for all categories of incentive, in a company.

Company W, Vice-President: *The system needs to be upgraded because the operational scale of the company grows larger and larger. Our previous system cannot satisfy the needs of our company and is affecting the working efficiency of our employees. Therefore, we planned to upgrade the system.*

Company W, IT Director: *Upgrading our ERP system is to meet the growth of our company, the expansion of our business operation scale, have more strict operational control, and reduce business loss due to human errors.*

Company S, IT Manager: *We chose to delay the upgrade and the reason is that basically, a new version usually has a higher bug rate than an earlier version, because it has not been used for a period of time in the market and the unknown system bugs and errors are relatively greater.*

Company T, ERP Team Leader: *Due to the timeframe for complying to the Government laws, i.e. the Financial Supervisory Commission requests that all listed companies must satisfy the IFRS regulation from 2013, we must upgrade and integrate our ERP systems. Furthermore, the maintenance support for the SAP R3 4.6C was terminated too, so it must be upgraded.*

Company R, Sales Key user (Supervisor): *We upgrade our ERP system because of our business expansion, the ever-changing business environment. The business operations of our enterprise include Mainland China, Hong Kong, Macau and Taiwan. Combining all information from these four locations into a single platform, using an ERP system is required, as this can help in unifying the business operations, and increasing the business process efficiency. The financial operation of the triangular trades among Mainland China, Hong Kong, Macau and Taiwan can be enhanced by the new ERP.*

Cross-case analysis is then conducted. The key cause-effect pattern (which is based on dependent and independent variables as listed in Proposition-1) is analysed by using tabular display & graph, and pattern-matching among the four cases, as shown in Figure 1.

The data analysis in Table 4 shows that Company W that upgrade its ERP system willingly emphasizes more on the strategic incentives and operational incentives in making its upgrade decision. This result is has a similarity with the case of Company R that weighs more heavily on strategic incentives and managerial incentives in making its upgrade decision. Conversely, Company S and Company T those upgrade their ERP systems unwillingly are failing to foresee the strategic incentives or business

Figure 1. Respondents expressing their perceived type of incentives derivable from a new ERP system

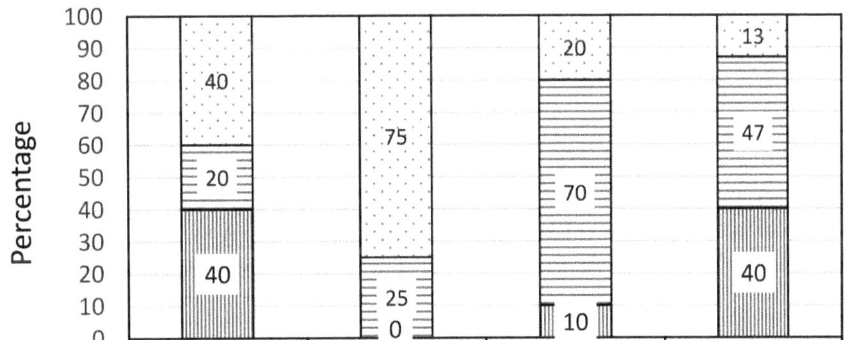

	Company W	Company S (forced upgrade)	Company T (forced upgrade)	Company R
Operational	40	75	20	13
Managerial	20	25	70	47
Strategic	40	0	10	40

values in a new ERP software. The incentives they perceive are prevailing more on the managerial incentives and operational incentives (see Figure 1). This shows that constant cause-effect patterns present between the independent and dependent variables. Although proposition-1 seems to be supported in this study, it still requires some modification as such – *strategic business benefit incentives* have strong positive impacts on making an ERP upgrade decision willingly.

Proposition 2: Positive Symbols Attached to an ERP System Have Strong Positive Impacts on Making an ERP Upgrade Decision Willingly

Interview transcripts coding for the concept of "symbols attached to an ERP system" are conducted for each case-company. A total of 141 descriptive codes is identified. For each case, the descriptive codes can be grouped into positive and negative symbols (Table 5). Some examples of the descriptive codes for the positive symbols are: friendly-user interface, increase the work efficiency, well-designed system, centralized database, unified information platform, agile, and support multiple languages. Examples of the interview quotes are as follows.

Company W, Financial Director: *An ERP system is a necessary system; it increases the efficiency of human operation.*

Company S, Vice President: *An ERP system is a tool capable of reinforcing and increasing the management efficiency of our company, monitoring the operation processes of all departments, increasing the production efficiency, and reducing production and other management costs.*

Company T, ERP Team Leader: *ERP provides the integration of all the important business operating activities within a company. With an ERP system, all the departments can obtain standardized and unified information across all functional areas, reduce rework processes, reduce waste of resources, and increase work efficiency.*

On the other hand, the examples of the negative symbols attached to an ERP system are: customizations are required, more complicated, massive system, lack of familiarity, expensive, limited flexibility, and maintenance contract. For instance,

Company T, Basis Member: *ERP is a massive and complicated system. As a result, its hardware and network requirements are also larger.*

Company R, Finance Key User (Supervisor): *ERP system is an expensive IS system, collects various operational data, its data input is complicated, and in order to use it to produce personalized reports customizations are required.*

Company R, Vice President: *It is a comprehensive business processes that provides an integrated database but it has limited flexibility for system customization.*

Quantitative content analysis is then conducted and the total number of positive symbol counts and negative symbol counts in each case-company is tabulated in Table 5, for cross-case comparison. As shown, both Company W and Company R have a higher percentage of positive symbols attached to an ERP system than the negative symbols. However, Company S and Company T, where their ERP upgrade decisions are forced, also have the same effects, i.e. having more positive symbols attached to their ERP systems than the negative ones.

A closer look at the case-by-case comparison, it is observed that although Company R has the highest negative symbols attached to their ERP system (compared to the other three cases), the company still makes the decision to upgrade their ERP system. In contrast, although Company S has the highest positive symbols attached to their ERP system, the company's ERP system upgrade decision is forced, after delaying for nine years. As a result, there are mixed results for the observed relationship between an upgrade decision and positive/negative symbols attached to the ERP system (Table 5). Thus, proposition-2 is not supported in this study.

This finding suggests that there is no obvious association between symbol attached and ERP upgrade decision. This means that an ERP upgrade decision is not socially constructed in a social setting. This also indicates that difference in perceptions (i.e. the symbols attached to the system) after using the system do not seem to have much impacts on the upgrade decision. This finding may suggest that the strategic business benefit incentive supersedes the role of the symbol attached to an ERP system, in the process of making an ERP upgrade decision.

Table 5. Case comparisons for proposition-2

	Symbols Attached to an ERP System*	
	Positive	**Negative**
Company W	16/19 (84%)	3/19 (16%)
Company S (forced upgrade)	24/25 (96%)	1/25 (4%)
Company T (forced upgrade)	42/54 (78%)	12/54 (22%)
Company R	26/43 (60%)	17/43 (40%)

*Note: x/y represents the ratio and (%) represents the percentage of number of codes for a particular category of symbol over the total number of codes for all categories of symbol, in a company.

Proposition 3: The Similarity Between a Firm and a New ERP System Business Processes Has Strong Positive Impacts on Making an ERP Upgrade Decision Willingly

The results of the coding performed on the interview transcripts, for the four case studies, for the core theme associated with the "similarity between a firm and a new ERP system business processes" produce 34 descriptive codes. Examples of these codes are: not the same, ERP system is able to satisfy the need of our company, they are some differences, it is the same, completely the same, not exactly the same, almost the same, and has a few differences. These 34 codes are then reduced to three common theme categories, i.e. not the same, almost the same and the same, as shown in Table 6. The following is some illustrations of the interview transcripts.

Company W, IT Director: *Most of the new ERP software business process flows are the same with ours.*

Company W, Financial Director: *The new ERP software business processes are almost the same with our existing processes, even though some differences are observed.*

Company S, Production Manager: *The business processes in our existing ERP system and the new ERP software are not the same. ... [However,] limited changes can be made to the production business processes, as our company wants to minimize modifications to the new ERP software due to our budget constraint.*

Table 6. Case comparisons for proposition-3

	Similarity between a Firm and a New ERP System Business Processes*		
	1= Not the Same	**2= Almost the Same**	**3= the Same**
Company W	1/11 (9%)	7/11 (64%)	3/11 (27%)
Company S (forced upgrade)	4/5 (80%)	0/5 (0%)	1/5 (20%)
Company T (forced upgrade)	5/8 (63%)	1/8 (13%)	2/8 (24%)
Company R	0/10 (0%)	2/10 (20%)	8/10 (80%)

*Note: x/y represents the ratio and (%) represents the percentage of number of codes for a particular category of similarity over the total number of codes for all categories of similarity, in a company.

Company T, ERP Team Leader: *The work processes [in our previous ERP software and the new ERP software] were not the same. All customizations done in the previous version need to be redeveloped and tested in the new version of the ERP system.*

Company R, SAP Team Leader: *We selected and designed our ERP system business blueprint based on the SAP best practices. ... The final ERP system is able to satisfy the need of our company.*

Subsequently, quantitative content analysis is conducted and the total number of codes belonging to each category is tallied and computed. The succeeding data analysis on Company W suggests that it has 91% of its descriptive codes belonging to "the same" and "almost the same" categories for "similarity between a firm and a new ERP system business processes." Company R, which implements its ERP upgrade willingly, also has the same result such that 80% of its descriptive codes for this theme falls into "the same" category. In comparison with the other two case companies, Company S and Company T, that prefer to delay their ERP upgrade (if they have the choice) have the highest percentage of descriptive codes for "not the same" for the "similarity between a firm and a new ERP system business processes." This indicates that there is a consistent pattern between the independent and dependent variables. Thus, there is a strong positive impact between the decision to upgrade an ERP system willingly and the similarity between a firm and a new ERP system business processes (see Figure 2). Based on this, the proposition-3 is supported by our empirical data here.

Proposition 4: Supports From Top Management Have Strong Positive Impacts on Making an ERP Upgrade Decision Willingly

The independent concept focused in this proposition is "top management supports." In this case, we concentrate the analysis of the interview transcripts, in each case study, on the interview questions that are particularly related to this concept. Thirty descriptive codes are produces for this concept. The descriptive quotes related to this core theme are found to be: interested in, surely interested, definitely provide the required supports, strongly supported, not interested, was not keen in supporting the upgrade, and did not really want to support the ERP system upgrade. These are categorized into two common themes, "not supporting" and "fully supporting." Examples of the quotes are as such:

Company W, Vice-President: *[The upgrade] is strongly supported by top management because the functionalities of the new system are superior to the previous one and it can increase the efficiency of users' business operations.*

Figure 2. Respondents expressing their perceived degree of similarity between their company and a new ERP system business processes

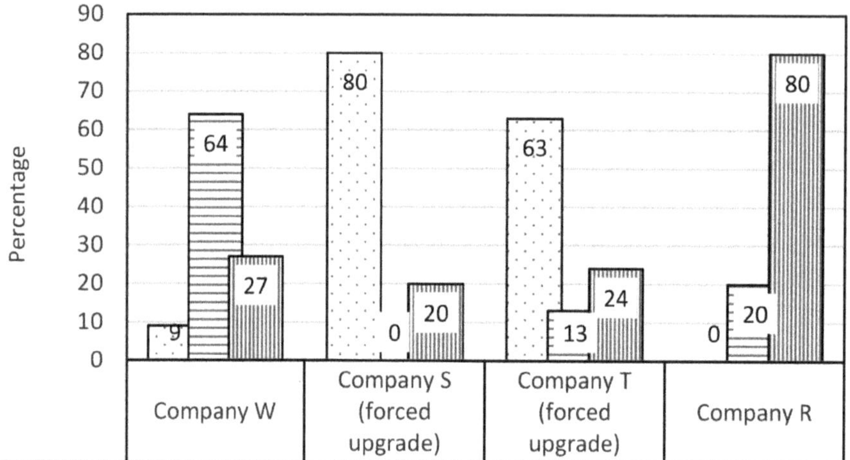

	Company W	Company S (forced upgrade)	Company T (forced upgrade)	Company R
Not the same	9	80	63	0
Almost the same	64	0	13	20
The same	27	20	24	80

Company S, Vice President: *Yes, we support our ERP upgrade. The efficiency and functionality, in the new ERP software, have been increased. These have been helpful to the overall business performance of our company.*

Company T, Accounting Vice-Manager: *The top management was not keen of supporting the upgrade of the previous ERP system. The reasons were the cost of upgrade was considerably expensive. Despite the fact that it was expensive, the ERP system must be upgraded due to the Government policies.*

Company T, Vice-President: *We did not strongly support the ERP upgrade because the performance of the new system upgrade and pricing were not clearly stated in the service contract of the ERP upgrade project, promoted by the ERP team.*

Company R, Material Manager: *The top management supports the system upgrade as there is a clear need to upgrade the system.*

In making the cross-case comparisons, it is found that the two cases, i.e. Company W and Company R in this study, that upgrade their ERP systems willingly do obtain full supports from their top management. Surprisingly, the other two case companies, where their upgrade decisions are not made willingly also have more than 50%

of their descriptive codes indicating the top management supports for their ERP upgrade decisions, see Table 7. Therefore, there is no stable pattern of cause-effect relationship between the ERP upgrade decision and top management supports. Thus, the empirical data in this study does not fully support our proposition-4.

We argue that top management supports are necessary for making an ERP upgrade decision but not a sufficient factor to justify for an ERP upgrade. This also indicates that ERP upgrade decisions are made rationally.

FURTHER ANALYSIS AND DISCUSSIONS

This study finds that ERP upgrade decision is highly related to the type of business benefits expected to be derived (or the type of business problems expected to be resolved by) from an ERP upgrade project. In general, it is observed that strategic business benefit has a relatively highest impact on the upgrade decision than the managerial and operational business benefits. The incentives or business benefits expected to be realized from an ERP upgrade does appear to be a strong factor influencing ERP upgrade decision (proposition-1). This finding is in line with prior studies conducted by Khoo and Robey (2007), and Dempsey et al. (2013).

Likewise, our empirical results here also suggest that the similarity between a firm and a new ERP system business processes has a strong impact on an ERP upgrade decision (proposition-2). This is consistent with the prior studies related to ERP system implementation success (Wang et al., 2008) and post-implementation system use success (Ng, 2013). However, symbols attached to an ERP system do not seem to be a strong differentiating- or salient-factor for the ERP upgrade decision (proposition-3). This finding is not consistent with Ng and Tan (2004). This is also

Table 7. Case comparisons for proposition-4

	Top Management*	
	Not Supporting	**Fully Supporting**
Company W	0/6 (0%)	6/6 (100%)
Company S (forced upgrade)	0/6 (0%)	6/6 (100%)
Company T (forced upgrade)	3/8 (40%)	5/8 (60%)
Company R	0/10 (0%)	10/10 (100%)

*Note: x/y represents the ratio and (%) represents the percentage of number of codes for a particular category of top management support over the total number of codes for all categories of top management support, in a company.

the case for top management supports, which fail to prove to be a strong factor influencing ERP upgrade decision (proposition-4).

Based on the pattern-matching of cause-effect relationships tested in this study (as shown in Table 8), it is argued that top management supports are necessary for making an ERP upgrade decision but not a sufficient factor to justify for an ERP upgrade, when there are lack of strategic business benefit incentives and similarity between a firm and a new ERP system business processes. This also indicates that ERP upgrade decisions are made rationally rather than habitually and socially defined. These empirical substantiations help us to refine our initial set of propositions in Table 2, and the modified propositions are as shown in Table 9.

Table 8. Pattern-matching of cause-effect relationships tested in this study

	Perceived Strategic Incentive ≥ 33%*	"Positive" Symbol Attached ≥ 60%**	"Almost the Same and the Same" Similarity ≥ 80%***	Full Top Management Support ≥ 80%****
Company W	✓	✓	✓	✓
Company S (forced upgrade)		✓		✓
Company T (forced upgrade)		✓		
Company R	✓	✓	✓	✓

* The percentage of perceived strategic business benefit incentive is equal to or larger than one-third (33%) of the total number of codes for all categories of incentives identified in each individual case company.

** The percentage of "positive" symbols is equal to or larger than 60% of the total number of codes for both categories of symbol identified in each individual case company.

*** The similarity between a firm and a new ERP system business processes – is belonging to the categories of "the same" or "almost the same" and its number of codes is equal to or larger than 80% of the total number of codes.

**** The percentage of "full top management support" is equal to or larger than 80% of the total number of codes for all categories of top management support identified in each individual case company.

Table 9. Refined theoretical propositions from this study

	Description
Proposition-1:	Strategic business benefit incentives have strong positive impacts on making an ERP upgrade decision willingly.
Proposition-2:	Symbols attached to an ERP system do not have strong positive impacts on making an ERP upgrade decision willingly.
Proposition-3:	The similarity between a firm and a new ERP system business processes has a strong positive impact on making an ERP upgrade decision willingly.
Proposition-4:	Top management supports are necessary but not a sufficient factor to justify for an ERP upgrade.

FUTURE RESEARCH DIRECTIONS

For future study, researchers can further improve the revised ERP upgrade propositions, as given in Table 9, by testing the propositions using survey research method, and examining if any other existing theories can be used or extended to explain the ERP upgrade decision.

Although this study finds that top management supports are not sufficient factor to justify for an ERP upgrade, it would be interesting to investigate whether different types of leadership style play a moderator role in influencing an upgrade decision, cf. (Rezvani, Dong, & Khosravi, 2017).

CONCLUSION

This study attempts to follow the rigor of positivist case study suggested by Dubé and Paré (2003) as far as possible in order to ensure validity and reliability of this study. This study provides a better understanding of ERP upgrade decision related best practices for practitioners. In particular, this study tells about when and what factors to consider in making a well-informed ERP upgrade decision, to improve the overall ERP upgrade success.

As for managerial implication, this study indicates that aligning more strategic business benefit incentives to an ERP upgrade are likely to gain more supports for the upgrade decision. Some of the latest strategic business benefit incentives may include linking organizational innovations such as cloud and mobile applications to enterprise systems (Sedera, Lokuge, Grover, Sarker, & Sarker, 2016), the use of big data analytics for analysing internal data (from ERP system) and external data for organizational performance evaluation and managerial decision-making (Appelbaum, Kogan, Vasarhelyi, & Yan, 2017), and integrating industrial internet of things (IoT) automation with ERP system to achieve better organizational agility and customer-demand responsiveness (Lavi, 2017).

The research contributions of this study are: (1) the findings here can function as a basis where one can build a stronger theory for ERP upgrade decision; and (2) it provides a support that the contingency factor (i.e. internal resource availability) considered in Khoo and Robey (2007) can be extended to include (i) vendor support termination, (ii) conformity to international standard, and (iii) the need for an upgrade.

ACKNOWLEDGMENT

This study was supported by two grants from the Ministry of Science and Technology: NSC 100-2410-H-155-012 and MOST 103-2410-H-155-023.

REFERENCES

Aberdeen Group. (2010, October 31). *SaaS ERP: Trends & Observations 2010*. Retrieved from http://www.aberdeen.com/aberdeen-library/6890/RA-enterprise-resource-planning.aspx

Acumatica. (2010, Aug. 13). *The importance of ERP deployment options*. Retrieved from http://erpcloudnews.com/2010/08/the-importance-of-erp-deployment-options/

Appelbaum, D., Kogan, A., Vasarhelyi, M., & Yan, Z. (2017). Impact of Business Analytics and Enterprise Systems on Managerial Accounting. *International Journal of Accounting Information Systems*, *25*, 29–44. doi:10.1016/j.accinf.2017.03.003

Beaty, R. C., & Williams, C. D. (2006). ERP II: Best Practices for Succesfully Implementing an ERP Upgrade. *Communications of the ACM*, *49*(3), 105–109. doi:10.1145/1118178.1118184

Beaumont, J. (2004). *Upgrading Your ERP System: Cognizant's Top 10 List*. Academic Press.

Bjorlin, C. (2008). *Customers upgrade to SAP ERP 6.0 for support, software consolidation*. Retrieved from http://searchmanufacturingerp.techtarget.com/news/1326125/Customers-upgrade-to-SAP-ERP-60-for-support-software-consolidation

Columbus, L. (2013, August 4). *Deciding If Upgrading Your Enterprise Software Is Worth It Or Not*. Retrieved from http://www.forbes.com/sites/louiscolumbus/2013/11/25/deciding-if-upgrading-your-enterprise-software-is-worth-it-or-not/

Dempsey, S., Vance, R., & Sheehan, L. (2013). Justification of an Upgrade of an Enterprise Resource Planning (ERP) System – The Accountant's Role. *Global Journal of Human Social Science Research*, *13*(1), 1–9.

Dubé, L., & Paré, G. (2003). Rigor in Information Systems Positivist Case Research: Current Practices, Trends, and Recommendations. *Management Information Systems Quarterly*, *27*(4), 597–635. doi:10.2307/30036550

Eisenhardt, K. M. (1989). Building Theories from Case Study Research. *Academy of Management Review*, *14*(4), 532–550.

Feldman, M. B., & March, J. G. (1981). Information in Organizations as Signal and Symbol. *Administrative Science Quarterly*, *26*(2), 171–186. doi:10.2307/2392467

Flick, U. (2006). *An Introduction to Qualitative Research* (3rd ed.). London: Sage Publications.

Herschberg, R. (2004). *Best Practices for Developing Your R/3 Upgrade Roadmap. Managing SAP Projects 2004* [Presentation slides]. Las Vegas, NV: Wellesley Information Services.

Jimenez, D.-Z., & Lee, W. (2011). Buyer Conversations: Coca-cola Bottling Co. Consolidated's ERP Upgrade Journey - APEJ View. *Asia/Pacific Business Applications and Information Management: Buyer Case Study*. Retrieved from ftp://public.dhe.ibm.com/software/hk/download/AP2670107T.pdf

Khoo, H. M., & Robey, D. (2007). Deciding to Upgrade Packaged Software: A Comparative Case Study of Motives, Contingencies and Dependencies. *European Journal of Information Systems*, *16*(5), 555–567. doi:10.1057/palgrave.ejis.3000704

Khoo, H. M., Robey, D., & Rao, S. V. (2011). An Exploratory Study of the Impacts of Upgrading Packaged Software: A Stakeholder Perspective. *Journal of Information Technology*, *26*(3), 153–169. doi:10.1057/jit.2011.1

Kimberling, E. (2010). *Tips for avoiding common pitfalls of ERP upgrades*. Retrieved from http://searchmanufacturingerp.techtarget.com/news/2240020512/Tips-for-avoiding-common-pitfalls-of-ERP-upgrades

Kimberling, E. (2017, July 25). *Now is a Terrible Time to Purchase New ERP Software*. Retrieved from https://www.panorama-consulting.com/now-is-a-terrible-time-to-purchase-new-erp-software/

Kumar, S. (2008). *GRC is a key business driver for SAP Upgrade*. Retrieved from http://www.free-press-release.com/news/200806/1212568140.html

Lavi, Y. (2017, July 20). *Industry 4.0: Harnessing the Power of ERP and MES Integration*. Retrieved from http://www.industryweek.com/supply-chain-technology/industry-40-harnessing-power-erp-and-mes-integration

Law, C., Chen, C., & Wu, B. (2010). Managing the Full ERP Life-Cycle: Considerations of Maintenance and Support Requirements and IT Governance Practice as Integral Elements of the Formula for Successful ERP Adoption. *Computers in Industry*, *61*(3), 297–308. doi:10.1016/j.compind.2009.10.004

Leonard-Barton, D., & Deschamps, I. (1988). Managerial Influence in the Implementation of New Technology. *Management Science*, *34*(10), 1252–1265. doi:10.1287/mnsc.34.10.1252

Maier, J. L., Rainer, K. R. Jr, & Snyder, C. A. (1997). Environmetal Scanning for Information Technology: An Enpirical Investigation. *Journal of Management Information Systems*, *14*(2), 177–200. doi:10.1080/07421222.1997.11518170

Miles, M. B., Huberman, A. M., & Saldaña, J. (2014). *Qualitative Data Analysis: A Methods Sourcebook* (3rd ed.). Thousand Oaks, CA: SAGE Publications, Inc.

Nah, F. F., & Delgado, S. (2006). Critical Success Factors for Enterprise Resource Planning Implementation and Upgrade. *Journal of Computer Information Systems*, *46*(5), 99–114. doi:10.1080/08874417.2006.11645928

Ng, C. S.-P. (2006). *A Resource-Based Perspective on Enterprise Resource Planning (ERP) Capabilities and Upgrade Decision*. Paper presented at the Pacific Asia Conference on Information Systems (PACIS), Kuala Lumpur, Malaysia.

Ng, C. S.-P. (2013). A Case Study on the Impact of Customization, Fitness, and Operational Characteristics on Enterprise-wide System Success, User Satisfaction and System Use. *Journal of Global Information Management*, *21*(1), 19–41. doi:10.4018/jgim.2013010102

Ng, C. S.-P. (2011). *Enterprise Resource Planning (ERP) Upgrade Decision: Toward A Unified View*. Paper presented at the 15th Pacific Asia Conference on Information systems (PACIS), Brisbane, Australia.

Ng, C. S.-P., & Chang, P. C. (2009). *Exploring the Links between Competitive Advantage and Enterprise Resource Planning (ERP) Upgrade Decision: A Case Study Approach*. Paper presented at the 16th ISPE International Conference on Concurrent Engineering, Taipei. 10.1007/978-1-84882-762-2_17

Ng, M. M. T., & Tan, M. T. K. (2004). *Symbolic Processes on ERP versus "Legacy" System Support.* School of Computing, National University of Singapore.

Olson, D. L., & Zhao, F. (2006). Critical Success Factors in ERP Upgrade Projects. In Research and Practical Issues of Enterprise Information Systems (Vol. 205, pp. 569-578). Boston: Springer. doi:10.1007/0-387-34456-X_58

Panorama. (2017). *2017 Report on ERP Systems & Enterprise Software.* Retrieved from https://www.panorama-consulting.com/wp-content/uploads/2017/07/2017-ERP-Report.pdf

Paré, G., & Elam, J. J. (1997). Using Case Study Research to Build Theories of IT Implementation. In A. S. Lee, J. Liebenau, & J. I. DeGross (Eds.), *Information Systems and Qualitative Research* (pp. 542–568). London: Chapman & Hall. doi:10.1007/978-0-387-35309-8_27

Paul, L. G. (2008). *How to avoid mistakes during ERP upgrades.* Retrieved from http://searchmanufacturingerp.techtarget.com/news/1325046/How-to-avoid-mistakes-during-ERP-upgrades

Paul, L. G. (2009). *ERP upgrade planning best practices demystified.* Retrieved from http://searchmanufacturingerp.techtarget.com/news/1345398/ERP-upgrade-planning-best-practices-demystified

Rahim, M. M., Shanks, G., & Johnston, R. B. (2011). A Cross Industry Comparison of Inter-Organisational Systems Implementation Activities. *Journal of Electronic Commerce Research, 11*(2), 215–243. doi:10.100710660-010-9074-9

Rezvani, A., Dong, L., & Khosravi, P. (2017). Promoting the Continuing Usage of Strategic Information Systems: The Role of Supervisory Leadership in the Successful Implementation Of Enterprise Systems. *International Journal of Information Management, 37*(5), 417–430. doi:10.1016/j.ijinfomgt.2017.04.008

Seddon, P. B., Calvert, C., & Yang, S. (2010). A Multi-Project Model of Key Factors Affecting Organizational Benefits from Enterprise Systems. *Management Information Systems Quarterly, 34*(2), 305–328. doi:10.2307/20721429

Sedera, D., Lokuge, S., Grover, V., Sarker, S., & Sarker, S. (2016). Innovating with Enterprise Systems and Digital Platforms: A Contingent Resource-based Theory View. *Information & Management, 53*(3), 366–379. doi:10.1016/j.im.2016.01.001

Shang, S., & Seddon, P. B. (2003). A Comprehensive Framework for Classifying the Benefits of ERP Systems. In G. Shanks, P. B. Seddon, & L. P. Willcocks (Eds.), *Second-Wave Enterprise Resource Planning Systems: Implementing for Effectiveness* (pp. 74–101). Cambridge, UK: Cambridge University Press. doi:10.1017/CBO9780511815072.004

Swanton, B. (2004, September 21). *Build ERP Upgrade Costs into the Business Change Programme - Not the IT Budget*. Retrieved from http://www.computerweekly.com/

Swanton, B., Samaraweera, D., & Klein, E. (2004). *Minimizing ERP Upgrade Costs Requires Synchronizing with Business Improvement Projects*. Retrieved from Boston: http://www.amrresearch.com/

Wailgum, T. (2010, November 18). *Why ERP Upgrade Fears Affect On-Premise versus SaaS Decisions*. Retrieved from http://www.cio.com/article/637874/Why_ERP_Upgrade_Fears_Affect_On_Premise_versus_SaaS_Decisions

Wang, E. T. G., Klein, G., & Jiang, J. J. (2006). ERP Misfit: Country of Origin and Organizational Factors. *Journal of Management Information Systems*, *23*(1), 263–292. doi:10.2753/MIS0742-1222230109

Wang, E. T. G., Shih, S.-P., Jiang, J. J., & Klein, G. (2008). The Consistency among Facilitating Factors and ERP Implementation Success: A Holistic View of Fit. *Journal of Systems and Software*, *81*(9), 1609–1621. doi:10.1016/j.jss.2007.11.722

Yin, R. K. (2003). *Case Study Research: Design and Methods* (3rd ed.). Thousand Oaks, CA: Sage Publications.

ADDITIONAL READING

Dumitraş, T., & Narasimhan, P. (2009). *Why Do Upgrades Fail And What Can We Do About It? Toward Dependable, Online Upgrades in Enterprise Systems.* Paper presented at the ACM/IEEE/IFIP Middleware Conference, Urbana-Champaign, IL.

Feldman, G., Shah, H., Chapman, C., & Amini, A. (2016). Enterprise Systems: The Upgrade Process Model. *Journal of Enterprise Information Management*, *29*(6), 822–840. doi:10.1108/JEIM-12-2014-0122

Oseni, T., Foster, S. V., Mahbubur, R., & Smith, S. P. (2017). A Framework for ERP Post-Implementation Amendments: A Literature Analysis. *AJIS. Australasian Journal of Information Systems*, *21*, 1–20. doi:10.3127/ajis.v21i0.1268

KEY TERMS AND DEFINITIONS

ERP Upgrade Decision: A decision related to replacing an existing installed enterprise resource planning (ERP) system with a newer version of the software, which is purchased either from the same or a different software vendor.

ERP Upgrade Incentives: The motivations behind an ERP upgrade decision. It is usually evaluated and measured based on the business benefits created by upgrading to a new ERP software. These business benefits can be usually categorized into strategic, managerial, and operational business benefits.

Managerial Business Benefits: The type of business benefits that can enhance an organization's business activities management, planning and controlling, business performance monitoring, capability in making a well-informed decision, and compliance to the business regulations.

Operational Business Benefits: The type of business benefits that can improve the effectiveness and efficiency in an organization's daily business operations. For example, a faster order fulfilment cycle, a real-time stock replenishment, and a better customer service provision.

Similarity Between Two Business Processes: The degree of alikeness between two business processes.

Strategic Business Benefits: The type of business benefits that can bring sustainable competitive advantages and bring in revenues to an organization, in the long run or in a few years from now. They are related to the future business and market share expansion, for example, creating an innovative way of doing business, innovations in new product/service, and developing new customer segments or market.

Symbol Attached to an ERP System: It is the perceptions, images, icons, signs, representations, or characteristics that one associates with an ERP system before or after using an ERP system. This symbol is either formed through a social setting/environment (i.e., influenced by other's opinions) or created through one's personal/own experience with an ERP system.

Top Management Support: An organization's senior-level executives backing, encouragement, and provision for various types of assistance and resources needed for a project implementation, such as an ERP upgrade project.

ENDNOTE

1. This paper is a major extension of a conference paper, i.e. Ng, C. S.-P., & Wang, E. T. G. (2014), "An Exploratory Study of the Emergent Theory for Enterprise Resource Planning Upgrade Decision," which is presented at the 25th Australasian Conference on Information Systems (ACIS), Auckland, New Zealand. This book chapter consists of around 50% new materials, not published.

Chapter 5
Towards an Agile and Secure IT Service Management

Sahid Abdelkebir
Hassan 1st University, Morocco

Yassine Maleh
Hassan 1st University, Morocco

Mustapha Belaissaoui
Hassan 1st University, Morocco

ABSTRACT

To support transformational business changes, IT must streamline the top-down process of new IT processes. In the ever-changing business world of today, no one knows what is around the corner, and to improve agility is the best way to organize to the test of the future. By defining IT maturity in your organization, you can map a route to successive levels of maturity and improved agility to reach a point where IT contributes to the execution, growth, and rapid transformation of the business. A successful IT service and asset management need to be efficient and agile to help transform from a traditional into a digital enterprise. In this chapter, the authors propose a global and practical strategic framework to improve ITSM service management processes with the additions of two drivers: agility control based on DevOps and security management based on SecOps.

DOI: 10.4018/978-1-5225-5393-9.ch005

INTRODUCTION

In the age of digitization, the world is evolving at a constant pace. Companies need to respond to changing conditions and often agility is the only guarantee of survival. Globalization means that there is more competition (Kumbakara, 2008). The life cycle of products is shorter than ever. A disruptive technology can change markets overnight.

The company faces challenging challenges in maintaining security and compliance while achieving its business objectives, complying with current regulations, and managing staff and technology. We understand that the IT staff must be able to react quickly to changing business needs while maintaining the existing infrastructure. We also know that the management objective so often quoted, "Doing more with less" is not only a goal, it is a corporate commitment (Mesquida, 2012).

Currently, with improved IT Service Management ITSM processes and the adoption of best practice guides and benchmarks such as ITIL (van Bon, 2007), ISO 20000 (ISO/IEC 20000, 2010). Compliance appears to be a need rather than a strategic choice to improve rapidly and easily decisions about IT and business processes. Get better agility, which allows the business to benefit from a faster Return On Investment ROI and a constant competitive advantage.

Recent developments in the field of IT governance and IT service management have led to the introduction of new technology and concepts such as service-oriented architecture SOA, decision-making, and of course agility (Uebernickel, 2006).

Over the last decade, agility has been proposed primarily around methods such as Scrum (Ken Schwaber, 2004), Extreme Programming XP (Beck, 1999), for lifecycle management of software and IT developments. However, with the strategic changes that companies are currently experiencing, agility is more a strategic choice than a simple development method, and it affects all business activities. There is no universally accepted definition of what looks like agility. There is no single model, framework or evaluation that will tell you what to do next. Different industries are subject to different pressures, and the impact of new technologies is different for each company so that each organization must have their own understanding of what business agility looks like for them. The result is that in a world of technology, it must be equally sensitive (Iden, 2015).

Naturally, there is a strong correlation between agility and computer maturity in one organization, as one allows the other. An immature IT function will struggle to support day-to-day operations. Driving a transformer change is not an option. Computer maturity allows agility and agility allow the flexibility and agility of the companies. Following a path to computer maturity (as defined by your organization, not a generic industry model), will allow you to improve both IT and business agility.

The management of IT services implies the adoption of an agile vision. Referential repositories such as ITIL define service design methods and processes. Agility adds a layer of flexibility and dynamism in this management (Chen, 2014).

The IT department's responsibility for maintaining and securing the IT environment now includes all devices employees use, but budgets and IT resources are limited. Agility is the right solution for IT departments to streamline IT processes and manage all aspects of end-user productivity. The objective is to reinforce the traditional IT services of the "control and control" type, oriented peripheral by a complete integrated approach, oriented user. ITSM increases the level of the communication efficiency between business departments and provides a structure to plan, research and implement IT services. The needs of IT service management in organizations can be changes in the ways they do business, communicate and also develop and innovate, gain market advantage and differentiate themselves to their customers (Brooks, 2006). Also, ITSM allows companies to internally govern and follow the set global standards (Mior, 2008). For a better understanding of the ITSM concept in the organization, reviewing the ITSM component would be useful. ITSM components consist of Process, Technology, Manpower (people), Organization, and Security, which is recently added to organization construction to improve the system security (McNaughton, 2010). Figure 1 illustrates the component of ITSM.

- **Processes:** The most important element to construct ITSM system (e.g.IT business process facilitates and keeps up IT service).
- **Organization:** To provide better IT service level and arranges proper tasks in the organization.
- **Technology and Security:** To provide best possible tools and automated solutions to develop a process in a higher level of efficiency and safety.

As mentioned earlier, IT service is connected to the four fundamentals of Information Technology Service Management (ITSM). Therefore, when IT is aligned with the business strategy and the organization, it can do what it wants to do. Furthermore, IT and new technologies enable the organization to do new things that were never possible before (Silva Molina, 2005). The strategic outcome is that the overall business benefits from effective IT-related service and IT benefits that are integral to the company's business plans will be delivered to the maximum economic value.

In the literature and even references such as ITIL, ISO 20000, Cobit (van Grembergen, 2009), there is no practical, concrete and agile model for the implementation of IT services management in organizations. In this work, we propose a global, practical and agile framework for supporting IT Service management ITSM. The proposed framework surpasses the limitations of existing methods/referential

Figure 1. ITSM components

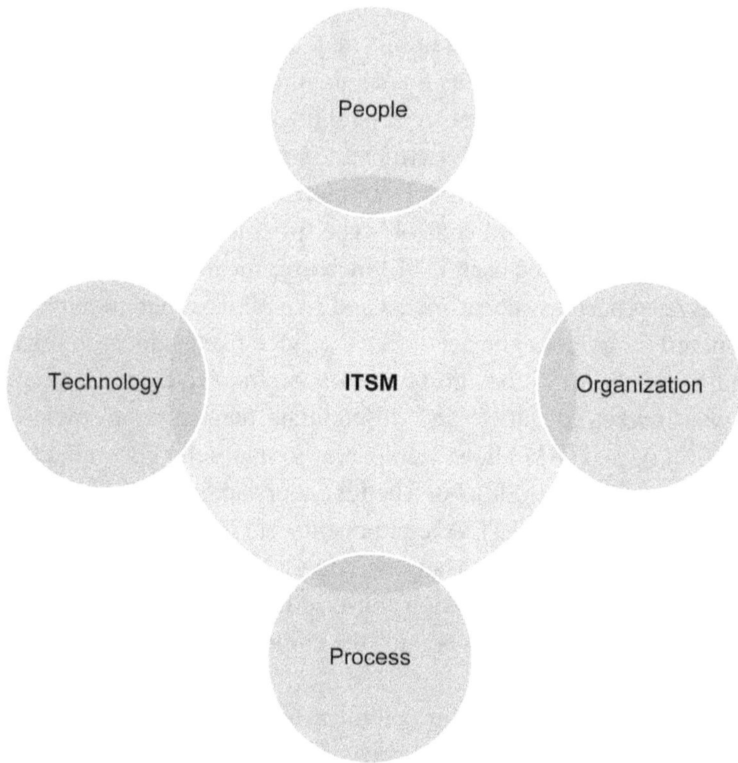

and meets the needs of international standards regarding flexibility and agility to improve ITSM processes. This generic framework will help any organization in the implementation of an agile, secure and optimal IT Service Center. We measure the proposed framework by adopting a continuous improvement process based on DevOps (DevOps is the concatenation of the first three letters of the word "development" and the usual abbreviation "ops" of the word "operations") and the PDCA Deming cycle.

RELATED RESEARCH

ITSM in Referential ITIL, ISO 20000

ISO 20000-1 is based on ITIL, which presents a set of best practices for the management of information systems. This approach and vision to IT service management highlight the importance of coordination and control of various functions, processes, and systems required to manage the full lifecycle of IT services. The following Figure 2

Figure 2. ITIL Process

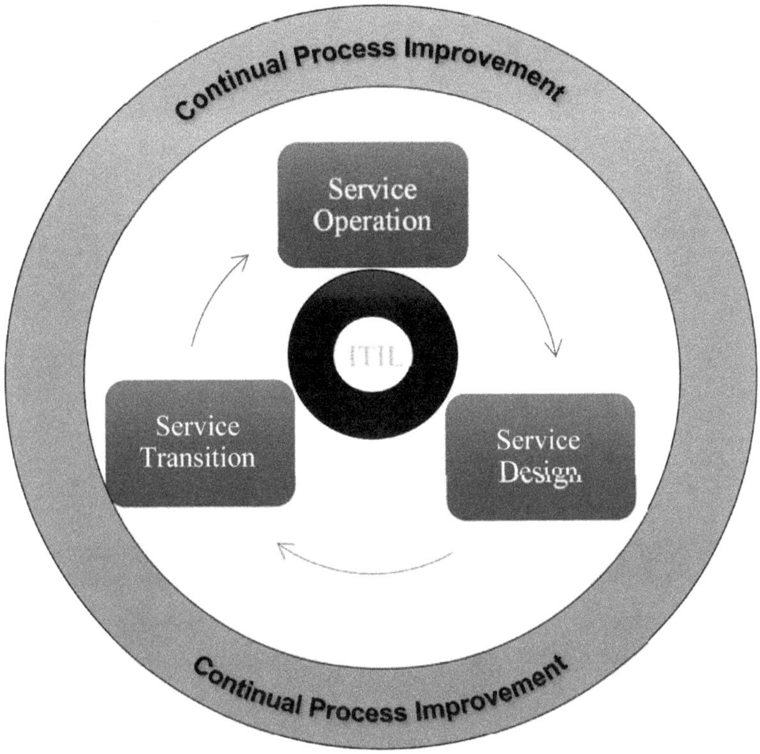

presents in a simplified way an overall representation of the process vision according to ITIL. The latter is broken down into a cycle consisting of five phases: service strategy, service design, service transition, the operation of services and continuous improvement of services. Also, document management, resource management, and service governance align with all phases of the service lifecycle, processes.

More explicitly, the following Figure 3 presents the existing processes in each phase of the service lifecycle in the context of ISO 20000.

ITSM in Scientific Research's

During the last two decades, the ITSM-related frameworks have provided a better systematic approach to the management of IT services in the fields of IT operation to continual improvement, implementation, and design (Marrone, 2011). For example, different studies have concentrated on the adoption of IT Service Management (ITSM) as a "particular service-oriented best practice". According to (Winniford, 2009), about 45% of US corporations are operating an ITSM while 15% are preparation its

Figure 3. The Process Model of ITSM_ISO 20000

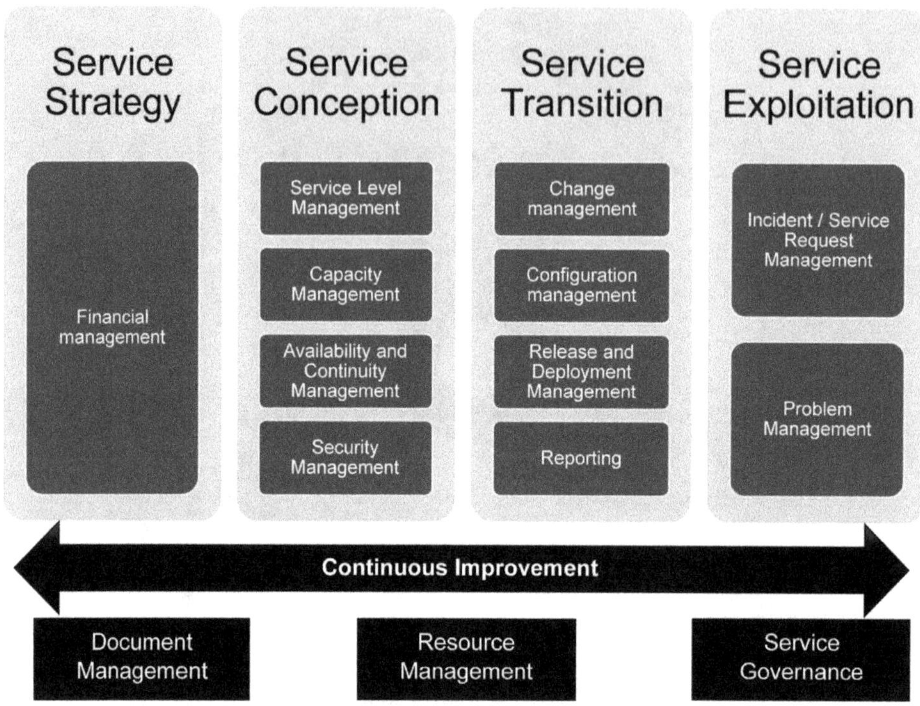

usage. IT service management is somehow the quality customer service that tries to ensure that customer needs and expectations are met at all times.

In "ITIL: What It Is And What It Isn't", (Hank, 2006) examined in the measuring techniques of successful companies when implementing the ITIL-best practice. He describes Service Support and Service delivery and explains its stress on an ITSM-ITIL best practice that it does not stand alone, and it could be successful when applying to other practices. The authors define three major tasks, which define appropriate goal setting through a Process Maturity Framework (PMF), rigorous auditing and reporting through a Quality Management System (QMS) and Project Management and a Continuous Service Improvement Program (CSIP), to support ITIL-usage. Furthermore, he also provided more information about business-aligned IT process and continuous improvement of the tactical and operational components especially those processes that focused on service quality by clients and users (Hank, 2006).

In "E-government: ITIL oriented Service Management Case Study", (Meziani, 2010) developed a service management self-assessment plans for the government agency to support continuous quality improvement of IT processes based on ITIL governance- gap analysis methods with respect to ITIL standards.

In Their work entitled "Managed IT-Services: the role of IT standards", (Kumbakara N., 2008) argues the practical issues based on standards and the management of IT services delivered by external or outsourced service providers. Here, the purpose of the authors is to assist IT organizations to recognise the significance of having a mutual standard for managing IT services.

(van Grembergen, 2009) illustrated a set of best guides and practices (COBIT Framework) for IT management control and assurance of information technology, and categorized them around a logical framework based on 34 IT processes.

(Marrone, 2011) studied the benefits of both operational and strategic of IT Service Management. The research outcome indicates that as the implementation of ITIL increased the number of realized benefits, like the levels of maturity of the Business-IT-Alignment.

In his book entitled "Information management: the evaluation of information systems investments" (Wilcocks, 2013). The author proposes different approaches to evaluating practice at strategic levels and during the pre-purchase phase of IS assessment. In the book "Asset management: A systematic approach to factor investing". The authors (Ang, 2014) introduces a comprehensive and new approach to the secular problem of where to place your money in the IT Asset Management. In recent works "Reducing the cost of test through strategic asset management" (Duane & Charlie, 2016). The authors explore the balance of the three fundamental aspects that make up asset management and will focus on how to implement strategies to reduce the total cost of ownership for the test.

Agility in the Literature

The concept of agility was first used in the literature of strategic management and industry at the beginning of the years ((Meade, 1997); (Vernadat, 1999) (Yusuf, Sarhadi, & Gunasekaran, 1999) (Richards, 1996) (Goldman, 1995)). Agility introduced and proposed in the literature with the argument that success in volatile industries requires a set of capacities different from those required for success in stable industries. In the literature, we deduced that is a lack of a unique definition of the agility concept; The Agility Research in (IS Agility) was been devised on several axes... (Lee, et al., 2006); (Fink & Neuman, 2009); (Holmqvist & Pessi, 2006); (Hong, Thong, Chasalow, & Dhillon, 2011).However, there is a lack of research regarding agility in IT Management Systems. Although the IT function, in all its dimensions, gains in flexibility, and in reactivity. Beyond that, the IT system function is at stake and must have the capability to accelerate its adaptation to business needs, market requirements, and the strategic alignment of the IS and the organization. Agility is the best solution to cope with the different internal/external changes ... DevOps is a set of best practices and change guidance that ensures development, assurance and quality improvement and operations to better respond effectively Customer needs. The word DevOps was invented by Patrick Debois during the organization of the first DevOps days in Ghent, Belgium, in October 2009.To ensure competitiveness, the organization must accelerate the delivery of new functionalities and software features. This is the idea behind agile application/software development processes that are now widely used by application delivery teams to reduce delivery cycle times. DevOps can be applied in the ITSM field, in order to benefit from it and to ensure an efficient and flexible ITSM in the organization. In recent work (Gene, Jez, Patrick, & John, 2016). The authors argue that more than ever, effective technology management is essential for business competitiveness. The book does not focus on tools such as infrastructure such as code, containers or configuration management. These are people, culture, and processes. The book creates a language to describe DevOps and a common understanding. Highly recommended, no matter if you have a professional or technical environment. The DevOps Handbook shows leaders/ practitioner how to reproduce these incredible results, showing how to integrate IT operations, development, product management, quality assurance, and information security to raise your business and win in the market.

THE PROPOSED ITSM FRAMEWORK

ITSM increases the level of the communication efficiency between business departments and provides a structure in order to plan, research and implement IT services. The needs of ITSM in organizations can be changes in the ways they operate, communicate and do business and also develop and innovate, gain a market advantage (Trusson, 2014) (Cots, 2015). In addition, ITSM allows companies to internally govern and follow the set global standards.

In this Table 1, attempted to manage the challenge of effective ITSM framework in IT corporations from two different views: the empirical findings and literature.

Table 1. ITSM drawbacks

Interview/ Findings	▪ Lack of maintenance objects/situation. ▪ Lack of ITIL support. ▪ Lack of knowledge evaluation framework by employee and management team. ▪ Problems in metrics level. ▪ Weakness in System performance and QS.
Literature	▪ Lack of users training and knowledge ▪ Lack of unit and cohesion structure between metrics. ▪ Insecurity and doubt about what to measure ▪ Lack of communication among users and producers of a Performance Indicator (PI).

With analysis of this challenge, it will be feasible to suggest some points address these issues.

We can confirm that there are many problems with having successful ITSM process. Conversely, as identified before, many good efforts have been done to improve these issues. The chapter aims to identify the important aspects that propose a comprehensive framework for ITSM efficiency. It was collected in a theoretical and empirical research study that generated answers to the sub-level research questions. We tried to extract a framework based on the literature review and various sources from the practical environment.

The IT department's responsibility for maintaining and securing the IT environment now includes all devices employees use, but budgets and IT resources are limited. The proposed ITSM framework exploits the good practices ITIL and ISO 2000 and integrates new strategic axes such as agility and security in order to propose an efficient and an agile ITSM. It replaces the traditional IT services of the "control and control" type, oriented peripherally by a complete integrated, user-oriented approach with the integration of four disciplines of IT management (Service management, Asset management, Agility Management and Security Management,). Figure 4 describes the architecture and the component of the proposed ITSM framework.

IT Service Management ITSM

Most of the ITSM Organizations consider Service Support process as a difficult task. Difficulties are mainly due to the following reasons:

Figure 4. The proposed ITSM model

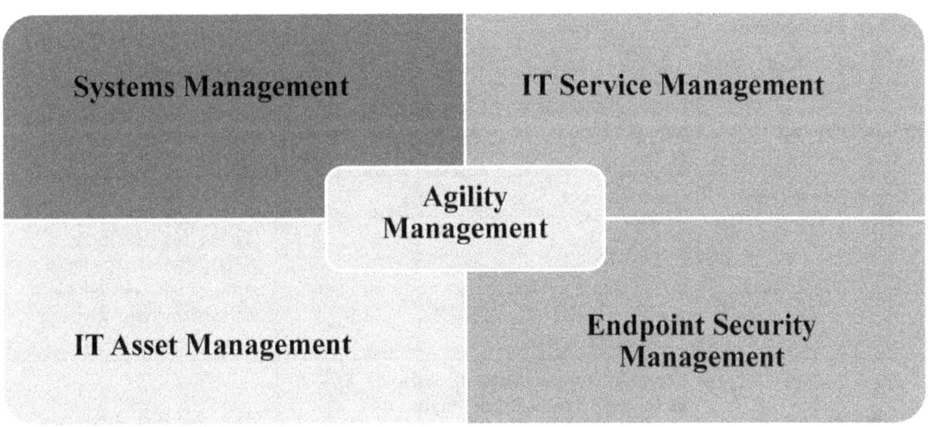

- IT organizations do not have a structured approach to measuring IT service and service management processes.
- Different tools exploited by IT Support Service Teams do not enable effective measurement.
- IT service management referential and standards do not provide practical guidelines and a roadmap to measure IT support process.
- Therefore, IT organization needs a structured approach to measuring IT service support process such as ITIL V2 /V3 or the other reliable sources to increase IT quality of services. So, implementations of the service support process are chosen as a priority to support as a result of continuous improvement in ITSM.

As it's illustrated in Table 2, IT service support process includes five main steps.

The scope of the evaluation would cover only the key processes of the service operation and the service transition. Data are collected through interviews, workshops, literature review and site visits. Visits to the service desk and data center may be required. A list of questions is often used. A time-based assessment would aim to determine the level of maturity of each ITIL process. Other data to be collected include the availability of tools, competencies, the role, and responsibilities of the organization, availability, and quality of documentation, evidence of continuous improvement, measurement and reporting, dissemination and the use of reports.

Table 2. IT service support process

Service Support Process	Description	Example
Incident Management	Restores normal service operations as quickly as possible	"Virus Attack, Server crashes. Hardware alarm, Turn down and decline of system performance"
Problem Management	Prevents incidents from happening and minimizes the impact of incidents that cannot be prevented	"All incidents that are not fixed basically with known errors"
Change Management	Controls the lifecycle of all changes	
Release Management	Implements approved changes to IT services	"To provide a solution for the problems like parameter, adjust, patch, configuration changes, upgrade of system version and server".
Configuration Management	Configuration management consists of managing the technical description of a system and its various components, as well as managing all the changes made during the evolution of the system.	"Tracking, Reporting and controlling all equipment's".

Based on the answers to the questions collected, the scores are tabulated using a spreadsheet tool and presented. A time-based assessment can use the 5-level ITSM maturity model to evaluate the individual process of ITSM as shown in Table 3.

IT Security Management

To manage and control the security management process to meet external/internal security requirements as it is found in SLAs, contracts, legislation and the company security policy. The ITSM must offer an efficient but above all secure service.

The threat environment continues to evolve rapidly and the volume of unique malware is growing, increasingly being applied and web-based. To complicate the puzzle, your users are different. They are more self-sufficient and, like water, they find the least resistant path to productivity. They bring things to the network and the information is just an application store and a credit card. The current approach to computer systems and security management must be more user-oriented.

Table 3. ITSM maturity model

Maturity Level	Description
Level 1: Initial	Awareness of the existence of the problem and the need to study it. However, there are no standardized processes, but approaches and processes in this direction tend to be applied autonomously on a case-by-case basis.The global management approach is not organized.
Level 2: Reproducible	The organization makes significant efforts to develop and establish the management process for ITSM services. The notions of reactivity and short-term are generally there. At this level, the organization is a little more advanced in its management. Generally, the activities related to this process are not all coordinated and are irregular. Commitment to the process is evident in the allocation of resources. However, IT service management is not always formalized or compliant.
Level 3: Defined	Describes a formalized service management process in which the objective, activities, inputs, and outputs have been defined. The performance is consistent and can be repeated throughout the organization. The process is well implemented and managed as a whole satisfactorily. The management process is identified and documented but there is no recognition of its role within the IT organizations as a whole. However, the process has a manager, formal objectives, and dedicated resources. A reporting is put in place to capitalize the experience.
Level 4: Managed	It is possible to monitor and measure ITSM compliance to standards and to act when processes do not seem to work properly. The management of the services is constantly improving and corresponds to a good practice. Automation and the use of tools are limited or partial.
Level 5: Optimized	IT service management has reached the level of best practice, following constant improvement and comparison with other similar contexts. The technology is used as an integrated way to automate workflows, providing tools that improve quality and efficiency and make the company quickly adaptable.

Companies' efforts to improve security can motivate them to react and buy high-tech products that can make them more secure rather than more secure. The problem is that this proliferation of advanced attacks does not allow you to be more responsive. Taking a more proactive approach to security involves the deployment of multiple layers of integrated protection that stifle network violations. Table 4 indicates some of the trends of reactive organizations versus those that are more proactive or have more mature IT security:

The best approach is to ensure that your members of the information security team respond to new threats and your IT team member's process mature systems. We propose a global model of maturity to achieve an effective IT security management framework, as shown in Table 5. The path to security maturity requires a diversified range of layered endpoint protection, management and capabilities Defensive, all integrated and fully automated. The bottom line on endpoint security is that today's threat environment is simply too dynamic for any single point solution to afford effective protection. The only practical and survivable defensive strategy are to move to a more mature security model that incorporate multiple layers of protective technology.

Agility Management

To take advantage of the digital age, companies are realizing that they need to deliver strategic responses more quickly and efficiently. ITSM teams are already focused on improving or constructing consistent, repeatable processes that reduce downtime and improve productivity (Robert, et al., 2016). Effective initiatives within the framework of the ITSM can extend the delivery and management of business services beyond the areas of computing. Service management teams become an advisory model for the company and your integrated, process-driven ITSM enables agility that supports business strategy (Giudice, Christopher, Amy, & Ian, 2016).

Table 4. Reactive\Proactive mature IT security

Reactive Organizations	Proactive Organizations
Low-level security	Multiple point solutions
Multi-layered security	Integrated security solution
Inefficient use of IT resources	Effective use of IT resources and alignment of IT processes
Manual methods to quarantine threats	Automatic ways to quarantine threats
IT Security manages all security processes	Security management processes are managed by IT operations, while IT security ensures surveillance and investigates threats.

Table 5. Security maturity model

Maturity of Capability Building Blocks		Level 1: Initial	Level 2: Basic	Level 3: Intermediate	Level 4: Advanced	Level 5: Optimizing
IT Service Security Management	Business continuity planning	- Ad hoc definition of information security strategy, policies, and standards. - The physical environment and the security of the computer components are only locally addressed. - There is no explicit consideration of budget requirements for information security activities - No systematic management of security risks - Access rights and policies are best managed using informal procedures. - IT security incidents and problems are managed on an ad hoc basis.	- Maturity reflects the linking of a basic information security strategy to business and IT strategies of the organization. - It also involves the development and review of information security policies and standards, typically after major incidents. - IT component and physical environment security guidelines are emerging. - There is some consideration of security budget requirements within IT, and requirements for high-level security features are specified for major software and hardware purchases. - A basic security risk-management process is established within IT based on perceived risk. - Access rights management is dependent on vendor-supplied solutions. - Processes or security management data throughout its life cycle are emerging. - Major security incidents are tracked and recorded within IT.	- Maturity reflects a detailed information security strategy that's regularly aligned to business and IT strategies and risk appetite across IT and some other business units. - Information security policies and standards are developed and revised based on a defined process and regular feedback. - IT and some other business units have agreed-on IT component and physical environment security measures. - IT budget processes acknowledge and provide for the most important information security budget requests in IT and some other business units. -The security risk-management process is proactive and jointly shared with corporate collaboration. - Access rights are granted based on a formal and audited authorization process. - Detailed processes for managing data security throughout its life cycle are implemented. - Security incidents are managed based on the urgency to restore services, as agreed on by IT and some other business units.	- Maturity is characterized by regular, enterprise-wide improvement in the alignment of the information security strategy, policies, and standards with business and IT strategies and compliance requirements. - IT component security measures on IT systems are implemented and tested enterprise-wide for threat detection and mitigation. Physical environment security is integrated with access controls and monitoring systems across the enterprise. - Detailed security budget requirements are incorporated in enterprise-wide business planning and budgeting activities. - A standardized security risk management process is aligned with the enterprise risk-management process. - Access rights are implemented and audited across the enterprise. - Data is effectively preserved throughout its life cycle, and data availability is effectively managed to meet business, regulatory, and security requirements. - Recurring incidents are systematically addressed enterprise-wide through problem-management processes that are based on root cause analysis.	- Maturity reflects an information security strategy that is regularly aligned to business and IT strategies across the business ecosystem. - Information security policies and standards are periodically reviewed and revised based on input from the business ecosystem. - The management of IT component security is optimized across the security framework layers. - Physical access and environmental controls are regularly improved. Security budget requirements are improved to provide adequate funding for current and future security purposes. - The security risk-management process is agile and adaptable, and tools can be used to address the business ecosystem's requirements. - Access rights and policies can deal effectively with the organization restructuring assignments and acquisitions. - Processes for managing data security throughout its life cycle are continuously improved. - Automated incident prediction systems are in place, and security incidents are effectively managed.
	IT Incident Management					
	Communication & Training					
	Security performance reporting					
IT Asset Security Management	Security budgeting					
	Resource effectiveness					
	Resource effectiveness					
	Tools & resources					
	Data identification & classifications					
	Access rights management					
Vulnerability and Risk Management	Security threat profiling					
	Security risk assessment					
	Security risk prioritization					
	Security risk monitoring					
	Data identification & classifications					
	Access rights management					
Compliance Management	Compliance control					
	Security assessment					
	IT services, processes, and systems comply with enterprise policies					

By agile, we do not just mean "fast", but it is a major element. Agility in ITSM is more a measure of responsiveness, and not just, how fast IT technicians process tickets or changes in version. Rather, true agility includes the entire IT team that solves service demands while respecting optimized labor costs. In short, true ITSM agility is achieved by implementing intelligent processes that work smarter and more efficiently.

The implementation (or transition) of a DevOps development process (integration of both development, operational teams and processes) has proven to be a tool capable of reducing publication time, automation Improved repetitive processes and a key element of Agile Development and Liberation. The DevOps approach is a philosophy, a way of thinking. It aims to establish closer and more effective collaboration between development and infrastructure teams by enabling faster deployments while reducing operational friction. It is a key element in the implementation of a Continuous Delivery process and translates into the application of different cultural and technological concepts. Adopting DevOps requires changes in the way teams are structured, how responsibilities are shared, and the need to integrate and deliver services that enable teams to succeed.

To understand the DevOps maturity of the core development and IT operations processes, we propose a proven DevOps maturity model based on Hewlett Packard HP (Hewlet Packard HP, 2016), IBM (Robert, et al., 2016) return of experience of the adoption of DevOps model of agility in their business strategy to accelerate innovation and meet market demands. This model looks at DevOps from three viewpoints IT service, process, assets, IT automation, and IT collaboration, and spans a series of clearly defined states on the path to an optimized DevOps ITSM environment. The DevOps maturity model described in Figure 5 represent a roadmap to achieve organization's maturity level in terms of ITSM standardization, IT automation tools, IT collaboration approaches, and end IT user security management, along with insights into your opportunities for a continuous IT service operations and organizational change improvement.

THE PROPOSED AGILE ITSM FRAMEWORK

In parallel with the development solutions and processes, ITSM plays a key role in supporting DevOps practices and objectives such as incident management, application deployment, and performance management, to name a few Than a few. The conception and implementation of new agile ITSM are a challenge. The proposed agile ITSM is shown in Figure 6.

Figure 5. Devops ITSM maturity model for continues organization's measure and improvement

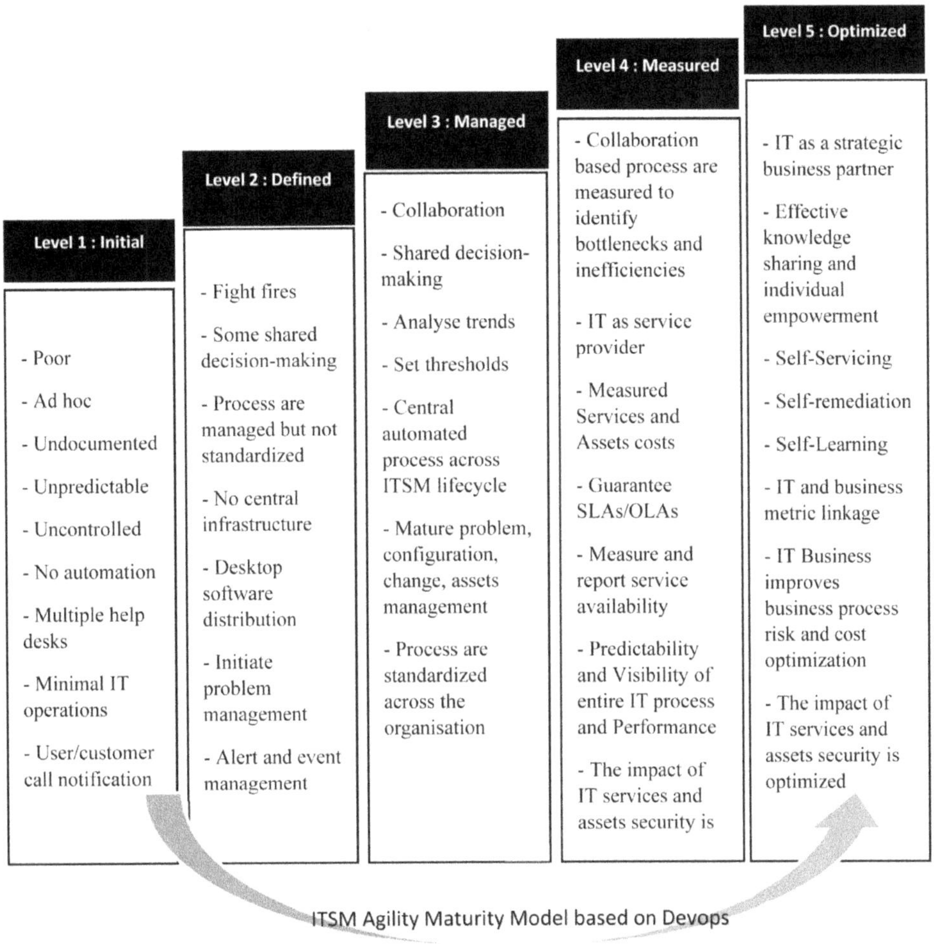

We conducted a study of the practices used by companies to manage the ITSM service center. This study is based on a questionnaire drawn up in a sample of 10000 IT professionals (Director, IT Manager, IT practical).

The objective is to have a return experience in relation to the IT services and assets management best methods and practices. To measure the contribution of our proposed framework on the company's IS performance.

To be able to meet the requirements of the proposed ITSM Framework, all employees must feel concerned and involved. To this end, the quality department has

Figure 6. The proposed agile ITSM framework

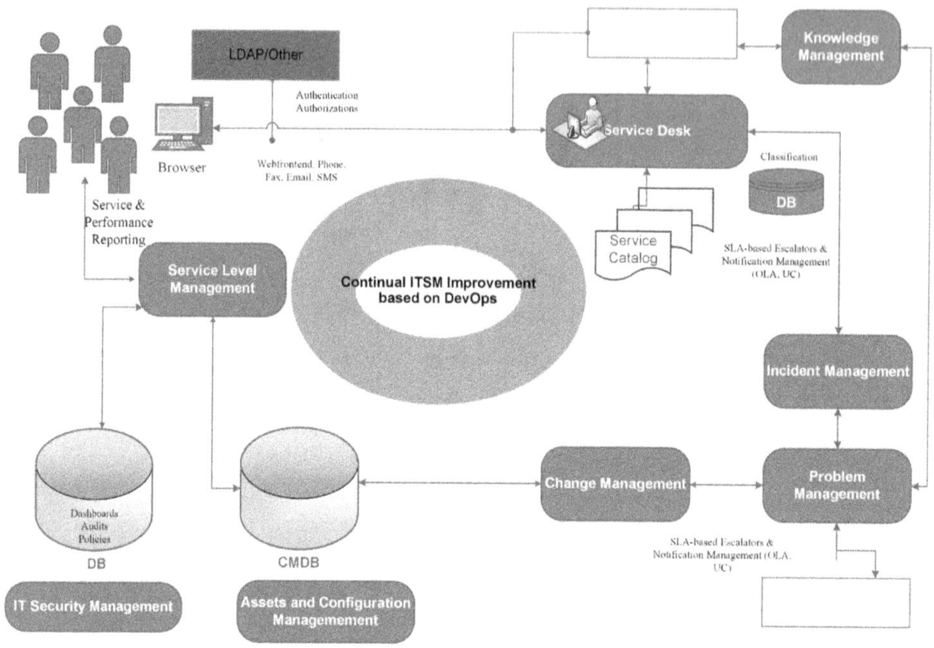

undertaken a series of strategic actions. These actions are planned following an agile model based on DevOps. Inspired by Deming wheel and DevOps, we organize the reports into four phases DDAO: Discover Do, Act, and Optimize, as shown in Table 6. Our goal is to develop a quality approach to continuous IT improvement. Starting with the auditing of all the functional and practical aspects of the management of the organization's services and the desired need, including the implementation of a roadmap for the desired organizations levels of maturity in terms of management of services, assets and IT security. We define an agile approach based on the proposed model DevOps, to guarantee a continuous improvement of the processes, services, security and organization, and contribution to the business of the organization.

Table 6. Continual quality improvement

DISCOVER	DO	ACT	OPTIMIZE
Vision and Strategy	Assessment	Organization	Performance Management
Auditing	Strategic Plan	Processes	Benchmarks
Key Performance Indicators	Roadmap	Tools And Technology	Continuous Improvement

Use Case

The questionnaire was carried out in several stages. A first version has been developed to take into account the different theoretical assumptions. This first version has been tested with IT service managers and consultants. This pre-test allowed rephrasing some questions to improve the comprehension of the questionnaire and to improve the quality of the given answers. In the end, the questionnaire consists of 100 questions divided into four topics: IT service management maturity, IT asset management maturity, IT security management maturity and IT agility maturity level as shown in the Appendix (Table 7).

Discover

The following section presents the part of the empirical study that concerns and identifies the measuring system of IT in the organization. During the empirical study, different possibilities in measuring and comparing the KPIs in different groups were found. In the following section, we will present measuring operations and visualization of measurements and auditing of IT services and security in the organization. IT managers described that there are different parts of ITIL that are incorporated in the fields of IT Support, Service desk SLA's, Incident and Problem management and Deployment fields. The most important parameters to measures are targeting Time Deliveries in different channels such as General Service management of core system functions, Business projects, Activities, Operational maintenance, and Admin. Another aspect that could be measured is Service improvement with providing surveys based on a yearly basis (on process and maintenance object level) to improve and monitor the overall performance of the systems.

ITSM Audit Score

We conducted an audit of the organization's ITSM practices. In order to define the current levels of maturity and to define the desired level to be attained by the organization. The Figure 7 shows the current ITSM maturity level. The maturity score 1 indicates the initial level (ad hoc), and the score 5 indicates the high score of maturity level (optimised).

IT Security Audit Result

Based on the model of security maturity on the table. We audit endpoint security of the organism that runs between the basic and intermediate level. Our objective is to

Figure 7. ITSM maturity score

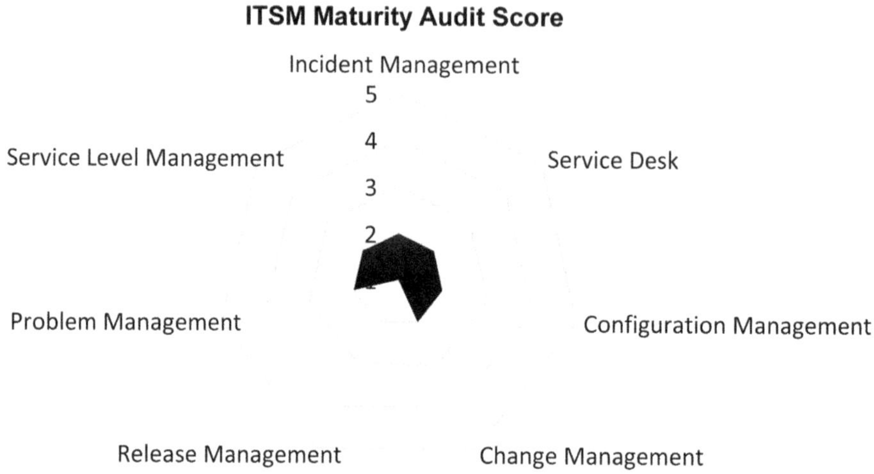

achieve an improved level of ITSM security and to be part of the overall governance of the organization's information security. The results of the audit are illustrated in Figure 8.

Do

The Practical Framework to Enhance ITSM Efficiency

In section 4, we have proposed different feedbacks about the system performance without modifying the new solutions for the future model. In this section, it would be helpful to be able to provide experimental model behavior, which has been missing in the Service Quality of IT Service Management process with some suggestion to improve different approaches, which we have evaluated. To conclude the issue, we could say that organizations should seriously take the advantage of learning from the system performance and should reduce the appropriate Incident management because successful approach and proper IT service management plan could make the difference between the organization's continued existence and sudden death. The suggested framework is a structured approach to increase the perception of ITSM efficiency and to reduce incident management in new start-up companies. In this part, we discuss the axes of improvement referring to the results of the empirical study and interviews with the IT managers in different axe of the ITSM.

Figure 8. IT security audit score

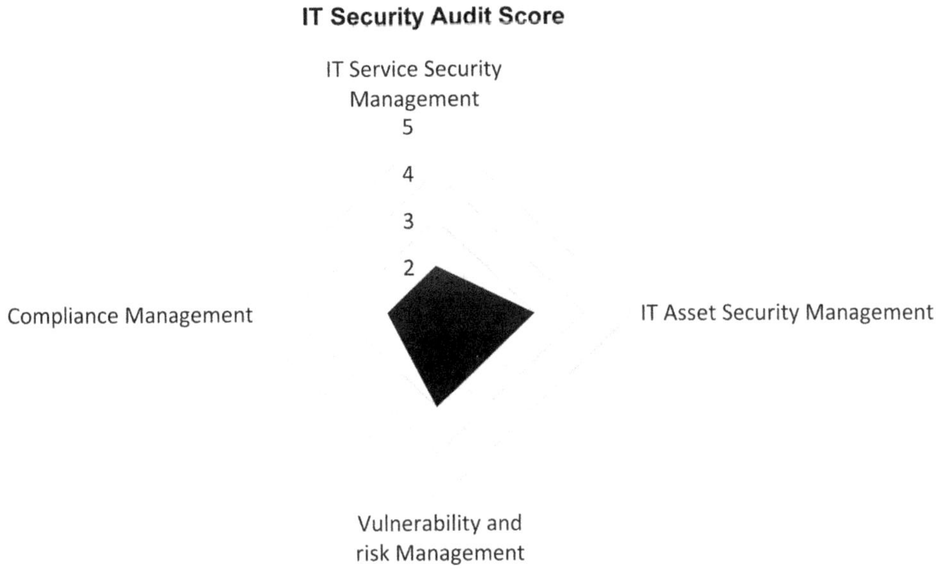

IT Service Management

In this part, we will discuss the improved points treated in terms of IT service management. The adoption of the proposed ITSM framework described in section 3.1 help the organization to increase the level of ITSM maturity to level 4: managed as shown in Figure 9.

User expectations have changed and the IT department has to develop other ways of communicating with them. The goal is to provide IT Service Management with a tool to anticipate their requests, optimize productivity, reduce downtime, and have all the necessary ITSM processes, including incident management, problem management, Changes, requests, self-service, as well as SLA management, etc. The proposed solution fits easily into IT operations.

- Control of the support center with fundamental processes
- Improved service and support performance, and reduced unforeseen costs and business risks.
- Support center solution is easy to use and administer
- IT administrators can easily configure, design and modify the support center system. IT teams can configure it without coding to meet the changing needs of the enterprise and achieve faster profitability without disrupting users.

Figure 9. ITSM maturity score after implementation

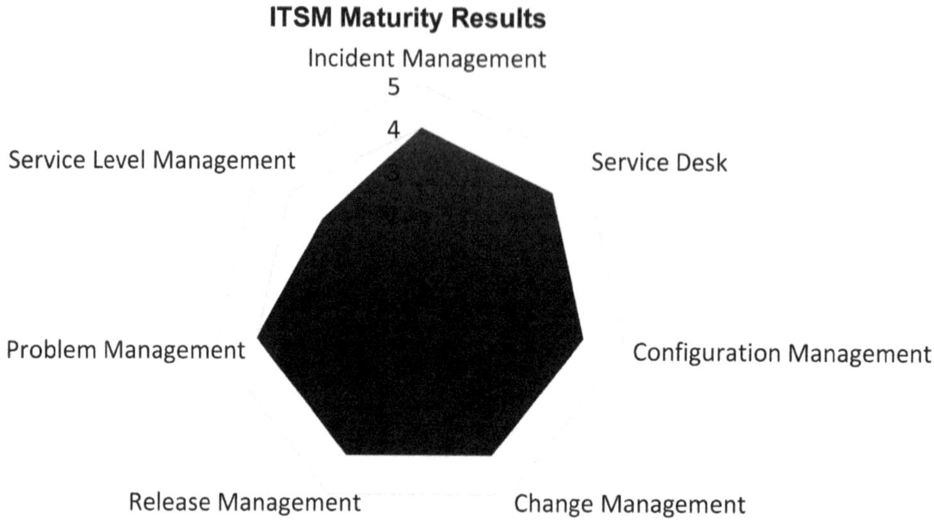

- Improved user satisfaction through the self-service portal: Secure self-service functions, available anywhere and all the time enable end users to log and resolve their own IT incidents, and display relevant information. The service catalogue allows the end user to view and use the services for which they have rights. Automatically provide and maintain services, linking them to the policy and objectives of the IT department.
- Improved visibility of operations through reports and dashboards: Quickly evaluate your performance against the company's goals, for continuous improvement. Easily create or configure multilevel reports based on the metrics used to demonstrate the value of IT Service Management (ITSM) for the enterprise. Dashboards with cascading analysis functions to trend charts based on KPIs to provide context for decision-making and planning. The benefits of the adoption of the practical ITSM framework are:
- 95 percent success rate on SLAs
- Reports meet auditor requirements
- 50 percent reduction in end-user calls
- Data confirms cost-cutting decisions
- Improved IT asset management and cost control
- Set up an agile approach to deal with the different changes in the SI
- Improving the management of the security of IT services
- Implement a continuous improvement strategy DDAO (Discover, Do, Act, Optimize).

IT Security Management

Organized cybercrime has only one target: user data. Data protection against the most complex threats. After auditing this axis, it appears that this component is not supported in the IT Service Management process, and the management of security incidents is not supported. We proposed to implement a security management solution based on the model defined in section 4.3, to offer better visibility of risks, facilitate compliance with current regulations and improve your overall level of security. Figure 10 illustrates the results of IT level of Security Maturity after implementation.

Act

This step will evaluate the decisions taken and the approach was taken. The quality department and management will study the results and judge the relevance of the decisions made. Moreover, this stage is required to reduce the gaps and dysfunctions deployed during each review or audit. The planned management review each year takes into account the steps taken during the year or the last six months in trying to define opportunities for improvement. We exploit DevOps approach to set up this step. DevOps brings fundamental changes to how application and execution teams interact and execute processes. It requires changes in technology, processes, and culture, and changes at this level can be difficult to resolve unless they are addressed in a systematic way. We measure the organization agility level by the proposed DevOps ITSM Maturity model for continues organization's measure

Figure 10. IT security maturity audit result after implementation

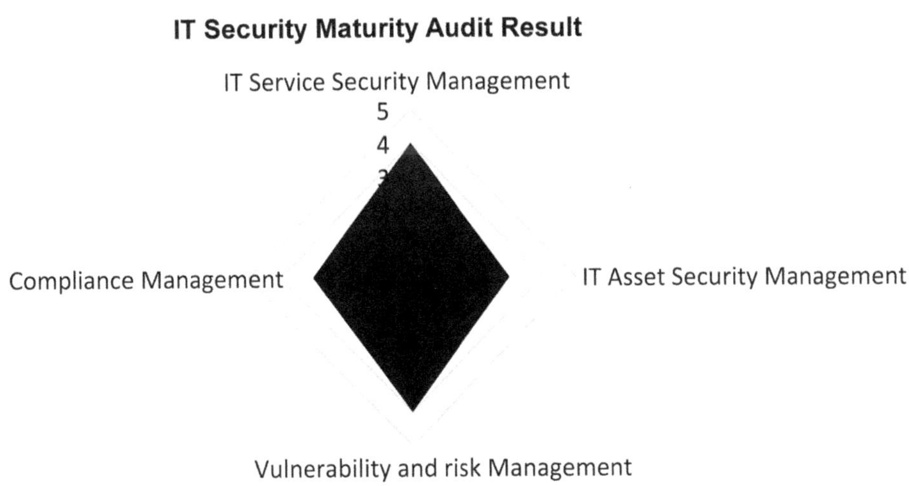

and improvement. The organization's level of agility is initial; our objective is to orient the ACT part towards an agile approach, in order to ensure a delicate change management and consequently a continuous improvement by supporting people, process and technology drivers. To creating an agile IT service/assets center that delivers quicker resolutions, increases user satisfaction and evolves with rapidly changing technologies, we suggest following these steps described in Figure 11.

The results obtained can be improved agile by adopting our agile approach based on DevOps. This approach will allow any organization to measure, control and manage IT services, asset and endpoint security costs and process.

Figure 11. Devops Continues IT improvement

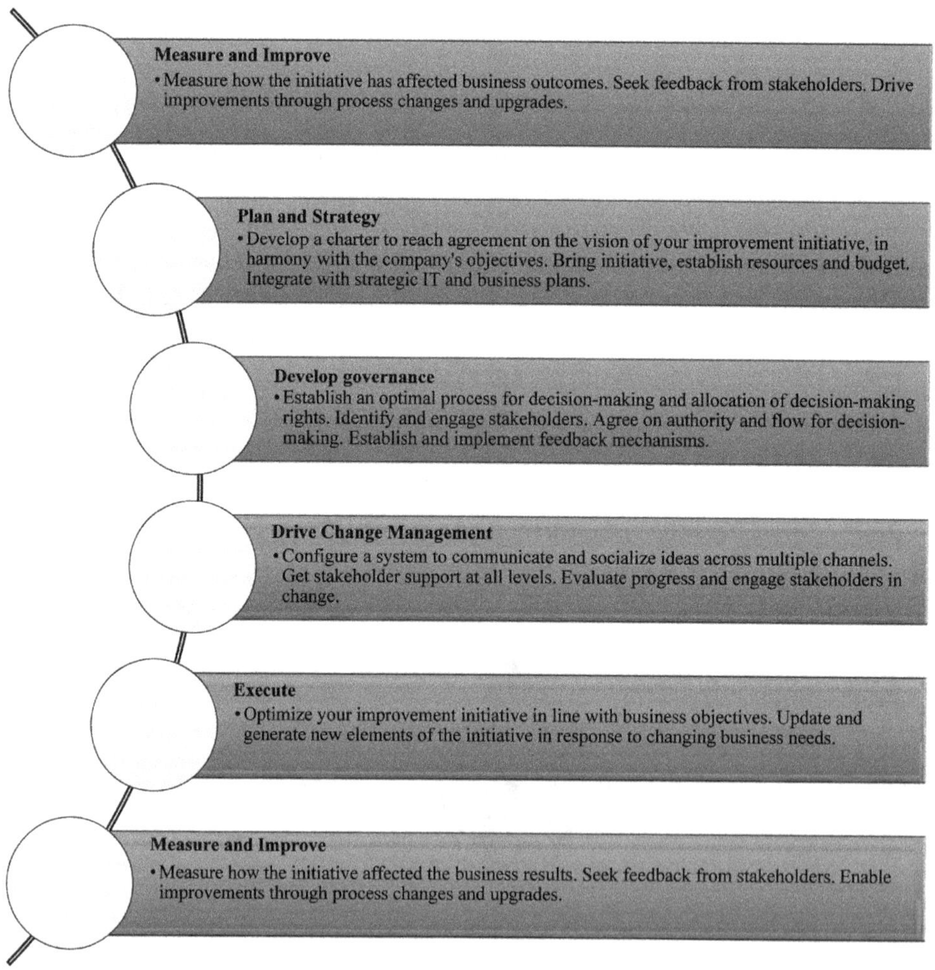

Optimize

The most important thing that organizations adopt agile practices is that there is no end to the journey and that they need to continuously improve to remain leaders. Customers always expect more, and competitors will always be there to deliver it if you don't do it first. Remaining a leader requires adapting to customer feedback and continually improving products and practices, and recognizing when it's time to pivot. New metrics are defined to measure and manage improvement, as well as value delivered.

CONCLUSION

An efficient, agile and practical approach to ITSM is vital for IT organizations to increase the quality of services they provide, to improve speed and agility of the service desk, and to improve user experience, all reducing the cost to run IT. The chapter aims to identify the important aspects that propose a practical agile framework for ITSM efficiency. It was collected based on a theoretical and empirical research study that generated answers to the sub-level research questions, and a return of experience analysis of the best practices in organizations.

In a theoretical study, the concept and the needs of ITSM in the organization are presented with applying different methods and improvements techniques, hence proving the most important of ITIL-ITSM best practice model. The objective of this work is to propose a global and practical ITSM framework based on 4 aspects (IT Service Management, IT Asset Management, Security Management and Agility Management). The proposed framework was defined based on empirical study and was implemented in the large-scale organization (+900 employees). The result of the adoption of this framework, gives a clear idea its efficiency, making it reusable in any other organization. Additionally, performing IT service management is a costly task. Small changes in the framework process can lead to major changes in profit and management process within the organization, like maintaining and operating an information infrastructure. Thus, firstly, it is important for an organization to choose the comprehensive ITSM framework, which fulfils its required aims from a specific task, and secondly which has a better performing quality in an IT service management model.

REFERENCES

Ang, A. (2014). *Asset management: A systematic approach to factor investing*. Oxford University Press. doi:10.1093/acprof:oso/9780199959327.001.0001

Beck, K. (1999). *Extreme Programming Explained: Embrace Change*. Addison-Wesley.

Chen, Y. W., Wang, Y., Nevo, S., Jin, J., Wang, L., & Chow, W. S. (2014). IT capability and organizational performance: The roles of business process agility and environmental factors. *European Journal of Information Systems*, *23*(3), 326–342. doi:10.1057/ejis.2013.4

Cots, S., & Casadesús, M. (2015). Exploring the service management standard ISO 20000. *Total Quality Management & Business Excellence*, *26*(5-6), 515–533. doi: 10.1080/14783363.2013.856544

Duane, L., & Charlie, S. (2016). *Reducing the cost of test through strategic asset management*. IEEE Autotestcon.

Fink, L., & Neuman, S. (2009). Exploring the perceived business value of the flexibility enabled by information technology infrastructure. *Information & Management*, *46*(2), 90–99. doi:10.1016/j.im.2008.11.007

Gene, K., Jez, H., Patrick, D., & John, W. (2016). *The DevOps Handbook: How to Create World-Class Agility, Reliability, and Security in Technology Organizations*. IT Revolution Press.

Giudice, D. L., Christopher, M. A., Amy, H., & Ian, M. (2016). *Agile And DevOps Adoption Drives Digital Business Success*. Cambridge, MA: Forrester Research. Retrieved from Transforming IT organizations into service providers: www.hp.com/hps/itsm

Goldman, S. N. (1995). *Agile Competitors and Virtual Organizations:Strategies for Enriching the Customer*. New York: Van Nostrand Reinhold.

Hank. (2006). ITIL: What It Is And What It Isn't. *Business Communications Review*.

Hewlet Packard, H. P. (2016). *HP Devops*. Retrieved from https://www.hpe.com: https://saas.hpe.com/fr-fr/software/devops-solutions

Holmqvist, M., & Pessi, K. (2006). Agility Through Scenario Development and ContinuousImplementation: A Global Aftermarket Logistics Case. *European Journal of Information Systems*, *15*(2), 146–158. doi:10.1057/palgrave.ejis.3000602

Hong, W., Thong, J. Y., Chasalow, L. C., & Dhillon, G. (2011). User acceptance of agile information systems: A model and empirical test. *Journal of Management Information Systems, 28*(1), 235–272. doi:10.2753/MIS0742-1222280108

Iden, J. &. (2015). The impact of senior management involvement, organisational commitment and group efficacy on ITIL implementation benefits. *Information Systems and e-Business Management,* 527-552.

ISO/IEC 20000. (2010). *ISO/IEC 20000 Information Technology.* ISO/IEC 20000.

Ken Schwaber. (2004). *Agile Project Management with Scrum.* Microsoft Press.

Kumbakara, N. (2008). Managed IT services: The role of IT standards. *Information Management & Computer Security, 16*(4), 336–359. doi:10.1108/09685220810908778

Kumbakara. (2008). Managed IT services: the role of IT standards. *Information Management & Computer Security.*

Lee, O., Banerjee, P., Lim, K., Kumar, K., Hillegersberg, V., & Wei, J. (2006). Agility in Globally Distributed System Development. *Communications of the ACM, 49*(10), 49–54. doi:10.1145/1164394.1164419

Marrone, K., & Kolbe, L. M. (2011). Uncovering ITIL claims: IT executives' perception on benefits and Business-IT alignment. *Information Systems and e-Business Management, 9*(3), 363–380. doi:10.100710257-010-0131-7

McNaughton, R., Ray, P., & Lewis, L. (2010). Designing an evaluation framework for IT service management. *Information & Management, 47*(4), 219–225. doi:10.1016/j.im.2010.02.003

Meade, L. M. (1997). Method for analyzing agility alternatives for business processes. In *Industrial Engineering Research - Conference Proceedings* (pp. 960-965). IIE.

Mesquida. (2012). IT Service Management Process Improvement based on ISO/IEC 15504: A systematic review. *Information and Software Technology.*

Meziani, S. (2010). E-government: ITIL-based service management case study. *The 12th International Conference on information integration and web-based applications & services.*

Mior. (2008). *The importance of ITSM. Malaysian Business.* Kuala Lumpur: New Straits Times Press.

Richards, C. (1996). Agile manufacturing: beyond lean. *Production & Inventory Management,* 60-4.

Robert, H., Isabell, S., Kiess, O., Ingo, B., Sacha, M., & Bradley, L. (2016). *IT Service Management for DevOps.* Retrieved from IBM: https://www.ibm.com/developerworks/community/files/form/anonymous/api/library/42529e82-173a-4f45-805b-93d9eb35ffa6/document/19b71c8c-1675-4727-a3ab-b259ba1d49e6/media/ITSM%20Reference%20Architecture%20-%20DevOps%20-%20Whitepaper.pdf

Silva Molina, L. F. (2005). How to Identify and Measure the Level of Alignment between IT and Business Governance. *Proceedings of the PICMET.*

Trusson, C. R., Doherty, N. F., & Hislop, D. (2014). Knowledge sharing using IT service management tools: Conflicting discourses and incompatible practices. *Information Systems Journal, 24*(4), 347–371. doi:10.1111/isj.12025

Uebernickel, B.-S. Z. (2006). Service-Engineering: A process model for the development of IS services. *Proceedings of the European and Mediterranean Conference on Information Systems (EMCIS).*

van Bon, E. (2007). *Foundations of IT Service Management based on ITIL v3.* Van Haren Publishing.

van Grembergen, H. (2009). *COBIT as a Framework for Enterprise Governance of IT.* Boston: Springer US. doi:10.1007/978-0-387-84882-2_5

Vernadat, F. (1999). Research agenda for agile manufacturing. *International Journal of Agile, 1*(1), 37–40.

Wilcocks, L. (2013). *Information management: The evaluation of information systems investments.* Springer Science Business Media.

Winniford, C. (2009). *Confusion in the Ranks: IT Service Management Practice and Terminology.* Academic Press.

Yusuf, Y., Sarhadi, M., & Gunasekaran, A. (1999). Agile manufacturing: The drivers, concepts and attributes. *International Journal of Production Economics, 62*(1-2), 33–43. doi:10.1016/S0925-5273(98)00219-9

APPENDIX

Table 7. ITSM Maturity Assessment Interview (Sample)

IT Service Management		Answer
Incident Management	Is there a clear understanding by the IT Staff in the organization of this process?	**Yes at least half of them are/do**
	Is there enough information captured about incidents when they are registered?	**Yes we did it once**
	Are incidents assigned a classification code that may point to the likely cause of the incident?	**Yes at least half of them are/do**
Problem Management	Is there a clear understanding by the IT Staff in the organization of this process?	**Yes we do it every few years**
	Is it clear who in the organization should be assigned problems to be dealt with?	**Yes at least half of them are/do**
	Is there sufficient time and budget allowed for training staff in this process area?	**Yes at least half of them are/do**
	Does the Process owner analyze incident information to look for incident trends?	**Yes a small percentage are/do**
Release Management	Is there sufficient time and budget allowed for training staff in this process area?	**Yes at least half of them are/do**
	Is there a published and accepted list of what is considered to be the highest priority components of the infrastructure?	**Yes a small percentage are/do**
	Is there a known and documented naming convention in place for all Configuration items (CI's)?	**Yes at least half of them are/do**
Change Management	Is there a clear understanding by the IT Staff in the organization of this process?	**Yes we do it every few years**
	Are change requests check and verified for completeness prior to their submission?	**Yes at least half of them are/do**
	Is there sufficient time and budget allowed for training staff in this process area?	**Yes we do it every few years**
	As the Change Advisory Board (CAB) been established with appropriate terms of reference (meeting times, authority, etc.)?	**Yes at least half of them are/do**
Service Level Management	Is there a clear understanding by the IT Staff in the organization of this process?	**Yes teams write/run their own**
	Is there a regular review of the activities associated with this process?	**Yes we do it every few years**
	Are there Service Level Agreements (SLA) in place that follows a defined structure?	**Yes we do it every few years**
	Does this process area exchange information with a variety of other process areas?	**Yes we do it every few years**
Availability Management	Are there regular reviews on the performance of this process area against documented Key Performance Indicators (KPI's)?	**Yes at least half of them are/do**
	Are the availability targets set by the organization SMART (Simple, Measurable, Achievable, Realistic, Time-bound)?	**Yes a small percentage are/do**
	Are electronic tools used in this process area well utilized?	**Yes at least half of them are/do**

continued on following page

Table 7. Continued

IT Service Management		Answer
Configuration Management	Is there a published and accepted list of what is considered to be the highest priority components of the infrastructure?	**Yes there is a standard set**
	Is there a known and documented naming convention in place for all Configuration items (CI's)?	**Yes, a small percentage are/do**
	Are there procedures in place to ensure that the process cannot be bypassed?	**Yes there is a standard set**
IT Financial Management	Do you have a good insight into the costs of running the IT environment?	**Yes, a small percentage are/do**
	Can costs of providing current services to the business be demonstrated easily?	**Yes, localized to business areas**
	Are actual costs compared to budgeted costs on a regular basis?	**No**
IT Security Management		**Answer**
IT Service Security Management	Is there a clear understanding in the organization of who or which department is responsible for IT security?	**Yes we do it every few years**
	Are there physical barriers in place preventing unauthorized access to critical IT equipment?	**Yes at least half of them are/do**
IT Asset Security Management	Have the security needs of the business been documented?	
	Is there a clear understanding in the organization of who or which department is responsible for IT security?	**Yes at least half of them are/do**
	Are there physical barriers in place preventing unauthorized access to critical IT equipment?	**Yes a small percentage are/do**
Vulnerability and Risk Management	Is there an IT Security Plan in place that is constantly reviewed and updated?	**Yes at least half of them are/do**
	Does the organization know what's required based on risk ratings?	**Yes a small percentage are/do**
Compliance Management	Is there a formal contract containing, or referring to all security requirements to ensure compliance with the organization's security policies and standards?	**Yes a small percentage are/do**
Agility Management		**Answer**
Strategy and Process	Is there a clear understanding by the IT Staff in the organization of this process?	**Yes in ad-hoc basis**
	Is there a regular review of the activities associated with this process?	**Yes a small percentage are/do**
Flexibility of Structure	Are users, IT Staff and providers gave roles and responsibilities for throughout the organization?	**Yes in ad-hoc basis**
	The enterprise has skilled and motivated people enabling agile responses to changing business conditions	**No**
	The enterprise provides processes, plans, and responsibilities for agile responses to a changing business environment	**Yes on an ad-hoc basis**
Staff competency and skills	Are responsibilities identified at the unit and at the division or enterprise level?	**Yes at least half of them are/do**
	T reaches out business unit leaders to explore the potential for IT to support business agility	**Yes a small percentage are/do**
	IT staff are encouraged to improve their technical skills and are trained in development methods and tools to support agile development	**Yes a small percentage are/do**
Organizational Agility	Optimize IT's resources to meet enterprise objectives for agility	**No**
	Define, maintain and approve functional requirements following expedient analysis of feasibility and alternatives	**No**

Chapter 6
Data Security Threats Sources:
An Empirical Examination of Institutional Characteristics

Nasim Talebi
University of Texas at San Antonio, USA

Emmanuel Ayaburi
University of Texas Rio Grande Valley, USA

Suhail Chakravarty
University of California – Santa Barbara, USA

ABSTRACT

Driven by the difficulty in achieving complete security with technical tools, business investigators are looking into organizational and behavioral issues that could help make systems more secure. This chapter looks at the security of systems from the organizational perspective. Specifically, this study attempts to identify if different organizations have different predisposition to particular type(s) of security threat sources. Using publicly available security breach data from a privacy rights clearinghouse to investigate which organizational characteristics predisposes an institution to an external or internal threat source, it was concluded that as size of organization and the number of its valuable documents increase by one unit, the organization's probability of suffering an internal attacks decrease. Furthermore, when executive members have a business degree rather than information-security-related degrees, the likelihood of suffering an internal attack increases. Also, the probability of an organization suffering an internal or external attack is not based on its industry type.

DOI: 10.4018/978-1-5225-5393-9.ch006

INTRODUCTION

Acts that affect the integrity and availability of business information systems as well as the privacy of business data threatens the security of those information systems. To achieve a secured system, the information systems must be protected from unauthorized access, use, disclosure, disruption, modification or destruction. As organizations continue to depend on complex information systems, the identification of sources of threat to these systems are very important (Warkentin & Willison 2009). Organizations of different types and sizes have different information security threats that they need to be aware of to ensure their sensitive information and assets are protected. The 2010/2011 Computer Security Institute's Computer Crime and Security Survey of 351 computer security practitioners revealed that most organizations experienced relatively less system security breaches over the years but the attacks are increasingly complex with some successful breaches resulting in huge financial loss (Warkentin & Willison 2009).

Prior studies on recent breaches have categorized potential sources of threats including cracking, malicious code, falsification and physical assault (Warkentin & Willison 2009). Another study developed a scoring system for vulnerabilities that pose threats to the systems. Some other studies which focused on the individuals within the organization, have suggested that individuals are the most important factor in protecting an information systems (Workman, Bommer, & Straub 2008).

Internal actors, according to findings by McAfee research, account for 43% of data loss and thus is a significant part of data loss. In the same study, they found that 68% of these incidents were significant enough to have a financially negative impact on the enterprise or firm (McAfee 2017). This means that insider threat and its financial consequences are issues that must be addressed and prevented for a company to succeed.

The threat of a data breach from an insider can come in multiple forms and have varying levels of dangers. A study by the Ponemon Institute in 2017 found in a survey of 874 incidents that the money lost from and the frequency of each type of insider breach. The data in the table adapted from a Ponemon Institute Infographic shows a comparison of insider breaches categorized under Malicious Insider, Negligent Insider, and Credential Theft. See Table 1.

Table 1. Adapted from Ponemon Institute 2016 infographic report: DTEX, 2017

Breach Type	% of Incidents	Cost to Contain	Annualized Cost
Malicious Insider	22%	$347,130	$1,227,812
Negligent Insider	68%	$206,933	$2,291,591
Credential Thief	10%	$493,093	$776,165

From the data presented, the Ponemon Institute concluded that although Credential Theft were the most expensive to contain, Negligent Insiders costed the most by sheer volume of incidents caused by human error. Given that 30% of data breaches that have negative financial impacts are insider breaches, it can be said that insider threat is a problem that firms must attempt to mitigate. In order to gain an understanding of the gravity of the problem, one must gain an understanding of how much it costs a firm to suffer an insider attack.

Insider Threat Cost Analysis and Examples

While it may seem that the containment of data breaches are the extent of the costs of a leak, there are many more underlying factors to the costs of an internal breach. Here are above the surface costs which are better known, as well as below the surface costs which might be less visible. Deloitte in an analysis of data breaches gave a list of above and below the surface consequences.

Some above the surface costs are:

- Technical Investigation
- Customer Breach Notification
- Regulatory Compliance
- Attorney Fees and Litigation
- Post Breach consumer protection
- Public relations
- Cybersecurity Improvements

While the below the surface costs are:

- Insurance Premium Increases
- Increased Cost to Raise Debt
- The Impact of Operational Disruption or Destruction
- Value of Lost Contract Revenue
- Devaluation of Trade Name
- Loss of Intellectual Property
- Lost Value of Customer Relationships

List adapted from Deloitte Infographic (Mossburg et al. 2016)

Using the caveats between the type of breaches and the opportunity cost, the costs of insider breaches can be explained with the different aspects of the price due to insider threat and are best illustrated using real world examples of insider breaches.

Stories of Costly Insider Breaches

Woolworths Negligent User Insider Breach

In another costly breach of data, the grocery store Woolworths lost a significant amount of money from an unintentional loss of data from an authorized user. GroupOn and Woolworths teamed up to sell "e-gift cards" at a discounted price and the customer would receive a voucher code to redeem for the Woolworths store credit. When customers were supposed to receive the pdf for their gift card, they instead received an email with a link to a spreadsheet that had the emails of thousands of customers and voucher codes that added up to $1,308,505. Opportunistic customers took advantage of the blunder and quickly redeemed both their own vouchers as well as those of other customers.

Many customers had their gift cards used before they were able to redeem it and as one customer reported, his gift card was used in a city 300km away (Reilly 2015).

The disclosure of voucher prices and customer emails was not a malicious attempt but rather was a result of negligence that not only resulted in financial loss but also resulted in a loss of customer satisfaction (Reilly 2015; Visentin 2015). Woolworths has agreed to refund the customers that have had their vouchers stolen but will lose all the money that had been stolen and used as a result of this debacle.

In the aftermath of the breach, Woolworths has to make investments beyond the reimbursement of customers. This would include retraining all the employees in better data management, notifying customers of the breach, and the below the surface

Australian Government Leak

The G20 summit is a meeting among world leaders from 19 of the largest world countries and the European Union. Being one of the most high profile events, the data available to the organizers is the most coveted and sensitive pieces of information in the world. Attendees included Vladimir Putin from Russia, President Barack Obama, President Xi Ping, and Prime Minister Narendra Modi (Farrel 2015). For the sake of efficiency, the immigration department must have access to all of the attendees' passport numbers, date of births and visa numbers. Given the valuable information to the immigration department, one would expect employees to err on the side of caution. However, that was not the case.

An employee, in an email, was meant to send these highly valued pieces of information to a colleague. However, the Australian government uses Microsoft Outlook which has an autofill function for email addresses. In a critical blunder, an employee of the Australian Immigration Department sent the email to the wrong person as a result of the autofill function. The passport numbers, among other vital pieces of information, of 31 international leaders attending the summit were sent to a member of the local organizing committee for the Asia Cup football tournament.

Given that this information was not spread further to the public by the recipient of the email, there was a comparatively tame effect on those whose information was compromised. The real problem stemmed from the government's reaction to the breach. None of the world leaders or their teams were notified of the breach until well after the issue had occurred. Just weeks before the leak, Australian government officials were urging citizens to trust them with personal data but after the blunder, Australian citizens were rightfully hesitant.

The costs as a result of the breach stemmed from public relations costs, retraining costs, and system improvements.

Financial Analysis of AT&T Malicious Insider Breach

One example of Insider Attacks that costed the firm a significant amount was an attack on the telecommunications giant AT&T between November 2013 and April 2014. In this time, call center employees from Mexico were paid by third parties to obtain and release customer information used to attempt to open stolen cell phones (Chabrow 2015). AT&T allows for cell phones to be fully unlocked for customers by asking for the customer's name and the last four digits of the customer's social security number with the expectation that only the customer and AT&T would have access to that data. However, with hopes of reselling the unlocked phones, the third party attempted to take advantage of the unlocking system by paying employees of call centers for names and Social Security Numbers. After gaining this information, the ring of cell phone thieves made 290,803 handset unlock requests with the information that had been compromised (National Cybersecurity Institute 2016).

Upon this incident, AT&T was forced to publicize its occurrence upon which the Federal Communications Commission launched its own investigation into the event. During the FCC's investigation, it was found that the three call center employees in Mexico gave information for 68,000 accounts. However, the FCC exposed further breaches taking place in Colombia and the Philippines. In the Colombian and Philippine facilities, an additional 40 employees had accessed 211,000 customer accounts (Federal Communications Commission 2015).

After the results of the investigation, the FCC took its biggest enforcement action by fining AT&T $25 million as well as requiring that all customers be notified, pay for credit monitoring services for customers affected by breaches in Colombia and Philippines. On top of the financial consequences, AT&T was required increase security by appointing a privacy certified senior compliance manager, conduct a privacy risk assessment, implement regular employee training and file compliance reports for the FCC (Federal Communications Commission 2015).

In order to fulfill the FCC's wishes, the fine was not the only cost AT&T suffered from the breach. According to Zurich Insurance Company, notifying a customer costs an average of $2.75, thus, that the cost of notifying the 279,000 account owners would come out to be $767,250 (Bailey 2014). According to the Ponemon Institute the cost of containment would cost at least $2.83 million for an average breach size of 24,089. Since the AT&T breach was 11½ times larger than the average breach, the cost of containment would be at least $32 million (Chabrow 2015). The cost to improve general security measures for a company with over 200,000 employees such as AT&T can be estimated at $70 million according to Deloitte (Mossburg et al. 2016). The total tangible costs of the AT&T breach thus comes out to be $128 million dollars. However, according to both Deloitte and the Kaspersky Institute, there are intangible losses and financial impacts such as customer loss and lost contracts as a result of the insider breach(Mossburg et al. 2016; Kaspersky 2015). Thus the loss that AT&T suffered as a result of the data breach in call centers is even larger than the tangible direct costs of the breach.

Why Is This Important?

While some of the costs from an insider breach are apparent, there are many hidden aspects that must be evaluated. Both malicious and negligent insiders can be trained or filtered with better training and awareness that could save a significant amount of money for any firm that is a target. Getting better insurance and training would cost the firm significantly less as is made clear by Philip Lieberman, president of IT security provider Lieberman Software, when he says "The cost to implement a control would be one-tenth - or vastly less - of the cost of the fine and other losses" (Ponemon 2017). The cost of insider breaches is undeniable and so is the necessity of better protection against the attacks given the financial and business consequences that come with insider threats. Identifying the factors that play into the susceptibility of a company is the ideal way to prevent such an attack.

However, due to resource constraints, organizations are not able to implement unlimited technical controls to protect their systems. Instead, they need to understand the major threat (external or internal) that systems will likely face so as to implement effective controls accordingly. This understanding stems from a 'self-awareness' about the respective type of industry and size of the firm as well as other additional factors.

This study attempts to identify if different organizations have different predisposition to particular type(s) of security threat. The ability to identify vulnerabilities will guide any investment of resources into protecting assets most likely to suffer an attack. Based on the review of past literature we developed four hypotheses which relate the firm size, industry type, Information Technology

(IT) competence and firm knowledge to external or internal types of threat. These hypotheses were tested empirically with security breach data gathered from Privacy Rights Clearinghouse and S&P Capital IQ providing company information. Following a statistical analysis of 35 reported security breaches using logistic regression, it was realized that as size of organization, reflected in the number of employees, increases, and as the amount of firm knowledge assets, reflected in the number of documents, the organization's probability of suffering an internal attacks decreases relative to external attacks. Also, the probability of suffering an internal attack relative to external attack for executives' business degree holders is higher. No statistically significant differences in threat source across industries was found in our analysis.

In subsequent sections, we will review the literature related to the subjects of information security threats and organizational factors. Then present the research model and hypotheses derived, outline the research methodology, report the results of the model testing, and discuss the findings and their theoretical and managerial implications. Then conclude with a discussion about the limitations and directions for future research.

BACKGROUND AND LITERATURE REVIEW

Categorization of breaches and mitigation strategies or techniques have been the predominant theme in most research. One such theme is the human factor and its influence on threat categories. A longitudinal study, (Warkentin & Willison 2009) found that the proportion of threat due to physical, false, malicious and cracking vulnerability categories have remained relatively stable over the years. Thus concluding that human error has been undervalued and should be regarded as a significant factor in protecting information systems. Herzog et al (2007) developed a web Ontology Language-based model which includes asset, threat, vulnerability, countermeasure and security goal and defense strategy as its core concepts. A general category of security threat sources introduced by Krausz (Chang & Ho 2006) hypothesizes that the actions a firm can take to prevent incidents depends on who, where and what the source of attack is. Given this hypothesis, four different categories of threats were devised: external versus internal, unintentional versus intentional, manual versus automatic, and human versus nature. Most researchers classify threats to information system security into two broad categories of external and internal (Workman & Bommer 2008). In addition, Al-Zubi (2010) is of the opinion that sources of threats can be divided into two internal and external classes, depending on the type of media used. Threats can then further be classified into groups depending on their location from the point of vulnerability.

An attempt to develop a vulnerability scoring systems for information systems has also been of interest to researchers. Mell et al. (2006) developed a common security scoring systems that generates consistent scores of vulnerabilities. Systems with higher scores need to be mitigated proactively. Some mitigation factors focus on the human dimension such as education and awareness of employees and third parties (Workman & Bommer 2008). Omissions and careless behavior by users threaten the security of most information systems. Workman et al. (2008), in an attempt to find out why there is omission of security measures among employees who should know the importance of securing a system, suggested that perceived severity of consequences employees will suffer from a breach influences how motivated they are to prevent breaches. Some other sources of threats include natural disasters, organization procedure and computer virus (Loch, Carr, & Warkentin 1992). This study extends from prior studies as it takes a focus on organizations' features and how those features influence these organizations' predisposition to either an internal or external attack on its information system.

STUDY OF POTENTIALS FACTORS THAT AFFECT SUSCEPTIBILITY

Issues, Controversies, Problems

Some of these threats sources include hostile cyber/physical attacks, human error or omission or disasters due to natural or man-made occurrence (Mell, Scarfone, Romanosky 2006). This study focuses on the first two sources since the third, disasters, affects all industries and there is little by way of effort organizations can do to prevent them from happening or predicted their occurrence. Threats due to attacks are usually carried out by adversaries who are not with the organization but are attempting to disrupt operation for either financial gain or for the joy of it. For the purpose of this study those types of threats sources are referred to as external threat sources while threats due to human omission or commission within the organization for any reason will be referred to as internal threats sources. One key factor in risk analysis is the consequence or assets that are affected (Chang, Ho 2006). Different organizations vary in the size and sensitivity of the assets they have. Therefore the type of threat source can be motivated by factors including type of target organization, the size of target organization, academic security knowledge of executive team members and the amount of precious documents. Next will be a discussion of these factors and their relationship to potential threat source.

1. Industry Type

Industry sector has been used in many previous research related to information security management and end-user security behavior (Ghobadian and Gallear 1997; Taylor and McGraw 2004; Stanton et al. 2005). Organizations have different needs for information systems in their operations. For some organizations, lack of availability of their information system means disruption in the provision of their services or products. These differences in information systems need appeal differently to different attackers since the attacker communities are not homogenous. For example, the attractiveness of a financial institution to an external attack by a hacker community is different compared to a non-profit organization. This is because there will be different type of challenges to the effort of an attacker and the attackers also benefit differently. A multi industry study in Korea revealed that there is differences across industries in the categories of information system security threats they face such that manufacturing considers interruption more serious, while academia and distribution firms considers modification and interruption more serious (Chang & Ho 2006). Therefore an organization's use of IT is influenced by the type of industry it operates in making organizations to be exposed to kinds of security threat. Thus we hypothesize that:

Hypothesis One: The industry type an organization operates in influences the source of security threat to its information system.

2. Organizational Size

Organizations in different sizes tended to handle information security differently with different levels of available resources and expertise (David 2002). While small organizations are generally resource poor and more sensitive to outside pressure (Ghobadian and Gallear 1997), larger ones encounter a problem due to the nature of the organization which is the more number of employees. Loach et al. (1992) are of the opinion that employees and organizational procedures are a greater threat to the security of information system infrastructure compared to other factors. As an organization increases in size the number of employees and documents produced increases. The likelihood of security breaches due to the number of employees also increases and makes the impact of the human element more pronounced. The human element is often referred to as the weakest link in the chain of security defense of information system. Possible ways to control for this factor is to create security awareness among employees or monitor their activities constantly. Employee compliant work practices are important to the security of IT operation. Therefore organizations must implement monitoring mechanisms to ensure compliance or detection of non-complaint behavior. With regard to these two remedies, larger companies have a tendency to underestimate the value of building awareness (Krausz 2015). In addition, the larger the firm the larger the cost involve in monitoring and securing the IT infrastructure. Therefore when the organization increases in size the human factor is more pronounced since the number of people to monitor on the network increases. Some employee work practices that have been identified as increasing the risk of a system includes resistance to adopting initiatives to improve security (Chang & Ho 2006). However, complete monitoring of employees might not be possible and managers cannot predict the intent of all employees. Hence we hypothesize that:

Hypothesis Two: The size of an organization influences the source of information system security threat such that large organizations are prone to internal attacks than small organizations do.

3. IT Competence

Information Technology (IT) competence makes it possible for a company to plan, organize, execute, and invest on information security effectively (DTEX 2017). More specifically, it is "the set of IT-related knowledge and experience that a business manager possesses" (Bassellier et al. 2003). It has been found in previous literature that the IT competence of business managers not only positively influence their attitudes toward practicing security controls and management (Bassellier et al. 2001; Hagen et al. 2008), but also makes them have proactive Information Security Management behaviors (Hagen et al. 2008). Majoring in IT or security related fields, executive managers can understand the necessity of allocating security investment budgets at the first place. Then, the need for building security awareness in employees through training programs along with focusing on employees as a potential threat to the overall security of systems are more understandable for them. Hence:

Hypothesis Three: IT competence of executive managers influences the source of security threat to its information system.

4. Firm Knowledge

Organizations are more dependent than ever on information systems (IS) to enhance business efficiency and effectiveness. Therefore, protecting those systems are of importance to organizations. However, most of the time the focus is only on either corporate computer assets or corporate IT systems, and information asset and data protection is utterly underestimated. Therefore, those information assets that organizations have makes them more attractive to outsiders such that the greater the size of the documents and the depth of data, the more hackers interested in. Not only outsider, but also insiders will become attracted to those knowledge assets. Park & Ho (2006) found that insiders have caused great damage and loss to corporate internal information assets. Hence:

Hypothesis Four: The total number of documents an organization have influences the source of information system security threat.

METHODOLOGY

Data

To study the research model depicted in Figure 1, we chose an empirical study approach using security breaches reported in the US as described below. An empirical methodology for this study is a good choice since evidence is needed to support the above hypothesis. Although the threat sources to information systems are varied, this study is concern about institutional factors that influence the type of threat source. Factors of interest are size of an organization, the industry type, IT competence of executive members, and firm knowledge. Data used to test the above hypotheses were obtained from Privacy Rights Clearinghouse's (PRC) repository of data breaches reported in the US along with S&P Capital IQ providing information on companies worldwide. Although 4669 breaches were reported from March 2005 to November 2015, not all breaches were usable because there were no reports

Figure 1. Research model

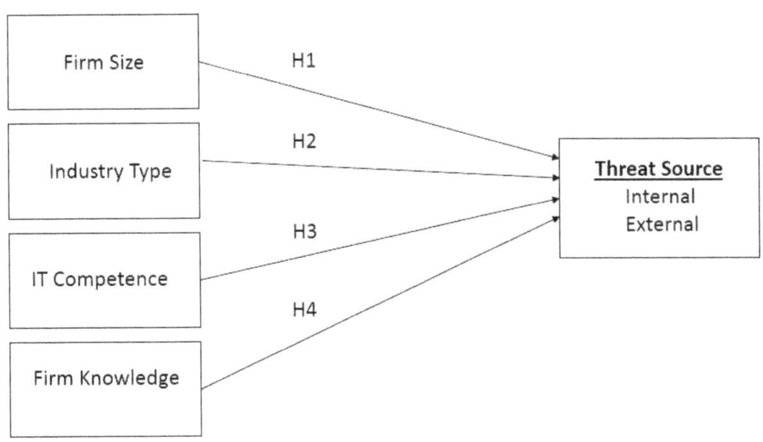

about the type of breach that occurred or the number of potential documents being accessed by fraudsters. After deletion of such data, the study ended up with 2211 useful observations for further analysis. Among those 2211 breaches we just were able to collect complete data for 41 organizations and focus on 35 of them to do hypotheses testing. Table 2 shows the descriptive statistics of the data.

Variables

Source of threat variable has two dimensions; internal and external threat source. External threat source are those breaches which can be traced to an individual or system outside the organization. Privacy Rights Clearinghouse reports the type of breaches on its website. For this study external threat sources are data breaches resulting from hacking or stealing of portability devices by third parties outside the organization. Internal threat sources on the other hand are those threats that can be traced to the actions of individuals within the organizations. Such threats include unintended disclosure, insider breach, loss of company information assets and employees falling for the activities of fraudster.

The size of the organization, which was measured using the number of employees, determines its exposure level to attackers. In fact, organizational total assets and revenue can also be used to represent the size of an organization. However, we use the number of employees because we believe human factors have great influence in determining an organization's security threats.

The type of industry an organization firm is in was based on the categories of organizations by PRC. In all seven categories were reported covering business, finance, education, health, not for profit and government. This categorization in the opinion of the author covers nearly all industries and the study therefore adopted their

Table 2. Data distribution

Threat Score Frequency	Percent
External 17	48.57
Internal 18	51.43
Total 35	100
Industry Type	
Financial 14	40
Medical 14	40
Others 7	20
Total 35	100

Table 3. Variables

Variable Name	Definition
Internal Threat (Internal)	Threat which is as a result of an action by an individual within the firm. These include unintended disclosure, insider breach and loss to fraudsters.
External Threat (External)	Breaches traced to an individual or system outside the organization. These include hacking and stealing by third parties.
Organizational Size (Trfirmsize)	Natural log of the total number of employees in an organization.
Industry Type (Industrytype)	Main type of activity carried out in the breached firm.
IT Competence (Majoruse)	Academic major the executive team hold.
Firm Knowledge (Trknowledgeasset)	Natural log of the total number of documents in an organization.

categorization. Due to the lack of data points in various industries, we used two main industries including financial coded as 1, medical coded as 2, and other industries coded as 3. The other category have instances from not for profit organizations, retail, and government institutions. The reference category used for analysis was the financial organization category. And since the continuous predictor variable of firm size, and firm knowledge were highly positively skewed, we used natural log transformation to make data ready for the analysis.

Results Analysis and Discussion

First proposed in the 1970s as an alternative technique to overcome the limitations of ordinary least squares regression in handling dichotomous outcomes, logistic regression analysis was used to predict the probability that a cyber-attack on a firm would come from an internal source relative to an external source.

A test of the final model with threat source as the dependent variable and firm size, industry type, IT competence, and firm knowledge as predictor variables compared with only the constant included null model was statistically significant with a Chi, $X^2 = 25.450$ with $p < 0.05$. Table 4 shows the logistic regression coefficient, Wald test, and odds ratio for each of the predictors. The odds and probability of an internal attack for each industry type is shown in Table 4 as well. Employing a 0.10 criterion of statistical significance, knowledge assets, firm size and IT competence of executive members were found to be significant.

One unit increase in firm size, the odds of suffering from an internal (1) attack decreases by (0.578-1)*100% = 42%. Also, the probability of getting an internal

Table 4. Variables in the Equation

Variables in the Equation

		B	S.E.	Wald	df	Sig.	Exp(B)	95% C.I.for EXP(B) Lower	Upper
Step 1[a]	Trknowledgeasset	-.415	.238	3.050	1	.081	.660	.415	1.052
	Trfirmsize	-.549	.249	4.863	1	.027	.578	.355	.941
	Industrytype			2.911	2	.233			
	Industrytype(1)	-2.469	1.515	2.657	1	.103	.085	.004	1.649
	Industrytype(2)	-2.258	1.530	2.178	1	.140	.105	.005	2.097
	Majoruse			4.054	2	.132			
	Majoruse(1)	3.401	1.689	4.054	1	.044	29.981	1.095	821.032
	Majoruse(2)	-17.159	40192.970	.000	1	1.000	.000	.000	.
	Constant	5.362	2.786	3.704	1	.054	213.242		

a. Variable(s) entered on step 1: Trknowledgeasset, Trfirmsize, Industrytype, Majoruse.

attack when the executive member holds a business degree is 29.98 times or 70% higher comparing to those who have IS degrees. In addition, one unit increase in the number of documentation, the odds of suffering from an internal attack decreases by (0.66-1)*100= 34%.

Thus, the data support H1 in a reverse direction, along with H3 and H4 in the predicated direction at the 10% significance level. However, the probabilities for an internal attack are not statistically different across financial, medical and other types of industries. The result of hypotheses testing is provided in Table 5.

Table 5. Results

	Hypotheses	**Result**
H1	*The* ***size*** *of an organization influences the source of information system security threat such that large organizations are prone to internal attacks than small organizations.*	**Supported - reverse**
H2	The **industry type** an organization operates in influences the source of security threat to its information system.	**Not supported**
H3	**IT competence** of executive managers influences the source of security threat to its information system.	**Supported**
H4	*The* **total number of documents** *an organization have influences the source of information system security threat.*	**Supported**

FUTURE RESEARCH DIRECTIONS

The results of this study should be interpreted with caution since there are many limitations to this study. First of all, the small sample size used in this study was the biggest concern of the authors. In addition, the use of reported breaches might not truly reflect the number and types of breaches organizations actually encounter as some organizations might be unwilling to disclose any news about a breach due to the impact it will have no its reputation.

Also, nearly half of the observations in the PRC data set were unusable due to the lack of information with regard to attack categorization. For instance, either the number of documents accessed or a potential source of attack was not made known as reported in the sample section of the methodology. Proper classification of these breaches and their inclusion in the analysis might potentially alter the results obtained in this study. In addition, since the sample is limited to the United States of America, it is suggested to replicate this study in other countries to reconfirm the result before using its implications. Finally, no interaction effect between the independent variables was examined. The interaction of those factors might impact the overall results obtained in this study. Future studies will exam the interactive effect of firm size and industry type.

CONCLUSION

Organizations face constant attacks on their information systems infrastructure and the data that they keep on a daily basis. These attacks could originate from an outside entity such as a hackers or actions and omissions from insiders who have privileged access to the systems. This study sought to investigate if the industry an organization belongs to, its size in terms of number of employees, the IT skills and knowledge of its executive member(s), or organization knowledge in the form of the amount of valuable documentation predisposes one organization to an internal attack relative to an external attack. Based on reviews of previous literature, the study investigated four hypotheses which state that the size of firm, along with the magnitude of documentations and academic knowledge and expertise of executive level are positively associated with its likelihood of suffering an internal attack and that the source of attacks vary by industry type. Following an execution of binary logistic regression on data set on publically announced security breaches, it was realized that larger organizations are not necessarily prone to internal attacks. Instead, smaller companies seem to be more prone to internal cyber attacks. A possible explanation for this is that while bigger companies probably face more internal attacks, these are more often successful in smaller companies due to a lack of investment in cyber attack prevention. This then makes one wonder if larger organizations are prone to external attacks instead. This unanswered question will be investigated in the future. However, the source of threat or an attack does not seem to differ across industries. In other words, firms experiencing internal threat source have fewer number of documents and are smaller in size, while their executive members hold a business degree versus an Information System or Information Security related degree.

This study highlights some concerns for managers in practice. The conclusion of this study appears to suggest that as firm become larger, they become attractive targets for hackers and thieves looking to the firm's assets.

ACKNOWLEDGMENT

This research was supported by National Science Foundation under grant number 1724725. Any opinions, findings, and conclusions or recommendations expressed in this material are those of the author(s) and do not necessarily reflect the views of the National Science Foundation.

REFERENCES

Al-Zubi, A. A. (2010). *Identification of Information Systems Threats Sources: An Analytical Study*. Academic Press.

Ashibani, Y., & Mahmoud, Q. H. (2017). Cyber physical systems security: Analysis, challenges and solutions. *Computers & Security*, *68*, 81–97. doi:10.1016/j.cose.2017.04.005

Bauer, S., & Bernroider, E. W. (2017). From information security awareness to reasoned compliant action: Analyzing information security policy compliance in a large banking organization. *ACM SIGMIS Database: the DATABASE for Advances in Information Systems*, *48*(3), 44–68. doi:10.1145/3130515.3130519

Chabrow, E. (2015, April 18). Insider Breach Costs AT&T $25 Million. In *GovInfoSecurity*. Skybox Security. Retrieved from www.govinfosecurity.com/insider-breach-costs-att-25-million-a-8089

Chang, S. E., & Ho, C. B. (2006). Organizational factors to the effectiveness of implementing information security management. *Industrial Management & Data Systems*, *106*(3), 345–361. doi:10.1108/02635570610653498

Colwill, C. (2009). Human factors in information security: The insider threat – Who can you trust these days? *Information Security Technical Report*, *14*(4), 186–196. doi:10.1016/j.istr.2010.04.004

Crossler, R. E., Bélanger, F., & Ormond, D. (2017). The quest for complete security: An empirical analysis of users' multi-layered protection from security threats. *Information Systems Frontiers*, 1–15.

Evesti, A., Kanstrén, T., & Frantti, T. (2017, June). Cybersecurity situational awareness taxonomy. In *Cyber Situational Awareness, Data Analytics And Assessment (Cyber SA), 2017 International Conference On* (pp. 1-8). IEEE.

Federal Communications Commission. (2015). Available at https://apps.fcc.gov/edocs_public/attachmatch/DOC-332911A1.pdf

Giovinazzi, S., Brown, C., Seville, E., Stevenson, J. R., Hatton, T., & Vargo, J. J. (2016). Criticality of infrastructures for organisations. *International Journal of Critical Infrastructures*, *12*(4), 331–363. doi:10.1504/IJCIS.2016.081303

Herzog, A., Shahmehri, N., & Duma, C. (2007). An ontology of information security. *International Journal of Information Security and Privacy*, *1*(4), 1–23. doi:10.4018/jisp.2007100101

Hu, Q., Hart, P., & Cooke, D. (2007). The role of external and internal influences on information systems security – a neo-institutional perspective. *The Journal of Strategic Information Systems*, *16*(2), 153–172. doi:10.1016/j.jsis.2007.05.004

Hurlburt, G. (2016). Good Enough" Security: The Best We'll Ever Have. *Computer*, *49*(7), 98–101. doi:10.1109/MC.2016.212 PMID:28003687

Im, G. P., & Baskerville, R. L. (2005). A longitudinal study of information system threat categories: The enduring problem of human error. *ACM SIGMIS Database*, *36*(4), 68–79. doi:10.1145/1104004.1104010

Initiative, J. T. F. T., & ... (2009). *800-53 Rev. 3*. SP: Recommended Security Controls for Federal Information Systems and Organizations.

Jung, B., Han, I., & Lee, S. (2001). S. Security threats to Internet: A Korean multi-industry investigation. *Information & Management*, *38*(8), 487–498. doi:10.1016/S0378-7206(01)00071-4

Kaspersky Lab. (2015). *Damage Control: The Cost of Security Breaches IT Security Risks Special Report Series*. Retrieved from https://media.kaspersky.com/pdf/it-risks-survey-report-cost-of-security-breaches.pdf

Krausz, M. (2015). *Managing information security breaches: Studies from real life. S.l.* IT Governance Ltd.

Loch, K.D., Carr, H.H., & Warkentin, M. E. (1992). Threats to Information Systems: Today's Reality, Yesterday's Understanding. *MIS Quarterly, 16*(2), 173.

Mell, P., Scarfone, K., & Romanosky, S. (2006). Common vulnerability scoring system. *IEEE Security & Privacy, 4*(6), 85–89.

Mossburg, E. (2017, September 15). *Beneath the surface | Deloitte US | Cyber Risk Services.* Retrieved November 17, 2017, from https://www2.deloitte.com/us/en/pages/risk/articles/hidden-business-impact-of-cyberattack.htm

Moteff, J. C. (2005). Risk Management and Critical Infrastructure Protection: Assessing, Integrating, and Managing Threats, Vulnerabilities and Consequences. *American Journal of Hospital Pharmacy, 47*(3), 533–543.

National Cybersecurity Institute. Excelsior College. (2016, July 11). *Insider Breach Costs AT&T $25 Million.* Retrieved from www.nationalcybersecurityinstitute.org/telecommunications/insider-breach-costs-att-25-million-2/

Peppard, J., & Ward, J. (2016). *The strategic management of information systems: Building a digital strategy.* John Wiley & Sons.

Ponemon Institute. (2017). *Cost of Data Breach Study.* Available at www.ibm.com/security/data-breach/index.html

Posey, C., Raja, U., Crossler, R. E., & Burns, A. J. (2017). Taking stock of organisations' protection of privacy: Categorising and assessing threats to personally identifiable information in the USA. *European Journal of Information Systems*, 1–20.

Reilly, C. (2015, May 31). *Data breach sees Woolworths gift cards leaked in email bungle.* Retrieved November 17, 2017, from https://www.cnet.com/au/news/data-breach-sees-woolworths-gift-cards-leaked-in-email-bungle/

Richardson, R. (2011). *2010/2011 Computer Crime and Security Survey.* Retrieved from http://gatton.uky.edu/FACULTY/PAYNE/ACC324/CSISurvey2010.pdf

Soomro, Z. A., Shah, M. H., & Ahmed, J. (2016). Information security management needs more holistic approach: A literature review. *International Journal of Information Management, 36*(2), 215–225. doi:10.1016/j.ijinfomgt.2015.11.009

Stewart, H., Stewart, H., Jürjens, J., & Jürjens, J. (2017). Information security management and the human aspect in organizations. *Information & Computer Security, 25*(5), 494–534. doi:10.1108/ICS-07-2016-0054

DTEX Systems. (2017). *The True Price Tag of Insider Threats: Findings from the New 2016 Cost of Insider Threats Report*. Retrieved from dtexsystems.com/true-price-tag-insider-threats-findings-new-2016-cost-insider-threats-report.

Thompson, M. (2016). *Harmonised Taxonomies of Security and Resilience: A Suitable Foundation for the Security Discipline* (Doctoral dissertation). University of New South Wales, Canberra, Australia.

van Schaik, P., Jeske, D., Onibokun, J., Coventry, L., Jansen, J., & Kusev, P. (2017). Risk perceptions of cyber-security and precautionary behaviour. *Computers in Human Behavior*, *75*, 547–559. doi:10.1016/j.chb.2017.05.038

Visentin, L. (2015, May). Woolworths Leaks $1 Million of Gift Cards in Massive Data Breach Debacle. *The Sydney Morning Herald*. Retrieved from www.smh.com.au/digital-life/consumer-security/woolworths-leaks-1-million-of-gift-cards-in-massive-data-breach-debacle-20150530-ghd8wl.html

Warkentin, M., & Willison, R. (2009). Behavioral and policy issues in information systems security: The insider threat. *European Journal of Information Systems*, *18*(2), 101–105. doi:10.1057/ejis.2009.12

Workman, M., Bommer, W. H., & Straub, D. (2008). Security lapses and the omission of information security measures: A threat control model and empirical test. *Computers in Human Behavior*, *24*(6), 2799–2816. doi:10.1016/j.chb.2008.04.005

Chapter 7
Social Internet of Vehicles:
A GCC (Gulf Cooperation Council) Perspective

Talal A. Butt
American University in the Emirates, UAE

Razi Iqbal
American University in the Emirates, UAE

Mounir Kehal
Higher Colleges of Technology, UAE

ABSTRACT

Advent of internet of things (IoT) has significantly enriched the opportunities of crafting state-of-the-art applications of smart connected objects. Intelligent transportation systems (ITS) are playing a vital role in the development of smart systems for transportation throughout the world. Based on IoT, the internet of vehicles (IoV) paradigm is emerging to revolutionize the field of ITS. In this paradigm, vehicles leverage the use of internet for socializing with other vehicles, infrastructures, passengers, and drivers. This concept of vehicle socialization is referred to as social internet of vehicles (SIoV). This chapter presents the GCC (Gulf Cooperation Council) perspective of SIoVs by highlighting the latest trends being followed by GCC countries in the broader field ITS. It also provides an insight into opportunities enabled by SIoV applications that can be availed by GCC countries along with the challenges and limitations.

DOI: 10.4018/978-1-5225-5393-9.ch007

INTRODUCTION

The Internet of Things (IoT) paradigm aims to lead us to a new era of computing where the Internet will expand to include billions of new types of devices. The IoT is based on the idea of integrating everyday smart objects equipped with sensors to the Internet. This way these heterogeneous objects become capable to communicate with each other and to provide ubiquitous services, which opens a new vista of possibilities. All this pervasiveness will be enabled by sensors that range from battery-less Radio Frequency Identification (RFID) to sensor devices equipped with many sensors. These devices sense different physical phenomenon and can actuate different tasks. The Cloud computing will provide the required infrastructure to gather and analyze the data generated by these sensors. This infrastructure will enable different applications by enabling the provision of end-to-end service. The analysis of this data will be important for businesses and governments, and eventually will become a key to create new business models.

The Social Internet of Things (SIoT) concepts envisions to enable consciousness in the IoT by enabling social networking among the IoT devices (Atzori, L., Iera, A., Morabito, G., & Nitti, M. (2012)). These devices will be able to socialize with each other and create social circles based on mutual interests and goals. This application of social networking will re-use the existing social network models and will address the IoT specific issues such as scalability. Furthermore, the IoT devices will build trust-based relationships and will leverage these relationships for service provisioning. SIoT will enable the feasibility of managing the ever-growing number of devices in IoT.

Internet of Vehicles (IoV) is an emerging concept derived from its parent domain, Internet of Things (IoT). The idea of IoV refers to the dynamic mobile communication between vehicles, infrastructure, drivers and the passengers. This communication is sub-divided in to V2V (Vehicle to Vehicle) when vehicles communicate with each other, V2I (Vehicle to Infrastructure) when vehicles communicate with RSUs (Road Side Units) and V2H (Vehicle to Human) when vehicles communicate with drivers or the passengers of the vehicles. The key advantage of IoV is information sharing between different entities that can greatly benefit in improving the traffic on road. IoV promises great commercial interest and wide horizon for research that attracts a lot of researchers and companies (Maglaras et. al, 2016). All time connected environment for vehicles on roads provides enormous opportunities for governmental and non-governmental organizations to connect with the drivers on the roads. For example, Traffic Regulatory Authorities can inform drivers to take an alternate route if there is an accident on the road ahead, or if construction work is in progress. This information can be directly integrated into vehicle navigation systems and effortlessly communicated through the Internet. This method of communicating with cars and drivers can significantly reduce the cost and effort by removing the expensive billboards on the roads.

Social Internet of Vehicles (SIoV) is the latest development in the area of IoV. It's following the trend of its sister concept, Social Internet of Things (SIoT) (Nitti, M., Girau, R., Floris, A., & Atzori, L. (2014). A key factor that makes SIoV exciting is the fact that vehicles can socialize with themselves and share information of common interests, e.g., road situations, nearby gas stations and hotels etc. Socializing in SIoV is not limited to vehicles only, as the network can include drivers, passengers and infrastructure as well.

The main objective of this chapter is to discuss the perspective of GCC towards the utilizations and limitations of SIoV. Adaptability of latest technologies in GCC countries make them an excellent choice for utilizing SIoV and its applications. However, SIoV is still in its early ages and hence require comprehensive research for development and deployment of these applications. The chapter will provide an insight in to challenges and limitations anticipated in providing SIoV solutions.

The rest of the chapter is organized as follows: The background section provides the introduction of SIoV through the review of literature. Main Focus of the chapter section presents the issues and challenges involved in designing and implementing SIoV applications in GCC countries. Solutions and Recommendations section delivers an insight into the proposed solutions to the challenges. Future Directions section provides the research directions in this field and finally the conclusion section concludes the chapter.

BACKGROUND

Social Internet of Vehicles (SIoV) is comprised of social characteristics, human behavior and network of vehicles. SIoV is sometimes referred to as Vehicular Social Networks (VSNs) that is assumed to be a group of vehicles and individuals having common interests. SIoV is considered an important concept as vehicles can share a lot like personal information (e.g., location, destination, pictures etc.), traffic information (e.g., accidents, road works, traffic jams) and other common interest information (nearby hotels, restaurant discounts, free parking slots etc.). Figure 1 further illustrates the typical SIoV model.

Social Internet of Vehicles (SIoV) is a perpetuation of VANETs (Vehicular Ad-hoc Networks). VANETs have been around for a few decades now and gained considerable attention from researchers. VANETs are network of vehicles that can communicate with each other, infrastructure and drivers. One of the major difference

Figure 1. Typical model of social internet of vehicles

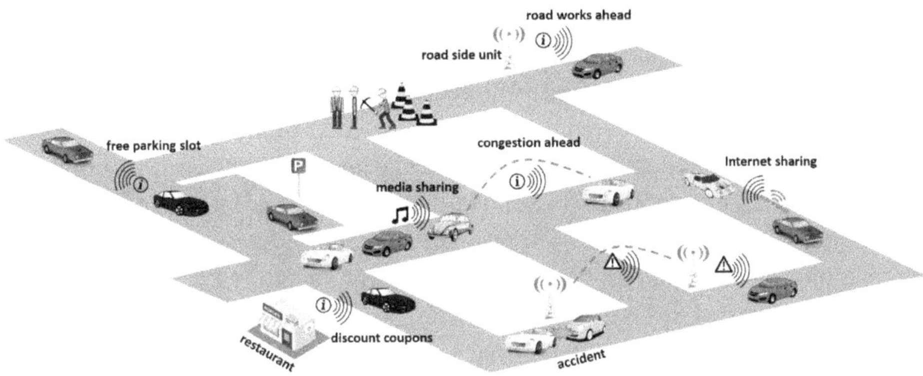

between VANETs and SIoV is that in VANETs, vehicles are not directly connected to the Internet and require an infrastructure (road side unit) for connection, whereas in SIoV all vehicles and infrastructure have Internet connectivity. Figure 2 further illustrates the typical VANET model.

SIoV is a fairly new concept in the field of ITS and mobile socializing and hence attracting researchers, academicians and industry professionals. Several research projects are underway for development and deployment of SIoV applications. This section provides the review of literature to build a solid foundation for discussing the state-of-the-art applications for GCC along with their challenges and limitations for the region.

Figure 2. Typical model of vehicular ad-hoc networks

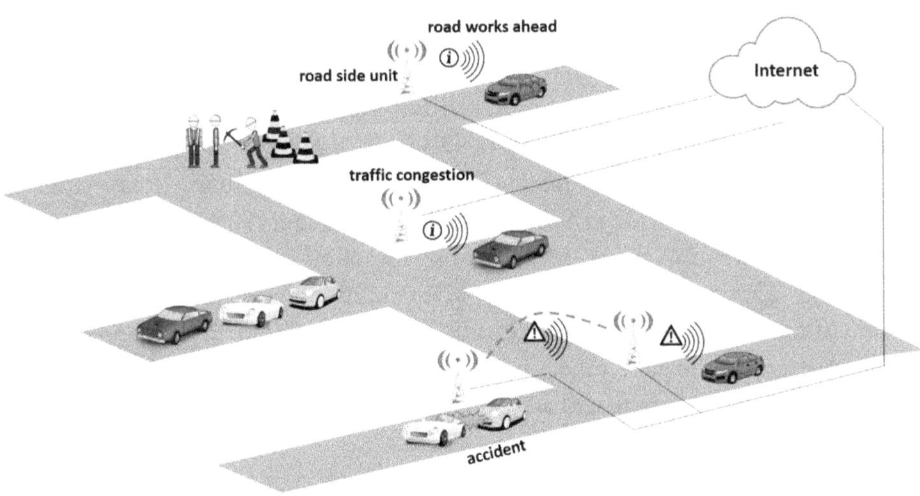

Lequerica, Longaron and Ruiz (2010) discussed a mobile application Drive and Share (DaS) which is installed on passengers' mobile phones in the vehicle. The application assists passengers in sharing road information such as traffic and infotainment based on their location using cellular network connection. Furthermore, the authors proposed an architecture that is expected to minimize the challenges of socializing in vehicular scenarios. The architecture is based on IP Multimedia Subsystems and the capabilities of vehicles to communicate with each other.

Bai, and Krishnamachari (2010) presented a generic framework for enabling information-rich vehicular network applications for social, safety and interactive services. They referred to this framework as IC NoW (Information Centric Networking on Wheels). The framework is proposed based on three key factors, space, time and user interest and it ensures that protocols and applications are employed in a distributed manner based on decisions made locally. The framework is designed in a way that it can be easily integrated with currently available infrastructure of cellular providers. Furthermore, this framework enables modular design, facilitating easy application development and creating a smooth migration path during the deployment evolution path.

Smaldone, Han, Shankar, and Iftode (2008) proposed a framework for building communities on the road to facilitate the commuters. As a proof-of-concept, they presented a design of a VSN system they referred to as RoadSpeak, that allows drivers to communicate with each other by joining different voice chat groups based on their location.

Maglaras et. al (2016) provide a comprehensive review of research and analysis of smart systems including smart vehicles. The authors believe that with growth in the autonomous nature of the cars, several applications are being developed for both cars and passengers that can facilitate these entities by sharing information between them. The article provides a detailed overview of components and technologies involved in SIoV, context awareness, social network analysis methods, security and trust issues and current challenges in drivers' privacy. The authors started by discussing the next generation of vehicles including self-driving cars, electric cars and the safety driving aspect of these future cars. Secondly, they highlighted the importance of enabling context awareness in vehicles while on road. The authors defined context awareness as the ability of the vehicles to adapt to the current contextual environment and provided three subsystems for it; sensing, reasoning and acting. Sensing helps in gathering information through sensors depending upon the environment, e.g., location of the vehicle, reasoning processes the collected information and extracts high level contextual data, e.g., detecting driver's fatigue level and finally, acting, facilitates in taking required action based on the data congregated, e.g., providing warning messages.

Furthermore, Social Network Analysis in SIoVs is provided by discussing the centrality of entities in SIoVs. Centrality of the entities is helpful as it provides a metric of finding entities that are central to a group of vehicles and can act as a relay node to ensure efficient information dissemination. Another important concept besides centrality is clustering or grouping of vehicles based on varying parameters like speed, location, distance and interests of the vehicles. This clustering of vehicles helps in avoiding broadcast storming (message duplication) problems, increasing throughput and improving bit error rate.

Finally, the authors have discussed the security and privacy issues by highlighting different potential attacks such as, denial of service, false message injection, masquerading and impersonation attacks.

SIoV relations and interactions can be very complicated as they yield low level details from the sensors and processing of this information is done at various layers before it can be delivered to the application layer. SIoV life cycle starts at the manufacturing site for the vehicles, where each vehicle is equipped with OBU (On-Board Unit) that forms a POR (Parental Object Relationship) with the manufacturer of the vehicle (Alam et. al, 2015). This relationship helps in providing information such as, repairs, maintenance and oil change etc. Another relationship of the vehicle is with HBU (Home Base Unit) through OBU that assists in connecting the vehicle to the owner's home, e.g., opening and closing of the garage gate etc. OBUs installed in vehicles can connect with RSUs (Road Side Units) to gather information like traffic congestion, alternate routes, free parking slots and road closures etc. Finally, OBUs communicate with OBUs of the vehicles in vicinity that helps them socialize with their peer vehicles without interference from any other unit.

It makes profound sense for vehicles to create a network while travelling through highways as the communication time, destinations, speed and topology are expected to be unchanged. Drivers of the vehicles can maintain a social profile like Facebook where they can share information and content like photos and videos while travelling. Individual drivers in this way can socialize with each other while driving on the highways that not only helps in keeping them up-to-date about the road conditions but also by making new contacts. Socializing on highways faces several challenges, however, two major challenges are vehicle high mobility and foreignness. To address these issues, Luan, Shen and Bai (2015) provides a Social on Road (SOR) model. To tackle the issue of high vehicle mobility, SOR provides a proactive technique of estimating connection time between peer vehicles and stipulates peers that are expected to communicate for longer time based on their destinations. To solve the problem of foreignness, SOR provides a safe solution to guard sensitive user information during social communications.

Literature delivers a solid knowledge and understanding of current state-of-the-art in the field of SIoV throughout the world by presenting the challenges and limitations identified by researchers along with the proposed solutions to these challenges. SIoV is currently in its early ages of development and hence requires extensive exploration that unleashes wide spectrum of opportunities for manufacturers, vendors developers and governmental bodies. Developing countries are keen in deploying SIoV applications to automate safety on road.

Following section will provide a discussion of available applications of SIoV, their benefits to the regulatory bodies along with the issues, challenges and problems in utilizing, developing and deploying of SIoV applications in GCC countries.

Benefits and Advantages

There has been a surge in the number of people living in the urban world. This trend will continue, and it is estimated that the urban population will increase to 6.3 billion by 2050. This surge will eventually increase the number of mega cities. In GCC, the urban population is over 55 Million and it is facing continued growth of local citizens and expatriates. There are many mega cities in the GCC composing the demographics of the constituent countries. Therefore, it's the right time to deploy smart city solutions to manage the ever-growing population in such cities. In a smart city, smart mobility makes top at the list of other smart solutions such as smart environment, smart healthcare, smart energy and smart industry. The main goal of the smart mobility is to ensure intelligent and safe transport by utilizing IoV paradigm.

The IoV paradigm relies on both direct and indirect perception of vehicles to gather real-time information. The direct perception is based on on-board sensor system that includes perceiving the vehicle, the driver and outside environment by using GPS, mileage recorder and other sensors in the vehicle. Whereas, indirect perception depends on the vehicle's communication with other vehicles, mostly within the same context. The data generated by both direct and indirect perception are communicated by either VANET or mobile (3G/4G) networks and is essential to enable existing and novel applications.

The SIoV focuses on enabling the social relationships among vehicles that offers multifaceted benefits to the governments and their citizens. These relationships are established based on the context that include location, owner's profile and mutual interests (Alam, K. M., Saini, M., & El Saddik, A. 2015). The governments can provide unique services to their people by leveraging these social relationships. These services can fulfill requirements of various applications by delivering useful information (Kaiwartya, O., Abdullah, A. H., Cao, Y., Altameem, A., Prasad, M., Lin, C. T., & Liu, X. 2016). The ITS system of a smart city can be enhanced with the SIoV to ensure ubiquitous connectivity of vehicles to collect real-time data and then managing these data after applying intelligent analytics. The SIoV enabled

ITS system, then works as a central hub where all data is collected and processed. This way the SIoV paradigm also enables governments to have more control in a smart city. This section explains the applications of SIoV with the focus on benefits offered to both government and citizens.

Safety Management

Ensuring traffic safety is the key goal of any ITS. The first category of safety applications utilizes sensors' data to improve the driver's performance. This is achieved by analyzing real-time sensed data to actuate automatic functions, such as wheel control, to enhance the quality of driving. Other applications rely on analytics of the real-time information shared between different vehicles. The SIoV guides different vehicles to decide what information needs to be shared with whom depending on the social relationships. This category of applications aid functions such as steering and speed control.

Another safety aspect is to monitor the overall condition of a vehicle and notify the driver and/or mechanic to book an appointment for repair. This diagnostic application depends on analytics of the vehicle sensor data sent to the cloud. The cloud applies analytics and predict when the vehicle will require a repair. If a vehicle is parked at home, then the diagnostic application can use the configurations to automatically book an appointment with the driver's personal mechanic or otherwise can recommend nearest or recommended service stations by using the social relationships with other vehicles. This application reduces the maintenance cost and avoids any technical faults that could lead to accidents.

In critical situations, these applications are beneficial to ensure safety in densely populated urban areas and highways. Furthermore, these applications trigger special calls in case of an emergency. These calls act like a black-box of the vehicle by providing context information such as location, number of passengers and other details regarding the cause of the emergency. This shared data is used to warn other vehicles about the hazard on the road to avoid any further accidents.

Traffic Control and Convenience

The SIoV enables many useful applications for the convenience of vehicles and better traffic management applications are dependent on social relationships based on current location information provided by the GPS. This information is essential for real-time traffic control application that is used in ITS to avoid congestions by effectively managing the traffic (Wan, J., Liu, J., Shao, Z., Vasilakos, A. V., Imran, M., & Zhou, K. 2016). The location data is communicated in real-time by vehicles using heterogeneous networks to the centralized or decentralized cloud. The ITS update other vehicles about the congested areas and suggest alternative routes. The electronic toll system uses the RFID chip information to ensure the smooth flow of traffic.

Convenient parking applications guide drivers to find the nearest empty parking spaces. These applications rely on accurate location information of the parked vehicles who have a social relationship based on being parked in same parking areas. The benefits of utilizing these applications include reduction in time required for parking that eventually leads to low carbon emission. Another important category of applications tailors the routes for users by using their profiles. These applications aim to optimize the resources such as fuel, comfort and money, by using multiple modes of transportation in the recommended routes. These multi-mode routes ensure to reduce the congestion and carbon emission in densely populated urban areas.

Some social relationships-based applications could help a driver to fix any hardware or software-based issues by connecting him to someone from his social circle who can guide him using text, audio or video chat. In case of no suitable match, the application can utilize cloud-based services to provide a related guidance tutorial. These applications aim to bring down the repairing and maintenance cost. Moreover, remote telematics applications allow drivers to remotely control their vehicles by replacing the traditional physical interaction-based operations. These applications use secure methods to ease the monitoring of vehicles and other operations such as remote locking a car.

Productivity

The SIoV based relationships can be exploited by novel applications to reduce the traffic and allow infotainment between vehicles. This can be achieved by creating social groups of cars whom the owners are willing to share their cars with potential car service seekers. Both owners allow their vehicles to join such groups where seekers are sharing their profile and requirements for car sharing. The owner configurations are matched to seekers profile and allocation is done between optimal candidates. The matching criteria could include information such as pickup and destination address, age, gender, and job designation. However, this type of service demands strict verification of seekers and car owners to ensure safety for both driver and passengers. Moreover, some infotainment applications allow vehicles to share their connectivity with other cars in their social circle using Wi-Fi Direct technology.

Commercialization

Insurance industry and other businesses can be benefited by using the data generated by vehicles and social relationships between them. The SIoV allows vehicles to join premier groups of safe driving practitioners based on the analytics of their recorded data. These data consist of months of data records to give insights on the driving behavior and the statistics of traffic rules violations during trips in different areas. Insurance companies can reward these elite group of vehicles by cutting their insurance cost. Other businesses can also buy their subscription to target their potential customers travelling in vehicles using tailored advertisements depending on the shared user information and other spatial or temporal context information. These applications rely on smart cloud-based services.

Issues, Controversies, Problems

The SIoV aims to integrate multiple vehicles and users using heterogeneous network technologies. The benefits of SIoV will enable the provision of services to a plethora of applications to provide a more reliable, efficient and manageable system. This section describes the issues that are instrumental in putting the limit to the adaptation rate of the SIoV. The discussion also provides a perspective of the GCC countries in the context of these challenges.

1. **Standardization:** One of the key issues in developing and implementing SIoV architecture and applications in GCC is the lack of standardization. Currently, no standards are available to tackle issues like interoperability, types of hardware and software, use of frequencies, protocols and communication technology. SIoV is expected to be influenced by different entities like governmental organizations for devising laws and policies, manufacturers of the vehicles for manufacturing smart vehicles that can socialize and third-party vehicle spare parts vendors for installing additional components like navigation systems and sensors etc. Presently, no standard, rule or policy is available for any of the above-mentioned entities. For example, no standard policy from governmental law enforcing agencies is available that can serve as a guideline for vehicles on how to socialize on roads. Similarly, no governmental rule is available regarding the use of communication technology on roads for vehicles. Furthermore, due to lack of policies, there is a gap between different vehicle manufacturers and different third-party vendors to unite at mutual parameters, e.g., use of communication technologies, protocols, hardware and software, etc. Due to this lack of unity, different vendors and manufacturers are delivering vehicles and their components at their own standards and hence creating difficulty in communication between vehicles and ultimately socialization of vehicles.
2. **Adaptability:** Embracing innovative technologies by people has always been an issue throughout the world. GCC countries have the same issues when it comes to accepting new technologies. SIoV is an emerging concept which is

currently lacking in applications; however, it has great potential for developing and implementing applications that can ease daily life operations. A major feature of SIoV is socializing and sharing of information, however, information sharing might not appeal a lot of users in GCC countries because of several factors such as, culture, privacy, trust, security, and anonymity and automation etc. Due to these issues, many people in GCC might not feel very comfortable in adapting to SIoV.

3. **Scalability:** Provision of better quality of experience is vital to the wide acceptance of SIoV in the GCC. The performance of SIoV is limited by the scalability of the infrastructure to handle dynamic rate of traffic in different areas. The traffic rates vary a lot the traffic surge during the peak periods a day and on special events. Moreover, the shape of the SIoT structure could add in to scalability issue by increasing the time for service provisioning in a dynamic vehicle network. The required quality of service for SIoV to provide better quality of experience is limited by the scalability issues that should be solved to attract the masses of GCC.
4. **Infrastructure:** Most of the GCC countries are developing at a rapid pace, however, they are still lacking in infrastructure when it comes to latest technological concepts like SIoV. Intelligent Transportation Systems (ITS) have started appearing in my GCC countries, e.g., Salik in Dubai for toll collection using RFID (Radio Frequency Identification). Although, GCC countries are supporting new concepts like ITS but still, SIoV might require more infrastructure than currently deployed, e.g., RSUs (Road Side Units), Parking Sensors, and OBUs etc. Development and deployment of these infrastructures require high cost which might be one of the major issues in pursuing towards adoption of SIoV by GCC countries at governmental level. Furthermore, as discussed earlier, currently, no standard policies are in place in GCC countries for developing and deploying infrastructure for SIoV, hence infrastructure vendors have no solid path for creating devices for SIoV for implementation in GCC countries.
5. **Lack of Applications:** The novel infotainment and user convenience applications are required to attract more users from GCC to actively engage in SIoV paradigm for its success. There are several applications of SIoV as was aforementioned. However, these applications only exist in theory and lack the novel infotainment third party applications. The big mobile software provider companies, Apple and Google have introduced CarPlay and Android Auto to compete for the in-car applications (Massaro, E., Ahn, C., Ratti, C., Santi, P., Stahlmann, R., Lamprecht, A., ... & Huber, M. 2017). The GCC governments will need to make sure that new business models are created of SIoV paradigm based on novel applications.

6. **Security:** The security of individual vehicles is critical in the context of SIoV. The consequence of comprising the security of even a single vehicle could be disastrous for the other vehicles in the context and even risk the reliable functioning of other components in the ITS infrastructure. The security issue is more challenging in SIoV domain that is enabled by heterogeneous and distributed technologies (Zheng, K., Zheng, Q., Chatzimisios, P., Xiang, W., & Zhou, Y. 2015). Furthermore, the connectivity between the location-based groups makes the security issue more complicated to address because of the several different locations, heterogeneous manufacturers and owners of vehicles. The security required to be foolproof at all links, including communication between vehicles, vehicles to infrastructure, between Infrastructure to cloud and between the cloud and applications. Therefore, the SIoV will be prone to different security threats and to successfully avoid these threats is still an open research challenge. The security risk of getting unreliable information that can result in hazardous situations poses a hurdle in the acceptance of SIoV in GCC.
7. **Privacy:** The privacy of user information is extremely important to be ensured to encourage the users to adopt to new technologies (Derikx, S., de Reuver, M., & Kroesen, M. 2016). In GCC, it's vital to ensure privacy because of the relatively conservative culture in most of the countries. In SIoV, the data is shared between different vehicles and analyzed by cloud to offer different services. The privacy becomes an issue because of the security risks at different stages of the SIoV. Moreover, the social groups can introduce other privacy issues such as identity theft. Therefore, the SIoV should follow the principles of privacy by design to satisfy the privacy requirements to ensure privacy such as anonymity and unlink-ability. In order to ensure anonymity, the data should be anonymized in such a way that the real identities of the users are revealed even the data is leaked from the system. After anonymity, the other aspects are that the attacker will be unable to link different data items to a single user. Moreover, the governments in GCC need come up with policies to enable transparency, so the people can trust the system and rather than being paranoid by itself.

INFORMATION MANAGEMENT IN SIOVS

Information management entails knowledge and various methods for communication, storage, interaction, data gathering, authentication, validation, data distribution and fault tolerance etc. In SIoVs, information can be categorized into safety and non-safety information, for instance. Information based on the safety of drivers, passenger and vehicles is essential in applications contributing towards providing ITS services like congestion information, accident warnings, alternate routes, traffic signals, dangerous curves, weather conditions, speed information, toll gates and infotainment such as sharing of media and hotspots etc. SIoV is vastly dependent on the information from various sources and requires processing of data to avoid information duplication, unreliability in data delivery and delay. Furthermore, information is expected to be secure from various attacks, should be coming from trustworthy sources, data delivery should be based on real time and privacy concerns should be properly addressed.

The security of the transportation network is a dynamic aspect of SIoVs, as the compromise of a vehicle can lead to life-threatening situations, as well as a general degradation of other components that use the SIoV as part of a city infrastructure. Hence, some major security threats for SIoVs could be resolved by the potential solutions that a respective information system ought to provide, for example issues in relation to:

- **Malware:** Such as viruses or worms, is usually introduced through outside unit software and firmware updates for example. Malware can infect vehicles and even allow remote adversaries to take control of individual vehicles. Remote access Trojans, paired with the advanced communication facilities that SIoVs may have, can gain control of the system and thus interrupt vital services.
- **Masquerading (or Camouflage Attack):** Through such attack a vehicle fakes its credentials and pretends to be legitimate in the network. Interlopers may conduct attacks, such as injecting false messages or having multiple identities to be multiple legitimate vehicles concurrently. They can disorder traffic and affect other drivers through the steering systems.
- **Distributed Denial of Service (DDOS):** Such attacks aim to prevent genuine users from accessing data or services in computer networks. In vehicular networks, this attack would flood and may gridlock the traffic with large volumes of extraneous messages that would negatively impact the communication between the network's nodes, on-board units and roadside units. Because the vehicle under attack is part of the wider infrastructure of the SIoV, there would be high-powered computing infrastructure near the targeted component.

In GCC countries, the population is increasing at a rapid pace. People living in these countries are embracing the modern technologies like other developing and developed countries. Introduction of SIoV systems in GCC is expected to catch attention of people because of its convenicnce, ease of use and diversity of applications. Growth in the adoption of SIoV systems in GCC is likely to surge the importance of information management for handling the data produced at an enormous pace. Information Management in SIoVs is hence essential for proper handling of information in SIoVs, especially in GCC.

SOLUTIONS AND RECOMMENDATIONS

There is a great scope and benefits of SIoV in the GCC region. However, there are undoubtedly various issues that need to be addressed for the successful deployment and adoption of SIoV in GCC. This section covers the details of such solutions and recommendations for successful deployment and adaptation of SIoV in GCC.

The GCC governments will have to work closely with vendors and manufactures to encourage the research and innovation in SIoV. These governments need to establish cross industrial cooperation to ripe the benefits of SIoV. Most of the GCC nationals travel across the GCC on a regular basis, therefore, the need for a common standard set is required in GCC. Consequently, the GCC governments will need to form a consortium to agree on the employment of different technologies and data sharing standards. Moreover, these countries will have to come up with mutual policies for SIoV.

The focus of GCC countries should be to take initiatives in promoting the SIoV applications to increase awareness of its adaptation in different sectors such as automobiles and insurance. These efforts should comply with the ultimate public demand of having convenient, safe and cost saving means of travel. Furthermore, the GCC governments should explore and fund the SIoV applications to be used in disaster management. Similarly, these governments need to agree on policies and law to address data privacy issues.

The whole process of deployment of SIoV system should be conducted in multiple stages. The early deployment stages can offer simple features to act like a test-bed environment. The systems need to be checked against different threats in the environments before they are made available to general public to improve the security. These early deployments can be based on basic vehicle communication to enable applications based on only critical data sharing between vehicles. The lessons learned from these deployments will provide a feedback loop for next stages to reduce the risk. This gradual deployment process will not only improve based on the users' feedback, it will also give time for adaptation.

FUTURE RESEARCH DIRECTIONS

To appreciate SIoVs, we need to study major topical issues such as: data redundancy, scalability, and synchronization. Thorough specification portrayal of SIoV is important to comprehend the impact of payload on VANETs infrastructure. A specialist domain ontology tailored to support the SIoV can be an important part of future work to inject intelligence and terminology-driven communication in the virtual entities. Strategies to leverage the smart connections in cyber-physical SIoV is also a viable future work. Additionally, practical deployment of a system and using it to collect real life IoV related multi-modal sensory data in city or urban areas can be another interesting direction, for the GCC.

There are different measures that can be taken to deal with the data redundancy, scalability and synchronization issues in a highly dynamic SIoV. The decentralized cloud based architecture (Fog computing) (Gerla, M., Lee, E. K., Pau, G., & Lee, U. 2014) should be considered by the GCC. This decentralized architecture will be helpful to improve the quality of experience for the SIoV users. Moreover, Software Defined Networking (SDN) and Network Function Virtualization (NFV) can provide reasonable solution for effective resource utilization during the traffic spikes in different regions (Salahuddin, M. A., Al-Fuqaha, A., & Guizani, M. (2015). Also, the SIoV social structure should be shaped to make the discovery and provisioning of services more efficient.

CONCLUSION

This chapter presents the evolution of VANET to SIoV and highlights the range of new services that can be enabled by this domain. Furthermore, it discusses different research efforts and applications that are being coined by the research community. It also focuses on the benefits and advantages of SIoV in GCC by discussing the impact of this new paradigm to novel applications to increase productivity and efficiency, while introducing new business models. It is also emphasized that the SIoV is a new domain and it has a range of technical as well as social issues that are pertinent to GCC dynamics. The role of information management will be key to manage the privacy while taking advantage of the SIoV potential. This work recommends various solutions and identify the future research directions to deal with the inherent issues of SIoV in GCC. The cooperative efforts of GCC governments to mutually design and implement policies for SIoV and then iteratively deploy its infrastructure by reflecting on the feedback are the key requirements for the successful adoption of this contemporary technology in the GCC.

REFERENCES

Alam, K. M., Saini, M., & El Saddik, A. (2015). Toward social internet of vehicles: Concept, architecture, and applications. *IEEE Access: Practical Innovations, Open Solutions*, *3*, 343–357. doi:10.1109/ACCESS.2015.2416657

Atzori, L., Iera, A., Morabito, G., & Nitti, M. (2012). The social internet of things (siot)–when social networks meet the internet of things: Concept, architecture and network characterization. *Computer Networks*, *56*(16), 3594–3608. doi:10.1016/j.comnet.2012.07.010

Bai, F., & Krishnamachari, B. (2010). Exploiting the wisdom of the crowd: Localized, distributed information-centric VANETs. *IEEE Communications Magazine*, *48*(5), 138–146. doi:10.1109/MCOM.2010.5458375

Derikx, S., de Reuver, M., & Kroesen, M. (2016). Can privacy concerns for insurance of connected cars be compensated? *Electronic Markets*, *26*(1), 73–81. doi:10.100712525-015-0211-0

Gerla, M., Lee, E. K., Pau, G., & Lee, U. (2014, March). Internet of vehicles: From intelligent grid to autonomous cars and vehicular clouds. In *Internet of Things (WF-IoT), 2014 IEEE World Forum on* (pp. 241-246). IEEE.

Kaiwartya, O., Abdullah, A. H., Cao, Y., Altameem, A., Prasad, M., Lin, C. T., & Liu, X. (2016). Internet of vehicles: Motivation, layered architecture, network model, challenges, and future aspects. *IEEE Access: Practical Innovations, Open Solutions*, *4*, 5356–5373. doi:10.1109/ACCESS.2016.2603219

Lequerica, I., Longaron, M. G., & Ruiz, P. M. (2010). Drive and share: Efficient provisioning of social networks in vehicular scenarios. *IEEE Communications Magazine*, *48*(11), 90–97. doi:10.1109/MCOM.2010.5621973

Luan, T. H., Lu, R., Shen, X., & Bai, F. (2015). Social on the road: Enabling secure and efficient social networking on highways. *IEEE Wireless Communications*, *22*(1), 44–51. doi:10.1109/MWC.2015.7054718

Maglaras, L. A., Al-Bayatti, A. H., He, Y., Wagner, I., & Janicke, H. (2016). Social internet of vehicles for smart cities. *Journal of Sensor and Actuator Networks*, *5*(1), 3. doi:10.3390/jsan5010003

Massaro, E., Ahn, C., Ratti, C., Santi, P., Stahlmann, R., Lamprecht, A., ... Huber, M. (2017). The Car as an Ambient Sensing Platform. *Proceedings of the IEEE*, *105*(1), 3–7. doi:10.1109/JPROC.2016.2634938

Nitti, M., Girau, R., Floris, A., & Atzori, L. (2014, May). On adding the social dimension to the internet of vehicles: Friendship and middleware. In *Communications and Networking (BlackSeaCom), 2014 IEEE International Black Sea Conference on* (pp. 134-138). IEEE.

Smaldone, S., Han, L., Shankar, P., & Iftode, L. (2008, April). Roadspeak: enabling voice chat on roadways using vehicular social networks. In *Proceedings of the 1st Workshop on Social Network Systems* (pp. 43-48). ACM. 10.1145/1435497.1435505

Wan, J., Liu, J., Shao, Z., Vasilakos, A. V., Imran, M., & Zhou, K. (2016). Mobile crowd sensing for traffic prediction in internet of vehicles. *Sensors (Basel)*, *16*(1), 88. doi:10.339016010088 PMID:26761013

Zheng, K., Zheng, Q., Chatzimisios, P., Xiang, W., & Zhou, Y. (2015). Heterogeneous vehicular networking: A survey on architecture, challenges, and solutions. *IEEE Communications Surveys and Tutorials*, *17*(4), 2377–2396. doi:10.1109/COMST.2015.2440103

Chapter 8
Information Problems in Competitive Markets and Their Impact on Labor Markets

Hasan Bilgehan Yavuz
Adana Science and Technology University, Turkey

ABSTRACT

Economic agents should be fully informed in order to maximize welfare by removing market disruptions. The full knowledge which is one of the assumptions of the traditional economic approach has been rejected in the recent studies and it is stated that the information is lacking and asymmetric and therefore market disruptions come to the forefront. Information created under certain conditions that economic agents use in their decisions and actions does not remove the problems of adverse selection and moral hazard. Information asymmetry among individuals will be minimized through institutions to be established in the obtaining, usage, and transfer of knowledge. Institutions such as signaling and discrimination, which will be created in the labor market in particular, will be able to provide economic efficiency by selecting qualified staff and paying based on efficiency.

INTRODUCTION

The traditional economic approach is working on the assumption that full competition markets and economic agents give rational decisions with full knowledge in the markets, and they are in balance. But the issue of equilibrium is a matter that has qualities beyond this assumption. Because the market has a complex structure, and there are many variables that affect the operation of markets.

DOI: 10.4018/978-1-5225-5393-9.ch008

One of the key elements that affects the operation of markets and the decisions and actions of economic agents is knowledge. The information mentioned here is the information about the quantity, quality and price of the product on the market, where the economic agent is acting or making the choice. The information on the quantity and the price of the product is the one that can be obtained easily and inexpensively, especially in the light of the developments in today's information technologies. But we can not say the same about the quality of goods or services. Uncertainties about quality have influenced individual actions and decisions in the past, and they are still affected today and these effects are expected to continue in the future.

Individuals have the opportunity to acquire some of the information they need in a variety of ways. However, we can not say that each individual has the same knowledge of one subject. While an information is missing for some individuals, it is too much scattered and asymmetric for others. This structure of knowledge also makes the output of knowledge different for each individual.

The fact that information is asymmetric causes many problems in the operation of markets. Due to asymmetric information, economic agents have to make adverse selections, invest in inefficient areas and consume poor quality goods and services at high prices.

Some institutional mechanisms are proposed to overcome this lacking and asymmetric information problem in the markets. These institutional mechanisms will be established by the economic authority as well as by the interaction of the units operating in the economic organization in the sector.

Unlike commodity markets, there is a lack of productivity in the labor market due to the lack of information. Since it will affect other commodity markets area, it needs to be focused on with precision. It is obvious that it is necessary to use quality input to produce quality goods and services. However, achieving full knowledge in terms of the labor force, which is the most important input item, has some difficulties. Employers who are willing to work to overcome these challenges and reach full and accurate information about the workforce focus on signaling what they are doing with their talents. The information obtained as a result of these activities not only affects the company's recruitment decision but also provides the employer with data to be used throughout the business life.

In this study, focusing on information problems in the markets, understanding the concepts of knowledge and uncertainty are explained, and the problems arising from asymmetric knowledge are addressed; a literature search is made on how these problems are solved in terms of labor market.

1. UNCERTAINITY

In economic science, there is a tendency towards the equilibrium situation in terms of the functioning of all markets. It is presumed that in a perfectly functioning market, especially at the markets where perfect competition conditions prevail, people have every kind of knowledge they need, as a result they are balancing their decisions or actions. A person's action can provide personal balance as a part of a specific plan. We can also assume that different actions of different individuals are balanced in a competitive system. This balance can be true for isolated individuals. However, it is impossible for the individuals to formulate their plans with different expectations and, more importantly, to discuss the balance in terms of all the individuals in the planning phase. For such a balance, the plans of all the individuals should be made in harmony with each other. However, an individual's plan will represent a data set for the other individual. Once this balance is achieved, it will continue until an external influence or new information emerges. (Hayek, 1937).

The only factor that affects the structure of markets is not equilibrium. The markets have a sophisticated complex structure. Because there are many variables affecting the functioning of markets (Hayek, 1974). These variables affect the distribution of the resources in the economy and ultimately affect the welfare level directly.

The flow of information between economic agents should be fully ensured so that the perfect functioning of the markets and troubles do not occur. Failing to provide information flow and sharing of all information lead to differences in knowledge among economic agents, thus causing disruptions in the functioning of markets and causing them to shift away from equilibrium (Çetinkaya, 2012).

Neoclassical economics approach, which is called as established economics, assumes that individuals have all the information they need to reach balance by maximizing their utility and therefore exhibit rational behavior. In other words, when individuals make a decision, they have information about all the available information on the market and the possible consequences of their decisions. However, for every economic agent there is some uncertainties. Because of these uncertainties, individuals can not make rational decisions. That is, individuals have limited rationality due to the uncertainties.

In the case of limited rationality, the individuals decide and choose under some certain rules. Because the real world is full of uncertainties. For this reason, it is accepted that most of the contracts made on the market are not completed (Şenalp, 2016).

The issue of uncertainty first came to light in 1921 with Knight's "Risk, uncertainty and profit" work and Keynes's "Investigation on Probability". It has been reported that Risk is measurable and includes a risk premium. However, uncertainty has been portrayed as an immeasurable quality (Akalın, Dilek, 2007). For example, entrepreneurs do not know what consumers want because of incomplete information, and take risk and make investment decisions. This risky investment they make with estimates is then returned as an entrepreneurial profit (Alp, 2010). In the uncertainty environment, the only source of information is the subjective beliefs and intuitions. In such an environment, individuals will not reach a balance where individual maximization is possible by making rational decisions (Buğra, 1999).

Uncertainty is the absence of information about past, present and future events and their effects. If the intensity of uncertainty is high, your confidence will also be hurt. The weakening of the sense of trust will affect the decisions and actions of economic agents, and they will make reliable decisions based on the amount of information they have (Telatar, 2004).

2. INFORMATION

In the literature review, it was seen that similar definitions were made about information. It is understood that in these definitions, utilitarian philosophy is analogous to the perceptions of human knowledge perceived by the senses.

According to this; information is defined as the whole of perceptions-values-concepts and principles that are obtained through learning, researching and observing in the meaning of the dictionary, in general terms through thinking and reasoning in the study of Alp, Karakaş, (2008) (Alp, Karakaş, 2008). In the study of Eğilmez (2016), he defined the knowledge as all of the knowledge and skills that a person acquires and learns after his or her training or experience (Eğilmez, 2016).

Kahveci (2015) distinguishes among information, data and information concepts while making a similar description of the information. Kahveci (2015) defines the knowledge as the intellectual product resulting from reasoning, thinking, judging, reading, researching, observing and experimenting; It is the building block of the starting point and the information to reach knowledge. Information is; (Kahveci, 2015) as raw data that are objectively categorized and classified as a systematic way of expressing objective requirements.

In Akalın, Dilek, (2007) study, she examined the information concept in terms of its accessibility, and explained open and implicit information in four different ways (Akalın, Dilek, 2007).

1. There is information that the consumer does not know, and he knows that he does not know.
2. The consumer has incorrect information.
3. There is information that the consumer does not depend on exact data, resulting in interpretation.
4. Information that the consumer knows and believes is correct. There is no need to do research or spend a fortune on such information.

Unlike other goods and services that have already been produced, information contains a public good within it. Some information may exclude others, but benefits may never be excluded. For this reason, every kind of information fragment is important in terms of actions and decisions of economic agents. Once information has been created and shared, it can never be undone or changed (Stiglitz, 2000). This information will be used on the market and will be increased and spread through appropriate communication tools (Hayek, 1945).

Information which is created under certain conditions is the basis of decisions and actions in terms of agents in the economy. The correct information thus obtained leads to correct decisions and actions to be taken in the right initiatives. However, here we can not be certain about the conditions under which the information is produced, the things that have been altered and the way they are used (Hayek, 1937).

Hayek has differentiated knowledge and information concepts in market socialization studies. While the information term expresses an initial level of knowledge, it also states that knowledge is broader and includes explicitly unspoken data (Alp, Karakas, 2008).

It is an inevitable situation for many researchers to face, even though it is problematic to create observational information in social sciences that conduct research on a complex structure involving human behaviors. In order to be able to analyse what is happening in the real world, it will be necessary to rely on some specific indefinite general information. Because the ability to find quantitative data is too small to be considered in terms of social sciences. The basis of this problem lies under trying to explain the basis of human behavior to the researchers. Although these problems are not known, it is expected that the researchers give definite information in social sciences.

One of the difficulties of informing about the uncertainties such as complex structures like market and human behavior and reaching the final judgments is the relationship and interactions of these variables with each other. For this reason, solving social problems in social sciences is not easy (Hayek, 1974). The market mechanism is specifically trying to solve the average information rather than the complete and correct information because this character, especially the rational economic order, is scattered and shared among the individuals. This average information will be needed again when planning every new action or decision. While average information has been influenced by beliefs, technology has also become an important factor in recent times. In this sense, we can see the price mechanism as a mechanism for transferring this average information (Hayek, 1945).

The concept of the information economy has been developed to form theories and policy propositions for the future, based on this, information passed from the past in economics. While the concept of information economy is being developed, it is stated that information is not perfect, it is scattered and missing at the markets, and that even with this structure, it is necessary to bear a certain financial burden in order to have information. Indeed, he argued that information acquisition at Hayek is a fundamental problem for every economy. The right to use information is not provided free of charge (Stiglitz, 2000).

Contrary to what has been explained above, traditional economic theory assumes that individuals have full information with the reason that markets are transparent and does not predict a cost to obtain information. Individuals were assumed to be able to easily access and use the information without cost, and to make rational decisions, thus sweeping the markets and providing efficient resource allocation.

In the real world, however, economic agents are researching and enduring some costs to be an information owner. This disrupts the efficient distribution of resources and makes information a commercial commodity. It is argued that the costs of production and transportation of information such as every commodity (Akalın, Dilek, 2007).

The cost of obtaining information in economic analysis is stated as the transaction cost. It has been argued that in the concept of modern information economy, transaction costs may be important outputs that will affect the standard results of welfare theory. According to the concept of information economy, authorities such as the state may need to intervene in order to reduce the costs, and to ensure pareto optimum.

Another issue that has led to the concept of transaction costs is incomplete contracts. Information deficiencies that exist in the marketplace will mean that contracts will not be completed either. If the information is perfect, the original contracts will be completed, and the completed and applicable contracts will be available. But in the real world there is no complete set of markets. This incomplete feature of the contracts is due to market failure (Stiglitz, 2000).

In the Dohlman (1979) study, there are research and information costs, contract and decision costs, implementation and execution costs. When examined, it will be seen that all of these costs are related to the concept of limited rationality. Because these costs are said to increase as they move away from full rationality.

Regulations can be ignored in an environment where transactions are free of charge. It can even change. In the real world, the competition, arbitrage and effective information feedback system provided by these conditions can provide the gains in the size of established economics that are close to zero transaction cost conditions (Şenalp, 2016).

3. INCOMPLETE INFORMATION

The information subject that has been studied from economics is accepted as a science branch in the 18. Century by Adam Smith, Alfred Marshall, Max Weber, John Stuart Mill, Jean Charles Leonardo Sismondi and Friedrich August Von Hayek. In the traditionally accepted teaching of economics, rational man and perfectly functioning markets have been defined, assuming that the information is complete. However, due to the fact that the information is not homogeneous and is unevenly distributed among the agents in the economy, the problem of efficiency arises in the actions and decisions of the agents.

As a result of this process called market failure, the complete information understanding of traditional economics has been criticized and new studies have focused on market failure under the assumption of uncertainty and incomplete information (Fidan, 2013).

The concept of incomplete information, together with the concept of uncertainty, was first introduced by Knight's "Risk, uncertainty and profit" and Keynes' "Probability on the study". Alfred Marshall emphasized that the lack of information in the labor market is especially high, as Knight pointed out that due to incomplete information, the actions and decisions of the agents differed from the expectations, which in turn disrupted the distribution of resources and income, leading to market failures (İşcan, 2010).

According to Kirzner, the economic rent due to lack of information is the essence of the market process. Lack of information is inevitable in terms of economic agents. Profit opportunities are dependent on agents seeing missing information and making rational estimates in actions and decisions. Thus, non-market information will be produced and spread on the market. In short, lack of information is natural.

This approach to information of the Austrian School is the most important issue that distinguishes the Austrian School from the full competition approach of Neo Classical Economics (Alp, 2010).

Similarly, in Hayek, the fact that all agents in the economy do not have to have the current information suggests that the price mechanism is sufficient to spread the information that the agents need. Thus, Hayek partially solves the problem arising from incomplete information in the competitive equilibrium model. A successful distribution and division will be achieved, even though the optimal allocation of resources and fair distribution of income can be achieved with neither the information that is not centrally determined nor the price system that is created by market dynamics (Stiglitz, 2000).

4. OBTAINING INFORMATION AND USING INFORMATION

It is also important that economic analysis focuses on understanding what is going on in the real world, and how information is collected and transmitted. Thus, it will be easier to explain what the market is as an empirical element of the market, and therefore what is happening in the real world (Hayek, 1937).

People guide their behavior to achieve specific goals. People's goals can be economic, social and psychological justification for action. We should also be knowledgeable about human behavior in order to understand the outcomes of people's actions, especially the output of their activities as economic agents. Information of human behaviors can be acquired through experience and from the outside world, as well as logical conclusions and communication activities. Apart from these qualities of acquired information, accuracy and objectivity are also important. The authenticity and objectivity of an acquired information is determined only when a communication is hold with other people and within a consensus (Buğra, 1999).

The most reliable information on the accuracy and objectivity of economic agents is the information gained based on past experience. The economic agent may either have information directly by conducting a research or may have information indirectly, by chance, meaning without the need of a research.

The most important source of information is the one obtained from specialists, vendors, acquaintances, goods or services. Besides, we may get some information about some goods and services when we watch television, listen to radio, read newspapers and do not make a special effort. In some cases, vendors have important advertising and marketing activities related to information disclosure (Akalın and Dilek 2007). While some of these information transfer processes are costly for receivers, the others are not. Some of the costs are paid by the vendors.

In the century we are in, most of the changes that took place in the economy come from the previous century at the end of the information transfer process. Information can not be regarded as any goods or services. It has its own characteristics and flaws. While there are infinite number of stores or producers where you can get service for a good, we can not mention the same property for information. This gives some advantages or differences to economic agents.

It is an important issue that needs to be addressed on how to create and spread the kind of information that will bc useful in the actions and decisions of economic agents. There are dimensions beyond the scarcity of being informed, and not knowing. Because information is likely to be the object.

In the process of formation and transfer of information, institutions such as the market or the price have important functions. Within the market process, not only prices but also economic agents and their activities are reported. Again, thanks to the price system, information such as the quality of economic agents and the patterns of behavior of households are transmitted (Stiglitz, 2000).

If the process of transferring information was seamless, there would be no need for conditional contracts. One of the important functions of contingent contracts arising from missing information is to convey information. For example, when sellers have all the information about the product, but the buyers do not have the information, it becomes compulsory to make contracts that include corporate regulations and warranty terms. Giving a guarantee does not provide information about the product, because the product may fail despite the warranty. However, this requirement is a source of confidence and forecast for the buyer. In contemporaneous contracts, the transfer of information shall be the subject of direct and continuous contact between the buyer and the seller. However, despite the fact that this contact is in the labor market, information can not be transferred completely, but it can be saved due to the presence of the resignation mechanism (Spence, 1976 b).

Some mechanisms that carry out the information transfer process systematically and not depending on a theory are included in the market processes. For example, structures such as the internet or social media will complete some of the missing information on the market, inform economic agents and affect the operation of markets. Again, these constructs will make it easier for buyers and sellers to get together, thereby increasing information sharing on the product and contributing to market equilibrium (Spence, 2002).

In economic activity, it is necessary to make research and to bear some costs in order to have information about the sellers and their products in terms of buyers. Because information to be obtained is a decisive factor in consumer decisions, as well as in investment decisions, recruitment and many other important actions (Stigler, 1961).

The first important ideas on the use of information were put forward by Hayek in the context of the ideas of the Austrian School in market socialization debates.

In socialist planning, the central planner has all the information. However, this information is not shared with other economic agents. Agents take part in the system under the supervision of their planner, using scattered information. This scattered information, which is circulating in the markets, is not organized, so it does not carry the quality of scientific information. Every individual decides and acts on the basis of the partial information he has in himself. It is important that the issue is to provide professional or personal development by using the information independently and in specific and local conditions.

This characteristic of information does not only apply to our economic behavior. It applies to all social occasions. Our civilization was created with the sum of the pieces of information transmitted throughout generations. This civilization is in action and makes_decisions about economic elements as well as social and social events, and uses this accumulated information.

In order to obtain the expected benefits from the information, many economic agents with partial information need to communicate with each other within the market system to share the information they possess. In this way, many problems can be solved and effective decisions can be made (Hayek, 1945).

When we look at social sciences, it is confusing with whom the information should be shared. Again the meaning is different from the point of view of the people, even if everyone is given the same information. For this reason, it may be the basis for the implementation of different actions and decisions. So the information is subjective. This character does not prevent contracting between economic agents. The contracts will also express a balance in social concept.

It is important to know what is happening in the real world, to know what kinds of experiences people experience by knowing what kind of information they have, to know what processes people go through, to understand what conditions are produced and shared, and to measure the effectiveness of actions and decisions of economic agents (Hayek, 1937).

In study of Akalın and Dilek (2007), it is stated that the consumers obtain the information, and the decision-making process takes place in three stages.

The first stage is defined as the psychophysical phase. At this stage, information is defined as a personal perception that can be presented to other agents using economic agents' information from their surroundings and the information available in their memory. The second stage; At the stage of consolidation, these perceptions are transformed into completed admissibility impressions, including the personal selection characteristics of the acquiring economic agent. The third stage is; The preference phase, at which point the agents have a preference for their particular decisions and actions (Akalın, Dilek, 2007).

5. ASYMMETRIC INFORMATION

The problem of asymmetric information has been technically first introduced to economics literature by G.A. Akerlof in 1970, "The matter for lemons: Quality, uncertainty and the market mecanism" and has been shaped by the thoughts of Stiglitz and Spence as well as Akerlof.

In Akerlof's study (1970) there was the examination of used car markets. It was found that sellers had full information about the car and the pricing was based on this complete information, but buyers did not have enough information about the quality of the vehicles, so he said that, the good cars and the bad cars, so-called lemon, will be bought for the same price and after a while, bad cars will be fired by the good cars from the market.

In the lemon problem, buyers will have more information about the car after a while, so that they will develop a new action with this new information they will obtain and that the market equilibrium price will be affected by this new action (Akerlof, 1970).

In his study of Spence (1978), Stiglitz (2000) stated that while oligopoly speaks about the existence of asymmetric information with collusion in the markets, important information asymmetries exist on the market and this information affects the actions and decisions of economic agents.

Asymmetric information has started to be seen as a market failure, especially when the work done after the 1980s was found to be quite extensive.

Although some theoreticians like Hayek emphasize that information is scattered, there is no significant difference between information asymmetry and distribution. In both cases, it is stated that the whole of the information is gathered in the market processes and the price system is going to give rise to this confusion or asymmetry (Cowen, Crampton, 2016). However, market failure theorists have distinguished between the concepts of information dissemination and asymmetry, and have pointed out that it is not possible to spread asymmetric information if all sides wants to benefit equally in the market process. Because some of the economic agents will have different information than others and this different information may not be shared (Alp, Karakaş, 2008).

If Hayek's information is to be disseminated and to be eliminated in the market process, Hayek should use information process and entrepreneurship together. The market is fragmented, scattered, gathered at certain points, and it has constantly changing and unexplainable structure, and it is processed by economic agents in the market processes to coordinate decisions, purposes and actions. This coordination, like game theory, will provide a certain gain to every economic agent that uses the market by a way of informing (Alp, 2010).

He has studied how asymmetric information influences the operation of markets in Spence. According to him, asymmetric information comes from the observable characteristics of the firm or the behavior of competing firms. If not all the attitudes of the company can be observed, there will be shortcomings in secret contracts.

These deficiencies will also be observed for the next contract and delayed in the reaction (Spence, 1978).

Spence (1976 b) pointed out two issues concerning the influence of asymmetric information on the market. First; The firm that has a quality product will determine its price as an average considering the prices of poor quality products. This average price may cause the product to be withdrawn from the market as it will prevent the product quality from being recognized. The second issue is; Sellers act to explain the product price and average prices to the buyer, which will also distort the structure of the action market, which is caused by asymmetric information (Spence, 1976 b). A similar issue is addressed in the work of Gibbons and Katz (2001), and it is stated that this process, which is valid for the labor market, will affect the output of the labor market (Gibbons and Katz, 2001).

It is very important for the development of the hypothesis theory that the agents in the economy have full information on the assumption of perfect competition market. However, it is not possible to have full information in all the markets and at all times. Thus, the conditions of the perfect competition market, which is supposed to be close to the ideal, will deteriorate. Because the other one knows what the market will not know. In terms of the more informed party, there will be a superiority and a power problem between those who have information and those who do not (Cetinkaya, 2012).

Economic theories, the problem of asymmetric information will not only mean bad goods or services for certain sectors. Asymmetric information is an element that totally disrupts the operation of markets. The fact that one of the parties in the market has a different information will cause changes in the price, quantity and quality of the goods or services subject to the exchange. Again, the agents will take decisions to develop some actions to remove these differences altogether. These new actions and decisions will also cause a new asymmetry problem on their own (Kahveci, 2015).

5.1. Asymmetric Information Problems

There are studies about the problems arising from asymmetric information in the literature surveyed, leading to many problems such as adverse selection, moral hazard, representation, principle-agent problem, signaling, distinction, reputation. However, this study will focus on the most common adverse selection, moral hazard problems, and the institutional mechanisms that will explain the notion of signaling and distinction, especially in the labor market, which will help solve the problem of asymmetric information.

5.1.1. Adverse Selection

Economic agents take decisions and take action by using all the possibilities and information they have to achieve their individual goals. Agents have no economic purpose alone. They act in the natural flow of life with other instincts. The basic element for any kind of behavior is the expected utility. However, people can not always make the right choices and make the right decisions because of the information they have or their motives (Buğra, 1999).

The problem of selection has been examined by dividing into two branches in the literature. The first arm is the selection made by informed economic agents for wealth, the second arm is the selection made by the uninformed agents. Economic agents can either do the choices they make on their own with the available information, or they can make a lot of research and find out the learning costs to acquire additional information.

There are many researchers' predictions about selection. When we look at the issue that focuses on the issue, Adam Smith's high interest rates are valid, and economic agents operating in financial markets are talking about the problem of an adverse selection where more risky customers give credit. Alfred Marshall also mentioned to the workers in the effective wage theorem that a high salary payment that is not proportional to their productivity would cause a certain increase in productivity.

Mirrles (1971), in his work on the social refinement contributions of the income tax system, argues that individual talents are known and equal to each other, but that the individual abilities are different because of the lack of such information, (Stiglitz, 2000).

Akerlof's controversial selection problem, which is related to used car markets, comes from the fact that economic agents have different information about each other before shopping or signing contracts (Alp, 2010). The fact that agents who are not likely to repay the loan in the financial system can get the loan first by accepting high interest in the financial institution is regarded as an adverse selection in terms of financial institutions. In fact, banks have an advantage in collecting information because they have long-term relationships with customers. However, the fact that economic agents can not recognize the crises, the failure to deal with the crisis, and the asymmetric information about the crisis necessitates banks to make adverse selection (Vardareri and Dursun, 2010).

Spence cited the asymmetric information problems in the labor market and said that the problem of adverse selection in the labor market would cause people who are not qualified in the market to find jobs and dominate the markets. This can be likened to the lemon problem mentioned in Akerlof's second-hand car market. Low-skilled workers identified as lemons may cause skilled workers to be unable to find jobs, be excluded from the market, or be unable to receive wages commensurate with their productivity (Fidan, 2013).

5.1.2. Moral Hazard

Another problem arising from information asymmetry, the moral hazard, arises as to the fulfillment of responsibilities that are expected from economic agents and can not be written on contracts to fulfill contracts. Examples in the finance, insurance and labor sectors are available in the literature.

When we look at financial markets, we see that a customer with a low repayment rate in the financial system is profitable if he or she invests in high-risk projects, but if he loses capital, he does not pay the loan. In this case, the borrower takes the non-moral activities according to the criteria of the borrower, thus hurting the interests of the borrower (Çetinkaya, 2012, Vardareri and Dursun, 2010).

In the evaluations made in terms of insurance markets; The person who took out the insurance does not show the necessary attention to the goods or services he / she has insured, as a moral hazard. After the signing of the contract on the insurance market, there is a secret action for the person insured (Sarıkaya, 2002). If individuals are insured against risk, they will not avoid taking risks. If the information is fully shared between the parties during the contracting, the actions of the agents will be added to the insurance contract with a clear requirement. Thus, agents' liabilities for moral behavior will be removed.

As an example, we can use land lease contracts to make this point clearer. A person who hires land with a right of 50% will not be in an effort to overdo it to get more products. However, if the same land is leased with 100% rights, everything that can be done to get the maximum product will be done. Thus, the anticipated return on the contrary comes as a factor to increase performance or reduce moral hazard.

Another market is the labor market where the moral risk problem can be encountered. In recruitment processes in the labor market, employers want to have full information of the talents and productivity of the people they will recruit. However, employers are unaware of the difficult conditions under which their employees work or other factors affecting their productivity. This leads to a moral hazard situation in the labor market. It is clear that the best contracts are wage contracts where information is perfect, but the wage contracts are also a bit of a moral hazard (Stiglitz, 2000).

Fidan (2013) stated that the behavior of economic agents as a result of all kinds of actions and decisions is a bit moral hazard (Fidan, 2013).

5.2. Institutions to Provide Asymmetrıc Information Problem

One of the most important inferences of the information economy teaching is; The problem of asymmetric information will never be solved completely (İşcan, 2010). Even if we look at the basis of human behaviors, the institutional structures that will be created by the laws of the authorities in the economy will be able to develop mechanisms that can reduce the effects even if they do not remove the information asymmetry problem.

While making decisions and choices in our daily life, the structure of society's institutions and dominant thought habits and behavioral patterns affect, limit and shape the decisions and actions of economic agents. The current institutional structure is the provision of information for economic agents who complete the information missing in the markets and act irrationally. With this information, individual interaction is pioneered, uncertainty is reduced and everyday life can become a rational structure (Şenalp, 2016).

The new concept of information economy also guides the formation of institutional structures that will enable economic agents to act rationally, as well as the role and importance of the structures in the process of operation of the markets. The most important institution defined in the market processes is the price mechanism. However, the price mechanism alone will not solve the problem of information scarcity. Together with other institutional structures, it will also affect the process of institutional formation, the process of change, and the selection and behavioral processes of economic agents. These intertwined processes due to their secret features will become more understandable with more complex institutional structures (Stiglitz, 2000).

Removing the asymmetric information problem altogether is the best solution the information theorists have revealed. Theoreticians such as Akerlof, Stiglitz, Spence have proposed many institutional structures to remove this problem. For example; Price system, guiding, quality, reputation and so on. However, it would be costly to remove such asymmetric information from the center by creating such institutional structures (İşcan, 2010). Instead, the problem of asymmetric information can be minimized (Stigler, 1961), through some economic or social organizations or institutions, which, as put forward by Stigler (1961), can reveal uncertainties in quality and establish trust between buyers and sellers.

In the work of Fedele and Tedeschi (2016), they hypothesized that the social norms to be created by society, under the assumption of competitive homogeneous firms and complete rational consumers, would provide a certain social order with the interactions between economic agents. The important element here is the reputation among economic agents. Because the relationship between buyers and sellers is a complex issue of hidden actions, confidential information, and confusing structures in which confidential action interacts with confidential information (Fedele and Tedeschi, 2016).

In his work Stigler (1961) also said that prestige is part of the quality, and that it affects the prices of goods and services. This reputation of a product or company that has earned a reputation for quality will eventually spread through the institutional structures established by the society and the interaction of economic agents (Stigler, 1961).

5.2.1. As an Institutional Structure: Quality

Akerlof's (1970) study which examined quality and uncertainty, is pointed to the existence of numerous institutional structures that would affect the properties of uncertainty. He showed branding and licensing applications as example.

In the lemon model of Akerlof, he stated that the risks related to the car subject to shopping originate from the information hidden by the sellers. The buyer's actions and decisions should focus on accurately determining the quality of the goods. The quality of the goods will be pushed out of the market. However, in cases where the reputation for quality goods is weak, bad goods may lead to good goods being fired from the market.

There are institutions for the discovery of qualifications for many markets. For example, interventions in this area of legal institutional structures can ensure that the welfare of economic agents is maximized. Or special institutional structures that will increase welfare outside legal institutions can be created within the market process. The existence of these institutions will cause sellers to drive higher quality goods to market, or to determine the price difference between quality goods and poor quality goods (Akerlof, 1970).

Reputation is an important issue when it is difficult to measure quality. Producing and selling goods at a low price for a monopolistic firm does not affect its relationship with its customers. The decision of the firm to produce goods at low quality does not leave the firm with any sanctions. Because the monopolist firm's production of goods at high quality is a non-rewarding act for the firm. For goods of high quality, a quality premium applies only to competitive markets.

On competitive markets, companies should offer low-priced, high-quality commodities to convince consumers. However, this mechanism does not apply to the markets where there are fully rational consumers. Because they will have information about future quality, looking at current prices. To put it briefly, the expectations about the quality of a good will depend on the quality of that good in the past and the price in the current period. Thanks to this information transfer, while good companies producing quality goods during the period obtain profit by providing reputation, firms producing bad goods are fired from the market together with loss of reputation.

The information about the quality and prices of the products produced by the companies in different periods can be spread by the other institutional structures in the society by way of advertisement, marketing, internet and TV. If social ties are low or low here, this spread on quality will be less. The result will be to increase quality competitiveness and in the long run, higher quality products will be available in the market at more affordable prices, and the asymmetric information on this issue will be lifted (Fedele, Tedeschi, 2016).

Cowen and Crampton (2016) emphasize how pricing determines quality. Quality is defined as a function of price, and prices of high-quality goods will be high (Cowen and Crampton, 2016).

6. ASYMMETRIC KNOWLEDGE IN TERMS OF LABOR MARKET

In competitive markets, companies should produce quality goods and sell them at low prices. In order to do this, they need to use good quality and cheap input. They want to have the right information about the price and quality of the entrants so that they can supply quality goods at low prices. The most important input that gives the firm competitive advantage is the labor force. Firms usually prefer to pay more for their employees who know their efficiency, training, competence and other qualifications than their outsiders because of the information they have. If the firm is unsure about the efficiency of the workforce, they will make a decision on the wage basis by looking at some of the signs.

Firms will do what they will research in order to obtain information about the quality and prices of inputs, the amount of capital they have, the information of top management's information on the subject, the expected benefits of the research and the structure of the market. Firms will make use of other economic agents, mass media, their own experiences, contracts and laws and some signs when doing this research. The most important research resources for the labor market are signs. That is, for someone to be hired, the firm will look at education, pleasure and preferences, habits, culture and traditions to determine the productivity and quality of the candidate.

In order to produce and compete with quality goods, the firm will want to have sufficient information not only of the labor market but also of the entire production process. Failure to obtain this information will reduce the courage of the enterprise. It is the duty of the institutional structure to eliminate this uncertainty that will adversely affect the economic growth process (Akalın, Dilek, 2007).

Gibbons and Katz (2001) stated that the asymmetric information problem can not be proved in terms of labor markets as a problem that is so significant as to affect the structure of the markets. The most important reason for this is the existence of the mechanism of resignation in the labor market.

The individual, the firm, and the market have symmetrical information about their abilities before a person starts to work. This information is not exact, but symmetrical. However, information becomes asymmetric after starting to work among these actors. Firms will not be able to adjust the wages of their employees according to their productivity. Because wages are usually sticky for labor market. Firms that are not able to set up a fee will want to remove their employees from the performance appraisal, which is very bad.

The important question at this point is how the firm will decide which worker to take. If a firm is working on who gets out of the business, it takes into account the signals that the workers have already given in the markets. According to this, employees who are inadequate in their talents are taken out of the company. This is because lowering wages will require lower wages for workers with higher productivity (Gibbons, Katz, 2001).

In Stiglitz (2000), similarly, employers have stated that they will want to know their employees' productivity, strengths and weaknesses. This request emphasizes a selection problem. The problem of selection is not just about selecting employees in labor markets. In addition, it is important for employers to know what difficulties employees are working under, and what risks employees take while they are avoiding from work accidents (Stiglitz, 2000).

Spence (1973) stated that employers in the labor market did not have enough information about the talents of the recruiters in his study of renting under uncertainty. In order for a job to be carried out in a quality way, it is necessary to obtain vocational training specifically for that job. This training involves time and cost. In addition, employers make their contracts annually and there is no question of re-contracting during the contract period. As a result of this investment decision, the recruitment process seems to be buying Spence lottery. Lottery is a monetary fee and this fee should be equal to the marginal contribution of the worker to the company.

In the recruitment process, which is similar to the lottery purchase process, the employer's first wage offer does not depend on the marginal product. Because the employer does not know about the marginal product of the employee who is not yet out. However, the age, gender, educational status, cultural status, traditions, etc. will be offered a fee by looking at their personal characteristics. The actual productivity of the recruited person will only be learned by the employer once he / she starts working. This learning means new information for the employer and the employer is expected to renew the remuneration proposal. The important thing is to propose an effective wage considering all employees (Spence, 1973).

In the efficient wage theory, it is said that the higher wage level will push the individuals to work harder. In the labor market, the employer does not know what difficulties the employees are working with. This is an asymmetric information problem. However, if employees prefer to work harder than to save, they know they will be charged more for their next job. Individuals think they will be fired at worst, but this can be a real opportunity for a new job rather than a loss. If the employer wants to improve his worker's performance, he has to pay a good premium. But at the same time this will cause some unemployment.

Behind the effective rate argument lies the opposite choice. In other words, proposals for high wages made in the first place with people who are out of work, fired or whose skills are unclear will attract these people and cause people with high productivity to be excluded from the market. This is also Akerlof's lemon problem in terms of labor market (Cowen, Crampton, 2016).

Now let's look at the issues of signaling and distinguishing among employers in the labor market as a method they use to deal with the asymmetric information problem they have when they make recruitment and remuneration decisions.

6.1. Signalling

The signaling is that the people who want to work in the labor market send signals to the employer that they can observe and interpret the quality and efficiency. The employer gives the decision on recruitment according to those signals of the person who wants to enter the job. The external appearance, certificate, work experience, age, gender, character traits, general culture, traditions and customs, and the environment in which they live are all signals (Kahveci, 2015). It is also perceived as a signal of time spending on the subject that someone is interested in (Spence, 2002).

Once the employers receive these signals, they will resolve their existing ambiguities and decide to recruit them. Regardless of the employer's preference, these signals will be distributed through personal communication. Thus, these signals will emerge as a social contract where the equilibrium state is valid. This social contract will also determine the quality and price of the products. Only firms that are new to the market will not benefit from these signals (Fedele and Tedeschi, 2016). Thus, these signals will cause all economic agents in the market to make more effective decisions (Spence, 2002).

The signaling is modeled by Spence's work. Spence focused on the reasons for companies to make recruitment decisions under asymmetric information or uncertainty. He considered the personal characteristics listed above as a data set belonging to those who wanted to enter the business.

This dataset created for the recruiters will also determine the structure of the market. Because, during the recruitment process, employers will use the information they receive with this signal set in subsequent recruitment processes and share it with other agents in the industry. In addition, these signals will apply not only to the decision to recruit but also to the remuneration of the worker.

Not all the signals given by recruiters are of the same quality. While some of them can change over time, some will stay constant. It may also be necessary to bear additional costs to replace the altered signals (Spence, 1973). However, it should not be forgotten; The signals provided by additional financial expenses, such as education, will be easily distinguishable from others and can be taken into account in the fee proposals.

The training signal on the job market can be given by the person in charge of the job, and firms can also train their employees and cause new signals about productivity capacities to emerge. This training activity will be an important signal for the employee's next job application in terms of productivity (Spence, 1976a).

All of the above-mentioned personal characteristics signals include a personal choice. Job seekers or signalers offer opportunities for their qualifications. In order for these signals to be effective, employers should not make a profit or profit in terms of low-skilled workers. If the snow is high, the marks on the quality point given to the signals may be ignored.

For companies producing high quality products, the cost of the signals they receive from their employees is lower. Because the people who come to apply for work offer certain signals and get ready signals. There is no need for the employer to receive a signal such as education in order to receive a signal. In addition, there is no respect for the signals given in oral explanations in terms of such companies. Because the word is described as something cheap. However, when the cost of signaling is high, it will be accepted in verbal signals.

Signaling has two qualitatively different characteristics. First; Conditional contracts. These include the terms of the contract the seller has spoken. The seller advocates these verbal conditions in order to see the ability for later products. Second; It is not clear how the signal works. The seller's activity requires a cost. So there is an external cost. For example, being educated and getting insurance.

In externally costly signals, there is a correlation between signaling activity and quality. In conditional contracts this correlation is provided by the behavior of the buyer. But there is an independent and costly activity of the seller from the buyer. For example, if the training function is taken as a signal, it has a net cost and is independent of the employer's behavior.

Although it is a real social cost, external signals are quite effective in transmitting information. However, such signals do not apply to every type of market (Spence, 1976b).

Due to the lack of information on the market, companies in competitive markets tend to imitate observing the behavior of their competitors. (Spence, 2002). A company that has a financial burden in signaling will be able to give delayed responses to signals to make it difficult to understand its behavior. In such cases, there may be confidential contracts between employers and recruiters. Failure to correctly observe behavior in the markets where secret contracts are concerned will lead economic agents to different outcomes. What is important here is to distinguish the company from other structural features of the observable features (Spence, 1978).

7. RESULT

As a result of this study, the dynamics of the deterioration of resource distribution are evaluated in terms of labor market due to the elimination of uncertainties and the problem of adverse selection caused by asymmetric information between economic agents;

The greater the uncertainty in the labor market, which is seen as the most important input, and the deeper the information asymmetry between economic agents, the more market failure will be the case. In terms of labor market, we can evaluate the market failure as employers' hiring of qualified people and the failure of them to work with the appropriate price.

In this process, employers are required to analyze the signals they receive from job applicants and to make a recruitment decision, and to offer them a step-by-step payment of qualifications. In the case of high wages for low-quality workers or vice versa, the efficiency and resource allocation of the markets will deteriorate. The problem here is not only the problem of correcting the quality of your workforce. Declines in the quality of other goods and services produced by an unqualified labor force will come into play.

In particular, institutional mechanisms are foreseen to create information and disseminate information in the labor market. These institutional mechanisms can be created by the economic authority, as well as the communication activities between economic agents themselves can be culturally created.

REFERENCES

Gibbons & Katz. (2001). Layoffs and lemons. *Journal of Labour Economics, 9*(4).

Akalin & Dilek. (2007). Belirsizlik altında tüketici kararları. *Zonguldak Karaelmas Üniversitesi Sosyal Bilimler Dergisi, 3*(6), 33-48.

Akerlof. (1970). The market for "lemons": Quality, uncertainity and the market mecanizm. *The Quarterly Journal Of Economics, 84*(3), 488-500.

Alp. (2010). Avusturya okulu bilgi teorileri ve E-Ticaret çerçevesinde Akerlof'un limon piyasa modelinin değerlendirilmesi. *Eskişehir Osmangazi Üniversitesi İİBF Dergisi, 5*(1), 175-190

Alp, & Karakaş. (2008). Asimetrik Bilgi teorisi karşısında Hayek'in ekonomik yaklaşımları: Karşılaştırmalı bir analiz. Liberal Düşünce Dergisi, 51-52.

Çetinkaya. (2012). Asimetrik bilginin piyasaya etkileri ve finansal krizlerdeki rolü. *Sakarya İktisat Dergisi*.

Cowen & Crampton. (n.d.). *Market failure or success: The new dabate*. Retrieved from http://www.Econ.canterbury.ac.nz/personel_pages/eric_crampton/bookintro.pdf

EĞİLMEZ. (2016). *Reputation and competition with social convention*. Retrieved from http://www.unibs.it/sites/default/files/ricerca/allegati/1105.pdf

Fidan. (2013). İktisadi açıdan bilgi kavramı ve bilgi kavramına yaklaşımlar üzerine bir inceleme. Süleyman Demirel Üniversitesi Vizyoner Dergisi, 4(9), 94-104.

Işcan. (2010). *İktisat teorisinde enformasyon teorisine yönelik yaklaşımlar*. Adana: Çukurova Üniversitesi, Sosyal Bilimler Enstitüsü, Doktora Tezi.

Spence. (1973). Job Market Signaling. *The Quarterly Journal of Economics, 87*(3), 355–374. doi:10.2307/1882010

Telatar. (2004). Politik İktisat Politikası. Ankara: İmaj Yayınları.

Sarikaya. (2002). Asimetrik bilgi çerçevesinde müzayedeler. Cumhuriyet Üniversitesi İktisadi ve İdari Bilimler Fakültesi Dergisi, 3(2).

Şenalp. (n.d.). Dünden bugüne Kurumsal İktisat. Retrieved from https://www.academia.edu/3340855/_2007_D ünden_Bugüne_Kurumsal_iktisat_Eyüp_özveren_der._Kurumsal_i ktisat_imge_Yayınevi_s._45-93

Spence, M. (2002). Signaling in Retrospect and the Informational Structure of Markets. *The American Economic Review, 92*(3), 434–459. doi:10.1257/00028280260136200

Spence. (1976a). Competition in salaries, credentials and signaling prerequisites for jobs. *Quarterly Journal of Economics, 90*, 51-74.

Spence. (1976b). Informational aspects of market structure: An introduction. *Quarterly Journal of Economics, 90*, 591-597.

Spence. (1978). Tacit co-ordination and imperfect information. *The Canadian Journal of Economics. Revue Canadienne d'Economique, 11*(3), 490–505. doi:10.2307/134318

Stiglitz. (2000). The contribution of the economics of information to twentieth century economics. The Quarterly Journal of Economics, 1441–1478.

Stigler. (1961, June). The economics of information. *Journal of Political Economy*, *69*(3), 213–225. doi:10.1086/258464

Kahveci. (2015). Tüketicilerin asimetrik enformasyon ve kurumsal itibar algısı: Seyahat acentası müşterileri üzerine bir araştırma. Balıkesir: Balıkesir Üniversitesi Sosyal Bilimler Enstitüsü, Yüksek Lisans Tezi.

Vardareri & Dursun. (2010). Asimetrik bilgi çerçevesinde 2008 küresel krizinin incelenmesi. Bilgi Ekonomisi ve Yönetim Dergisi, 5(1).

Von Hayek. (1945, September). The use of knowledge in society. *The American Economic Review*, *35*(4), 519–530.

Von Hayek. (n.d.a). Economics and knowledge. Retrieved from http://www.jstor.org/stable/2548786

Von Hayek. (n.d.b). The pretence of knowledge. Retrieved from http://about.jstor.org/terms

Chapter 9
Mobile Cyber Information Leakage:
Users' Attitudes and Information Protection Strategies

Hongbo Lv
Zhejiang Wanli University, China

Zhiying Zhou
Zhejiang Wanli University, China

ABSTRACT

With the wide use of smartphones, mobile cyber has become an indispensable part of our lives. While smartphones are used almost every aspect of our lives, awareness of personal information protection is underdeveloped, and information leak has become one particular problem on mobile cyber. At the same time, personal information resources have become more valuable than ever. This chapter investigates users' attitudes toward cyber information leakage and methods to protect personal information. The software SPSS 19 was used to analysis the relationship among cyber environment, applicability and practicability of protection methods, economic cost, and overall evaluation (satisfaction). A suggestion that may promote personal information awareness and promote cyber security from technical, legal, and social aspects is also provided.

DOI: 10.4018/978-1-5225-5393-9.ch009

1. INTRODUCTION

With the rapid development of mobile communication technology, information interactions between individuals are now more frequent than ever. Smart phones are the preferred device for web browsing, emailing, using social media and making purchases. Personal information is also transferring from PC (personal computer) to smart phones. The global smartphone users are 2.1 billion in 2016, with smartphone penetration rates still increasing. China, the most populous country in the world, leads the smartphone industry. The number of smartphone users in China is around 563 million in 2016. It is projected that approximately half of the Chinese population will use a smartphone by 2020 (Statista, 2016). Information security has become a major concern and the security of mobile cyber information is also facing with unprecedented challenges. Many lawless merchants and enterprises found methods to exploit personal information into their offense, especially through personal information value research by the social research institutions. There is a rapid expansion of information leakage in mobile network.

Most mobile apps require personal information to demonstrate authenticity and authority. However, improper authority will lead to a direct access to information by smartphone apps, which may cause personal information to leak occasionally or deliberately. In 2016, China's Android mobile phone privacy security report pointed out that,58% of Android apps leak users' private information. They provided users' data to developers, advertisers and third parties of unidentified identities. There are a lot of leakage problems in apps. The user information is hard to protect. Wang et al. (2015) found that smartphone users in China were vulnerable to malware than anywhere else through multiple data comparisons. In addition to spam messages and harassing phones, malicious software such as decoy fraud, system destruction, malicious deductions, privacy theft and others have been constantly evolving.

This chapter will discuss the growing concern about mobile information security. A strategy to use questionnaire is discussed for investigating and analysis the information leakage state, as well as for information cognition and protection. Possible reasons for the mobile cyber information leakage are explored, and suggestions for preventing information leakage are provided.

2. CATEGORIES OF MOBILE INFORMATION LEAKAGE

Smartphone has become an indispensable part of modern life. With the growing maturity of mobile cyber technology, the use of mobile network is ever increasing. A series of O2O business apps, such as Baidu Takeout[1], Didi Kuaidi[2], and Uber allow phone users to do what they want to do without leaving their homes. Feng (2016) mentioned that social apps, such as QQ and WeChat[3] are must-have SNS(Social Networking Services) apps in almost every smartphone in China. Watching videos on phones is also getting easier. The Statistical Report on Internet Development in China (2017) showed that the utilization rates of mobile network were 67.1% and 70.8% for watching video and listening to music online, respectively.

The mobile network makes life better and smoother. It provides convenience support for model life and travels. However, at the same time risks of information leakage increased. The risks can mainly dividend into two categories. One category is that data stolen by direct intrusion, which can implement by viruses or irregular apps. Tan (2014) envisioned that the smartphones have become a new virus disaster area. Ma (2016) mentioned that because of diversity and openness of the smartphones, malicious attackers, as part of software developers, can also get the users' app authority. They use users' network, access to users' communication record and SMS, charge users, and provide "service" for them. All these greatly increased the security risks of mobile cyber users. Another category is the leakage caused by the users' information sharing by themselves. Such leaks usually occur during online account registration, online shopping, commercial app downloading and uses SNS apps for self sharing. The popularization of real name network makes users use their real information during websites and game id registering. Commercial apps need use real information to fulfill its accurate service. It makes accurate personal information transmitted into the network and promotes the risk of information leakage. Personal information is in an open state as users are using social apps while filling their information. This is one of the easiest ways for information to be stolen. Vorobyov et al. (2015) demonstrated that the more frequently use of information, the higher risk of information leakage. Although the current network is well developed, it is not completely safe.

3. INVESTIGATION AND ANALYSIS OF MOBILE CYBER INFORMATION LEAKAGE

3.1 Questionnaire Design

In order to further analyze the status of information leakage, we designed a questionnaire from four aspects.

1. Personal information. This includes user's age, gender, occupation, and annual income, etc. This information will allow researchers assess factors causing information leakage among different users.

2. Usage of mobile network. This part will collect basic information about usage on mobile network. We then analyze users' awareness level of non-invasive leakage in the mobile network and clarify users' main use of mobile network. We will further acquire users' mobile operation steps and possible causes of information leakage.
3. Status of information leakage. We will check the extent of information leakage among mobile users, explore users' awareness of information leaked, search users feedback method, find out connections between information leakage with economic benefits, and collect information of how much users pay attention to their personal data.
4. Satisfaction about mobile cyber information security. This information will help us to conduct further research and generate constructive suggestions to protect personal information and enhance cyber security.

The questionnaires were distributed through both online and offline at the same time. Online questionnaire was issued to the public living forums, bulletin board systems (BBS), and opening public platforms. Offline questionnaire was distributed in business centers, living areas, and public spaces. After 5 days, we received 432 questionnaires, among them 418 were valid, resulting in a valid rate of 96.8%. The questionnaire sample size is sufficient for the analysis of this chapter.

3.2 Mobile Cyber Information Leakage Status Analysis Based on Questionnaire

3.2.1 Main Usage of Mobile Network

The distribution of mobile cyber usage is shown in Figure 1. It shows that SNS apps rank the highest among smartphones usage, with a proportion of 97.1%. Smartphones use various kinds of SNS apps, which collect our private data. SNS apps mostly have hidden information security risk. Their credential management would allow an attacker to view personal information stored on the server (2016). Private data leakage, as a potential hazard, is caused by the current design flaws in the app industry, which is increasing in size but with various level of personal information protection security. Other usages of mobile network, such as online entertainment and online shopping, are also have large proportion, as shown in Figure 1. Entertainment information, taking online game as an example, needs real name register information supervised by official. Information leakage will occur if the personal information is spread out or sold to profiteers. Online shopping apps

Figure 1. Distribution of mobile cyber usage

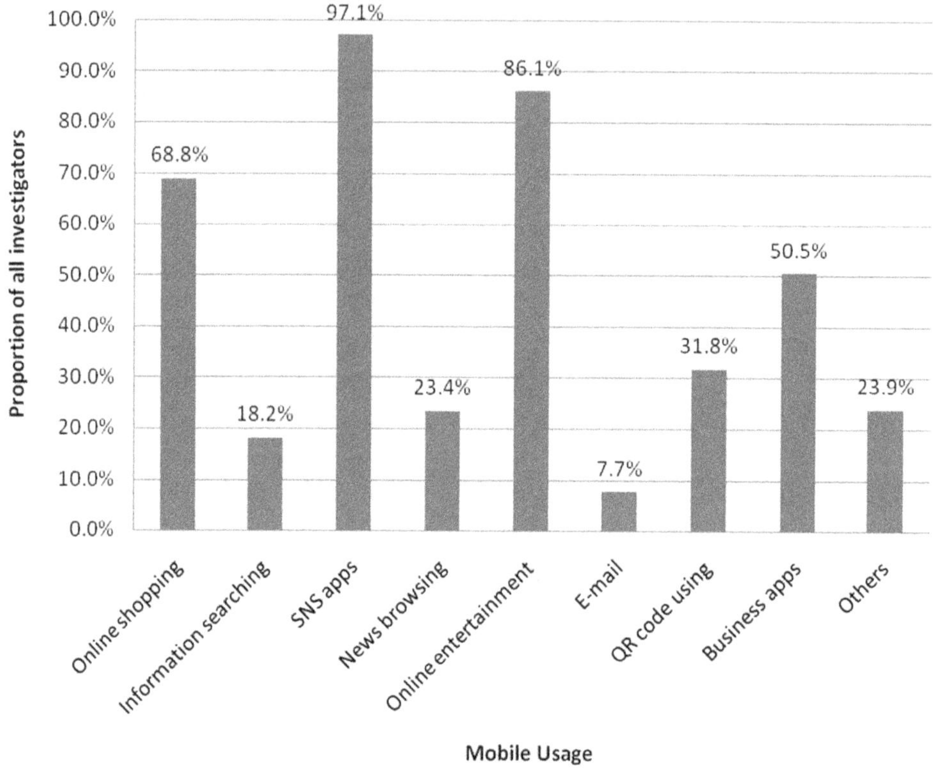

information can also be obtained by sellers, and then be used as target of propaganda or promotion. Other remainder usage proportions are relatively low. They are not main channels of information leakage.

3.2.2 Attitude Toward Information Leakage

The problem of information leakage is quite common among questionnaire responders. According to questionnaire data, 87.1% of the responders believe that their information have been leaked, and only 12.9% users believe that their data have never been leaked. As for the attitude about information leakage, as shown in Table 1, 35 of the responder are seriously concerned about personal information, 52 are not much concerned, while the rest are at a normal concern level.

Table 1 also shows that only 2.11% male responders are seriously concerned about information leakage, and 33.8% feel indifferent to it. In contrast, female

Table 1. Attitude toward personal information leakage

	Seriously Concerned		Normal		Indifferent	
	Number	Percent	Number	Percent	Number	Percent
Male	3	2.11%	91	64.08%	48	33.80%
Female	32	11.47%	243	87.10%	4	1.43%
Total	35	8.38%	334	79.90%	52	12.44%

responders are more seriously about personal information. A fraction of 11.47% female responders are seriously concerned about information leakage, and only 1.43% responders feel indifferently. It shows that females pay more attention to information leakage than males.

3.2.3 Type and Frequency of Information Leakage

Based on the questionnaire, there is no large proportion of direct benefits lost about information leakage, only 14 among 418 (3.3%) questionnaire responders suffered economic lost. The percentages of responders suffered from phone harassment and spam message harassment are relatively high (Table 2). In particular, all responders received spam messages at various frequencies, among whom 46.7% often received spam harassment. Unwanted advertising message caused by the leakage of phone numbers is one of the cheapest advertising methods. Currently, there is no relevant law that regulates this type of activity. Because it is not deemed illegal and its risks are lower than those of internet account embezzlement or fraudulent phone, profiteers use this channel to advertise. This is the reason for such high occurrence of spam message harassment.

Table 2. Statistics of type and frequency of information leakage

	Often		occasionally		Never	
	Number	Percent	Number	Percent	Number	Percent
Stolen of account password	2	0.5%	121	29.0%	295	70.6%
Phone harassment	74	17.7%	269	64.4%	75	17.9%
Spam message harassment	195	46.7%	223	53.4%	0	0.0%
Telephone fraud	31	7.4%	119	28.5%	268	64.1%
Others	97	23.2%	141	33.7%	180	43.1%

3.2.4 Methods to Prevent Information Leakage

In the questionnaire, we designed four choices, i.e., *software protection, download app from authority, not fill in real information*, and *no protections* to investigate users' preference to protect personal information. According to the collected data, most users (91.2%) prefer protective software, followed by *download app from authority* (38.5%). There are 99 users among the 418 responders do not take any protective measures.

As shown in Table 2, 100% questionnaire responders suffered from spam message harassment at least occasionally. We investigated the methods taken by people to prevent such harassment and found that 69.1% of them chose to block information from the harassment source. Table 2 also shows that 29.0% users suffered from account number being stolen. Among these victims, 84.5% chose to modify their password, indicating that not all of them chose to modify password even they found that the password was stolen. Only less than 1% victims chose to use law to defend their own interest. This is likely caused by the perception of high legal cost and long time to settle the case leading the victim to think not worthwhile pursuing the legal route.

The questionnaire also collected information about the responder's occupation, whether or not related to network. Among all of those who provided valid responses, the occupations of 77 responders were irrelevant to network while those of the remaining 341 responders were relevant. Table 3 summarizes main causes for information leakage. It shows that information *Left over* and *Be sold* were the main reasons, independent of whether their occupation is computer relevant or not. The proportion was all over 70%. A total of 55.3% of responders think their information was leaked because of *friend list sharing*. Only 29.2% of the leakage was caused by *virus*, and that by *others reason* was 15.6%.

Table 3. Statistics of main causes for information leakage

Way of Information Leakage	Irrelevant(77)		Relevant(341)		Total(418)	
	Number	Percent	Number	Percent	Number	Percent
Left over	67	87.0%	244	71.5%	311	74.4%
Virus	40	51.9%	82	24.0%	122	29.2%
Friend list sharing	24	31.2%	207	60.7%	231	55.3%
Be sold	61	79.2%	237	69.5%	298	71.3%
others	11	14.3%	56	16.4%	67	15.6%

3.2.5 Satisfaction About the Information Security

Figure 2 shows questionnaire responders' perception for causes of personal information leak. Most responders believed that the main reason for information leakage is that sellers think that personnel information profitable. Therefore, sellers will collect all kinds of buyers' information. The under-developed legal system regarding personal information protection is the second cause. An improved legal system will significantly reduce cases of personal information leak. Another 31.6% responders believe that the information leakage is caused by the ineffective network supervision. Only 14.6% responders think that the society does not pay enough attention to the information leakage problem.

3.2.6 Regression Analysis

To further mine the 418 valid questionnaire responses, we used SPSS19.0 to analyze the reliability and validity of designed variables and the correlation among five variables: *cyber environment, easy-to-use of methods, practicability of protection methods, economic cost and overall evaluation(satisfaction).*

Figure 2. Causes for personal information leakage

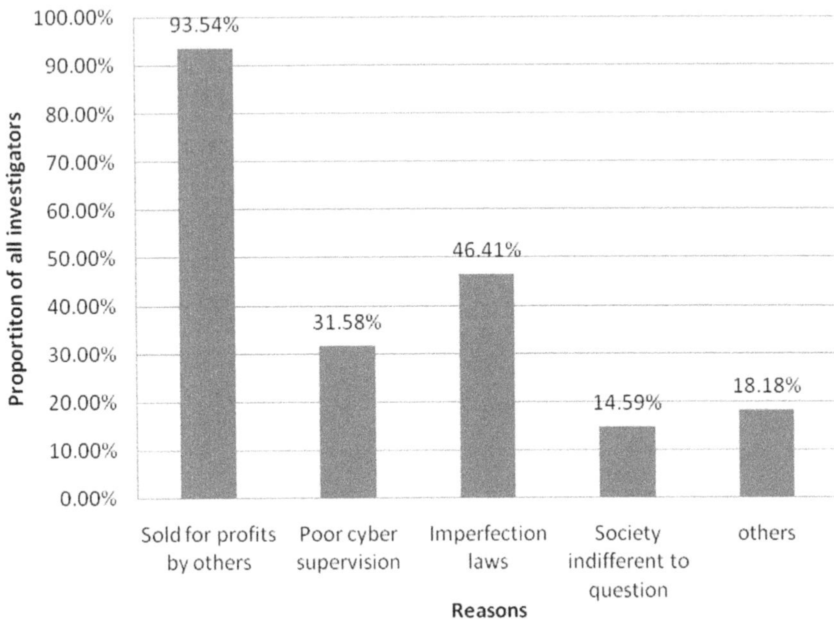

1. Reliability analysis.

Reliability analysis is to study the effectiveness of the designed variables and to determine the reliability of the questionnaire. Cronbach's alpha is usually used as an indicator for reliability analysis. Its value is between 0 and 1. 0, with 0 indicating not reliable while 1 indicating absolutely reliable. Analysis results are shown in *Table 4*.

As seen from *Table 4*, all Cronbach's alpha values are larger than 0.79, indicating that they have good reliability for further analysis.

2. Validity analysis.

Validity refers to the validity or accuracy of the measurement. It is closely connected with reliability analysis. Factor analysis is usually used to assess validity. Only high values of KMO (Kaiser-Meyer-Olkin) can be used for factor analysis. Its value is between 0 and 1. 0, with 0 indicating not validate while 1 indicating absolutely suit for further validity analysis. The KMO values calculated by SPSS19 for this study are listed in *Table 5*:

The KMO values are all larger than 0.7, indicating that the chosen variables have a good internal consistency and that they are suitable for factor analysis. Further results of factor analysis are shown in *Table 6*.

Table 4. Cronbach's alpha of each variables

Variable	Cronbach's Alpha
Cyber environment	0.837
Easy-to-use of methods	0.792
Practicability of protection methods	0.931
Economic cost	0.916
Overall evaluation(Satisfaction)	0.802

Table 5. KMO values for factor analysis

Variable	KMO Value
Cyber environment	0.733
Easy-to-use of methods	0.862
Practicability of protection methods	0.801
Economic cost	0.794
Overall evaluation(Satisfaction)	0.753

Table 6. Factor analysis of variables

Factor	Questions	Factor Loading	Variance (%)
Cyber environment	1	0.865	71.654
	2	0.853	
	3	0.846	
Easy-to-use of methods	4	0.952	86.384
	5	0.924	
	6	0.912	
Practicability of protection methods	7	0.864	70.796
	8	0.848	
	9	0.836	
Economic cost	10	0.869	80.021
	11	0.923	
	12	0.884	
Overall evaluation(Satisfaction)	13	0.926	83.956
	14	0.895	
	15	0.926	

All values of *Cyber environment*'s *factor loading* are higher than 0.8 with a total variance of 71.654%, indicating that the variable *Cyber Environment* has a good construction validity. Similarly, the others four variables all have the good construction validity, indicating that a good validity analysis has been achieved and correlations between variables can be calculated.

3. Correlation analysis.

The correlation analysis checks the internal relationship among variables. The correlation coefficients (r) are summarized in *Table 7. Cyber Environment, Easy-to-use of methods* and *Practicability of protection methods* all have positive impact on *Overall evaluation(Satisfaction)* of modern cyber information security. *Cyber Environment* has the highest degree of influence with a r value of 0.881; *Practicability of protection methods* ranks the second with a r value of 0.761; and the third is the *Easy-to-use of methods* with a r value of 0.632. Yet *Economics Cost* has a negative influence on *Overall evaluation(Satisfaction)*with a r value of -0.532.

Table 7. Correlation coefficient between variables

	Cyber Environment	Easy-to-use of Methods	Practicability of Protection Methods	Economic Cost	Overall Evaluation (Satisfaction)
Cyber Environment	1	0.543	0.532	-0.765	0.811
Easy-to-use of methods	0.543	1	0.891	-0.673	0.632
Practicability of protection methods	0.532	0.891	1	-0.611	0.761
Economic cost	-0.765	-0.673	-0.611	1	-0.532
Overall evaluation(Satisfaction)	0.811	0.632	0.761	-0.532	1

4. Regression analysis.

The above correlation analysis shows that *Cyber Environment* is best correlated with overall evaluation. Here we take *Cyber Environment* as the predictor variable and *Overall evaluation(Satisfaction)* as the dependent viable for the regression analysis (further analyze shows that the other three factors are all have significant probability big than 0.1, not fit for further regression analysis). The results are shown in *Tables 8* and *9*. According to the analysis results in *Table 9*, the statistical value of the model is 61.541 and the significant probability is 0.000 (<0.05), indicating that the overall regression effect of the model is statistically significant.

Table 8. Model Summary[b] and Anova[b]

Model	R	R Square	Adjusted R Square	Std. Error of the Estimate	F	Sig
1	0.793[a]	0.629	0.614	0.71334	61.541	0.000 [a]

Table 9. Coefficient

Model		Unstandardized Coefficients		Standardized Coefficients	t	Sig
		B	Std. Error	Beta		
1	Constant	2.694	0.511		5.482	0.000
	Cyber environment	0.604	0.085	0.427	7.070	0.000

a. **Predictors:** (Constant), Cyber Environment.
b. **Dependent Variable:** Overall Evaluation (satisfaction).

As shown in Table 9, the regression coefficient of *Cyber Environment* on *Overall Evaluation (satisfaction)* is 0.793, and the significant probability of *t* value is less than 0.05, indicating that *Cyber Environment* can be used to explain *Overall Evaluation (satisfaction)*. Furthermore, its impact on *Overall Evaluation(satisfaction)* is positive, i.e., the better the cyber environment, the more users will trust and be satisfied with the mobile network. The standard regression equation from this analysis is: *Overall evaluation (satisfaction) = 2.694 + 0.793* Cyber environment.*

According to the analysis of the results of the questionnaire investigation, we make the following observations and preliminary conclusions:

1. In mobile devices, a high proportion of users use SNS apps. The possibility of information leakage through SNS apps is high.
2. Users, independent of gender, do not pay enough attention to their personal information.
3. The mainly risk of personal information leakage lies in the little legal consequence.
4. Information harassment is very serious, with all responders being a victim at least once.
5. The majority of users use security software to protect personal information. However, there are still a large proportion of users who do not take any measures to protect their personal information.
6. The advantages and disadvantages of the whole cyber environment are the most direct and fundamental factors of whether the users perceiving the mobile network is safe.
7. If the methods of protection and feedback channels are too complicated, users will choose to give up taking actions.

4. STRATEGIES FOR MOBILE CYBER INFORMATION PROTECTION

4.1 Ways to Reduce the Information Leakage Risk

1. Using security software.

Xu and Gong (2016) pointed out that in facing of the current mobile cyber information leakage, security software can effectively reduce the urgent problem. Base on the questionnaire analysis, 69.6% of the responders chose at least one security software to protect information leakage. And within those taking protection methods, the percent of using software protection is 91.2%. The high percent use of security software also proves that it can provide effective protection. Nowadays security software can protect the user's information from many aspects. Firstly, security software can effectively resist the invasion of the virus. A total of 29.1% of the users thought their information leakage was caused by virus, indicating that virus has a certain degree of threat to information. Security software has been an effective first line of defense against virus. Strengthening the usage of security software can effectively reduce the occurrence of information leakage caused by the virus. Secondly, some malwares will automatically be detected when they apply for mobile authority permission. In that case, users can intuitively judge whether authority should be given and prevent direct access to mobile information effectively. Third, part of the security software has the function of blocking advertising information. Our data analysis shows that the proportion of SMS harassment is up to 100%. That is to say, after the information is leaked, it will most likely lead to the harassment of SMS. And some of the security software has the function of advertisement filtering, which can effectively reduce the harassment of SMS.

2. Avoid installing unknown software and browsing unknown sites.

There are lots of free cyber software and a wide range of websites online now. However, except a few of high-profile websites, the majority of the websites' privacy statements are lack of standardization. There is a lack of relevant regulation that requires the privacy statement to include which part of information. Therefore, the content, collecting methods, security requirements for information usages, corresponding secrecy measures, duration of information retention about personal data are not clearly defined. Website managers can easily find loopholes in them, sell users' personal information or make use of it for profits. If there's an unknown website requires user registration, one should avoid filling in the real and effective information for protection from information leakage. Now most of apps need specific privileges before installation. If the user does not provide permissions to those apps at will, it will not let them any chance to access or steal information from smartphones. Then it won't cause any economic loss, either. In facing this situation, users must know well about the content of mobile access management, decide whether to give permission or not. Then they can effectively prevent malwares from stealing information.

3. Prudently sharing of personal information.

The results of the questionnaire show that 97% of the investigators transmitted their personal or family information on mobile network. If one does not know the importance of information and the danger that might cause, the transmitted information might be in an unknown environment. The result of the questionnaire also shows that SNS apps were the most popular in smartphones apps. The proportion is up to 97.1%. Such a high ratio of usage, information security must be paid attention to. There are two main reasons for the leakage of personal information through SNS apps. The first reason is sharing information within friends list. One should consider whether the information will cause personal information leak before releasing the information within the friends list. After being shared, the information is in an open state. It could be randomly shared by friends and friends' friends and it can be obtained by strangers after two or more times of re-sharing. If the information contains important message it would be exploited by others. Therefore, before information release one should consider the risk of re-sharing. The second reason is to fill in the personal information of an account. Now even well-known dating websites have reports of information leakage occasionally. So one should be careful when logging into these kinds of websites. At least one should hide part of the important personal information during registration.

4.2 Strategies for Preventing Information Leakage

1. Technical aspect.

Nowadays people pay more attention to the protection of personal information on mobile network. However, modern technologies in changing this situation still have a long way to go. Our questionnaire results show the frequency of SMS harassment and phone harassment are high. The proportion of SMS harassment is up to 100% and the phone harassment is 82.06% among all responders. The cause of harassment information mainly due to personal information leak. Hiding part of the contact information using technical methods would reduce the occurrence of information leak. Today's network phone can partly conceal information and effectively realize this technique. Two kinds of methods can be used.

The first method is to make temporary web phone exist for a certain time. The questionnaire results show that about half (211 of the 418) responders used O2O type of business apps, such as Baidu Takeout and Didi Kuaidi. These kinds of apps require sharing personal contact information for the sellers to offer service. Take Didi Kuaidi as an example. When Didi Kuaidi was first launched, it transferred uses' real names and the real phone numbers to drivers (service provider). After users and drivers reported harassment information during the first stage, the company switched the real data to a web phone. This switch shields both the users and the drivers from obtaining the real phone numbers, thereby protecting user's information. However, this method has its drawbacks. The web phones are unable to persist for a long time after the phone hung up. It makes it unable to re-contact when the users use a temporary account. The web phone is an approach for personal information protection, but it needs more technical development to resolve the current shortcomings.

The second method is to use QR code to generate web phone contacts. The results of the questionnaire shows that 64.8% of the responders used mobile shopping online. At same time, up to 100% investigators have been harassed by business ads caused by cell phone numbers breach. Therefore, it is necessary to hide the contact information. Yet in the face of online shopping users must provide effective contact information. To solve this dilemma, users can use some apps to transfer personal information into a QR code on both customers and sellers sides. If couriers need to communicate buyers, they scan the QR code to generate a temporary web phone contact again to reach the customer. Once the transaction completes, the user can choose to cancel that QR code at any time. This can be a good way to avoid harassment SMS.

2. Legal aspect.

According to the questionnaire data, illegal activities involving fraud and account embezzlement that are prohibited by laws have lower occurrences than those not explicitly prohibited by a law. The problems caused by information leakage usually do not cause direct economic losses or personal injury, but in a form of advertising which is beyond severe legal punishment. Our data also shows that only 1% of the responders will take legal actions to defend their interests due to the high cost and long duration of the legal process. In our opinion, the legal system should be improved from the following three aspects to for personal information protection.

First, make clear what kind of advertisement is illegal. Our questionnaire data show that 3.3% of the responders incurred direct economic losses because of information leakage. These low-risk and high-frequency behaviors are spread among businesses. It is necessary to develop regulations to restrict unsolicited anonymous calls and spam messages, clearly states the legal provisions, and forbid spreading advertisements randomly or targeted to others smartphones without the users' consent. Once such a legal system is in place, the problem of information leakage can alleviate.

Second, clearly legislate accountability the infringement of personal information. For the reasons of information leakage, 46.4% of the responders believed that the current law was imperfect. Many of the low danger of information leakage activities are beyond the current laws. It is necessary to determine the infringement responsibility of personal information. Guo (2012) called for improving legislation to meet the challenges in the current mobile cyber world. This need is ever increasing with the increasing number of cases of personal information infringement in the big data age. Therefore, a state needs to increase the punishment of personal information theft and transaction, strengthen the protection of personal information rights, and make full use of various forms of responsibility.

Third, simplify legal complaints channels. In the survey of users' satisfaction to current network, the questionnaire set up questions for ways of simplicity feedback and attributed it to *Usability of protection methods*. From the overall analysis of data, the correlation coefficient of *Usability of protection methods* and *Overall evaluation (satisfaction)* is 0.632. The simplicity of feedback channels is an issue that we deeply concern. The reason is that the cost of using the law as a means of feedback is too high and the steps are too time-consuming. It is necessary to establish a relatively convenient way of feedback. One approach might be setting up a special complaint web page on the websites, where all users need to do is only to provide the illegal advertising information and business information online. This way more feedback can be collected.

3. Social aspect.

According to our data analysis, the impact of *Cyber environment* on *Overall evaluation (satisfaction)* is up to 0.811. It shows that users now have a high level of concern about the cyber environment. The embodiment of cyber environment is mainly on the protection of network and the quality of cyber merchants. A total of 31.5% responders believed that the reasons for information leakage were attributed to poor supervision. It also proved that the current cyber regulation is not in place. The improvement of cyber merchants' quality can put an end to unhealthy competition. A total of 93.5% responders believed that the fundamental reason for the information leakage was that the business was making a profit from it. This means that sellers can effectively prevent information from leakage once unhealthy competition is removed. All aspects of society need to give publicity to promote the importance of personal information. Only 8.37% of responders are seriously concerned about their information. This situation is more prominent among male responders, and only 2.11% of the males surveyed are very concerned with personal information. This is partly because males do not pay enough attention to personal information. It is necessary to make the public understand the importance of personal information.

The information leakage can't be solved by law and technology alone. Take the virus as an example, the protection of security software is undoubtedly a very favorable barrier. But new viruses will ceaseless appear. What security software can do is to reduce the probability of the problem and reduce the losses. Technology is only a tool for an inanimate network, and only people's self-discipline can eradicate the nature of virus. There will be a qualitative change in the improvement of business autonomy. The mobile network is just like a society: if the social atmosphere become well, the surrounding crime rate will decline. Technologies and laws are necessary in dealing with information leakage, but it is impossible to solve the problem of information leakage by them only. Information leakage is not a single aspect that can be completely eradicated, and the whole society needs to work together.

CONCLUSION

The rapid development of mobile network gives us unprecedented convenience. Our lives have also undergone a dramatic change. However, the hidden problems behind the prosperity are increasingly sharpened. Information leakage leads to economic losses, injury of mind, and harass of life.

This chapter starts from the cognition and experience of information security in modern mobile network. In the form of questionnaire survey, we collected users' view on the security of modern mobile network. The data was analyzed to gain further insights into the extent, causes, and perception of personal information leak. We found that the cyber security is not so optimistic. A total of 87.1% of the users discovered information leakage by themselves. However, the loss of the economy after information leakage is not as serious as we imagined. Only 3.5% responders have had substantial economic losses. Most leakage causes SMS harassment; all questionnaire responders experienced SMS harassment. It showed that the result of information leakage harassment occurs mostly by the way of this kind of smaller form of illegal responsibility. The satisfaction of responders on mobile cyber security is basically in the middle of a mediocre attitude, neither perfect nor worthless. They all think they are under safe protection, but it should be strengthened. Combined with the state cyber environment, we put forward feasible suggestions from three aspects of technology, law and society. Suggestions to achieve the better development of the mobile cyber information security are also provided.

REFERENCES

Chen, P., & Huang, Z. (2012). *Ibm SPSS 19 statistical software application guide*. Beijing, China: People's Health Press.

Choi, J., Na, G., & Yi, J. H. (2016). Hardware-assisted credential management scheme for preventing private data analysis from cloning attacks. *Multimedia Tools and Applications*, *75*(22), 1–16. doi:10.100711042-016-3271-z

CNNIC. (2017). *Statistical Report on Internet Development in China*. Retrieved from http://www.cnnic.net.cn/

Dai, W., Qiu, M., Qiu, L., Chen, L., & Wu, A. (2017). Who moved my data? privacy protection in smartphones. *IEEE Communications Magazine*, *55*(1), 20–25. doi:10.1109/MCOM.2017.1600349CM

Fan, X. (2016). *Last year, the national 4G user reached 386 million permeability to 29.6*. Beijing, China: Beijing Daily.

Feng, Z. (2016). *Research on network privacy in the big data age: from rights protection to personal choice* (Unpublished doctoral dissertation). Jilin University, Changchun, China.

Guo, M. (2012). *Protection of the tort law of personal information rights*. Beijing, China: Legal Publishing House.

Ma, L. (2015). On privacy leaks in mobile Internet social networks. *News Knowledge*, (6), 3-5.

Statista. (2016). *Number of smartphone users worldwide from 2014 to 2020 (in billions)*. Retrieved from https://www.statista.com/statistics/330695/number-of-smartphone-users-worldwide/

Tan, J. (2014). *Research and system implementation of mobile phone virus network detection and system implementation* (Unpublished doctoral dissertation). South China University of Technology, Guangzhou, China.

Vorobyov, K., Krishnan, P., & Stocks, P. (2012). A Low-Overhead, Value-Tracking Approach to Information Flow Security. *International Conference on Software Engineering and Formal Methods*, (73), 367-381. 10.1007/978-3-642-33826-7_26

Wang, Y., Liao, Z. & Xia, C. (2015). Discussion on the information security of smart phones. *Technology Square*, (11), 50-60.

Xing, K. (2014). *College students mobile phone: mobile market share accounted for about 70%*. Retrieved from http://news.youth.cn/gn/201404/

Xu, H., & Gong D. (2016). Research on the way, hidden danger and prevention strategy of personal information leakage. *Legal System*, (13), 176-177.

APPENDIX

Mobile Cyber Information Leakage Questionnaire

Dear Mr. / Miss:

To better understand the encounter and understanding of the information leakage of the mobile network. We launched this questionnaire. This survey is used only for academic research. Your answer is very important to us. Thank you very much for your help.

1. Your gender ()
   A. Male B. Female
2. Is your occupation related to the computer ()
   A. Y B. N
3. How much is your monthly cost of living?()
   A. lower than 1000 B.1000-1499 C.1500-1999 D. more than2000
4. Do you often get, transfer, and share information through mobile networks (mobile phones, tablet and other mobile terminals)? ()
   A. Often B. Occasionally C. Never
5. What is the main use of your mobile brower ()(Multi-choice)
   A. Online shopping
   B. Finding out information
   C. SNS apps
   D. Browse news
   E. Entertainment (games, movies)
   F. Message passing (E-mail)
   G. Use of QR code
   H. Others
6. Is there any disclosure of information that has been leaked? ()
   A. Yes B. No
7. What do you think of the cause of your information leak? ()(Multi-choice)
   A. Sold by bad merchants after account register.
   B. Necessary cyber information left over (Online shopping, Takeouts, Didi Kuaidi)
   C. Virus
   D. Friend list sharing
   E. Others
8. What are the usual hazards after the information leak? How about the frequency? (Table 10)

Table 10. Frequency of information leakage

	Often	Occasionally	Never
Account password is stolen			
phone harassment			
Spam message harassment			
telephone fraud			
Other method			

9. Is there any economic loss after information leakage ()
   A. Yes B. No
10. Do you care about the leakage of personal information ()
    A. Yes B. Don't like but don't dig into it ether C. Indifferent to me
11. What action did you take if information leaked ()(multi-choice)
    A. Shielded harassment source
    B. Modify account password
    C. Reflect to the operator
    D. Take no steps
    E. Take legal actions
    F. Others
12. What do you think is the reason for the disclosure of information()
    A. For profit by website administer
    B. Poor cyber supervision
    C. The relevant law is not perfect enough
    D. The society does not pay enough attention to the problem
    E. Others
13. What do you do to protect your information ()(multi-choice)
    A. Software protection
    B. Download App from authority
    C. Not fill in real information
    D. No any measures be taken
    F. Others
14. Your attitude with the current mobile cyber information security

Table 11. Attitude of cyber information security

		1 Totally Disagree	2	3	4	5 Totally Agree
Cyber Environment	**1. I feel safe about the network software**					
	2. Sellers won't hurt my interests					
	3. Few seller steal information					
Usability of protection methods.	**4. Protection software are easy to use**					
	5. The way of feedback is simple and convenient					
	6. The method of reducing and avoiding harm is simple					
Practicability of protection methods	**7. Protection software puts my mind in peace**					
	8. There will be no loss of information by downloading regular software					
	9. Reporting to operators can be a good way to curb information leaks					
economic cost	**10. The cost of pay ware is reasonable**					
	11. Protection software is free					
	12. The lower the software sales standard, the more user					
Overall evaluation (Satisfaction)	**13. Protection software can be good for protecting information**					
	14. Normal software does not steal user information					
	15. My current security assessment for mobile networks is good					

1An online food ordering-and-delivery company.

2A major ride-sharing company, providing transportation services for more than 450 million users across over 400 cities in China.

3 QQ and Wechat are Chinese social media (instant messaging, commerce and payment services) mobile application software developed by Tencent.

Chapter 10
A Modelled Management Information System for Information Diffusion and Management in Nigerian Universities

Muhammad Laminu
Ramat Polytechnic Maiduguri, Nigeria

Sufian Yousef
Anglia Ruskin University, Nigeria

Babagana Umara Zulum
University of Maiduguri, Nigeria

ABSTRACT

The rapid evolution of the communication technology started with the diffusion of information between connected computers to the present system in which voice, video, etc. are being exchange between systems. Driven by the global educational challenge in the twenty-first century, the Nigerian University Commission had stated that Nigerian university system will now go paperless as it has launched a portal called NUSMAP. The major set-back to the realization of the objectives of NUSMAP is that most Nigerian universities still handle their information system manually by using paper as a delivery vehicle. Some use the single management system. Other universities employ the LAN management model, where each department and/or unit has its own established management information system on the LAN. Very few universities use a campus network where departments/units can share information. In view of the above, the researchers propose a campus network that will be a modelled management information system for information diffusion and management in Nigerian universities.

DOI: 10.4018/978-1-5225-5393-9.ch010

INTRODUCTION

Nowadays, educational institutions create and use enormous quantities of information as compared to the past. Information has become a treasured asset to educational institutions especially universities. Information backs day-to-day tasks, decision making and virtually any function in the university. Universities spend huge amount in Information Systems as they have proven to deliver information needed to make decisions, control operations, analyse problems, and create new products or services via its three activities of input, processing, and output. The input activity of the information system collects raw data from within the university or from its external environment; while processing converts this raw input into a meaningful form and the output activity transfers the administered information to the people who will use it or to other accomplishments for which it will be used.

An information system in a university can technically be defined as a set of interconnected components that collect, process, store, and diffuse information to support decision making, planning and control in a university. In addition to backing decision making, management, and control, information systems may also support university administrators/supervisors/monitors and other staff of the institutions analyse problems, create new products and envisage composite issues. Information systems comprise information about students, staff, departments, faculty, accommodation, etc. and other things within the university or in the surrounding environment.

Management Information Systems (MIS) literally is the combination of management and information system is defined by Daoleng, Oyerinde and Vem, (2014) "as computer systems in an organisation that provide information to support managers to make decisions in a functional area of an organization". Hence, in the university setting, Management Information System can be defined as a set of interrelated systems in a university that provide information to support university administrators/monitors (NUC as in Nigeria) to make decision in the university. The position of management information systems is revealed through its influence on improved information flow from top down management levels and vice versa, and direct transfer of information to the operational level employees at an effective cost (Stamatovic and Kurij, 2003),

The field of management information systems (MIS) tries to achieve this broader information systems literacy which Laudon and Laudon, (2014) referred to as information which includes an understanding of the management and organizational dimensions of systems as well as the technical magnitudes of systems. Computer literacy on the other hand, focuses principally on understanding of information technology. MIS deals with behavioural issues as well as technical issues surrounding the development, use, and impact of information systems used by managers and employees in the university (Laudon and Laudon, 2014).

The technological evolution in the world today has created a global world in which national borders, distances and time zones are no longer an excuse. Networking has become an important aspect in the current globalization of the internet which contributed immensely to the development of networks. Researchers in the field of networking are developing new products and services designed to take advantage of the network capabilities" (Cisco Networking Academy, 2010), and internet plays an important role in the success of their developments.

The rapid evolution of the communication technology which started with the diffusion of information between connected computers to the present system in which voice, video, etc. are being exchange between systems. These changes instigated challenges for the development of various communication techniques for direct diffusion of information (voice, texts, Instant messages, video, etc.) directly between many systems and societies. "The immediate nature of communication over the internet encourages the formation of global communication." (Cisco Networking Academy, 2010).

Propelled by the global educational challenge in the 21st century, the Nigerian University Commission, NUC, whose primary responsibility is to coordinate, finance and develop universities and also ensures the maintenance of standards in the universities had stated that Nigerian University system will now go paperless as it has launched a portal called Nigerian University System Management Portal, NUSMAP (Vanguard Newspaper, 2013).

NUSMAP is an "online programme designed to enable Nigerian universities process, share and communicate data with the NUC, the public and other government agencies for proper planning and management" (The Nigerian University Commission).

However, NUSMAP ultimately captures complete information on students' bio-data, academic data, including their O-Level results, JAMB/UTME entry qualifications, hobbies, skills, computer knowledge, and membership of institutional and professional bodies, amongst others. It also captures information on staff including their designation, areas of specialization, employment details, and knowledge of ICT, membership of institutional and professional bodies, amongst others. The process involves reading information from different information systems at each point in time and uploading the data to the portal at the academic office or quality assurance office of the university. This is because NUSMAP and the university systems lacks basic communication standard for data exchange. The process automatically inherits all the risk associated with data migration. NUSMAP is extremely people dependent and it is seen as an unsustainable approach to ever growing demands for secure and timely access to highly accurate educational data. In addition, NUSMAP does not cater for easy access to educational data by other agencies that might need it (Ise, 2014).

The Nigerian universities are confronted with challenges of managing a huge amount of information for quite a number of times, thus making them gradually depending on MIS for its input, process and output. With the support of Management Information System, Nigerian universities have improved access to relevant, accurate, up-to-date information on their students, staff and research activities for decision making. The rapid evolution in information technology has made the option to MIS in management of universities in particular and the educational sector in general vital (Daoleng, Oyerinde and Vem, 2010).

In order to comply with the developments in information technology, Nigerian Universities have developed Web portals, available on the Internet, for capturing and processing of data from staff and students. This has made it possible for University administrators to take informed, timely and accurate decisions at the tip of their fingers tips. Beside the ease of administration, it has led to the consideration and involvement of most Nigerian Universities and Higher Educational Institutions in the World Webometric Ranking of Universities (Daoleng, Oyerinde and Vem, 2010).

The major bottleneck to the realization of the objectives of NUSMAP is that most Nigerian universities still handle their information system manually by using paper as a delivery vehicle. Some uses the single management system. This model has no established computer network and the exchange of information between computers is not achievable. These institutions according to Li, (2014) still remain in the sector-oriented individual level and are liable to loss of data. Other universities employ the LAN management model, where each department and/or units have its own established management information system on the LAN. That is, each department/unit can store and share data within the department. This model has the limitation of not sharing data between departments/units. While very few universities (mostly private) uses a campus network where departments/units can share information.

In this chapter, the authors concentrate on creating a campus network model management information system with the aim of connecting the various faculties/departments/units within the university. Thereby providing the information required by NUSMAP, hence, clearing the above mentioned bottleneck and ease the diffusion and management of Information in the university.

BACKGROUND

Management Information System

Prior to the emergence of computer and network technology, management information system in universities is done manually with paper as a delivery vehicle. With the advent of computer and network technologies and applications, this original management information processing methods have been gradually paved away by the computer. The computer became the carrier of the campus network and the delivery of electronic information processing replaced, which is called the information system with the influence of information technology which is made up of computer technology and network technology, universities employ computer network. The formation of campus network according to Li, (2014) generally has two features: the external network connections and; the use of modern ways of improving the quality of teaching and management with network technology. The external network is the internet which is the world's biggest and most broadly used network. The Internet is a universal "network of networks" that practices international standards to connect millions of diverse networks with nearly 2.3 billion users in over 230 countries around the world (Laudon & Laudon, 2014). The Internet has fashioned a new "universal" technology foundation on which universities can build new products, services, and strategies. This same technology platform can provide connectivity to link different systems and networks within the university. The World Wide Web is a service provided by the Internet that practices universally accepted standards for storing, retrieving, formatting, and displaying information in a page format on the Internet. With an internet connection, the university will be able to provide the university's information services, integrate into the world information flow; comprehend the outside world, strengthen academic exchanges and cooperation between other universities with an established management information system. The use of modern means to improve the quality of teaching and management level through the network, can be achieved by using computers and communications equipment that can be connected in networks for sharing voice, data, images, sound, and video. These multimedia and communication technologies according to Li (2014) can provide: for remote teaching; faculty realize complementarily with relatively sound management information system and; network applications expansion.

University Management Information System Models

Campus Network unlevelled the development of information systems; they currently coexist in three modes according to Li, (2014).

1. **Single Management Model:** In this model, there is no established computer network. Hence there is no exchange data and information sharing between computers. The universities which adopt this model according to Li (2014) still remain in the sector-oriented individual transaction level and this situation often determines their system data inconsistencies, prone to data loss, virus infections and other issues.

2. **LAN Management Model:** This model can provide one with the opportunity to carry out the work on the network, such as establishment of management information systems on the LAN. Here, the data set in the department server and this provide the department's management staff to share data within the department. This model which provide for the management of work within the department has played a catalytic role in resolving the intra-departmental data redundancy and inconsistency. The limitations of this model are that: applications are completed on a computer terminal and it overloaded the server just for file storage, data storage and print sharing; low network utilization; many departments/units have their own campus LAN and individual actions cannot achieve data sharing between different units, hence there is no rational flow of information resources.
3. **The Campus Computer Network:** In this model, there is exchange of information between departments such as covering the whole school for the management of information systems, electronic document flow, management information, upload issues, the information systems to management systems based on various departments. Here, departments manage data in addition to the use of internal staff to meet outside the department, but also for other sectors and even other university staff to provide information services.

Requirements for Management Information Systems

Management Information System in Universities in particular and tertiary institutions in general is faced with the following requirements:

1. To strengthen scientific and technological information exchanges both within the university, country and abroad;
2. Provide primary information region for the university by the use of transaction processing system, and clearing channels of information between various departments based on the establishment of the university shared database;
3. Replacement of the traditional manual office by the establishment of modern office support environment thereby improving office efficiency;
4. Establishment of Web-based online network teaching system. The campus network can be used to provide a teaching medium, transmit teaching content, implementation of teaching and conducting online campus teaching management, and online testing and online communication.

University Management Information System Implementation

According to the analysis of the general university system setting, (Ping Li, 2014) draws the information needs for universities as services, office information, management information and teaching information. These needs which determine the university information system is a university-wide, open, distributed multimedia information systems. The establishment of university management information system based on these information needs requires information subsystems, specifically integrated information services, office automation, administration, information and network teaching system. These subsystems encounters diverse variety of users and data is organised in various ways. In order to meet the need to take different technical solutions to solve for the domestic and international, internal and external users of the system, the user www browser is the most convenient in the functions of management. Most of the information in university MIS is structured data with operators of complex operations, the database should be manage mainly in the flow of information between the various offices, such as notification, referrals, reports, etc. For most of unstructured data, it is often needed to determine the marking process based on the content, hence one cannot use fixed data structure database technology to transfer processes, and should take advantage of Lotus Notes data organisation. The system is running structure the data flow of information online (Li, 2014).

The management information system implementation methods are:

1. World Wide Web technology with the development of integrated information service system
2. Database technology development and management information systems

Modelling Management Information System

Modelling of a management information system is made up of many complicated steps which have to be done before its usage as a system. The application of modern modelling techniques and technologies plays a vital role in the development of management decision process that will enable universities and other institutions to be successful in a fast revolving environment. Significantly, simulation modelling is now considered an essential feature of decision making in companies that actively employ modern information technologies.

Though there are many approaches to develop new information system in which different strategy, methodology, modelling techniques or life cycle can be used, modern modelling components should expedite reciprocated indulgent at the various organizational levels when making strategic management decisions thus closing the gaps between its execution and the institutions' vision.

Modern professional simulation modelling components employ distinct software, programming languages and systems to develop models of institutional or university processes, relations between student, academic/management staff and departments/faculties for optimization in the institutional structure as a whole Serova (2013).

Classification of Modelling Methods

The term model is widely used in all fields of knowledge and modelling is a representation of a reality, i.e., the real university campus. Thus establishing a classification of all possible types of modelling is not an easy task. Nevertheless, Serova (2013) classified modelling as: conceptual; physical; structured functional; mathematical and simulation models.

All these types of modelling are not mutually exclusive and can be employed to develop complex management information systems at the same time, or in certain combinations. Conventionally, computer modelling or computer simulation falls within the class of simulation and is deals with the analysis or syntheses of composite management information systems in order to support students, academic staff and management staff in decision analysis undertakings. The aim of computer modelling can include: the activity of the institution or university, campus network, technological process or any real object or process.

The major difference between computer simulation and structure-function analysis is that the former produces both qualitative and quantitative effects (Serova, 2009).

University Portal

An Internet portal can be defined as "a single integrated, ubiquitous, and useful access to information (data), applications and people." Portal, though similar to a Web site as the subsequent logical step in the evolution in the direction of a digital culture, but it is far more as it serve as a gate, a door, or entrance that brings together all the information that users need in a single place, available in an intelligible way that provides for improved productivity. It is an application that has link with a database. Unlike static website which serves as a gateway to portal, portal is dynamic in the sense that it is more interactive whereby one can actually input data and also get the information in it.

A University Portal or Institution Portal on the other hand, is a one-stop client-oriented web site that personalizes the portal's tools and information to the precise requests and characteristics of the person visiting the site, using information from the faculty databases. A University web site differs from university portal in the sense that, the information is available on the website, but it is up to the guest to find it by either using a search engine, or navigating the links on the University's web page (Cronin, 2001) (Muhammad, and Idris, 2010). While in a "University Portal", the guest introduces himself to the portal by either signing up or login in. The portal then provides the detailed knowledge the faculty has about the guest and presents the information which could be generic publicly accessible information, or confidential information specific to that individual (like course grades or payroll information) to the guest in one place. The information provided by a portal has shifted from a public web site showing on-line pamphlets to a user-oriented web site that provides tools, reports, and services specifically designed for that specific guest (Muhammad, and Idris, 2010).

Benefits of Portals to the University

The possible benefits realized from a campus-wide portal are far-reaching and spin around increased efficiency and the ability to provide university communities with access to information. Some notable benefits according to Muhammad, and Idris, (2010) include:

1. User identification through a single log-on account;
2. Centralized administration and enforcement of security driven by user authentication protocols;
3. A common entry point for all services available at the university;
4. A common architecture for integrating administrative systems, course management tools, and content from disparate systems and providers;
5. Consistent appearance and behaviour, facilitating improved user experience and improved relationship with and between constituents; and
6. The ability to engage, empowers, and retains constituents by providing a sense of membership in an academic community.

The main reason for the deployment of portal according to Daigle and Cuocco, (2002) is "to improve productivity by increasing the speed and customizing the content of information provided to internal and external constituencies." They also recommend that portals serve a knowledge management function by "dealing with information glut in an organized fashion."

In Olsen, (2002) view, Web portals have been used to streamline and automate administrative functions in higher education by creating a point of access for administrative functions for staff and students. Portals also simplify knowledge transfer through the addition of several communication channels, such as message boards and directories; moving beyond the one-sided information exchange found in traditional web sites (Muhammad and Idris; 2010).

Campus Network

The campus network according to Tao, Shaoqian, Minglian and Baozhu, (2012) "is a collection of teaching, research, administrative, educational administration, general management functions into one integrated network which has an aligned Waiting function, to meet such requirements as internet services, remote education services, electronic bulletin board, video conferencing and odd-campus data communication services, etc. With the rapid development and wider application of computer and network technology, the campus network plays a very important role for staff and students work, study, living, etc. thereby providing a great convenience in the university teaching and management in particular and the education system in general. Hence, this in turn is about to modify the traditional teaching and management model" (Tao, et al; 2012).

Universities and other Higher Education Institutions (HEIs) moved into a totally new era of the e-campus with the introduction of the China Education and Research Network (CERNET) in 1994. 'E-campus' at this juncture means an institution established on a campus network with the incorporation of digital resources, building up and e-educational administration portal, e-learning, distance education and multimedia broadband network, campus management information system, etc. This ultimately forms maximize digital environment so as to increasingly spread the application of information technology all over the campus (Li and Lei, 2005) (Guodong and Zhongjiao; 2010).

A 10 gigabit campus network to provide appropriate solution for the large campus network was presented by Lianzhi, Guangming, and Rongshen, (2010). The proposed plan which uses the 10G Ethernet for its construction is a high-speed campus network model to satisfy the need for a real time and half-time performance in a campus. Though the capacity is high, the cost of 10G Ethernet is also high for a University campus.

Xie, (2011) provides a good solution to the normal teaching and systematic research work in order to meet future development needs by making a detailed analysis on a campus network to achieve a higher overall performance. The study is mainly meant to apply to the construction of the campus network and network upgrade.

Quang, Bio, Shurong, and Amei, (2012) presents an integrated management system in University laboratory based on campus network. The system is intended to improve work efficiency by standardizing the laboratory management and the acceleration of the development of the university.

Lan (2012) proposes an IT Service Management System of College or University campus network by analysing the practical function, structure and development methodology of college or university campus network service management module. He went further to analyse the existing problems and causes of college or university campus network management, learning from the structure and core process of ITIL, pointing out the improvement directions of the college or university campus network management and design the process of IT Service management of college or university campus network.

The construction of a campus network group system design based on the basic unit of campus network on IP was introduced by Yang, (2012) and proposes the development of remote information site, the network classroom, campus network groups and information centre for video monitoring in the large data flow requirements, the campus network monitoring system, cloud computing solutions and key technologies. He went further to implement the actual network system.

Wei, Shengzhong, and Hong, (2010) considers the limitations of a campus network at the preliminary stage of development which include the absence of unified norms or criteria for the organization of data among different work sections; the impossibility for different sections to share information effectively; users' inconveniences and construction of information by universities. They finally propose a newly defined plan of Unified Identity Authentication based on university website portal which can organize relevant tasks and screen irrelevant tasks.

Campus Network Characteristics

The structure of a campus network can be divided into three layers, namely the core data layer, the convergence layer and the access layer. The type of campus network can also be divided into teaching, office and dormitory subnet, etc. Juels, (2006) stated that one of the Characteristics of campus network is the diversity of accessing methods, which include dial-up authentication access, Local Area Network (LAN) access, wireless access, etc., and the beneficiaries of Campus network which comprises of students, faculties and the staff in campus business office are also very complex. Additionally, the export structure on the campus network is generally made up of multiple links (Tao, Jia, and Yang; 2011).

Guodong and Zhongjiao (2010), outline four characteristics of e-campus as follows:

1. The digital storage of resources;
2. Information transfer via network;
3. Automation of management; and
4. Personalisation of communication.

"As it were, e-campus is a brand new model for teaching, scientific research and campus management in colleges and universities, and to some extent promoting the steady development and reform of universities" (Guodong and Zhongjiao; 2010).

The Nigerian University Commission

The National Universities Commission (NUC) is a statutory body which was created by Decree No. 1. Of 1974 was initially established in 1962 as an advisory agency in the Cabinet Office to serve as a channel of communication between Nigerian Universities and the Federal Government through the Federal Ministry of Education (The Nigerian University Commission).

Thus, the NUC is the agent of the Federal Government for coordinating, financing, maintenance of high standard, avoidance of unnecessary and wasteful duplication of academic programmes and orderly development of the Universities with the vision and mission "to be a dynamic regulatory agency acting as a catalyst for positive change and innovation for the delivery of quality university education in Nigeria" and "to ensure the orderly development of a well-coordinated and productive university system that will guarantee quality and relevant education for national development and global competitiveness" respectively (The Nigerian University Commission).

These can be achieved through the attainment of a stable and crisis-free University System; work with Nigerian Universities to achieve full accreditation status for at least 80% of the academic programmes; initiate and promote proficiency in the use of ICT for service delivery within the Commission and the Nigerian University System; upgrade and maintain physical facilities in the Nigerian University System for delivery of quality university education; match university graduate output with national manpower needs and; foster partnership between the Nigerian University System and the private sector. With the mandates of approving courses and programmes, determination and maintenance of minimum academic standards, accreditation of academic programmes and provision of guidelines and processing of applications for the establishment of private universities.

The Commission has the Executive Secretary (ES) as the Chief Executive Officer and a Deputy Executive Secretary has twelve Departments which are Department of Academic Standards, Department of Inspection and Monitoring, Department of Management Support Services, Department of Students Support Services, Department of Research and Innovations, Department of Information and Communications Technology, Department of Finance and Accounts, Department of Quality Assurance, Department of Physical Planning and Development, Department of Open and Distance Education, Liaison Office Department and the Executive Secretary's Office. Each of the departments is headed by a Director (The Nigerian University Commission).

The Nigerian University System Management Portal (NUSMAP)

The development of Management Information System (MIS) in the Nigerian Educational System started in the late 1980's. This was made possible by the NUC in collaboration with the British Council. In 1992, some universities piloted the establishment of a Nigerian University Management Information System (NUMIS) managed by the NUC. About a decade later, the NUMIS project was abandoned by the NUC due to some challenges which include bureaucracy, communication difficulties and other associated challenges (Daoleng, Oyerinde and Vem, 2010).

The Nigerian University System Management Portal (NUSMAP) is designed to combine the functions of the Universities Programme Accreditation, Universities Academic Standards and University System Annual Review Meeting (USARM). The software has facilities to harness and generate all reports in these three key NUC programmes under the Directorates of Quality Assurance and Academic Standards. It will enable the universities generate information on: Enrolment/ Statistics; Academic programmes; Physical facilities; Budgets and Expenditures; Staff information; Student information; Research and Innovations; and Information Help Desk (Welcome to NUSMAP).

The portal is a storage and retrieval system which enables the directors of academic planning/quality assurance in all universities to communicate online the information required by regulatory agencies – National Universities Commission (NUC) and the Ministry of Education. It helps them fill their Online Universities Programme Accreditation Portal without any further challenge or visits to the various departments or faculties of the institution to request for information needed for accreditation. It also provides the university a reliable source of concrete data for making future projections.

The portal is totally under the control of directors of academic planning or quality assurance of the university. They have the key and can create passwords for any official of the university that is required to perform any function in the system.

The Portal (NUSMAP) Paul (n.d.) is the best solution for harnessing all relevant data of all universities in the country, which had hitherto eluded education planners. NUSMAP is running and has been verified by some universities and the public can seek NUC support online in matters relating to students and staff information, university and course status etc.

"The Academic world has gone beyond the era of planning without data. Education planners and regulators can also no longer accept unverifiable, if not questionable data from universities. This software is designed to achieve data integrity. Any claim by an institution can easily be verified, since all universities are required to submit all claims in data form. Staff and student data must be submitted to NUC or

Federal Ministry of Education as requested and this does not, in any way, impinge on university autonomy.

The implementation of this system will put to rest the numerous challenges faced by the universities in harnessing their data for academic planning and, in the long run, improve their ratings"(Paul, n.d).

How to Use the Portal

The directors of academic planning/quality assurance and staff appointed by them will login using the Staff Login Panel which is located at the top right hand corner of this page with their staff number and password; they then select any of the links by the side menu of the subsequent page to get started (Welcome to NUSMAP).

Features of the NUSMAP Application

The Nigerian University System Management Portal (NUSMAP) user guide presents the following features of NUSMAP.

1. **Robust Administration:** It has secured control panels for the universities (Directors of Academic Planning (DAPs)/Directors of Quality Assurance (DQAs)), as well as for the National Universities Commission (NUC). It gives the DAPs and NUC administrators' full control over their respective sections, allowing them to: i) Create administrators to manage separate sections of the software ii) Assign privileges and roles to staff. iii) Block any USER from using the system.
2. **Secured Login System:** NUSMAP application is designed to provide secured login and has provision for restriction of staff to specific areas, such that, no user can view/print pages that he/she is not authorized to.
3. **Unique Identity for Each University:** NUSMAP application is designed to be unique for each institution. All data for any particular institution can be view and used only by that institution and its appointed staff.
4. **User Friendly:** The NUSMAP application was designed with simplicity in mind and has a unique graphical user interfaces which is friendly and easy to use. Each page has instructions and guidelines on what to do and thus makes it easy for anyone using the software.
5. **Captures a Vast Range of Information:** It captures complete information on students' bio-data, academic data, including their O-Level results, JAMB/UTME entry qualifications, hobbies, skills, computer knowledge, and membership of institutional and professional bodies, amongst others. It also captures information on staff including their designation, areas of specialization, employment details,

and knowledge of ICT, membership of institutional and professional bodies, amongst others.

6. **Automatic Population of Database From Records in School's Portal or From an Excel File:** The NUSMAP application can connect to the Edu-Portal of the university to automatically fetch records of students as they register. So at any point in time, the full record of students can be accessed at the click of a button. There is also provision for records to be fetched from an excel file, for schools that do not have the Edu-Portal.
7. **Generation of Printable Reports in NUC-Specified Format:** The NUSMAP application generates printable reports that follow NUC-specified format and therefore reduces the time wasted in trying to compile such reports in the specified format, manually. The reports also have the added benefit of being customized with the school's logo as header.
8. **Export Feature:** The NUSMAP Application, in addition to generating printable reports, also enable the export of such reports to excel format, this enables the school to have a softcopy of the report on their local computers.
9. **Sending of Reports to NUC:** The NUSMAP Application enables the sending of reports to the NUC within its environment. Whenever request for reports are made to the school, the DAP can upload the relevant data requested by NUC into the NUC Central Database via NUSMAP. This reduces paperwork between NUC and the university and also frequent visit to the university by NUC.
10. **Provision for NUC to View Submitted Reports:** The NUSMAP Application has provision for NUC to view and collate reports that have been submitted by the various institutions. These reports are categorized into groups, namely: Budget/Expenditure, Enrolment/Statistics, Physical Facilities, Academic Programmes, Staff and Students groups. These groups have sub-categories into which the reports required by the NUC are categorized.
11. **Automatic Calculation of Full Time Equivalent (FTE):** The NUSMAP Application Automatically calculates the Full time Equivalent (FTE) of students enrolments based on captured students data. This eliminates the strain of performing such complex calculation manually.
12. **Automatic Summation/Calculation Capability:** The NUSMAP application enables automatic summation of records, in the Budget/ Expenditure sections, as well as in the Enrolment/Statistical section. In addition, the NUSMAP Software can calculate the total number of staff in various grade levels automatically, and can give a detailed list of staff and students, based on specified criteria such as: Faculty, Department, State of Origin, Gender, level, Grade Level, Staff category, State & Department and rank.

13. **Automatic Notification on Expiry of a Project's Master Plan:** The NUSMAP application enables staff assigned to the Physical Facilities Section, to receive notification via the Physical Facilities section of NUSMAP whenever the expiration date of the master plan of any project under their supervision elapses. This enables the staff to know which projects are due for review.
14. **Automatic Generation of Annual Payroll Report:** The NUSMAP application automatically calculates annual estimate of cost on total staff salaries, non-salaries, goods and services sorted by staff categories.
15. **Staff Progression/Staff Area of Specialization at a Glance:** The NUSMAP application enables the area of specialization of staff to be viewed at a glance. It also contains record of a staff's progression from one grade level to another.
16. **Facilitates Online Universities Programme Accreditation:** It facilitates the generation of detailed reports required by NUC during Accreditation exercise, and also provides data, which can be used to fill the NUC accreditation portal online.
17. **USARM Now Online:** the Universities Annual Review Meeting (USARM), which is usually an annual assembly of all universities in the federation, could hold online with the birth of NUSMAP. The risk of Universities coming to Abuja to defend their stewardship for the year will be reviewed online. This will remove the risk of travelling and reduce cost incurred by the universities and NUC for this event.

The Nigerian University Commission

Assessing Some Nigerian University Portals

Muhammad, and Idris (2010) selected ten (10) Nigerian University portals for design assessment which is based on the best practices of Personalisation, Timely and Relevance, Building Relationships Using E-mail, Mail and Telephone, Track Inquiries, Integration and Make the System Easy to Manage. The result is presented in tabular form and then a chart drawn for the data presented in table 1. "In an effort to best understand our universities existing systems and processes, and to avoid redundancies in future systems and processes, everyone whose job impacted the admission enrolment process need to be invited to attend the needs assessment" Muhammad, and Idris, 2010).

"Generally, from the analysis of the data in the table 1above and figure 1 below, it is easy to say that most Nigerian University portals are averagely designed. Thus, they don't take full advantage of the functions which a well-designed portal can provide. It is also easy to deduct that the University of Lagos and Federal University of Technology Minna portals have one of the best portal design within the country.

Table 1. Some Nigerian university portals – assessment table

	Nigerian Universities Portals	1. F.U.T. Minna, www.futminna.edu.ng	2. B.U.K. Kano, www.bukportal.com	3. A.B.U. Zaria, www.abuportal.net	4. University of Nigeria, Nsukka, http://portal.unn.edu.ng	5. University of Abuja, www.unibujaportal.com	6. Madonna University Elele, Rivers, www.madonnauniversityportal.com	7. University of Lagos, http://unilagcomm.com	8. University of Ibadan, http://www.ui.edu.ng	9. University of Benin, http://www.uniben.edu	10. Ladoke Akintola University of Technology, Ogbomoso http://www.lautech.edu.ng/
	Best Practices										
A	Personalization (10)	7	7	7	7	8	6	8	8	6	7
B	Timely and Relevant(10)	4	4	4	3	4	2	4	3	3	3
C	Building Relationships Using E-mail and Telephone (10)	5	3	5	3	3	4	5	6	5	4
D	Track Inquiries (10)	6	5	3	5	2	7	4	4	3	5
E	Integration (10)	5	5	4	6	4	6	5	4	5	4
F	Make the System Easy to Manage (10)	6	7	6	6	6	6	7	7	8	7
	Total Scores(60)	**33**	**31**	**29**	**30**	**27**	**31**	**33**	**32**	**30**	**30**

Source: Muhammad, and Idris (2010).

The University of Abuja portal design comes under our hammer for relatively poor design" (Muhammad, and Idris, 2010).

Assessing Nigerian University Network

Nigerian universities still handle their information system manually by using paper as a delivery vehicle. Some uses the single management system. This model has no established computer network and the exchange of information between computers is not achievable. These institutions according to Li (2014) still remain in the sector-oriented individual level and are liable to loss of data. Other universities employ the LAN management model, where each departments and/or units have its own established management information system on the LAN. That is, each department /unit can store and share data within the department. This model has the limitation of not sharing data between departments/units. While very few universities (mostly private) uses a campus network where departments/units can share information.

Figure 1. Assessment of some Nigerian University portals chart
Source: Muhammad, and Idris (2010)

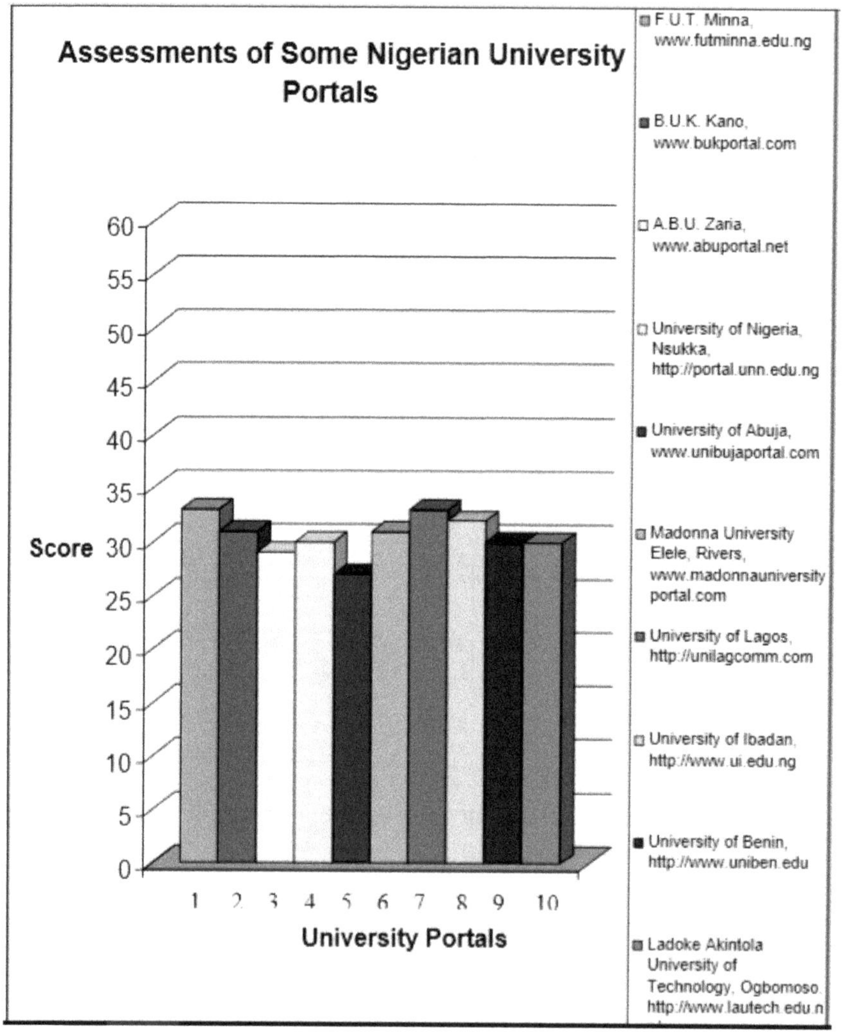

NETWORK MODEL: EXTENDED NUSMAP

The Hierarchies of Information

Looking at the point at which information is collected and used, there are three main levels of information in the Modelled Management Information System for Information Diffusion and Management in Nigerian Universities.

The Department level, at which detailed information about individual students, lecturers and staff (including their name, age, sex, grade, home address, academic performance, qualification, salaries, etc.), as well as information about the department (e.g., area, number of offices, laboratories, classrooms/theatres equipment, etc.) have to be kept for the smooth running of the departments concerned;

The Faculty level, where not all the data kept by the department are required. Only summary statistics such as the number of students by age, sex and grade, and the amount of recurrent expenditures are required for individual departments/units; and

The Campus level, where, depending on the extent of decentralization, detailed information on individual departments may not be required. Only summary information is collected at the Directorate or faculty level.

On the other hand, subject to the usage, information could be distinguished between that for planning, management control, and operation. Preferably, information at the department, faculty, and campus level should be integrated and shared in one, or one network, of data base(s). For example, information kept in the departments could be digitalised, and only the relevant data would be extracted and passed to the computer system kept at the faculty/directorate level; and the similar procedure could apply to the flow of information between the faculty and campus level. This could assist in the avoidance of a lot of duplication of work, and also solve the problems of quality of data and the time lag in producing the information. With the use of personalized data bases, more precise information could be made available about students and lecturers flow, which is exceptionally useful in planning at the departmental position, and lecturer demand and supply. The personalised data base could also reduce considerably the data problems confronting educational researchers, NUC and NUSMAP. Likewise, the same can be said of information for planning, management control and operation. For example, a simple ledger accounting system, if judiciously planned and computerized, could provide a wealth of information beneficial in observing spending, analysing cost structure and efficiency, as well as for forecasting and planning educational expenditures.

The modelled network, E-NUSMAP which will serve as an extension of the Nigerian University System Management Portal, E-NUSMAP was designed to support standard office applications including email, web browsing, database access and file transfer. The E-NUSMAP consists of two main offices: Academic and Establishment. The Academic is situated in the Academic Planning office which is connected to the various faculties (Engineering, Science, Management, Social Sciences, Pharmacy, Medical College and Education (as in the case of University of Maiduguri)) and Admission office. The departments in the various faculties are connected to their respective faculty offices in the form of a LAN network.

The Academic Planning office was designed to support database, web browsing and email and the offices attached to it rely on the dedicated servers in the centre. The faculty offices through the various departments provide information on Academic performances, physical facilities and student information while the admission office provides information on student enrolment and statistics.

The Establishment office system is located at the establishment unit in the office of the Registrar and supports e-mail and database. It has two branches connected to it which depends on the main establishment office. The branches are Bursary and staff office. The bursary office provides such information as Budgets and Expenditure while the staff office provides information regarding staff of the University.

To prevent data loss, the E-NUSMAP is supported by a backup of approximately 20 Gigabytes of data and is designed to support voice. The architecture of the E-NUSMAP is as shown in figure 2 below (Youssef, 2013).

PERFORMANCE OF THE E-NUSMAP

The performance of the Modelled Management Information System – E-NUSMAP were analysed based on the following: Email, FTP (backup), and HTTP (web

Figure 2. An architecture of E-NUSMAP

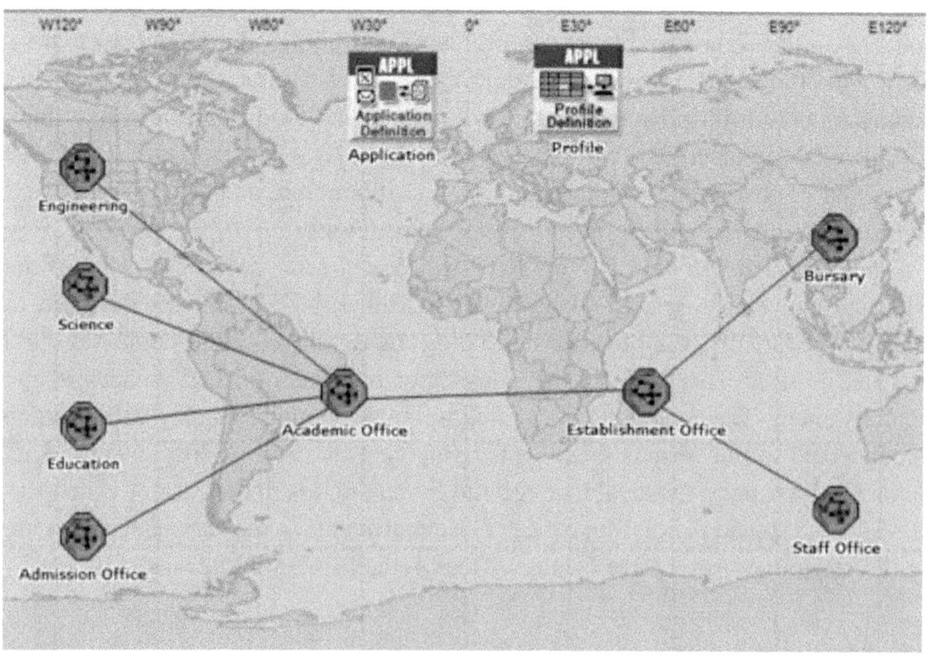

browsing). In evaluating Email, the download response time, traffic sent and received in packets/second are considered; in file transfer, the download and upload response time, traffic sent and received in packet/second are evaluated. In the HTTP, the result is analysed regarding the page response time (Sethi, and Hnatyshyn, 2013).

E-Mail

Time elapsed between sending request for emails and receiving emails from email server in the network. This time includes signalling delay for the connection setup. Average number of packets per second forwarded to all email applications by the transport layers in the network. Average number of packets per second submitted to the transport layers by all email applications in the network. The time it takes for e-mail message to arrive from the server in response to the users' request is as shown in figure 3a below. In addition, the average departure and arrival rate for all e-mail deployed in the network is shown in (b) and (c).

Figure 3. (a) Time average in e-mail downloads time (sec); (b) Time average in e-mail traffic sent; (c) Time average in e-mail traffic received

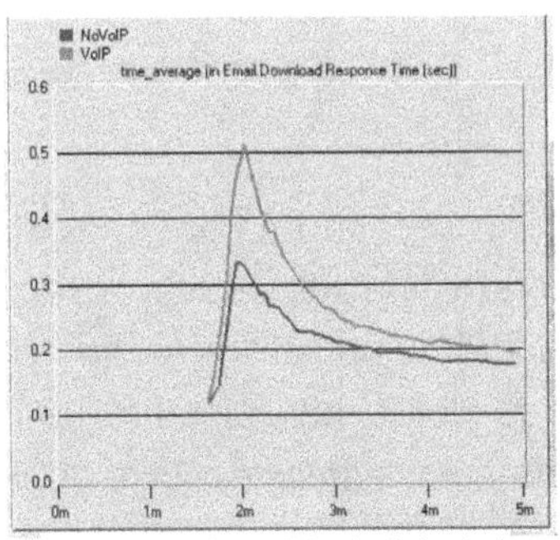

(a) Time average in e-mail downloads time (sec)

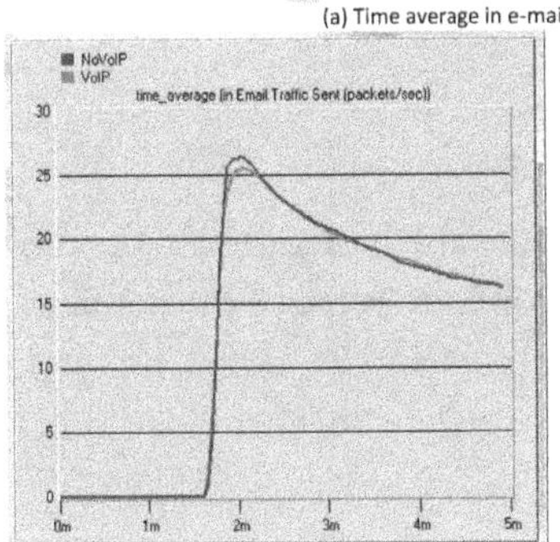

(b) Time average in e-mail traffic sent

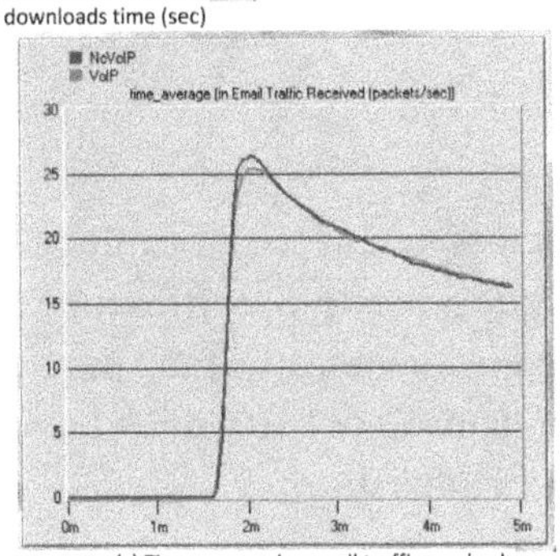

(c) Time average in e-mail traffic received

Figure 4. (a) Time average in FTP downloads response time; (b) Time average in FTP upload response time; (c) Time average in FTP traffic sent (Pac/sec) received (Pac/Sec); (d) Time Average in FTP traffic

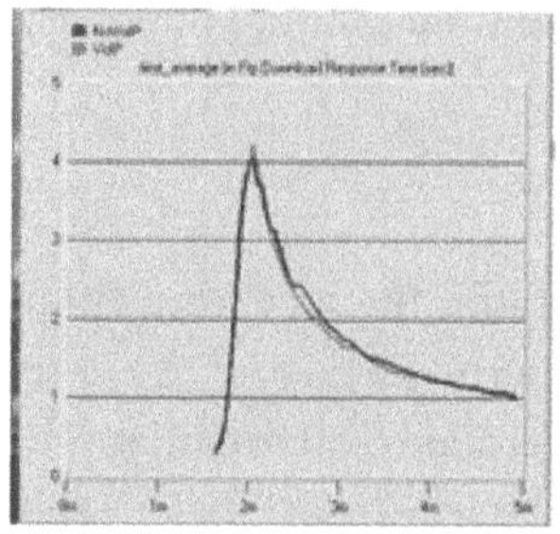

(a) Time average in FTP downloads response time (second)

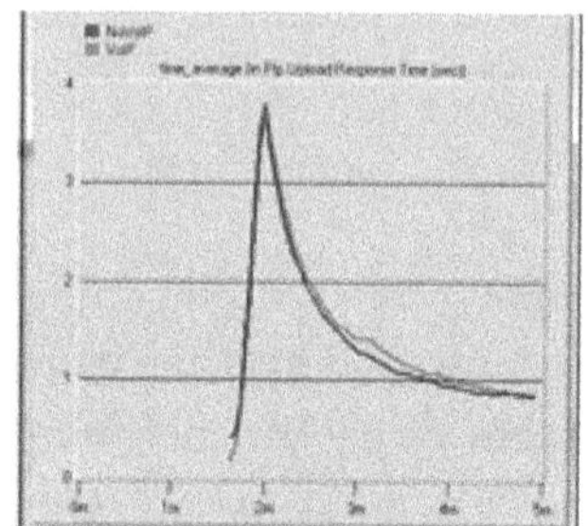

(b) Time average in FTP upload response time (second)

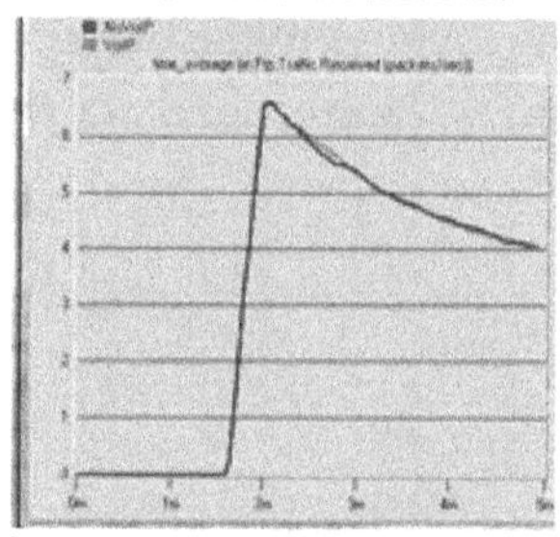

(c) Time average in FTP traffic sent (Pac/sec) received (Pac/sec)

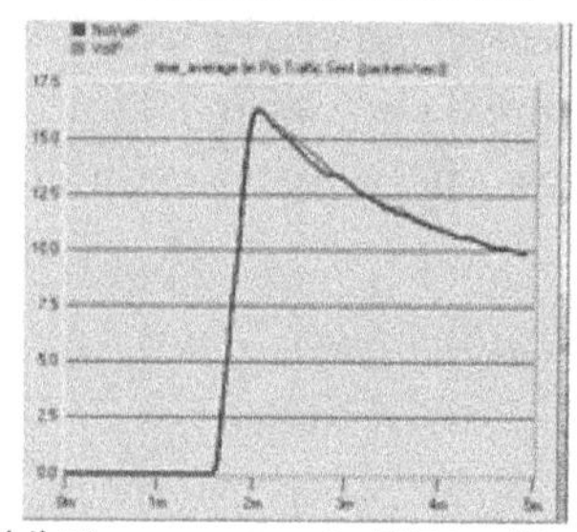

(d) Time average in FTP traffic

FTP

Average number of packets per second forwarded to all FTP applications by the transport layers in the network. Average number of packets per second submitted to the transport layers by all FTP applications in the network. The figure 4 below shows the time it takes to download and upload a file from/to the server starting from the time the user sends a get request/receive ACK; and the average traffic departure and arrival.

HTTP

The time it takes to retrieve an entire HTML page including all-lined objects is as shown in figure 5 below. Specifies time required to retrieve the entire page with all the contained inline objects. If the page contains a video that is not preloaded (i.e., streamed on-demand or live video), then the retrieval of that video is not taken into account for this statistic.

Figure 5. Time average in HTTP Page response time (sec)

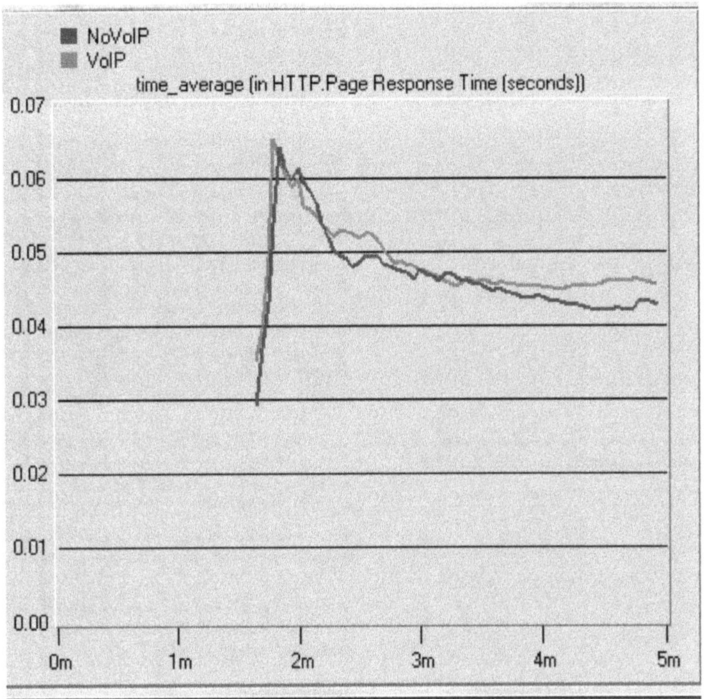

Time average in HTTP Page response time (sec)

FUTURE RESEARCH DIRECTIONS

New Trends in Management Information System

There are three interrelated changes in the technology area according to Laudon and Laudon, (2014), these are:

1. The emerging mobile digital platform,
2. The growing business use of "big data," and
3. The growth in "cloud computing," where more and more business software runs over the Internet.

Table 2. New trends in MIS

CHANGE	BUSINESS IMPACT
TECHNOLOGY	
Cloud computing platform emerges as a major business area of innovation	A flexible collection of computers on the Internet begins to perform tasks traditionally performed on corporate computers. Major business applications are delivered online as an Internet service (Software as a Service, or SaaS).
Big data	Businesses look for insights from huge volumes of data from Web traffic, e-mail messages, social media content, and machines (sensors) that require new data management tools to capture, store, and analyze.
A mobile digital platform emerges to compete with the PC as a business system	The Apple iPhone and Android mobile devices are able to download hundreds of thousands of applications to support collaboration, location-based services, and communication with colleagues. Small tablet computers, including the iPad, Google Nexus, and Kindle Fire, challenge conventional laptops as platforms for consumer and corporate computing.
MANAGEMENT	
Managers adopt online collaboration and social networking software to improve coordination, collaboration, and knowledge sharing	Google Apps, Google Sites, Microsoft Windows SharePoint Services, and IBM Lotus Connections are used by over 100 million business professionals worldwide to support blogs, project management, online meetings, personal profiles, social bookmarks, and online communities.
Business intelligence applications accelerate	More powerful data analytics and interactive dashboards provide real-time performance information to managers to enhance decision making.
Virtual meetings proliferate	Managers adopt telepresence videoconferencing and Web conferencing technologies to reduce travel time, and cost, while improving collaboration and decision making.
ORGANIZATIONS	
Social business	Businesses use social networking platforms, including Facebook, Twitter, and internal corporate social tools, to deepen interactions with employees, customers, and suppliers. Employees use blogs, wikis, e-mail texting, and messaging to interact in online communities.
Telework gains momentum in the workplace	The Internet, wireless laptops, smartphones, and tablet computers make it possible for growing numbers of people to work away from the traditional office. Fifty-five percent of U.S. businesses have some form of remote work program.
Co-creation of business value	Sources of business value shift from products to solutions and experiences, and from internal sources to networks of suppliers and collaboration with customers. Supply chains and product development become more global and collaborative; customer interactions help firms define new products and services.

Source: Laudon and Laudon, (2014)

Source: Laudon and Laudon, (2014)

CONCLUSION

The modelled network which will serve as an extension of the Nigerian University System Management Portal can be utilized within the university, for the diffusion and management of the information required by NUSMAP. The simulation results indicate that the system if implemented will really improve the service performance and resource utilization of NUSMAP. Hence, it contributes to the statement that the Nigerian University will now go paperless.

REFERENCES

Cisco Networking Academy. (2010). *CCNA Exploration Course Booklet- Network Fundamentals Version 4.0*. Indianapolis, IN: Cisco Press.

Cronin, B. (2001). Knowledge management, organizational culture and Anglo-American higher Education. Journal of Information Science, 27(3), 129-137. doi:10.1177/016555150102700302

Daigle, S. L., & Cuocco, P. M. (2002). Portal Technology Opportunities, Obstacles, and Options: A View from the California State University. In *Web Portals and Higher Education, Technologies to Make IT Personal* (pp. 109-123). Boulder, CO: Educause. Available at: http://www.educause.edu/ir/library/html/pub5006.asp

Daoleng, G., Oyerinde, O., & Vem, S. (n.d.). *Towards a Pleasurable University Experience for UniJos Students*. Academic Press.

Design Evaluation of Some Nigerian University Portals: A Programmers Point of View. (2010). *GESJ: Computer Science and Telecommunications, 5*(28).

Guodong, Z., & Zhongjiao, J. (2010). From e-campus to e-learning: An overview of ICT applications in Chinese higher education. *British Journal of Educational Technology, 41*(4), 574–581. doi:10.1111/j.1467-8535.2010.01085.x

Guodong, Z., & Zhongjiao, J. (2010). From e-campus to e-learning: An overview of ICT applications in Chinese higher education. *British Journal of Educational Technology, 41*(4), 574–581.

Ise, O. A. (2014). Towards a Unified University Information System: Bridging the Gap of Data Interoperability. *American Journal of Software Engineering*, 2(2), 26–32. doi:10.12691/ajse-2-2-3

Juels, A. (2006). RFID Security and Privacy: A Research Survey. IEEE Journal on Selected Areas in Communications, 24(2), 381-394. doi:10.1109/JSAC.2005.861395

Lan, R. (2012). Design and Implementation of IT Service Management System of College of University Campus Network. *Proceedings of the 7th International Conference on Computer Science and Education (ICCSE)*, 299 – 304.

Laudon, K. C., & Laudon, J. P. (2014). *Management Information Systems: Managing the Digital Firm* (13th ed.). Pearson Education Limited.

Li, F., & Lei, H. (2005). *The construction of e campus*. Beijing: Educational Technology Institution of Tsinghua University.

Li, P. (2014). College Campus Network Management Information System Research and Implementation. Frontiers of Manufacturing and Design Science IV. *Applied Mechanics and Materials*, *496-500*, 2265–2268. doi:10.4028/www.scientific.net/AMM.496-500.2265

Lianzhi, G., Guangming, H., & Rongshen, W. (2010). Design and Performance Research of 10 Gigabit Campus Network. *Proceedings of the 2nd International Conference on Information Science and Engineering*, 4488 – 4491.

Mader, M. (2012). Monitoring networking between higher education institutions and regular actors. *Journal of Cleaner Production, 49*, 105-113. Retrieved from www.elsevier.com/locate/jclepr

Muhammad, A. S., & Idris, I. (2010). Design Evaluation of Some Nigerian University Portals: A Programmers Point of View. *GESJ: Computer Science and Telecommunications, 5*(28).

Olsen, F. (2002). The Power of Portals. *The Chronicle of Higher Education*, *48*(48), A32–A34.

Paul, A. (n.d.). Nigerian University System Management Portal (NUSMAP). *User Guide. Academic Press.*

Quang, L., Bio, L., Shurong, H., & Amei, C. (2012). Design and Exploitation of Integrated Management System in University Laboratories. *Proceedings of the 2nd International Conference on Consumer Electronics, Communications and Networks*, 962 – 965.

Security Analysis on China Campus Network and Construction on Network Security System. (2011, November). *Journal of Convergence Information Technology*, *6*(11). doi:10.4156/jcit.vol6.issue11.19

Serova, E. (2013). The Role of Agent Based Modelling in the Design of Management Decision Processes. *The Electronic Journal Information Systems Evaluation, 16*(1), 71-80. Available online at www.ejise.com

Sethi, A. S., & Hnatyshyn, V. Y. (2013). *The Practical OPNET Users Guide for Computer Network Simulation*. Boca Raton, FL: CRS Press.

Stamatović, M., & Kurij, K. (2003). Introducion to Strategic Managemet. Savez in enjera i tehni ara Srbije – Centar za razvoj, Belgrade.

Tao, M., Shaoqian, W., Minglian, L., & Baozhu, W. (2012). The Research on Strategy of Building Campus Network Security Based on University Management. *Proceedings of the 2012 International Conference on Mechanical and Electrical Engineering*, 142 – 147. Available online at www.sciencedirect.com

Tao, X., Jia, C., & Yang, C. (2011). Security Analysis on China Campus Network and Construction on Network Security System. *Journal of Convergence Information Technology*, *6*(11). doi:10.4156/jcit.vol6.issue11.19

The Nigerian University Commission. (n.d.). Retrieved from www.onlinenigeria.com

Vanguard Newspaper. (2013). *NUC. Nigerian Varsities go paperless.* Retrieved from www.vanguardngr.com

Wei, W., Shengzhong, Y., & Hong, H. (2010). Design of Portal-Based Uniform Identity Authentication System in Campus Network. *Proceedings of the International Conference on Multimedia Communications*, 112 – 115.

Welcome to NUSMAP! (n.d.). Retrieved from https://nusmap.nucdp.edu.ng/institution_login.aspx

Xie, S. (2011). Planning, Designing and Building Large-Scale Network at Campus. *Proceedings of the 3rd International Conference on Computer Research and Development*, 495 – 498.

Yang, L. (2012). Campus Network Group Design Based on Cloud Computing. *Proceedings of the 7th International Conference on Computer Science and Education (ICCSE)*.

Youssef, S. (2013). *Network Modelling and Simulation Lecture Notes*. Anglia Ruskin University. (Unpublished)

Chapter 11
Information Systems Governance:
The Case of the Largest Companies in Portugal

Almiro de Oliveira
Portuguese Catholic University, Portugal

Pedro Fernandes Anunciação
Polytechnic Institute of Setubal, Portugal

ABSTRACT

The complexity of the environment and economical operation, tightly integrated with information and communication technologies, have challenged the management to adopt new paradigms and new approaches associated with new operating models. Internet of things, cloud computing, governance, and urbanism are some examples of new paradigms and new approaches in the area of information systems, which highlight the information as a basic resource for economic activity and justify the need to ensure appropriately the functions of production, storage, and distribution insofar as of its quality and availability depends on the effectiveness of corporate governance. This chapter, carried out by the European Club for Information Systems Governance in 2011 and 2012, provides evidence about the governance practices adopted in the area of information systems by large economic organizations in Portugal.

DOI: 10.4018/978-1-5225-5393-9.ch011

INTRODUCTION

Information and communication technologies (ICT) have assumed an increasingly important role in the development of economic activities and support for organizational activities. Economic activities are strongly dependent on ICT and they play a conditioning role in the respective management options. Through them, managers seek to improve levels of organizational efficiency and effectiveness, as well as levels of knowledge. However, organizations are simultaneously confronted with increments of organizational complexity resulting from new economic and commercial dynamics that are established supported in more interactive systems of technological characteristics.

Expressions like cloud computing, big data; information systems project management; organizational impacts; sustainability, networks privacy, ethics, return on investment; supply chain, business analytics, enterprise systems, ICT platforms, Chief Information Officer strategy, economic focus on technologies, ICT investments and associated costs, payback, security of Information Systems (IS), among other aspects, highlight the doubts associated with these issues and, consequently, the dimensions of Information Systems Governance in economic organizations (Pearlson & Saunders, 2013). Questions such as the economic value gained or the gains in competitiveness achieved through IS/ICT are examples that managers are currently facing. The answer to these and other associated questions passes through the value obtained with the main current economic resource, the information. Understanding the central role of information in the current context of society and the economy, known as the Information Society, is often hampered by the absence of an architectural framework in economic organizations.

OECD (2017) highlights some central recommendations to Government responsibilities, considering the global trends in the context of the information society challenges:

- What are the latest developments in government innovation? The recommendations for Governments are:
  - Signal innovation as a priority;
  - Enable connections across and beyond government;
  - Promote trust through transparency and responsiveness;
  - Forge partnerships with all relevant players;
- Human and machine: pairing human knowledge with innovative tools. The key recommendations are:
  - Manage data as an asset for many uses and users;
  - Open data to fuel innovation;

    - Develop open checks and balances;
    - Integrate resilience in system design;
- Zoom in or zoom out: scaling government. The key recommendations are:
    - Provide a common ground for collaboration;
    - Build shared approaches to encourage innovation;
    - Be a willing and responsive partner;
    - Build trust through transparency;
- Citizens as experts: redefining citizen-government bounderies. The key recommendations are:
    - Provide a common ground for collaboration;
    - Develop government-wide engagement strategies;
    - Arm public employees and citizens with tools to connect and establish dialogue;
    - Build evaluation into the innovation process;
    - Take feedback into account and reconnect with citizens;
- Mass or personalized services: the next generation of services delivery. The key recommendations are:
    - Clarify rules and regulations;
    - Promote interaction among civil servants;
    - Catalogue data comprehensively;
    - Be transparent about data collection and use;
    - Engage partners with shared values
- Experimental government: small bets with big potencial. The key recommendations are:
    - Provide empowerment and space for innovation and experimentation;
    - Ensure the system is flexible;
    - Build the institutional infrastructure to scale-up successes;
    - Consider ethics protocols for experimentation;
- Breaking the norms: rethinking the machinery of government. The key recommendations are:
    - Do not accept the system as a given
    - Undertake systems analysis through an innovation lens;
    - Invest in human capacity;
    - Encourage cross-government networks.

Only an architectonic or even urbanistic framework makes perceptible the usefulness and value of information as "raw material" for management, and "intelligible" the system and the information technologies associated with the respective treatment.

In this context of the Information Society, the balance between the social, economic and technological factors inherent in the organizational mission and the control of the complexity and turbulence associated with the development of organizational activities in the competitive context are assumed as the prime conditions for the development of profit and nonprofit organizations. Only through reference to the set of resources and associated factors will it be possible to understand the breadth and depth of Information Systems.

The current economic time has extremely short production and availability cycles, providing increasingly smaller "windows of opportunity", which increases the difficulties of optimizing IS/ICT management practices. The organizational environment in this area is also conducive to some difficulties and some confusion, not only in relation to the objectives to be attained or the underestimation of the importance that IS/ICT have in the profit and nonprofit organizations (Oliveira, 2010) but even about the concepts of IS and ICT itself (Oliveira, 2009).

The pressure of technological innovations on economic organizations and the commercial power of "constraint" of the respective suppliers contribute to aggravate the traditional difficulties of framing, understanding and managing the complexity associated with Information Systems. This pressure has led to strategic decisions by Top Management of delegation in external organizations the responsible for the functions that are inherently associated with it.

Considering the Information Systems essential to the functioning of economic organizations and assuming them to be strategically relevant in their development, it becomes evident the responsibility of Top Management in this field. According Pearlson & Saunders (2013), the reasons why business managers should participate in information systems decisions are the following:

- IS must be managed as a critical resource,
- IS enable change in the way people work together,
- IS are part of almost every aspect of business,
- IS enable or inhibit business opportunities and new strategies, and
- IS can be used to combat business challenges from competitors.

In this sense, it will be with propriety that it can be considered that these are functions of Governance, whose scope goes beyond the traditional scope of IS/ICT management. The concept of IS governance has a dimension that has not always been easy to understand and achieve. The reason for this, is due to the fact that the management of IS/ICT is often poorly understood in relation to the essential responsibilities and competences to an organizational and functional evaluation of the value of IS/ICT, and their role in other organizational areas, in particular as regards its decision-making capacity and authority.

The functions traditionally associated with the IS area have not always been visible, clearly and unequivocally assumed among professionals who have authority and responsibility in this area. Not always:

- Is perceptible who is responsible or who has authority over IS/ICT;
- Is evident and assumed the power and dependence of ICT providers, often referred to as partners;
- The objectives set out, where they exist, are clear and acceptable for the IS.

Similarly, we could also add that often, not always:

- The costs and income derived from the use of IS/ICT are evaluated;
- IT insertion projects in organizations are managed with the same rigorous management requirements that often apply to other investments in other organizational areas;
- The fundamental performances inherent to the acquisitions and allocations of resources for the design and use of IS/ICT are controlled, disregarding the economic calculation and rigor of the investment analysis.

The IS must capture and not undervalue the interests, wants and objectives of the various organizational stakeholders and, in this sense, must be perfected within the vision and the organizational objectives, and should be economically defensible. Knowing that all organizations are information based, that there is no organizational functioning without IS and that there is no management without Information, it becomes evident that policies associated with IS have to be a competence of Top Management.

Integrating IS a set of resources (people, data and information, hardware and software) that, in an interrelated way (organization and rules) aim at the achievement of a certain purpose (timely information, quality and in adequate quantities, in the first instance, in order to support decision-making at second instance), the need to adopt an IS Governance logic is much more urgent and profound than the traditionally ICT only dimension. This dimension of IT Governance, which is currently so much addressed, calls for a segmented view of the IS concept, focusing only on a restricted and restrictive part of it. Applying the concept of Governance only in this sense corresponds to a strongly conditioning and penalizing limitation of the wealth, value and role of IS in relation to the development of organizational activities. Therefore, secondarily to this theme means assuming real and opportunity costs that are difficult to justify in the short and medium term by Top Management of organizations and stakeholders.

CONCEPT, SCOPE, AND DEPTH OF THE THEME

Very often we confuse the governance of information systems and the computer systems. It is true, the words are neighbours. But they cover very different realities for the information system of a company can't be identified with its computer system. This fuzziness is the source of confusion. Indeed, the mechanisms used are not the same and the consequences are different. To appreciate this difference is sufficient to recall that in an enterprise computer system costs are about 1 to 2% of revenues while the cost of the information system is about 15 to 30% of the turnover. We are in a ratio of 1 to 10, more (ISGec, 2011).

The IS integrate a systemic set of physical, logical, human, and procedural/organizational elements (people, hardware, software, communication networks and data and information resources), which require clear and objective rules of organization and relationship, whose purpose is to collection, production, provision, storage and distribution of information (Morais & Carvalho, 2000) (Bravo, 2000) (Zwass, 1998) (O`Brien, 1996). Its objectives are to support the corresponding operations, the interactions between the organization and its environment, support management functions and decision making, facilitate control and follow-up of the organization's development, among others. These are objectives within the responsibilities of the Top Management. Some questions that can help frame this responsibility are as follows: who is responsible for the decision to invest in IS/ICT? Who should be responsible for organizational differentiation and competitiveness? Who should be responsible for the efficiency and effectiveness of organizational activities? These and other questions should make us reflect on the lack of responsibility in this context, there has been among the top managers in relation to IS.

The breadth and depth of the factors related to these and other questions highlight the wide diversity of activities and responsibilities associated with IS Governance, such as those related to the following domains (ISGec, 2010):

- Investments,
- Centralization, decentralization, empowerment,
- Human resources,
- Partnerships in the productive process,
- Level of integration,
- Innovation, research & development,
- Differentiation and competitiveness,
- Internal marketing of available solutions,
- Information distribution & research,

- Paperless Office,
- Security,
- **Economics:** Costing, overheads, charge back, ...

It is the assumption of information as a fundamental resource of economic activity and its configuration as a structuring element of management and organizational cohesion, which justifies the need to ensure the proper form of the system or systems required for its production, storage and distribution (Oliveira, 1999; Oliveira, 1996) insofar as of its quality and availability depends the effectiveness of Corporate Governance.

For all that has just been exposed, it becomes evident the need and relevance of the existence of specific activities related to making policy and strategic decisions about the IS and above all in relation to the vitality of its compliance with the Corporate Governance. It is the coherence between the policies and strategies defined in the IS and its compatibility with the lines identified for Corporate Governance that depends on performance and organizational development.

Governance also presupposes responsibility for the management of IS, insofar as it is important to be able to operationalization of the policies and strategies defined. The phenomenological complexity that traditionally characterizes the IS, resulting, among other things, from the great variety and value of the resources involved (human, physical, logical, communications, consumables,...) and from the fact that any employee of the company is a consumer and producer of information, integrating and participating in a diversity of flows, emphasizes the central role that IS can have as dynamic or conditioning elements of competitiveness and organizational sustainability.

For all these reasons, the responsibility of the IS can not and should not be secondary or subaltern to the highest responsibility of economic organizations or other activities or management functions. In this area, information and management correspond to two sides of the same coin, and therefore cannot be decoupled.

IS Governance (Legrenzi & Salzman, 2012; ISGec, 2010) encompasses all the activities related to Political and Strategic decision making on IS and its compatibility with Corporate Governance). For Hubert (2014) we can understand governance as the authoritative policy-making and implementation about collective problems and interests. Information Governance, under the responsibility of the President of the Institution, should aim for:

- The election and clarification of the objectives to be achieved with investments in IS (Oliveira, 2004);
- The organization model of IS and their compatibility with the Macro Structure of the Institution;

- The definition and characterization of the IS Management Model at the various levels (operational, tactical and strategic);
- The definition and characterization of the solutions of IS Urbanism and Architecture: objectives, morphology, functionalities, levels of integration of the applications, relations between users and stakeholders (Anunciação & Zorrinho, 2006; Anunciação, 2004; Anunciação, 1997);
- The design, development and control of the implementation process and the performances of the IS;
- The definition of Organization forms and exploration models to be adopted in Architecture and IS Engineering.

Because this theme should provide an analytical framework for raising the awareness of management regarding the importance of the discussion of activities associated with Information Systems, the Information Systems Governance European Club decided to analyze the practices adopted by the largest companies, Public Administration and Banking and Insurance in Portugal.

STUDIES AND METHODOLOGY ADOPTED

Within the activities of the Information Systems Governance European Club – Portugal, two studies were developed. The first study took place in 2011 and aimed to analyze the governance practices adopted by the economic organizations in the field of information systems in relation to 2010. The second study was conducted in 2012 and aimed to analyze these practices for 2011. Both studies included the largest Companies, Administration and Public Organizations, Banking and Insurance in Portugal.

To this end, we designed a questionnaire in which he addressed four areas intrinsic to the concept of governance of the SI, namely:

- Information System Management,
- Organizational Model,
- Analysis and Decision on investments in Information Systems, and
- Ethic.

With regard to Information System Management, the existence of Information Technologies in support of organizational activities is not enough for the company to solve its problems of information processing (Domínguez & Garrido, 2010). Information, technologies and activities should be conveniently integrated with the other elements, such as human resources, procedures and economic objectives, within an organizational framework. This integration requires management skills in the architecture of Information Systems, and, in terms of technologies, also include technical and business knowledge.

In this first area of analysis, we tried to verify, through 15 questions, the following aspects considered essential for the management of Information Systems:

- The existence of a budget to assess the costs associated with the IS;
- The weight of these costs relative to the total costs of the organization;
- The average evolution over the last three years;
- The nature of the costs;
- The existence of policies and practices for internal allocation of IS costs for services rendered to other departments;
- The nature of the value logic associated with the IS area (such as cost center or profit center);
- A systematic evaluation of productivity, efficiency and effectiveness in relation to the IS and indicators adopted;
- The existence of quality assessment practices, variables used and responsibility in their evaluation;
- The existence of practices for the evaluation of the systematic control of SI performance, as well as the identification of responsibility for this evaluation;
- The performance of audits and their frequency.

The second domain of analysis included the Organizational Model. One of the central objectives of the IS is to make information available to the various organizational areas, on the activities carried out, in order to analyze the fulfillment of the company's objectives, as well as the support to the accomplishment and coordination of the respective activities. These activities, carried out by Departments or Services, presuppose specific information needs according to the requirements underlying the specificity of the various tasks that integrate them.

The existence of an organizational function in Information Systems derives, among other aspects:

- The relevance of its role in the competitiveness of enterprises;
- Its indispensability in the decision-making process;
- The comprehensiveness and coverage of all organizational areas;
- The integration, horizontally and vertically, of information flows in organizations;
- The need for integration and functional cohesion of the different areas within organizations.

The organizational function associated with the Information Systems is responsible for the promotion, coordination and collaboration with the aim of articulating the activities and procedures for optimizing the functioning of information systems and technologies, namely, in the capture, architecture, validation, selection, manipulation, processing, preservation, storage and communication of information. In addition, it also assumes responsibility for the acquisition and management of technologies by selecting and making available hardware and software appropriate to the needs of system users, supporting policy and strategy formulation, planning, decisions. Its noblest function is thus associated with architecture, with responsibility for ensuring the compatibility of the data format used by the various organizational departments and the suitability of technological resources for the identified treatment needs.

In this second area of analysis, we tried to assess, through 7 questions, the following aspects associated with the Organizational Model:

- The existence of a management function of Information System in the organizational macro-structure, its level, functional content and to whom it reports its responsible;
- The existence of an architecture model for the IS (objectives, morphology, functionalities, among others), the degree of intervention of the administration in this architecture and the levels contemplated.

The third area of study focused on the Analysis and Decision on Investments in IS. The problem of the insertion of information and communication systems and technologies in the organizational context is reflected in the variety of resources to be used and in the complexity of tasks and specialized activities to be developed, which cannot be left to the empiricism of performance or voluntarism of the players, not even the willingness and interests of the suppliers of equipment or services (Oliveira, 2004). Such recognition raises the need to establish a critical path, a schedule of logical activities, rationally linked according to the investment objective and, inexorably, the use of a methodology.

In this study, we tried to assess, through 5 questions, the following nuclear aspects related to the analysis and decision on investments in IS:

- The existence of quantified and specific objectives associated with investments in IS, and their degree of accomplishment;
- The practice of the economic-financial analysis associated with the investment, as well as the identification of the indicators adopted.

The last area of analysis focused on Ethics. The relevance of this issue stems from the fact that, in particular with regard to the commercial relations established between customers and suppliers, these may appear asymmetric due to the specific nature of the activities carried out, the nature and urgency of the need and the different domain of knowledge and power detained by the various parties (Anunciação, 2014). The lack of knowledge and technical expertise to cope with the complexity and demands of economic and organizational challenges leads many organizations to seek, in the subcontracting of activities associated with IS, a way to solve the problems they face in this field.

In this context, we have tried to identify, through 4 questions, existing practices regarding the following aspects:

- Who makes the information needs explicit;
- Who makes explicit the needs of software and hardware;
- Who provides training in the field of IS;
- What is the nature of the relationship between the supplier and the company.

As mentioned previously, the universe studied included the largest companies, Administration and Public Organizations, and Banking and Insurance, and 223 entities were surveyed in the first study and, in the second study, 231.

The survey was directed to the senior managers of the organizations, namely, Presidents of the Boards of Directors and General Directors, having clearly identified the purpose of the study and the entity responsible for it. In this sense, two documents prepared by ISGec were also sent with the survey, namely 'European Manifesto for Governance of Information Systems' (ISGec, 2009) and 'Governance of Information Systems - Why?' (ISGec, 2010; Oliveira, 2009), in order to raise the analysis and discussion of these issues at the highest level of organizations.

In the specific case of the 2nd investigation, we went a little further. Having found, through the answers to the 1st survey, some confusion as to the concepts present in it, it was decided to make them explicit in the cover letter with a view to their uniformity in the answers given. The concepts adopted, using a short glossary, was as follows:

- **Information System Architecture:** Integrated and harmonious design of a solution for the Information System in support of Management and Business;
- **Governance of Information Systems:** A set of activities related to Political and Strategic decision-making related to the Information System and its compatibility with Corporate Governance;
- **Information System:** Set of elements (physical, logical, human and procedural/organizational) that, through appropriate relationship rules and previously defined purposes, aim at the production and availability of Information;

- **Computer System:** Automated or automated part of the Information System;
- **Information and Communication Technologies:** A set of technological devices (physical and logical) that integrate the computer system and allow the collection, processing, storage and distribution of information.

RESULTS OF THE STUDIES

In both studies two calls were made whose overall distribution is shown in Table 1.

Verifying the validity of the sample to carry out the study, appeared in a first level of analysis, the interrogation of the reduced number of replies. Faced with this reality, it is justified a first reflection regarding any and / or real reasons that could be the source of this. Thus, it will be legitimate for us to question whether this reality will be a:

- The lack of time with which management is confronted daily?
- Underestimation of IS governance issues?
- The lack of relevance of the IS themes?
- The complexity of these themes?
- The inopportuneness of the inquiry?
- Ignorance of governance issues within the organization itself?

The results for each of the groups and questions raised in the survey were as follows:

Table 1. Summary of studies carried out

Sector	1st Study – 2011			2nd Study – 2012		
	Number of Surveys	**Number of Replies**	**%**	**Number of Surveys**	**Number of Replies**	**%**
Largest companies	102	10	9,8	100	27	27
Administration and public entities	89	31	34,8	103	45	43,7
Banking and insurance	32	3	9,4	28	9	32,1
Unidentified	---	2	---	---	---	---
Total	223	46	20,6	231	81	35,1

1. Information System Management

1. **Budget for SI Costs:** It is found in both years that almost all organizations claim to have a budget for SI costs, as evidenced in Table 2.
2. **The Weight of the IS Costs of the Total Costs of the Company:** For the companies that responded affirmatively, as regards the existence of a budget for the costs of the IS, it is found in both years that most of the companies surveyed refer to a weight ratio of less than 5%, as shown in Table 3.
3. **Average Annual Growth in the Last Three Years:** It is evident, as can be seen in Table 3, a reduction, both in 2011 and 2012, of the overall costs of IS in most companies.
4. **The Nature of Costs:** It can be seen from Table 5 that the most significant factors in the cost structure associated with IS are equipment (acquisition, depreciation, maintenance, etc.) and human resources. However, consumables and licenses (operating systems, applications, ...) are also of importance. Generally, between 2011 and 2012, they all increase, except for the costs associated with human resources, which remain practically unchanged.

The organizations surveyed indicated that they considered other types of costs, mentioned the following: Supplies and External Services, Consulting, Outsourcing, Services and Software Development, Maintenance, among others.

Table 2. Budget for SI costs

	1st Study- 2011 -	2nd Study- 2012 -
Yes	95,7%	91,3%
No	4,3%	6,2%
Do not know / Do not respond	0,0%	2,5%

Table 3. Weight of IS costs in the total costs of the company

	1st Study- 2011 -	2nd Study- 2012 -
Lower than 5%	65,9%	64,8%
Between 5% and 10%	20,4%	16,2%
Between 10% and 15%	9,1%	8,1%
Greater than 15%	2,3%	6,8%
Do not know / Do not respond	2,3%	4,1%

Table 4. Average annual evolution of the last three years

	1st Study- 2011 -	2nd Study- 2012 -
Descending	54,5%	52,7%
Growing less than 5%	15,9%	12,1%
Growing by more than 5%	13,6%	14,9%
Growing between 5% and 10%	6,8%	8,1%
Growing between 10% and 15%	4,6%	1,4%
Growing by more than 15%	4,6%	5,4%

Table 5. Nature of SI costs

	1st Study- 2011 -	2nd Study- 2012 -
Equipment (Acquisition, depreciation, maintenance, ...)	91,1%	97,3%
Human Resources	95,5%	95,9%
Licenses (Operating Systems, applications, ...)	53,3%	66,2%
Communications	62,2%	60,8%
Consumables	71,1%	86,5%
Others	40,0%	35,1%
Do not know / Do not respond	2,2%	0,0%

5. **Policies and Practices for Internal Allocation of IS Costs to Other Departments:** As regards the existence of policies and practices for internal allocation of IS costs for services rendered to other departments, as shown in Table 6, it is noted that the majority, in 2011, refers to the lack of such practices. However, in 2012 there is a reversal of the trend identified in 2011, in which the majority refers to the imputation of SI costs to other departments.
6. **IS Area as Cost Center (CC) or Result Center (CR):** The answers to the question whether the IS area is considered as a cost center or results center show that most companies assume it as a cost center, it is possible to see in Table 7. However, a slight tendency change is noticeable.
7. **Performance Evaluation of Productivity, Efficiency and Effectiveness of IS:** In relation to the evaluation of productivity, performance, efficiency and effectiveness of IS, most companies assume that in 2011 this evaluation was not carried out. However, in 2012, a change of attitude in this area is evident, as shown in Table 8.

Table 6. Policies and practices for internal allocation of IS costs

	1st Study- 2011 -	2nd Study- 2012 -
Yes	34,8%	49,4%
No	63,0%	45,7%
Do not know / Do not respond	2,2%	4,9%

Table 7. IS area as Cost Center / Results Center

	1st Study- 2011 -	2nd Study- 2012 -
Cost Center (CC)	91,3%	87,6%
Result Center (CR)	4,3%	6,2%
CC + CR	2,2%	2,5%
Do not know / Do not respond	2,2%	3,7%

Table 8. Systematic evaluation of productivity performance, efficiency and efficacy of IS

	1st Study- 2011 -	2nd Study- 2012 -
Yes	34,8%	54,3%
No	63,0%	43,2%
Do not know / Do not respond	2,2%	2,5%

8. **Instruments Adopted in the Evaluation of the Performance of the Productivity, Efficiency and Effectiveness of the IS:** With respect to the instruments adopted the surveyed organizations, who answered Yes to the previous question, indicated Satisfaction Surveys, Service Levels, Performance Indicators, Uptime of systems and networks, Incidents in the applications, Key performance indicators (KPI), Quantity and degree of resolution of support interventions, IT Cost/Total Costs, Project performance, Operating costs, Response times, among others.
9. **IS Quality Assessment:** For IS quality assessment most companies assume that this assessment is carried out, although there is a decrease between 2011 and 2012, as we can be seen in Table 9.
10. **Variables Used in Quality Assessment:** Regarding the variables used in quality assessment, the surveyed organizations indicated the following:

Table 9. IS quality assessment

	1st Study- 2011 -	2nd Study- 2012 -
Yes	71,7%	58,0%
No	26,1%	38,3%
Do not know / Do not respond	2,2%	3,7%

Ability to respond to business changes, User satisfaction, Meeting deadlines and requirements, Service Level Agreement, System availability, Uptime of systems and networks, Incidents in applications, Information quality, Quality of services, among others.

11. **Appraiser of the Quality of the IS:** In relation to who evaluates the SI quality, the weight of the person in charge of the Business in this evaluation is prevailing, as can be seen in Table 10. However, it should be pointed out that in 2012 other entities than those mentioned assume a preponderance in the evaluation of the quality of the IS (12.8%). It should also be noted that in any of the years it`s evident a dispersion of the answers regarding this question.
12. **Existence of a Process to Control IS Performance:** Most companies report a systematic process of SI performance, as can be seen from Table 11.
13. **Responsible for Controlling the Performance of the IS:** The responsibility for this control of the performance of the IS, in relation to the surveyed organizations that responded Yes, is carried out according to the organizational specificity of these organizations. The organizational areas referenced for this control were: Department of Information Systems, Administration, Systems Administration, IT Governance Area, Executive Committee, IS Manager, Management Control, IT Office, Administration and Quality Committee, among others.
14. **Carrying Out Audits to the IS:** The importance of the audits expressed in the high percentage of affirmative answers is evident in any of the years under analysis, as can be seen in Table 12.
15. **Frequency of IS Audits:** The responses showed in the first survey a greater preponderance of audits without a defined period and, in the second survey, the annual audit as a practice mostly adopted by the organizations, as evidenced in Table 13.

In this first area of analysis, considering the results obtained, we can draw the following conclusions regarding the Management of Information Systems:

- Globally, the results show a weak acuity in the management practices of IS, even though there are some inconsistencies;

Table 10. Appraiser of the quality of the IS

	1st Study- 2011 -	2nd Study- 2012 -
Information Systems (IS)	5,9%	6,4%
Information Technology (IT)	2,9%	4,3%
Business	17,7%	10,6%
Administration	5,9%	4,3%
IS + IT	2,9%	6,4%
IS + Business	5,9%	
IS + Administration	2,9%	6,4%
IS + Other		2,1%
IT + Administration	2,9%	2,1%
IT + Business		2,1%
IT + Other		2,1%
Business + Administration	2,9%	2,1%
Business + Other	2,9%	
Administration + Other	8,8%	6,4%
IS + Business + Other	2,9%	2,1%
IS + Administration + Other		2,1%
Business + Administration + Other	8,8%	
IS + IT + Business		6,4%
IS + Business + Administration		6,4%
IS + IT + Business + Administration	8,8%	4,3%
IS + IT + Business + Administration + Other	2,9%	
IT + Business + Administration + Other		2,1%
IS + IT + Administration + Other		2,1%
IS + IT + Business + Other		2,1%
IS + Business + Administration + Other		2,1%
Other	8,8%	12,8%
Do not know / Do not respond	5,9%	2,1%

Table 11. Process to control IS performance

	1st Study- 2011 -	2nd Study- 2012 -
Yes	67,4%	60,5%
No	32,6%	35,8%
Do not know / Do not respond	0,0%	3,7%

Table 12. Audits of the IS

	1st Study- 2011 -	2nd Study- 2012 -
Yes	82,6%	75,3%
No	17,4%	22,2%
Do not know / Do not respond	0,0%	2,5%

Table 13. Frequency of IS audits

	1st Study- 2011 -	2nd Study- 2012 -
Annual	31,6%	55,7%
No defined period	47,4%	31,1%
Annual + No defined period	2,6%	
Annual + When inconsistencies / incidents are detected	5,3%	6,6%
No defined period + When inconsistencies / incidents are detected	5,3%	3,3%
When inconsistencies or incidents are detected	7,8%	3,3%

- The budgetary dimension of IS management (95.7% in 2011 and 91.3% in 2012) is evident, but it is not apparent whether these decreasing costs reflect an increase in productivity, efficiency or effectiveness;
- There is a limited view of the IS area, when it is considered a Costs Center and not a Results Center, even if there is no imputation of the different nature of costs in a significant part of the surveyed organizations;
- This finding is reinforced, considering the data from 2011, whereby there is no evidence of efficiency, efficacy and productivity evaluation practices at the IS level (63%). However, 67.4% say that they systematically control IS performance, although 47.4% do so without a defined period;
- The evaluation of the IS quality assumes great importance (71.7%). However, despite the preponderance of those in charge of the business, IS and IT managers also assume the same importance. In addition, there is a great dispersion of responsible persons who participate in this evaluation of IS quality;
- Only 7.8% of surveyed organizations audit their systems when they detect inconsistencies.

2. Organizational Model

16. **Macro-Organizational Structure for IS Management:** The vast majority of organizations have a function for the management of information systems in their organizational macro-structure, as evidenced in Table 14.
17. **Level of the IS Management Function in the Macro-Organizational Structure:** The great majority of organizations in 2011 assume a division between the department and another that is not considered, being more predominant the Other. In 2012 the preponderance is the departmental level, although the option of a level other than those mentioned will still have a significant expression, as can be seen in Table 15.
18. **Functional Content of the IS Management Function:** The most obvious functional content is information systems in both survey results. However, the dispersion of responses to this question is evident, as can be seen in Table 16.
19. **Hierarchical Level of the SI Management Function:** Most companies, according to Table 17, indicate that the person in charge of the IS management function depends hierarchically on a manager at the top management level. There is a significant number reporting to the Chairman of the Board of Directors.
20. **Existence of an IS Architecture Model:** In the answers obtained and although most companies mention the existence of a model of the specification of the IS Architecture, with regard to the objectives, morphology, functionalities, level of integration of applications, relations between users and stakeholders,

Table 14. IS Management function in the Macro-Organizational Structure

	1st Study- 2011 -	2nd Study- 2012 -
Yes	91,4%	88,9%
No	4,3%	9,9%
Do not know / Do not respond	4,3%	1,2%

Table 15. Level of the IS Management function in the Macro-Organizational Structure

	1st Study- 2011 -	2nd Study- 2012 -
Department	37,9%	50,0%
Service	13,3%	9,7%
Other	44,4%	38,9%
Do not know / Do not respond	4,4%	1,4%

Table 16. Functional content of the IS Management function

	1st Study- 2011 -	2nd Study- 2012 -
Information system	44,4%	36,1%
Computer System	4,4%	8,3%
Information Technology	13,4%	12,5%
Information System + Computer System	2,2%	2,7%
Information System + Information Technologies	11,1%	5,6%
Information System + Other	2,2%	
Computer System + Other		1,4%
Computer System + Information Technologies		1,4%
Information Technology + Other		1,4%
Information System + Computer System + Information Technologies	13,4%	15,3%
Information System + Information Technologies + Other		1,4%
Information System + Computer System + Information Technologies + Other	6,7%	5,6%
Other	2,2%	8,3%

Table 17. Hierarchical level of the IS Management function

	1st Study- 2011 -	2nd Study- 2012 -
Chairman of the Board of Directors	24,4%	30,6%
Member of the Board of Directors	42,3%	41,7%
1st Line Manager	15,6%	15,3%
2nd Line Manager	2,2%	1,4%
Member of the Board of Directors + Other	2,2%	
Chairman of the Board of Directors + Member of the Board of Directors		1,4%
Member of the Board of Directors + 1st Line Manager		1,4%
Other	13,3%	8,2%

it can be pointed out that this majority is not expressive of the centrality of architecture in information systems, as can be seen in Table 18.

21. **Intervention Degree of the Administration in the IS Architecture:** The results present two extremes in the approach that the organizations make regarding the degree of intervention of the Administration in the conception of

Table 18. Existence of an IS architecture model

	1st Study- 2011 -	2nd Study- 2012 -
Yes	56,5%	60,5%
No	39,1%	37,0%
Do not know / Do not respond	4,4%	2,5%

the IS Architecture. In 2011, there is a participation of more than 50%, while in 2012 this participation is around 10%, as can be seen in Table 19.

22. **Levels Contemplated in the Definition of IS Architecture:** The results show that the levels considered in the definition of the IS architecture are business, information and technologies, as can be seen in Table 20.

In this second area of analysis, the conclusions that we can draw from the analysis of the results obtained on the Organizational Model are as follows:

Table 19. Intervention degree of the administration in the IS architecture

	1st Study- 2011 -	2nd Study- 2012 -
10%	25,0%	51,0%
20%	17,9%	22,4%
30%	17,9%	6,1%
40%	0,0%	4,1%
+ 50%	39,2%	16,4%

Table 20. Levels contemplated in the definition of IS architecture

	1st Study- 2011 -	2nd Study- 2012 -
Business, Information and Technologies	84,1%	83,7%
Physical Technologies only	0,0%	0,0%
Logical technologies only	0,0%	2,0%
Physical and logical technologies	9,1%	2,0%
Business only	0,0%	0,0%
Information only	0,0%	0,0%
Business and Information only	0,0%	
Business, Information and Technologies + Physical and logical technologies	4,5%	10,3%
Do not know / Do not respond	2,3%	2,0%

- The results indicate the existence of an organizational function associated with IS. However, it is clear that this function differs from the ones mentioned (44.4%), not having a direct hierarchical relationship with a member of the Board of Directors (42.5%) and the level.
- Although most refer to their functional content as IS (44.4%), there is some confusion about the concepts Information System, Computer System and Information Technology.
- The relevance of the architecture in IS is assumed by only half of the respondents (56.6%). However, in cases where it exists, there is some inconsistency in that the Business has a participation of 0.0% and Management more than 50% in the respective specification.
- The three levels contemplated in the architecture specification are: business, information and technologies.

3. Analysis and Decision on Investments in Information Systems

23. **Objectives of Investments in IS:** On the question of whether IS investments comply with quantified and specific objectives, most of the answers show a management attitude towards this, as can be seen in Table 21.
24. **Control Degree of the Achievement of IS Investment Objectives:** The results show that most of the surveyed organizations carry out a check on the objectives of investments made in IS, as evidenced in Table 20.
25. **Control Mechanisms for Investments in IS:** The degree control of the investments in Information Systems is made, according to the surveyed organizations, through: Management and control of the return of the investment, KPI`s, value of the investment + Timings, Business valuation, Performance evaluation and budget control, Budgets and quantified benefits, Indicators and targets, among others.
26. **Economic and Financial Analysis of Investments in IS:** The results show that most of the companies make a priori an economic and financial analysis

Table 21. Objectives of investments in IS

	1st Study- 2011 -	2nd Study- 2012 -
Yes	86,9%	80,2%
No	13,1%	17,3%
Do not know / Do not respond	0,0%	2,5%

Table 22. Control degree of IS investment objectives

	1st Study- 2011 -	2nd Study- 2012 -
Yes	95,0%	81,6%
No	5,0%	16,9%
Do not know / Do not respond	0,0%	1,5%

of the investment. However, it is noted that a significant number of companies do not use this management tool, as can be seen in Table 23.

27. **Indicators used in economic and Financial Analysis:** The main indicators used are the following: Return On Investment, Payback, Investment Costs vs. Savings Generated, Net Present Value of Investment/Budget, Risk, Cost-Efficiency, Cost-Benefit.

In this third area of analysis some of the conclusions that can be drawn from management practices in the field of analysis and decision on investments in IS are as follows:

- It is in the investments in IS that the relevance of the role and responsibility of the management emerges (86.9%);
- The degree of implementation (95.0%) of the investment objectives is controlled;
- However, only about 2/3 carry out an economic-financial analysis (69.6%).

4. Ethic

28. Explanation of Information needs – The results show that it is the owner of the business that makes explicit the information needs, as shown in Table 24.
29. **Explanation of Software and Hardware Requirements:** The results show that it is also the owner of the business that explains the software and hardware needs, as shown in Table 25.

Table 23. Economic and financial analysis of SI investments

	1st Study- 2011 -	2nd Study- 2012 -
Yes	69,6%	65,4%
No	30,4%	32,1%
Do not know / Do not respond	0,0%	2,5%

Table 24. Explanation of Information Needs

	1st Study- 2011 -	2nd Study- 2012 -
Provider	0,0%	2,5%
Company	97,8%	92,6%
Both	2,2%	3,7%
Do not know / Do not respond	0,0%	1,2%

Table 25. Explanation of Software and Hardware Requirements

	1st Study- 2011 -	2nd Study- 2012 -
Provider	4,4%	2,5%
Company	89,1%	87,7%
Both	6,5%	8,6%
Do not know / Do not respond	0,0%	1,2%

30. **Training in the Field of IS:** The results show a dispersion of the answers between the different hypotheses. However, they point out that this responsibility, as can be seen from Table 26, is shared between suppliers, the company itself and the schools / training centers.
31. **Supplier/Company Relationship:** The results show that most companies assume that the relationship with suppliers is autonomous, as can be seen from Table 27.

Table 26. Who conducts training in IS

	1st Study- 2011 -	2nd Study- 2012 -
Provider	8,7%	12,4%
Company	10,9%	17,3%
Schools / Training Centers	15,2%	12,4%
Provider + Company	15,2%	16,1%
Provider + Schools / Training Centers	17,4%	7,4%
Company + Schools / Training Centers	10,9%	8,6%
Provider + Company + Schools / Training Centers	21,7%	24,8%

Table 27. The supplier/company relationship

	1st Study- 2011 -	2nd Study- 2012 -
Autonomy	69,6%	76,5%
Dependency	23,9%	16,0%
Partnership	2,2%	0,0%
Autonomy + Dependency	4,3%	5,0%

In this last field of analysis, Ethics, the conclusions that can be drawn on this point are as follows:

- Explanation of information, software and hardware needs is made by the reporting organizations;
- Most organizations share the training responsibilities with Suppliers and Training Centers / Centers;
- The surveyed organizations recognize sufficient knowledge for training in the area of IS;
- There is doubt about the real participation of companies in all stages of the cycle: identification of information needs, specification of software and hardware needs and training;
- About 2/3 of the surveyed organizations assume a relationship of autonomy with respect to suppliers, with only 2.2% considering having a partnership relationship.

GENERAL CONCLUSIONS

Considering that this study covers the largest Portuguese Companies, Public Administration and Banking and Insurance Companies, we consider that the way for IS Governance is still long, in so far as:

- There is evidence of some inconsistencies with regard to the principles and best practices in IS Governance;
- The adoption of budgetary logic in the management of IS overlaps with one of results, i.e. efficiency and effectiveness of solutions;
- The lack or absence of practices to evaluate efficiency, effectiveness and productivity, suggests that there are difficulties in the strategic framework of SI investments;

- The weak relevance of architecture as "cornerstone" is a conditioning factor in the management and devclopment of IS;
- On IS investments, although there is a quantification of objectives, the necessary economic and financial analysis is not carried out;
- There is a weak identification of the relationship between IS Governance and Corporate Governance.

REFERENCES

Anunciação, P. F. (1997). *Information Systems Urbanism.* CETOP Publishing. (in Portuguese)

Anunciação, P. F. (2004). Banking Information Systems – The example of a "Securities" subsystem. *Management Studies – Portuguese Journal of Management Studies*, *9*(1), 3 –51. (in Portuguese)

Anunciação, P. F. (2014). *Ethics, Sustainability and Information and Knowledge Society*. Lisbon: Chiado Editora. (in Portuguese)

Anunciação, P. F., & Zorrinho, C. (2006). *Organizational Urbanism - How Managing Technological Shock in Companies*. Lisbon: Sílabo Publishing. (in Portuguese)

Bravo, D. G. (2000). *Information Systems in the Enterprise – Concepts and Applications*. Pirámide Publishing. (in Spanish)

Hubert, L. (2014). *The Integrity of Governance – What It Is, What We Know, What Is Done, and Where to Go*. Palgrave Macmillan.

ISGec – Information System Governance European Club. (2009). *Information Systems Governance Manifest.* Retrieved from http://www.cegsi.org/index.php/qui-sommes-nous/o-que-e-o-cegsi

ISGec – Information System Governance European Club. (2010). *Why the Corporations are asking for an information systems governance?* Retrieved from http://www.cegsi.org/index.php/documents/telechargement-du-document-la-gouvernance-des-systemes-d-information-pourquoi/la-gouvernance-des-systemes-d-information-pourquoi

ISGec – Information System Governance European Club. (2011). *The Importance of the Information Systems Approach in the Governance of Organizations*. Retrieved from http://www.cegsi.org/index.php/documents/l-importance-de-l-approche-par-les-systemes-d-information/the-importance-of-the-information-systems-approach-for-governance-organizations (in French)

Legrenzi, C., & Salzman, C. (2012). *Les concepts de base de la Gouvernance d'entreprise, gouvernance informatique et gouvernance des systèmes d'information*. Retrieved from http://www.cegsi.org/index.php/documents/les-concepts-de-base-de-la-gouvernance/les-concepts-de-base-de-la-gouvernance-informatique-d-entreprise-des-systemes-d-information

Morais, P., & Carvalho, J. A. (2000). A Taxonomy of Computer Systems to Support the Development Process of Information Systems. [in Portuguese]. *Information Systems*, *13*, 7–29.

O'Brien, J. (1996). *Management Information Systems – Managing Information Technology in the Networked Enterprise*. IRWIN.

OECD. (2017). *Embracing Innovation in Government - Global Trends*. Retrieved from http://www.oecd.org/gov/innovative-government/embracing-innovation-in-government-global-trends.htm

Oliveira, A. (1996). The Potential Value of Information Systems. [in Portuguese]. *Management Studies*, *3*(1), 3–18.

Oliveira, A. (1999). The Importance of Information Systems for Industry [in Portuguese]. *Information Systems*, (11), 21–26.

Oliveira, A. (2004). *Analysis of the Investment in Systems and Technologies of the Information and the Communication*. Sílabo Publishing. (in Portuguese)

Oliveira, A. (2009). *Information & Information Systems – Facts, myths, mitifications, mystifications, dangerous half-truths & lack of common sense*. Refertelecom Publishing. (in Portuguese)

Oliveira, A. (2010). Governance of Information Systems – Why. ISGec Conference, Madrid, Spain.

Pearlson, K. E., & Saunders, C. S. (2013). *Managing and Using Information Systems – A Strategic Approach*. Hoboken, NJ: John Wiley & Sons.

Zwass, V. (1998). *Foundations of Information Systems*. McGraw-Hill.

Compilation of References

Aaker, D. A. (1991). *Managing Brand Equity*. New York: The Free Press.

Aaker, D. A. (1995). *Building Strong Brands*. New York: The Free Press.

Aaker, D. A. (1996). Measuring Brand Equity across Products and Markets. *California Management Review, 38*(3), 102–120. doi:10.2307/41165845

Aaker, J. (1997). Dimensions of Brand Personality. *JMR, Journal of Marketing Research, 34*(3), 347–356. doi:10.2307/3151897

Aberdeen Group. (2010, October 31). *SaaS ERP: Trends & Observations 2010*. Retrieved from http://www.aberdeen.com/aberdeen-library/6890/RA-enterprise-resource-planning.aspx

Acton, T., & Golden, W. (2003). Training the knowledge worker: a descriptive study of training practices in Irish software companies. *Journal of European Industrial Training, 27*(2/3/4), 137–146. 10.1108/03090590310468958

Acumatica. (2010, Aug. 13). *The importance of ERP deployment options*. Retrieved from http://erpcloudnews.com/2010/08/the-importance-of-erp-deployment-options/

Agarwal, M. K., & Rao, V. R. (1996). An empirical comparison of consumer-based measures of brand equity. *Marketing Letters, 7*(3), 237–247. doi:10.1007/BF00435740

Aggarwal, P. (2004). The Effects of Brand Relationship Norms on Consumer Attitudes and Behaviour. *The Journal of Consumer Research, 31*(1), 87–101. doi:10.1086/383426

Ahearne, M., Bhattacharya, C. B., & Gruen, T. (2005). Antecedents and Consequences of Customer–Company identification: Expanding the Role of Relationship Marketing. *The Journal of Applied Psychology, 90*(3), 574–585. doi:10.1037/0021-9010.90.3.574 PMID:15910151

Ailawadi, K. L., Scott, A. N., & Karen, G. (2001). Pursuing the Value Conscious Consumer: Store Brands Versus National Brand Promotions. *Journal of Marketing, 65*(1), 71–89. doi:10.1509/jmkg.65.1.71.18132

Akalin & Dilek. (2007). Belirsizlik altında tüketici kararları. *Zonguldak Karaelmas Üniversitesi Sosyal Bilimler Dergisi, 3*(6), 33-48.

Akerlof. (1970). The market for "lemons": Quality, uncertainity and the market mecanizm. *The Quarterly Journal Of Economics, 84*(3), 488-500.

Alam, K. M., Saini, M., & El Saddik, A. (2015). Toward social internet of vehicles: Concept, architecture, and applications. *IEEE Access: Practical Innovations, Open Solutions, 3*, 343–357. doi:10.1109/ACCESS.2015.2416657

Albert, N., & Merunka, D. (2013). The Role of Brand Love in Consumer-Brand Relationships. *Journal of Consumer Marketing, 30*(3), 258–266. doi:10.1108/07363761311328928

Alp, & Karakaş. (2008). Asimetrik Bilgi teorisi karşısında Hayek'in ekonomik yaklaşımları: Karşılaştırmalı bir analiz. Liberal Düşünce Dergisi, 51-52.

Alp. (2010). Avusturya okulu bilgi teorileri ve E-Ticaret çerçevesinde Akerlof'un limon piyasa modelinin değerlendirilmesi. *Eskişehir Osmangazi Üniversitesi İİBF Dergisi, 5*(1), 175-190

Al-Zubi, A. A. (2010). *Identification of Information Systems Threats Sources: An Analytical Study*. Academic Press.

Ang, A. (2014). *Asset management: A systematic approach to factor investing*. Oxford University Press. doi:10.1093/acprof:oso/9780199959327.001.0001

Anunciação, P. F. (2004). Banking Information Systems – The example of a "Securities" subsystem. *Management Studies – Portuguese Journal of Management Studies, 9*(1), 3 –51. (in Portuguese)

Anunciação, P. F. (1997). *Information Systems Urbanism*. CETOP Publishing. (in Portuguese)

Anunciação, P. F. (2014). *Ethics, Sustainability and Information and Knowledge Society*. Lisbon: Chiado Editora. (in Portuguese)

Anunciação, P. F., & Zorrinho, C. (2006). *Organizational Urbanism - How Managing Technological Shock in Companies*. Lisbon: Sílabo Publishing. (in Portuguese)

Appelbaum, D., Kogan, A., Vasarhelyi, M., & Yan, Z. (2017). Impact of Business Analytics and Enterprise Systems on Managerial Accounting. *International Journal of Accounting Information Systems, 25*, 29–44. doi:10.1016/j.accinf.2017.03.003

Appiah, D., Ozuem, W., & Howell, E. K. (2016). Towards a Sustainable Brand Loyalty*: Attitudinal Loyalty Perspective. Eighteenth Annual International Conference*. Global Business and Technology Association.

Appiah, D., Ozuem, W., & Howell, K. E. (2017). Brand Switching in the Smartphone Industry: A Preliminary Study. *Global Business and Technology Association Conference*, Vienna, Austria.

Arnett, D. B., German, S. D., & Hunt, S. D. (2003). The Identity salience Model of Relationship Marketing success: The case of Non-profit Marketing. *Journal of Marketing, 67*(4), 89–105. doi:10.1509/jmkg.67.2.89.18614

Arnold, D. (1992). *The handbook of brand management*. Century Business. The Economist Books.

Aron, A., Aron, E. N., & Smollan, D. (1992). Inclusion of Other in the Self–Scale and the Structure of Interpersonal Closeness. *Journal of Personality and Social Psychology*, *63*(4), 596–61. doi:10.1037/0022-3514.63.4.596

Ashibani, Y., & Mahmoud, Q. H. (2017). Cyber physical systems security: Analysis, challenges and solutions. *Computers & Security*, *68*, 81–97. doi:10.1016/j.cose.2017.04.005

Ashok, K., Dillon, W. R., & Yuan, S. (2002). Extending Discrete Choice Models to Incorporate Attitudinal and Other Latent Variables. *JMR, Journal of Marketing Research*, *39*(2), 31–46. doi:10.1509/jmkr.39.1.31.18937

Attaran, M. (2004). Exploring the relationship between information technology and business process reengineering. *Journal of International Management*, *41*(5), 585–596.

Atzori, L., Iera, A., Morabito, G., & Nitti, M. (2012). The social internet of things (siot)–when social networks meet the internet of things: Concept, architecture and network characterization. *Computer Networks*, *56*(16), 3594–3608. doi:10.1016/j.comnet.2012.07.010

Azize, S., Hakan, K., & Cemal, Z. (2013). Creating Commitment, Trust and Satisfaction for a Brand: What is the Role of Switching Costs in Mobile Phone Market? *Procedia: Social and Behavioral Sciences*, *99*, 496–502. doi:10.1016/j.sbspro.2013.10.518

Bagozzi, R. P. (1975). Marketing as Exchange. *Journal of Marketing*, *39*(10), 32–39. doi:10.2307/1250593

Bagozzi, R. P., & Utpal, M. D. (2006). Antecedents and Purchase Consequences of Customer Participation in Small Group Brand Communities. *International Journal of Research in Marketing*, *23*(1), 45–61. doi:10.1016/j.ijresmar.2006.01.005

Bai, F., & Krishnamachari, B. (2010). Exploiting the wisdom of the crowd: Localized, distributed information-centric VANETs. *IEEE Communications Magazine*, *48*(5), 138–146. doi:10.1109/MCOM.2010.5458375

Bandyopadhyay, S., & Martell, M. (2007). Does Attitudinal Loyalty Influence Behavioural Loyalty? A Theoretical and Empirical Study. *Journal of Retailing and Consumer Services*, *14*(1), 35–44. doi:10.1016/j.jretconser.2006.03.002

Bansal, P., & DesJardine, M. R. (2014). Business sustainability: It is about time. *Strategic Organization*, *12*(1), 70–78. doi:10.1177/1476127013520265

Barnes, S. J., & Scornavacca, E. (2004). Mobile Marketing: The Role of Permission and Acceptance. *International Journal of Mobile Communications*, *2*(2), 128–139. doi:10.1504/IJMC.2004.004663

Batra, R., Lehmann, D. R., & Singh, D. (1993). The Brand Personality Component of Brand Goodwill: Some Antecedents and Consequences. In Brand Equity and Advertising. Hillsdale, NJ: Lawrence Erlbaum Associates.

Bauer, S., & Bernroider, E. W. (2017). From information security awareness to reasoned compliant action: Analyzing information security policy compliance in a large banking organization. *ACM SIGMIS Database: the DATABASE for Advances in Information Systems, 48*(3), 44–68. doi:10.1145/3130515.3130519

Beaty, R. C., & Williams, C. D. (2006). ERP II: Best Practices for Succesfully Implementing an ERP Upgrade. *Communications of the ACM, 49*(3), 105–109. doi:10.1145/1118178.1118184

Beaumont, J. (2004). *Upgrading Your ERP System: Cognizant's Top 10 List*. Academic Press.

Beck, K. (1999). *Extreme Programming Explained: Embrace Change*. Addison-Wesley.

Belk, R. W. (1988). Possessions and the Extended Self. *The Journal of Consumer Research, 15*(9), 139–168. doi:10.1086/209154

Benn, S., & Dunphy, D. (2014). *Can democracy handle corporate sustainability? Constructing a path forward*. Retrieved from http://www.tandfonline.com/doi/abs/10.5172/impp.2004.6.2.141#.VT8jsiGqqko

Bennett, K., Layzell, P., Budgen, D., Brereton, P., Macaulay, L., & Munro, M. (2000). Service-based software: the future for flexible software. In *Proceedings Seventh Asia-Pacific Software Engeering Conference. APSEC 2000* (pp. 214–221). IEEE Comput. Soc. 10.1109/APSEC.2000.896702

Berne´, C., Mu'gica, J. M., & Yague, M. J. (2001). The Effect of Variety-Seeking on Customer Retention in Services. *Journal of Retailing and Consumer Services, 8*(6), 335–345. doi:10.1016/S0969-6989(01)00002-9

Berry, L. L. (2000). Cultivating Service Brand Equity. *Journal of the Academy of Marketing Science, 28*(1), 128–137. doi:10.1177/0092070300281012

Bharadwaj, G. B., Tuli, R. K., & Bonfrer, A. (2011). The Impact of Brand Equity on Shareholder Wealth. *Journal of Marketing, 75*(9), 88–104. doi:10.1509/jmkg.75.5.88

Bhat, S., & Srinivas, K. R. (1998). Symbolic And Functional Positioning Of Brands. *Journal of Consumer Marketing, 15*(1), 32–43. doi:10.1108/07363769810202664

Bhattacharya, C. B., & Lordish, L. (2000). *Towards a System for Monitoring Brand Health from Store Scanner Data*. MSI working Paper, Report No. 00-111.

Bhattacharya, C. B., Rao, H., & Glynn, M. A. (1995). Understanding the bond of identification: An investigation of its correlates among art museum. *Journal of Marketing, 59*(4), 46. doi:10.2307/1252327

Bhattacharya, C. B., & Sanker, S. (2003). Consumer-Company Identification: A Framework for Understanding Consumers' Relationship with Companies. *Journal of Marketing, 67*(4), 76–88. doi:10.1509/jmkg.67.2.76.18609

Biel A. L, (1993). Converting Image into Equity. In *Brand Equity and Advertising: Advertising's Role in Building Strong Brands*. Hillsdale, NJ: Lawrence Erlbaum Associates.

Bjorlin, C. (2008). *Customers upgrade to SAP ERP 6.0 for support, software consolidation.* Retrieved from http://searchmanufacturingerp.techtarget.com/news/1326125/Customers-upgrade-to-SAP-ERP-60-for-support-software-consolidation

Boehm, B. W. (1988). A spiral model of software development and enhancement. *Computer, 21*(5), 61–72. doi:10.1109/2.59

Bolton, R. N., Parasuraman, A., Hoefnagels, A., Migchels, N., Kabadayi, S., Gruber, T., ... Solnet, D. (2013). Understanding Generation Y and Their Use of Social Media: A Review and Research Agenda. *Journal of Service Management, 24*(3), 245–267. doi:10.1108/09564231311326987

Bower, J. L., & Christensen, C. M. (1995). Disruptive Technologies: Catching the Wave. *Harvard Business Review*, (2-3), 43-53.

Boyd, D. M., & Ellison, N. B. (2007). Social Network Sites: Definition, History, and Scholarship. *Journal of Computer-Mediated Communication, 13*(1), 210–230. doi:10.1111/j.1083-6101.2007.00393.x

Brakus, J. J., Bernd, H. S., & Shi, Z. (2008). Experiential Attribute and Consumer Judgments. In *Handbook on Brand and Experience Management*. Cheltenham, UK: Edward Elgar Publisher. doi:10.4337/9781848446151.00022

Brakus, J. J., Bernd, H. S., & Zarantonello, L. (2009). Brand Experience: What Is It? How Is It Measured? Does It Affect Loyalty? *Journal of Marketing, 73*(3), 52–68. doi:10.1509/jmkg.73.3.52

Bravo, D. G. (2000). *Information Systems in the Enterprise – Concepts and Applications*. Pirámide Publishing. (in Spanish)

Breitner, H. G. H. (2005). E-Learning (M. H. Breitner & G. Hoppe, Eds.). Heidelberg, Germany: Physica-Verlag HD. doi:10.1007/3-7908-1655-8

Bresciani, P., Perini, A., Giorgini, P., Giunchiglia, F., & Mylopoulos, J. (2004). Tropos: An Agent-Oriented Software Development Methodology. *Autonomous Agents and Multi-Agent Systems, 8*(3), 203–236. doi:10.1023/B:AGNT.0000018806.20944.ef

Brewer, M. B. (1979). In group Bias in the Minimal Intergroup Situation: A Cognitive–Motivational Analysis. *Psychological Bulletin, 86*(2), 307–324. doi:10.1037/0033-2909.86.2.307

Cagnin, C. H., Loveridge, D., & Butler, J. (1999). *An Information Architecture to Enable Business Sustainability*. Academic Press.

Cagnin, C. H., Loveridge, D., & Butler, J. (2013). Business Sustainability Maturity Model. *Computer Communication Review*, 1–15.

Campo, K., Gijsbrechts, E., & Nisol, P. (2000). Towards understanding consumer Response to Stock outs. *Journal of Retailing, 76*(2), 219–242. doi:10.1016/S0022-4359(00)00026-9

Carpenter, G. S., Glazer, R., & Nakamoto, K. (1997). *Reading on Market-Driving Strategies: Towards a New Theory of Competitive Advantage*. Addison Wesley.

Cecere, G., Corrocher, N., & Battaglia, R. D. (2015). Innovation and Competition in the Smartphone Industry: Is there a Dominant Design? *Journal of Telecommunications Policy,* (39), 162-175.

Çetinkaya. (2012). Asimetrik bilginin piyasaya etkileri ve finansal krizlerdeki rolü. *Sakarya İktisat Dergisi.*

Chabrow, E. (2015, April 18). Insider Breach Costs AT&T $25 Million. In *GovInfoSecurity*. Skybox Security. Retrieved from www.govinfosecurity.com/insider-breach-costs-att-25-million-a-8089

Chang, S. E., & Ho, C. B. (2006). Organizational factors to the effectiveness of implementing information security management. *Industrial Management & Data Systems*, *106*(3), 345–361. doi:10.1108/02635570610653498

Chaplin, L. N., & Roedder, D. J. (2005). The Development of Self-Brand Connections in Children and Adolescents. *The Journal of Consumer Research*, *32*(1), 119–129. doi:10.1086/426622

Chaudhuri, A., & Holbrook, M. B. (2001). The Chain of Effects From Brand Trust And Brand Affect To Brand Performance: The Role Of Brand Loyalty. *Journal of Marketing*, *65*(2), 81–93. doi:10.1509/jmkg.65.2.81.18255

Checkland, P. (2000). Soft systems methodology: A thirty year retrospective. *Systems Research and Behavioral Science*, 17.

Cheng, C. C. J., Yang, C., & Sheu, C. (2014). The link between eco-innovation and business performance: A Taiwanese industry context. *Journal of Cleaner Production*, *64*, 81–90. doi:10.1016/j.jclepro.2013.09.050

Chen, P., & Huang, Z. (2012). *Ibm SPSS 19 statistical software application guide*. Beijing, China: People's Health Press.

Chen, Y. W., Wang, Y., Nevo, S., Jin, J., Wang, L., & Chow, W. S. (2014). IT capability and organizational performance: The roles of business process agility and environmental factors. *European Journal of Information Systems*, *23*(3), 326–342. doi:10.1057/ejis.2013.4

Chernev, A., Hamilton, R., & Gal, D. (2011). Competing for Consumer Identity: Limits to Self-Expression and the Perils of Lifestyle Branding. *Journal of Marketing*, *75*(3), 66–82. doi:10.1509/jmkg.75.3.66

Choi, J., Na, G., & Yi, J. H. (2016). Hardware-assisted credential management scheme for preventing private data analysis from cloning attacks. *Multimedia Tools and Applications*, *75*(22), 1–16. doi:10.100711042-016-3271-z

Christensen, C. M. (1997). *The Innovators Dilema: When New Technologies Cause Great Firms to Fail.* Boston: Harvard Business School Press.

Cisco Networking Academy. (2010). *CCNA Exploration Course Booklet- Network Fundamentals Version 4.0.* Indianapolis, IN: Cisco Press.

CNNIC. (2017). *Statistical Report on Internet Development in China*. Retrieved from http://www.cnnic.net.cn/

Cobb-Walgren, C. J., Ruble, C. A., & Donthu, N. (1995). Brand Equity, Brand Preference, and Purchase Intent. *Journal of Advertising*, *24*(3), 2540. doi:10.1080/00913367.1995.10673481

Colomo-Palacios, R. (2012). *Professional Advancements and Management Trends in the IT Sector*. IGI Global. Retrieved from https://books.google.com/books?hl=en&lr=&id=8qSeBQAAQBAJ&pgis=1

Columbus, L. (2013, August 4). *Deciding If Upgrading Your Enterprise Software Is Worth It Or Not*. Retrieved from http://www.forbes.com/sites/louiscolumbus/2013/11/25/deciding-if-upgrading-your-enterprise-software-is-worth-it-or-not/

Colwill, C. (2009). Human factors in information security: The insider threat – Who can you trust these days? *Information Security Technical Report*, *14*(4), 186–196. doi:10.1016/j.istr.2010.04.004

Copeland, M. T. (1923). Relation of Consumer's Buying Habits to Marketing Methods. *Harvard Business Review*, *1*, 282–289.

Costanza, R., & Patten, B. C. (1995). Defining and predicting sustainability. *Ecological Economics*, *15*(3), 193–196. doi:10.1016/0921-8009(95)00048-8

Cots, S., & Casadesús, M. (2015). Exploring the service management standard ISO 20000. *Total Quality Management & Business Excellence*, *26*(5-6), 515–533. doi:10.1080/14783363.2013.856544

Coutre, L. (2016). *Cleveland Clinic announces top 10 medical innovations for 2017*. Retrieved July 24, 2017, from http://www.modernhealthcare.com/article/20161027/news/161029924

Coviello, N., & Munro, H. (1997). Network relationships and the internationalisation process of small software firms. *International Business Review*, *6*(4), 361–386. doi:10.1016/S0969-5931(97)00010-3

Cowen & Crampton. (n.d.). *Market failure or success: The new dabate*. Retrieved from http://www.Econ.canterbury.ac.nz/personel_pages/eric_crampton/bookintro.pdf

Crichton, D. (2015). Fear Not the Robot: Automation Will Continue to Raise Our Quality of Life. *National Review*. Retrieved on August 1, 2017, from https://www.nationalreview.com/nrd/articles/417033/fear-not-robot

Cronin, B. (2001). Knowledge management, organizational culture and Anglo-American higher Education. Journal of Information Science, 27(3), 129-137. doi:10.1177/016555150102700302

Cron, W. L., & Sobol, M. G. (1983). The relationship between computerization and performance: A strategy for maximizing the economic benefits of computerization. *Journal of International Management*, *6*(3), 171–181.

Crossler, R. E., Bélanger, F., & Ormond, D. (2017). The quest for complete security: An empirical analysis of users' multi-layered protection from security threats. *Information Systems Frontiers*, 1–15.

Crouch, G. I., Perdue, R. R., Timmermans, H. J. P., & Uysal, M. (2004). *Consumer Psychology of Tourism, Hospitality and Leisure*. Oxon, UK: CABI. doi:10.1079/9780851997490.0000

Daigle, S. L., & Cuocco, P. M. (2002). Portal Technology Opportunities, Obstacles, and Options: A View from the California State University. In *Web Portals and Higher Education, Technologies to Make IT Personal* (pp. 109-123). Boulder, CO: Educause. Available at: http://www.educause.edu/ir/library/html/pub5006.asp

Dai, W., Qiu, M., Qiu, L., Chen, L., & Wu, A. (2017). Who moved my data? privacy protection in smartphones. *IEEE Communications Magazine*, *55*(1), 20–25. doi:10.1109/MCOM.2017.1600349CM

Daoleng, G., Oyerinde, O., & Vem, S. (n.d.). *Towards a Pleasurable University Experience for UniJos Students*. Academic Press.

Davies, J. B., & Ward, P. (2005). Exploring the Connections between Visual Merchandising and Retail Branding. An Application of Facet Theory. *International Journal of Retail & Distribution Management*, *33*(7), 505–513. doi:10.1108/09590550510605578

Davis, F. (1986). *A Technology Acceptance Model for Empirically Testing New End-User Information Systems: Theory and Results* (Unpublished Doctoral Dissertation). MIT Sloan School of Management, Cambridge, MA.

Davis, L. M. (2016). *CT Scan (CAT Scan, Computerized Axial Tomography)*. Retrieved July 24, 2017, from http://www.emedicinehealth.com/ct_scan/article_em.htm

Davis, F., & Venkatesh, V. (1996). A Critical Assessment of Potential Measurement Biases in the Technology Acceptance Model: Three Experiments. *International Journal of Human-Computer Studies*, *45*(1), 19–45. doi:10.1006/ijhc.1996.0040

Day, G. S. (1969). A Two-Dimensional Concept of Brand Loyalty. *Journal of Advertising Research*, *9*, 29–35.

de Chernatony, L., & Dall'Olmo Riley, F. (1998). Defining Brand: Beyond the Literature with Expert Opinion. *Journal of Marketing Management*, *14*(5), 417–443. doi:10.1362/026725798784867798

de Chernatony, L., & MacDonnald, M. (1992). *Creating Powerful Brands*. Oxford, UK: Heinermann and Butterworth.

de Chernatony, L., & McWilliam, G. (1990). Appreciating Brands as Assets through using a Two-Dimensional Model. *International Journal of Advertising*, *9*(2), 111–119. doi:10.1080/02650487.1990.11107137

Dell Rio, A. B., Vazquez, R., & Iglesias, V. (2001). The Effects of Brand Associations on Consumer Response. *Journal of Consumer Marketing*, *18*(5), 410–425. doi:10.1108/07363760110398808

Dempsey, S., Vance, R., & Sheehan, L. (2013). Justification of an Upgrade of an Enterprise Resource Planning (ERP) System – The Accountant's Role. *Global Journal of Human Social Science Research, 13*(1), 1–9.

Denning, D. E. (2012). Stuxnet: What Has Changed? *Future Internet, 4*(3), 672–687. doi:10.3390/fi4030672

Derikx, S., de Reuver, M., & Kroesen, M. (2016). Can privacy concerns for insurance of connected cars be compensated? *Electronic Markets, 26*(1), 73–81. doi:10.100712525-015-0211-0

Design Evaluation of Some Nigerian University Portals: A Programmers Point of View. (2010). *GESJ: Computer Science and Telecommunications, 5*(28).

Dibrell, C., Davis, P., & Craig, J. (2008). Fueling Innovation through Information Technology in SMEs. *Journal of Small Business Management, 46*(2), 203–218. doi:10.1111/j.1540-627X.2008.00240.x

Dick, A., & Basu, K. (1994). Customer Loyalty: Towards an Integrated Conceptual Framework. *Journal of the Academy of Marketing Science, 22*(2), 99–113. doi:10.1177/0092070394222001

Dickinson, J. E., Ghali, K., Cherrett, T., Speed, C., Davies, N., & Norgate, S. (2014). Tourism and the smartphone app: Capabilities, emerging practice and scope in the travel domain. *Current Issues in Tourism, 17*(1), 84–101. doi:10.1080/13683500.2012.718323

Dimitriades, Z. S. (2006). Customer Satisfaction, Loyalty and commitment in service organisations: Some evidence from Greece. *Management Research News, 29*(12), 782–800. doi:10.1108/01409170610717817

Dion, D., & Arnould, E. (2016). Persona-fied Brands: Managing Branded Persons through Persona. *Journal of Marketing Management, 32*(1-2), 121–148. doi:10.1080/0267257X.2015.1096818

Dolich, I. J. (1969). Congruence Relationships between Self Images and Product Brands. *JMR, Journal of Marketing Research, 6*(1), 80–84. doi:10.2307/3150001

Dotinga, R. (2015). One in Five Teens May Be Bullied on Social Media. *HealthDay News*. Retrieved July 28, 2017, from http://health.usnews.com/health-news/articles/2015/06/22/1-in-5-teens-may-be-bullied-on-social-media

Downes, L. (2012). Who Really Stopped SOPA, and Why? *Forbes*. Retrieved from https://www.forbes.com/sites/larrydownes/2012/01/25/who-really-stopped-sopa-and-why/#2f883dfc7b76

Doyle, P. (1994). *Marketing Management and Strategy*. Englewood Cliffs, NJ: Prentice-Hall.

DTEX Systems. (2017). *The True Price Tag of Insider Threats: Findings from the New 2016 Cost of Insider Threats Report*. Retrieved from dtexsystems.com/true-price-tag-insider-threats-findings-new-2016-cost-insider-threats-report.

Duane, L., & Charlie, S. (2016). *Reducing the cost of test through strategic asset management*. IEEE Autotestcon.

Dubé, L., & Paré, G. (2003). Rigor in Information Systems Positivist Case Research: Current Practices, Trends, and Recommendations. *Management Information Systems Quarterly*, *27*(4), 597–635. doi:10.2307/30036550

Dwivedi, A. (2015). A higher-order model of consumer brand engagement and its impact on loyalty intentions. *Journal of Retailing and Consumer Services*, *24*, 100–109. doi:10.1016/j.jretconser.2015.02.007

Dwyer, F. R., Schurr, P. H., & Oh, S. (1987). Developing buyer-seller relationships. *Journal of Marketing*, *51*(2), 11–27. doi:10.2307/1251126

Dyllick, T., & Hockerts, K. (2002). Beyond the business case for corporate sustainability. *Business Strategy and the Environment*, *11*(2), 130–141. doi:10.1002/bse.323

Ebrahim, R., Ghoneim, A., Irani, Z., & Fan, Y. (2016). A Brand Preference and Repurchase Intention Model: The Role of Consumer Experience. *Journal of Marketing Management*, *32*(13-14), 13–14, 1230–1259. doi:10.1080/0267257X.2016.1150322

Edell, J. A., & Burke, M. C. (1987). The power of feelings in understanding advertising effects. *The Journal of Consumer Research*, *14*(3), 421–433. doi:10.1086/209124

EĞİLMEZ. (2016). *Reputation and competition with social convention*. Retrieved from http://www.unibs.it/sites/default/files/ricerca/allegati/1105.pdf

Eisenhardt, K. M. (1989). Building Theories from Case Study Research. *Academy of Management Review*, *14*(4), 532–550.

Elliott, R., & Wattanasuwan, K. (1998). Brand as Symbolic Resources for the Construction of Identity. *International Journal of Advertising*, *17*(2), 131–144. doi:10.1080/02650487.1998.11104712

Elsbach, K. D., & Kramer, M. K. (1996). Members' Responses to Organizational Identity Threats: Encountering and Countering the Business Week Rankings. *Administrative Science Quarterly*, *41*(3), 442–76.

Erb, J. J., & James, S. R. (2017). *Global Logistics for Dummies*. Chichester, UK: John Wiley & Sons, Ltd.

Escalas, J. E. (2004). Narrative Processing: Building Consumer Connections to Brands. *Journal of Consumer Psychology*, *14*(1-2), 168–180. doi:10.120715327663jcp1401&2_19

Escalas, J. E., & Bettman, J. R. (2003). You Are What You Eat: The Influence of Reference Groups on Consumers' Connections to Brands. *Journal of Consumer Psychology*, *13*(3), 339–348. doi:10.1207/S15327663JCP1303_14

Escalas, J. E., & Bettman, J. R. (2005). SelfConstrual, Reference Groups, and Brand Meaning. *The Journal of Consumer Research*, *32*(12), 378–389. doi:10.1086/497549

Evesti, A., Kanstrén, T., & Frantti, T. (2017, June). Cybersecurity situational awareness taxonomy. In *Cyber Situational Awareness, Data Analytics And Assessment (Cyber SA), 2017 International Conference On* (pp. 1–8). IEEE.

Fan, X. (2016). *Last year, the national 4G user reached 386 million permeability to 29.6.* Beijing, China: Beijing Daily.

Faraj, S., & Sproull, L. (2000). Coordinating Expertise in Software Development Teams. *Management Science*. Retrieved from http://pubsonline.informs.org/doi/abs/10.1287/mnsc.46.12.1554.12072

Farhana, M. (2014). Implication of Brand Identity Facets on Marketing Communication of Lifestyle Magazine: Case Study of a Swedish Brand. *Journal of Applied Economics and Business Research.*, *4*(1), 23–24.

Farquhar, P. H. (1989). Managing brand equity. *Marketing Research.*, *1*(3), 24–33.

Federal Communications Commission. (2015). Available at https://apps.fcc.gov/edocs_public/attachmatch/DOC-332911A1.pdf

Feldman, M. B., & March, J. G. (1981). Information in Organizations as Signal and Symbol. *Administrative Science Quarterly*, *26*(2), 171–186. doi:10.2307/2392467

Felix, R. (2015). *The state of the Global Smartphone Market. Statista Infographics.* Retrieved from: https://www.statista.com/charts/2512/smartphone-market-share

Feng, Z. (2016). *Research on network privacy in the big data age: from rights protection to personal choice* (Unpublished doctoral dissertation). Jilin University, Changchun, China.

Fenny, D. (2001). *Making Business Sense of the E-Opportunity*. Retrieved April 28, 2015, from http://sloanreview.mit.edu/article/making-business-sense-of-the-eopportunity/

Fidan. (2013). İktisadi açıdan bilgi kavramı ve bilgi kavramına yaklaşımlar üzerine bir inceleme. Süleyman Demirel Üniversitesi Vizyoner Dergisi, 4(9), 94-104.

Fink, L., & Neuman, S. (2009). Exploring the perceived business value of the flexibility enabled by information technology infrastructure. *Information & Management*, *46*(2), 90–99. doi:10.1016/j.im.2008.11.007

Flick, U. (2006). *An Introduction to Qualitative Research* (3rd ed.). London: Sage Publications.

Fournier, S. (1998). Consumers and Their Brands: Developing Relationship Theory in Consumer Research. *The Journal of Consumer Research*, *24*(3), 343–373. doi:10.1086/209515

Galbreath, J. (2009). Addressing sustainability: A strategy development framework. *Int. J. of Sustainable Strategic Management*, *1*(3), 303–319. doi:10.1504/IJSSM.2009.026284

Gardner, B. B., & Levy, J. S. (1955). The Product and the Brand. *Harvard Business Review*, *33*(3-4), 33–39.

Gartner. (2016). *Worldwide Smartphone grew 9.7 percent in Fourth Quarter of 2015*. Retrieved from: http://www.Gartner.com/newsroom

Gene, K., Jez, H., Patrick, D., & John, W. (2016). *The DevOps Handbook: How to Create World-Class Agility, Reliability, and Security in Technology Organizations*. IT Revolution Press.

Gerla, M., Lee, E. K., Pau, G., & Lee, U. (2014, March). Internet of vehicles: From intelligent grid to autonomous cars and vehicular clouds. In *Internet of Things (WF-IoT), 2014 IEEE World Forum on* (pp. 241-246). IEEE.

Gibbons & Katz. (2001). Layoffs and lemons. *Journal of Labour Economics, 9*(4).

Gilroy, L., & D'Amato, T. (2011). *How many patents does it take to build an iPhone?* Retrieved August 1, 2017, from https://inovorg2011-2.wikispaces.com/file/view/2.1-How+many+patents+does+it+take+to+build+an+iPhone.pdf

Giovinazzi, S., Brown, C., Seville, E., Stevenson, J. R., Hatton, T., & Vargo, J. J. (2016). Criticality of infrastructures for organisations. *International Journal of Critical Infrastructures, 12*(4), 331–363. doi:10.1504/IJCIS.2016.081303

Giudice, D. L., Christopher, M. A., Amy, H., & Ian, M. (2016). *Agile And DevOps Adoption Drives Digital Business Success*. Cambridge, MA: Forrester Research. Retrieved from Transforming IT organizations into service providers: www.hp.com/hps/itsm

Glavič, P., & Lukman, R. (2007). Review of sustainability terms and their definitions. *Journal of Cleaner Production, 15*(18), 1875–1885. doi:10.1016/j.jclepro.2006.12.006

Gleick, J. (2011). How Google Dominates Us. *The New York Review of Books*. Retrieved July 26, 2017, from http://www.nybooks.com/articles/2011/08/18/how-google-dominates-us/

Goldman, S. N. (1995). *Agile Competitors and Virtual Organizations:Strategies for Enriching the Customer*. New York: Van Nostrand Reinhold.

Goldsmith, R. E. (2000). Characteristics of the Heavy User of Fashionable Clothing. *Journal of Marketing Theory and Practice, 8*(4), 21–28. doi:10.1080/10696679.2000.11501877

Govette, J. (2016). 15 Amazing Healthcare Technology. *Innovations*. Retrieved from https://getreferralmd.com/2016/01/healthcare-technology-2016/

Greenhow, C., & Askari, E. (2017). Learning and Teaching with Social Network Sites: A Decade of Research in K-12 Related Education. *Education and Information Technologies, 22*(2), 623–645. doi:10.100710639-015-9446-9

Greenhow, C., Robelia, B., & Hughes, J. E. (2009). Learning, Teaching, and Scholarship in a Digital Age: Web 2.0 and Classroom Research: What Path Should We Take Now? *Educational Researcher, 38*(4), 246–259. doi:10.3102/0013189X09336671

Gremler, D. D., & Brown, S. W. (1996). Service Loyalty; its Nature, Importance and Implications. In B. Edvardsson, S. W. Brown, R. Johnston, & E. Scheuing (Eds.), *QUIS V: Advancing Service Quality: A Global Perspective*. New York, NY: ISQA.

Griffin, M., Babin, B. J., & Modianos, D. (2000). Shopping Values of Russian Consumers: The Impact of Habituation in a Developing Economy. *Journal of Retailing*, *76*(1), 33–52. doi:10.1016/S0022-4359(99)00025-1

Guadagni, P. M., & Little, J. D. C. (1983). A Logit Model of Brand Choice Calibrated on Scanner Data: A Logit Model of Brand Choice Calibrated on Scanner Data. *Journal of Marine Science*, *2*(3), 203–238. doi:10.1287/mksc.2.3.203

GuardChild.com. (2017). *Cyber Bullying Statistics*. Retried July 28, 2017, from http://www.guardchild.com/cyber-bullying-statistics/

Guodong, Z., & Zhongjiao, J. (2010). From e-campus to e-learning: An overview of ICT applications in Chinese higher education. *British Journal of Educational Technology*, *41*(4), 574–581.

Guodong, Z., & Zhongjiao, J. (2010). From e-campus to e-learning: An overview of ICT applications in Chinese higher education. *British Journal of Educational Technology*, *41*(4), 574–581. doi:10.1111/j.1467-8535.2010.01085.x

Guo, M. (2012). *Protection of the tort law of personal information rights*. Beijing, China: Legal Publishing House.

Hallowell, R. (1996). The Relationships of Customer Satisfaction, Customer Loyalty, and Profitability: An Empirical Study. *International Journal of Service Industry Management*, *7*(4), 27–42. doi:10.1108/09564239610129931

Hank. (2006). ITIL: What It Is And What It Isn't. *Business Communications Review*.

Hanselman, S. E., & Pegah, M. (2007). The wild wild waste. In *Proceedings of the 35th annual ACM SIGUCCS conference on User services - SIGUCCS '07* (pp. 157–162). New York: ACM Press. 10.1145/1294046.1294083

Hansen, L. (2003). Service Layer Essential for Future Success. *Ericsson Mobility World*. Available at: http://www.ericsson.com

Han, Y. J., Joseph, C. N., & Drèze, X. (2010). Signaling Status with Luxury Goods: The Role of Brand Prominence. *Journal of Marketing*, *74*(4), 15–30. doi:10.1509/jmkg.74.4.15

Harenber. (2011). *Online Piracy*. Retrieved on July 31, 2017, from http://piracy.web.unc.edu/brief-history-of-online-piracy/

Hartmans, A. (2017). 15 Fascinating Facts You Probably Didn't Know about Amazon. *Business Insider*. Retrieved November 28, 2017, from http://www.businessinsider.com/jeff-bezos-amazon-history-facts-2017-4/#amazon-wasnt-the-companys-original-name-1

Helgeson, J. G., & Supphellen, M. (2004). A Conceptual and Measurement Comparison of Self-Congruity and Brand Personality. *International Journal of Market Research*, *46*(2), 205–233. doi:10.1177/147078530404600201

Herschberg, R. (2004). *Best Practices for Developing Your R/3 Upgrade Roadmap. Managing SAP Projects 2004* [Presentation slides]. Las Vegas, NV: Wellesley Information Services.

Hersh, M. A. (1999). Sustainable decision making: The role of decision support systems. *IEEE Transactions on Systems, Man and Cybernetics. Part C, Applications and Reviews*, *29*(3), 395–408. doi:10.1109/5326.777075

Herzog, A., Shahmehri, N., & Duma, C. (2007). An ontology of information security. *International Journal of Information Security and Privacy*, *1*(4), 1–23. doi:10.4018/jisp.2007100101

Hewlet Packard, H. P. (2016). *HP Devops*. Retrieved from https://www.hpe.com: https://saas.hpe.com/fr-fr/software/devops-solutions

Highsmith, J., & Cockburn, A. (2001). Agile software development: The business of innovation. *Computer*, *34*(9), 120–127. doi:10.1109/2.947100

Hirschman, E. C., & Holbrook, M. B. (1982). Hedonic consumption: Emerging Concepts, Methods and Propositions. *Journal of Marketing*, *46*(3), 92–101. doi:10.2307/1251707

Hofmeyr, J., & Rice, B. (2000). *Commitment-Led Marketing*. Chichester, UK: Wiley.

Hogan, E. J., & Armstrong, G. (2001). Toward a Resource Based Theory of Business Exchange Relationships: The Role of Relational Asset Value. *Journal of Business-To-Business Marketing*, *8*(4), 3–28. doi:10.1300/J033v08n04_02

Holbrook, M. B., & Corfman, K. P. (1985). Quality and Value in the Consumption Experience: Phaedrus Rides Again. In C. V. S. How, J. J. Merchandise, & J. C. Olson (Eds.), *Perceived Quality*. Lanham, MD: Lexington Books.

Holbrook, M. B., & Hirschman, E. C. (1982). The Experiential Aspects of Consumption: Consumer Fantasies, Feelings, and Fun. *The Journal of Consumer Research*, *9*(2), 132–140. doi:10.1086/208906

Holmqvist, M., & Pessi, K. (2006). Agility Through Scenario Development and ContinuousImplementation: A Global Aftermarket Logistics Case. *European Journal of Information Systems*, *15*(2), 146–158. doi:10.1057/palgrave.ejis.3000602

Holwell, S. (2000). Soft Systems Methodology: Other Voices. *Systemic Practice and Action Research*, *13*(6), 773–797. doi:10.1023/A:1026479529130

Homburg, C., & Giering, A. (2001). Personal Characteristics as Moderators of the Relationship between Customer Satisfaction and Loyalty— an Empirical Analysis. *Journal of Psychology and Marketing*, *18*(1), 43–66. doi:

Hong, P., Kwon, H., & Jungbae Roh, J. (2009). Implementation of strategic green orientation in supply chain. *European Journal of Innovation Management, 12*(4), 512–532. doi:10.1108/14601060910996945

Hong, W., Thong, J. Y., Chasalow, L. C., & Dhillon, G. (2011). User acceptance of agile information systems: A model and empirical test. *Journal of Management Information Systems, 28*(1), 235–272. doi:10.2753/MIS0742-1222280108

Hoyer, W. D., & MacInnis, D. J. (1997). *Consumer Behaviour*. Boston: Houghton Mifflin Publishers.

Hoyer, W. D., & Ridgway, N. M. (1984). Variety seeking as an explanation for exploratory behaviour: A theoretical model. In T. C. Kinnear (Ed.), *Advances in Consumer Research* (Vol. 11, pp. 114–119). Provo, UT: Association for Consumer Research.

Hsu, L. C., & Liou, D. K. (2017). Maintaining Customer-Brand Relationships in the Mobile Industry: The Mediation Effects of Brand Relationship Benefits and Quality. *International Journal of Mobile Communications, 15*(4), 388. doi:10.1504/IJMC.2017.084861

Hubert, L. (2014). *The Integrity of Governance – What It Is, What We Know, What Is Done, and Where to Go*. Palgrave Macmillan.

Hu, Q., Hart, P., & Cooke, D. (2007). The role of external and internal influences on information systems security – a neo-institutional perspective. *The Journal of Strategic Information Systems, 16*(2), 153–172. doi:10.1016/j.jsis.2007.05.004

Hurlburt, G. (2016). Good Enough" Security: The Best We'll Ever Have. *Computer, 49*(7), 98–101. doi:10.1109/MC.2016.212 PMID:28003687

Hutton, J. G. (1997). A Study of Brand Equity in an Organisational-Buying Context. *Journal of Product and Brand Management, 6*(6), 428–439. doi:10.1108/10610429710190478

Iden, J. &. (2015). The impact of senior management involvement, organisational commitment and group efficacy on ITIL implementation benefits. *Information Systems and e-Business Management,* 527-552.

Im, G. P., & Baskerville, R. L. (2005). A longitudinal study of information system threat categories: The enduring problem of human error. *ACM SIGMIS Database, 36*(4), 68–79. doi:10.1145/1104004.1104010

Initiative, J. T. F. T., & ... (2009). *800-53 Rev. 3*. SP: Recommended Security Controls for Federal Information Systems and Organizations.

Işcan. (2010). *İktisat teorisinde enformasyon teorisine yönelik yaklaşımlar*. Adana: Çukurova Üniversitesi, Sosyal Bilimler Enstitüsü, Doktora Tezi.

Ise, O. A. (2014). Towards a Unified University Information System: Bridging the Gap of Data Interoperability. *American Journal of Software Engineering, 2*(2), 26–32. doi:10.12691/ajse-2-2-3

ISGec – Information System Governance European Club. (2009). *Information Systems Governance Manifest*. Retrieved from http://www.cegsi.org/index.php/qui-sommes-nous/o-que-e-o-cegsi

ISGec – Information System Governance European Club. (2010). *Why the Corporations are asking for an information systems governance?* Retrieved from http://www.cegsi.org/index.php/documents/telechargement-du-document-la-gouvernance-des-systemes-d-information-pourquoi/la-gouvernance-des-systemes-d-information-pourquoi

ISGec – Information System Governance European Club. (2011). *The Importance of the Information Systems Approach in the Governance of Organizations*. Retrieved from http://www.cegsi.org/index.php/documents/l-importance-de-l-approche-par-les-systemes-d-information/the-importance-of-the-information-systems-approach-for-governance-organizations (in French)

ISO/IEC 20000. (2010). *ISO/IEC 20000 Information Technology*. ISO/IEC 20000.

Itami, H., & Roehl, W. T. (1987). Mobilizing Invisible Assets. Harvard University Press.

Jacoby, J. (1971). A Model of Multi-Brand Loyalty. *Journal of Advertising Research*, *11*(3), 25–31.

Jacoby, J., & Kyner, D. B. (1973). Brand Loyalty vs. Repeat Purchasing Behaviour. *JMR, Journal of Marketing Research*, *10*(1), 1–9. doi:10.2307/3149402

Jimenez, D.-Z., & Lee, W. (2011). Buyer Conversations: Coca-cola Bottling Co. Consolidated's ERP Upgrade Journey - APEJ View. *Asia/Pacific Business Applications and Information Management: Buyer Case Study*. Retrieved from ftp://public.dhe.ibm.com/software/hk/download/AP2670107T.pdf

Jones, S. (2002). *3G Launch Strategies, Early Adopters, Why & How to make them yours*. Tarifica Report.

Juels, A. (2006). RFID Security and Privacy: A Research Survey. IEEE Journal on Selected Areas in Communications, 24(2), 381-394. doi:10.1109/JSAC.2005.861395

Jung, B., Han, I., & Lee, S. (2001). S. Security threats to Internet: A Korean multi-industry investigation. *Information & Management*, *38*(8), 487–498. doi:10.1016/S0378-7206(01)00071-4

Kahn, B. E., & Louie, T. A. (1990). Effects of Retraction of Price Promotions on Brand Choice Behaviour for Variety-Seeking and Last-purchase Loyal Consumers. *JMR, Journal of Marketing Research*, *27*(3), 279–289. doi:10.2307/3172586

Kahveci. (2015). Tüketicilerin asimetrik enformasyon ve kurumsal itibar algısı: Seyahat acentası müşterileri üzerine bir araştırma. Balıkesir: Balıkesir Üniversitesi Sosyal Bilimler Enstitüsü, Yüksek Lisans Tezi.

Kaiwartya, O., Abdullah, A. H., Cao, Y., Altameem, A., Prasad, M., Lin, C. T., & Liu, X. (2016). Internet of vehicles: Motivation, layered architecture, network model, challenges, and future aspects. *IEEE Access: Practical Innovations, Open Solutions*, *4*, 5356–5373. doi:10.1109/ACCESS.2016.2603219

Kanchanapibul, M., Lacka, E., Wang, X., & Chan, H. K. (2014). An empirical investigation of green purchase behaviour among the young generation. *Journal of Cleaner Production, 66*, 528–536. doi:10.1016/j.jclepro.2013.10.062

Kapferer, J. N. (2001). *Reinventing the Brand: Can Top Brands Survive the New Market Realitie?* London: Kogan Page.

Kaptein, M. (2008). Developing a Measure of Unethical Behavior in the Workplace: A Stakeholder Perspective. *Journal of Management, 34*(5), 978–1008. doi:10.1177/0149206308318614

Kaspersky Lab. (2015). *Damage Control: The Cost of Security Breaches IT Security Risks Special Report Series*. Retrieved from https://media.kaspersky.com/pdf/it-risks-survey-report-cost-of-security-breaches.pdf

Keller, K. L. (2001). Building Customer-Based Brand Equity. *Journal of Marketing Management, 10*(2), 16–26.

Keller, K. L. (1993). Conceptualizing, Measuring and Managing Customer-based Brand Equity. *Journal of Marketing, 57*(1), 1–22. doi:10.2307/1252054

Keller, K. L. (2008). *Strategic Brand Management: Building, Measuring, and Managing Brand Equity* (3rd ed.). Upper Saddle River, NJ: Pearson Education, Inc.

Keller, K. L., & Lehmann, D. R. (2006). Brands and Branding: Research Findings and Future Priorities. *Journal of Marine Science, 25*(6), 740–759. doi:10.1287/mksc.1050.0153

Ken Schwaber. (2004). *Agile Project Management with Scrum*. Microsoft Press.

Kerlinger, F. N., & Lee, H. B. (2000). Foundations of Behavioural Research (4th ed.). Holt, NY: Harcourt College Publishers.

Khoo, H. M., & Robey, D. (2007). Deciding to Upgrade Packaged Software: A Comparative Case Study of Motives, Contingencies and Dependencies. *European Journal of Information Systems, 16*(5), 555–567. doi:10.1057/palgrave.ejis.3000704

Khoo, H. M., Robey, D., & Rao, S. V. (2011). An Exploratory Study of the Impacts of Upgrading Packaged Software: A Stakeholder Perspective. *Journal of Information Technology, 26*(3), 153–169. doi:10.1057/jit.2011.1

Kimberling, E. (2010). *Tips for avoiding common pitfalls of ERP upgrades*. Retrieved from http://searchmanufacturingerp.techtarget.com/news/2240020512/Tips-for-avoiding-common-pitfalls-of-ERP-upgrades

Kimberling, E. (2017, July 25). *Now is a Terrible Time to Purchase New ERP Software*. Retrieved from https://www.panorama-consulting.com/now-is-a-terrible-time-to-purchase-new-erp-software/

Kim, C. K., Han, D. C., & Park, S. B. (2001). The Effect of Brand Personality and Brand Identification on Brand Loyalty: Applying the Theory of Social Identification. *The Japanese Psychological Research*, *43*(4), 195–206. doi:10.1111/1468-5884.00177

King, S. (1973). *Developing New Brands*. Bath, UK: Pitman Publishing.

Klamo, L., Wang, K. L., Le, T., & Huang, W. (2006). Successfully Implementing e-Government: Fundamental Issues and a Case Study in USA. *Electronic Government: An International Journal*, *3*(2), 158–173. doi:10.1504/EG.2006.009216

Kleine, S. S., Kleine, R. E. III, & Allen, C. T. (1995). How is a Possession 'Me' or 'Not Me'? Characterizing Types and Antecedents of Material Possession Attachment. *The Journal of Consumer Research*, *22*(12), 327–343. doi:10.1086/209454

Klewitz, J., & Hansen, E. G. (2014). Sustainability-oriented innovation of SMEs: A systematic review. *Journal of Cleaner Production*, *65*, 57–75. doi:10.1016/j.jclepro.2013.07.017

Kottler, P., & Amtrong, G. (1994). *Principles of Marketing*. Prentice Hall.

Krausz, M. (2015). *Managing information security breaches: Studies from real life. S.l.* IT Governance Ltd.

Kressman, F., Sirgy, M. J., Hermmann, A., Hubber, F., Hubber, S., & Lee, D. J. (2006). Direct and Indirect Effects of Self-Image Congruence on Brand Loyalty. *Journal of Business Research*, *59*(9), 955–964. doi:10.1016/j.jbusres.2006.06.001

Krohmer, H., Malär, L., & Nyffenegger, B. (2007). The Fit between Brand Personality and Consumer's Self: The Importance of Self-Congruence for Brand Performance. *AMA Winter Educators' Conference Proceedings*.

Kumar, S. (2008). *GRC is a key business driver for SAP Upgrade*. Retrieved from http://www.free-press-release.com/news/200806/1212568140.html

Kumar, V., & Shah, D. (2004). Building and Sustaining Profitable Customer Loyalty for 21st century. *Journal of Retailing*, *80*(4), 317–330. doi:10.1016/j.jretai.2004.10.007

Kumbakara. (2008). Managed IT services: the role of IT standards. *Information Management & Computer Security*.

Kumbakara, N. (2008). Managed IT services: The role of IT standards. *Information Management & Computer Security*, *16*(4), 336–359. doi:10.1108/09685220810908778

Kuusik, A., & Varblane, U. (2009). How to Avoid Customers Leaving: The Case of the Estonian Telecommunication Industry. *Baltic Journal of Management*, *4*(1), 66–79. doi:10.1108/17465260910930458

Laine, M. (2014). Defining and Measuring Corporate Sustainability: Are We There Yet? *Social and Environmental Accountability Journal*, *34*(3), 187–188. doi:10.1080/0969160X.2014.967956

Lam, S. K., Ahearne, M., Mullins, R., Hayati, B., & Schillewaert, N. (2013). Exploring the Dynamics of Antecedents to Consumer–Brand Identification with a New Brand. *Journal of the Academy of Marketing Science*, *41*(2), 243–252. doi:10.100711747-012-0301-x

Lam, S. K., Ahearn, M., Hu, Y., & Schillewaert, N. (2010). Resistance to Brand Switching When a Radically New Brand Is Introduced: A Social Identity Theory Perspective. *Journal of Marketing*, *74*(6), 128–146. doi:10.1509/jmkg.74.6.128

Lan, R. (2012). Design and Implementation of IT Service Management System of College of University Campus Network. *Proceedings of the 7th International Conference on Computer Science and Education (ICCSE)*, 299 – 304.

Lancaster, K. J. (1966). A New Approach to Consumer Theory. *Journal of Political Economy*, *74*(2), 132–157. doi:10.1086/259131

Latimer, M. T. (2004). Patenting Inventions Arising from Biological Research. *Genome Biology*, *6*(1). *Article*, *203*, 1–9.

Laudon, K. C., & Laudon, J. P. (2014). *Management Information Systems: Managing the Digital Firm* (13th ed.). Pearson Education Limited.

Lavi, Y. (2017, July 20). *Industry 4.0: Harnessing the Power of ERP and MES Integration.* Retrieved from http://www.industryweek.com/supply-chain-technology/industry-40-harnessing-power-erp-and-mes-integration

Law, C., Chen, C., & Wu, B. (2010). Managing the Full ERP Life-Cycle: Considerations of Maintenance and Support Requirements and IT Governance Practice as Integral Elements of the Formula for Successful ERP Adoption. *Computers in Industry*, *61*(3), 297–308. doi:10.1016/j.compind.2009.10.004

Leckie, C., Munyaradzi, W. N., & Johnson, L. W. (2016). Antecedents of Consumer Brand Engagement and Brand Loyalty. *Journal of Marketing Management*, *32*(5-6), 5–6, 558–578. do i:10.1080/0267257X.2015.1131735

Lee, J. W. (2009). Relationship between Consumer Personality and Brand Personality as Self-Concept: From the Case of Korean Automobile Brands. *Academy of Marketing Studies Journal*, *13*(1), 25–44.

Lee, O., Banerjee, P., Lim, K., Kumar, K., Hillegersberg, V., & Wei, J. (2006). Agility in Globally Distributed System Development. *Communications of the ACM*, *49*(10), 49–54. doi:10.1145/1164394.1164419

Legrenzi, C., & Salzman, C. (2012). *Les concepts de base de la Gouvernance d'entreprise, gouvernance informatique et gouvernance des systèmes d'information.* Retrieved from http://www.cegsi.org/index.php/documents/les-concepts-de-base-de-la-gouvernance/les-concepts-de-base-de-la-gouvernance-informatique-d-entreprise-des-systemes-d-information

Leonard-Barton, D., & Deschamps, I. (1988). Managerial Influence in the Implementation of New Technology. *Management Science*, *34*(10), 1252–1265. doi:10.1287/mnsc.34.10.1252

Lequerica, I., Longaron, M. G., & Ruiz, P. M. (2010). Drive and share: Efficient provisioning of social networks in vehicular scenarios. *IEEE Communications Magazine*, *48*(11), 90–97. doi:10.1109/MCOM.2010.5621973

Lester, S. (n.d.). *Soft systems methodology*. Retrieved from https://www.umsl.edu/~sauterv/analysis/F2015/Soft Systems Methodology.html.htm

Levy, S. J. (1959). Symbols for Sale. *Harvard Business Review*, *37*(7/8), 117–124.

Levy, S. J. (1999). Symbols for Sale. In *Brand Consumers Symbols and Research*. London: Sage Publications. doi:10.4135/9781452231372.n18

Lianzhi, G., Guangming, H., & Rongshen, W. (2010). Design and Performance Research of 10 Gigabit Campus Network. *Proceedings of the 2nd International Conference on Information Science and Engineering*, 4488 – 4491.

Li, F., & Lei, H. (2005). *The construction of e campus*. Beijing: Educational Technology Institution of Tsinghua University.

Ligas, M., & Cotte, J. (1999). The Process of Negotiating Brand Meaning: A Symbolic Interactionist Perspective. *Advances in Consumer Research. Association for Consumer Research (U. S.)*, *26*(1), 609–614.

Li, P. (2014). College Campus Network Management Information System Research and Implementation. Frontiers of Manufacturing and Design Science IV. *Applied Mechanics and Materials*, *496-500*, 2265–2268. doi:10.4028/www.scientific.net/AMM.496-500.2265

Liu, T. C., Wu, L. W., & Hung, C. T. (2007). The Effects of Inertia and Switching Barriers on Satisfaction-Retention Relationship: A Case of Financial Service Industries. *Journal of Management*, *24*, 671–687.

Liz, M. (2007). *The Rise of Brands*. Oxford, UK: Berg Publishers.

Loch, K.D., Carr, H.H., & Warkentin, M. E. (1992). Threats to Information Systems: Today's Reality, Yesterday's Understanding. *MIS Quarterly*, *16*(2), 173.

Luan, T. H., Lu, R., Shen, X., & Bai, F. (2015). Social on the road: Enabling secure and efficient social networking on highways. *IEEE Wireless Communications*, *22*(1), 44–51. doi:10.1109/MWC.2015.7054718

Luftman, J., Lyytinen, K., & Zvi, T. (2017). Enhancing the Measurement of Information Technology (IT) Business Alignment and Its Influence on Company Performance. *Journal of Information Technology*, *32*(1), 26–46. doi:10.1057/jit.2015.23

Lury, C. (2004). *Brands: The Logos of the Global Economy*. London: Routledge.

Lu, Y., & Abeysekera, I. (2014). Stakeholders' power, corporate characteristics, and social and environmental disclosure: Evidence from China. *Journal of Cleaner Production*, *64*, 426–436. doi:10.1016/j.jclepro.2013.10.005

Lu, Y., & Ramamurthy, K. (2011). Understanding the Link between Information Technology Capability and Organizational Agility: An Empirical Examination. *Management Information Systems Quarterly*, *35*(4), 931–954. doi:10.2307/41409967

Lyytinen, K., & Rose, G. M. (2003). The Disruptive Nature of Information Technology Innovations: The Case of Internet Computing in Systems Development Organizations. *Management Information Systems Quarterly*, *27*(4), 557–596. doi:10.2307/30036549

Ma, L. (2015). On privacy leaks in mobile Internet social networks. *News Knowledge,* (6), 3-5.

Mader, M. (2012). Monitoring networking between higher education institutions and regular actors. *Journal of Cleaner Production, 49*, 105-113. Retrieved from www.elsevier.com/locate/jclepr

Maglaras, L. A., Al-Bayatti, A. H., He, Y., Wagner, I., & Janicke, H. (2016). Social internet of vehicles for smart cities. *Journal of Sensor and Actuator Networks*, *5*(1), 3. doi:10.3390/jsan5010003

Maier, J. L., Rainer, K. R. Jr, & Snyder, C. A. (1997). Environmetal Scanning for Information Technology: An Enpirical Investigation. *Journal of Management Information Systems*, *14*(2), 177–200. doi:10.1080/07421222.1997.11518170

Malär, L., Krohmer, H., Hoyer, W. D., & Nyffenegger, B. (2011). Emotional Brand Attachment and Brand Personality: The Relative Importance of the Actual and the Ideal Self. *Journal of Marketing*, *75*(4), 35–52. doi:10.1509/jmkg.75.4.35

Mano, H., & Oliver, R. L. (1993). Assessing the Dimensionality and Structure of the Consumption Experience: Evaluation, Feeling, and Satisfaction. *The Journal of Consumer Research*, *20*(3), 451–466. doi:10.1086/209361

Marrone, K., & Kolbe, L. M. (2011). Uncovering ITIL claims: IT executives' perception on benefits and Business-IT alignment. *Information Systems and e-Business Management*, *9*(3), 363–380. doi:10.100710257-010-0131-7

Marshall, J. D., & Toffel, M. W. (2005). Framing the elusive concept of sustainability: A sustainability hierarchy. *Environmental Science & Technology*, *39*(3), 673–682. doi:10.1021/es040394k PMID:15757326

Massaro, E., Ahn, C., Ratti, C., Santi, P., Stahlmann, R., Lamprecht, A., ... Huber, M. (2017). The Car as an Ambient Sensing Platform. *Proceedings of the IEEE, 105*(1), 3–7. doi:10.1109/JPROC.2016.2634938

Massoud, S., & Gupta, O. K. (2003). Consumer perception and attitude toward mobile communication. *International Journal of Mobile Communications*, *1*(4), 390–408. doi:10.1504/IJMC.2003.003993

Mayergoyz, A. (2009). Lessons from Europe on How to Tame U.S. Patent Trolls. *Cornell International Law Journal, 42*(2), 241-270.

McCorvey, J. J. (2013). Amazon Fresh is Jeff Bezos' Last Mile Quest for Total Retail Domination. *Fast Company*. Retrieved July 26, 2017, from https://www.fastcompany.com/3014817/amazon-jeff-bezos

McCracken, G. (1988). *The Long Interview*. London: Sage. doi:10.4135/9781412986229

McFadden, D. (1986). The Choice Theory Approach to Market Research. *Journal of Marine Science*, *5*(4), 275–297. doi:10.1287/mksc.5.4.275

McGrath, R. G. (2011, January). When your Business Model is in Trouble. *Harvard Business Review*, 96–98.

McKenzie, S. (2004). *Social Sustainability - Towards Some Definitions*. Retrieved April 28, 2015, from https://atn.edu.au/Documents/EASS/HRI/working-papers/wp27.pdf

McNaughton, R., Ray, P., & Lewis, L. (2010). Designing an evaluation framework for IT service management. *Information & Management*, *47*(4), 219–225. doi:10.1016/j.im.2010.02.003

Meade, L. M. (1997). Method for analyzing agility alternatives for business processes. In *Industrial Engineering Research - Conference Proceedings* (pp. 960-965). IIE.

Meenaghan, T. (1995). The Role of Advertising in Brand Image Development. *Journal of Product and Brand Management*, *4*(4), 23–34. doi:10.1108/10610429510097672

Mell, P., Scarfone, K., & Romanosky, S. (2006). Common vulnerability scoring system. *IEEE Security & Privacy, 4*(6), 85–89.

Memon, Z. A., Wei, Y.-M., Robson, M. G., & Khattak, M. A. O. (2014). Keeping track of "corporate social responsibility" as a business and management discipline: Case of Pakistan. *Journal of Cleaner Production*, *74*, 27–34. doi:10.1016/j.jclepro.2014.03.057

Merz, M. A., Yi, H., & Vargo, S. L. (2009). The Evolving Brand Logic: A Service-Dominant Logic Perspective. *Journal of the Academy of Marketing Science*, *37*(3), 328–344. doi:10.100711747-009-0143-3

Mesquida. (2012). IT Service Management Process Improvement based on ISO/IEC 15504: A systematic review. *Information and Software Technology*.

Meziani, S. (2010). E-government: ITIL-based service management case study. *The 12th International Conference on information integration and web-based applications & services.*

Miles, M. B., Huberman, A. M., & Saldaña, J. (2014). *Qualitative Data Analysis: A Methods Sourcebook* (3rd ed.). Thousand Oaks, CA: SAGE Publications, Inc.

Miller, J. J. (2015). Modern Pollster: The Profession Must Adapt to Cell Phones and the Internet. *National Review*. Retrieved July 31, 2017, from https://www.nationalreview.com/nrd/articles/415667/modern-pollster

Mingers, J. (2000). An Idea Ahead of Its Time: The History and Development of Soft Systems Methodology. *Systemic Practice and Action Research*, *13*(6), 733–755. doi:10.1023/A:1026475428221

Mintel Group. (2017). *Smartphone Purchasing Process*. London: Author.

Mior. (2008). *The importance of ITSM. Malaysian Business*. Kuala Lumpur: New Straits Times Press.

Mitchell, R., Hutchinson, K., Quinn, B., & Gilmore, A. (2015). A framework for SME retail branding. *Journal of Marketing Management*, *31*, 17-18, 1818-1850.

Mitchell, V.-W. (1999). Consumer Perceived Risk: Conceptualisations and Models. *European Journal of Marketing*, *33*(1/2), 163–195. doi:10.1108/03090569910249229

Mollerup, P. (1997). *Marks of Excellence: The History and Taxonomy of Trademarks*. London: Phaidon.

Montiel, I., & Delgado-Ceballos, J. (2014). Defining and Measuring Corporate Sustainability: Are We There Yet? *Organization & Environment*, *27*(2), 113–139. doi:10.1177/1086026614526413

Moon, H., & Sprott, E. D. (2016). Ingredient Branding for a Luxury Brand: The Role of Brand and Product Fit. *Journal of Business Research*, *69*(4), 5768–5774. doi:10.1016/j.jbusres.2016.04.173

Morais, P., & Carvalho, J. A. (2000). A Taxonomy of Computer Systems to Support the Development Process of Information Systems. [in Portuguese]. *Information Systems*, *13*, 7–29.

Mossburg, E. (2017, September 15). *Beneath the surface | Deloitte US | Cyber Risk Services*. Retrieved November 17, 2017, from https://www2.deloitte.com/us/en/pages/risk/articles/hidden-business-impact-of-cyberattack.htm

Moteff, J. C. (2005). Risk Management and Critical Infrastructure Protection: Assessing, Integrating, and Managing Threats, Vulnerabilities and Consequences. *American Journal of Hospital Pharmacy*, *47*(3), 533–543.

Muhammad, A. S., & Idris, I. (2010). Design Evaluation of Some Nigerian University Portals: A Programmers Point of View. *GESJ: Computer Science and Telecommunications, 5*(28).

Mulder, K. (2014). Strategic competencies, critically important for Sustainable Development. *Journal of Cleaner Production*, *78*, 243–248. doi:10.1016/j.jclepro.2014.03.098

Muniz, A. M. Jr, & O'Guinn, T. C. (2001). Brand Community. *The Journal of Consumer Research*, *27*(4), 412–432. doi:10.1086/319618

Murphy, J. (1990). *Brand Strategy*. Cambridge: Director Books.

Murphy, J. (1992). What is Branding? In J. Murphy (Ed.), *Branding, a key marketing tool* (pp. 1–12). London: Macmillan. doi:10.1007/978-1-349-12628-6_1

Murugesan, S. (2008). Harnessing Green IT: Principles and Practices. *IT Professional, 10*(1), 24–33. doi:10.1109/MITP.2008.10

Nah, F. F., & Delgado, S. (2006). Critical Success Factors for Enterprise Resource Planning Implementation and Upgrade. *Journal of Computer Information Systems, 46*(5), 99–114. doi:10.1080/08874417.2006.11645928

Nah, F. F.-H., Zhao, F., & Zhu, W. (2003). Factors influencing Users' Adoption of Mobile Computing. In J. Mariga (Ed.), *Managing E-commerce and Mobile Computing Technologies Book*. Hershey, PA: Idea Group Inc.

Nam, J., Ekinci, Y., & Whyatt, G. (2011). Brand Equity, Brand Loyalty and Consumer Satisfaction. *Annals of Tourism Research, 38*(3), 1009–1030. doi:10.1016/j.annals.2011.01.015

National Cybersecurity Institute. Excelsior College. (2016, July 11). *Insider Breach Costs AT&T $25 Million*. Retrieved from www.nationalcybersecurityinstitute.org/telecommunications/insider-breach-costs-att-25-million-2/

Ng, C. S.-P. (2006). *A Resource-Based Perspective on Enterprise Resource Planning (ERP) Capabilities and Upgrade Decision*. Paper presented at the Pacific Asia Conference on Information Systems (PACIS), Kuala Lumpur, Malaysia.

Ng, C. S.-P. (2011). *Enterprise Resource Planning (ERP) Upgrade Decision: Toward A Unified View*. Paper presented at the 15th Pacific Asia Conference on Information systems (PACIS), Brisbane, Australia.

Ng, C. S.-P., & Chang, P. C. (2009). *Exploring the Links between Competitive Advantage and Enterprise Resource Planning (ERP) Upgrade Decision: A Case Study Approach*. Paper presented at the 16th ISPE International Conference on Concurrent Engineering, Taipei. 10.1007/978-1-84882-762-2_17

Ng, C. S.-P. (2013). A Case Study on the Impact of Customization, Fitness, and Operational Characteristics on Enterprise-wide System Success, User Satisfaction and System Use. *Journal of Global Information Management, 21*(1), 19–41. doi:10.4018/jgim.2013010102

Ng, M. M. T., & Tan, M. T. K. (2004). *Symbolic Processes on ERP versus "Legacy" System Support*. School of Computing, National University of Singapore.

Nitti, M., Girau, R., Floris, A., & Atzori, L. (2014, May). On adding the social dimension to the internet of vehicles: Friendship and middleware. In *Communications and Networking (BlackSeaCom), 2014 IEEE International Black Sea Conference on* (pp. 134-138). IEEE.

NoBullying.com. (2017). *A Comprehensive View of Cyberbullying in the USA*. Retrieved July 28, 2017, from https://nobullying.com/cyberbullying-in-usa/

Norazah, M. S. (2013). Students' dependence on smart phones: The influence of social needs, social influences and convenience. *Campus-Wide Information Systems, 30*(2), 124–134. doi:10.1108/10650741311306309

O'Brien, J. (1996). *Management Information Systems – Managing Information Technology in the Networked Enterprise*. IRWIN.

O'Keeffe, A., Ozuem, W., & Lancaster, G. (2016). Leadership Marketing: An Exploratory Study. *Journal of Strategic Marketing*, *24*(5), 418–443. doi:10.1080/0965254X.2014.1001867

OECD. (2017). *Embracing Innovation in Government - Global Trends*. Retrieved from http://www.oecd.org/gov/innovative-government/embracing-innovation-in-government-global-trends.htm

Oliveira, A. (2010). Governance of Information Systems – Why. ISGec Conference, Madrid, Spain.

Oliveira, A. (1996). The Potential Value of Information Systems. [in Portuguese]. *Management Studies*, *3*(1), 3–18.

Oliveira, A. (1999). The Importance of Information Systems for Industry [in Portuguese]. *Information Systems*, (11), 21–26.

Oliveira, A. (2004). *Analysis of the Investment in Systems and Technologies of the Information and the Communication*. Sílabo Publishing. (in Portuguese)

Oliveira, A. (2009). *Information & Information Systems – Facts, myths, mitifications, mystifications, dangerous half-truths & lack of common sense*. Refertelecom Publishing. (in Portuguese)

Oliver, R. (1980). A cognitive Model of The Antecedents and Consequences of Satisfaction Decisions. *JMR, Journal of Marketing Research*, *17*(4), 460–469. doi:10.2307/3150499

Oliver, R. L. (1997). *Satisfaction: A Behavioural Perspective on the Consumer*. New York: Irwin/McGraw-Hill.

Oliver, R. L. (1999). Whence Consumer Loyalty? *Journal of Marketing*, *63*(10), 33–44. doi:10.2307/1252099

Olsen, F. (2002). The Power of Portals. *The Chronicle of Higher Education*, *48*(48), A32–A34.

Olson, D. L., & Zhao, F. (2006). Critical Success Factors in ERP Upgrade Projects. In Research and Practical Issues of Enterprise Information Systems (Vol. 205, pp. 569-578). Boston: Springer. doi:10.1007/0-387-34456-X_58

Orth, U. R., & De Marchi, R. (2007). Understanding The Relationships Between Functional, Symbolic, And Experiential Brand Beliefs, Product Experiential Attributes, And Product Schema Advertising-Trial Interactions Revisited. *Journal of Marketing Theory and Practice*, *15*(3), 219–233. doi:10.2753/MTP1069-6679150303

Oswald, L. R. (1999). Culture Swapping: Consumption and the Ethnogenesis of Middle-Class Haitan Immigrants. *The Journal of Consumer Research*, *25*(3), 303–318. doi:10.1086/209541

Ozuem, W., Howell, K. E., & Lancaster, G. (2008). Communicating in the New Interactive Marketplace. *European Journal of Marketing*, *42*(9/10), 1059–1083. doi:10.1108/03090560810891145

Ozuem, W., Patel, A., Howell, K., & Lancaster, G. (2017). An exploration of consumers' response to online service recovery initiatives. *International Journal of Market Research, 54*(1).

Ozuem, W., Thomas, T., & Lancaster, G. (2016). The Influence of Customer Loyalty on Small Island Economies: An empirical and Exploratory Study. *Journal of Strategic Marketing, 24*(6), 447–469. doi:10.1080/0965254X.2015.1011205

Panorama. (2017). *2017 Report on ERP Systems & Enterprise Software*. Retrieved from https://www.panorama-consulting.com/wp-content/uploads/2017/07/2017-ERP-Report.pdf

Paré, G., & Elam, J. J. (1997). Using Case Study Research to Build Theories of IT Implementation. In A. S. Lee, J. Liebenau, & J. I. DeGross (Eds.), *Information Systems and Qualitative Research* (pp. 542–568). London: Chapman & Hall. doi:10.1007/978-0-387-35309-8_27

Park, R. E. (1959). Race and Culture. Glencoe, IL: The Free Press.

Park, C. S., & Srinivasan, V. (1994). A Survey-Based Method for Measuring and Understanding Brand Equity and Its Extendibility. *JMR, Journal of Marketing Research, 31*(2), 271–288. doi:10.2307/3152199

Park, C. W. B., Jaworski, J., & Maclnnis, D. J. (1986). Strategic Brand Concept-Image Management. *Journal of Marketing, 50*(4), 135–145. doi:10.2307/1251291

Park, C. W., Eisingerich, A. B., & Park, J. W. (2013). Attachment– Aversion (AA) Model of Customer–Brand Relationships. *Journal of Consumer Psychology, 23*(2), 229–248. doi:10.1016/j.jcps.2013.01.002

Park, C. W., MacInnis, D. J., & Priester, J. R. (2009). Research Directions on Strong Brand Relationships. In D. J. MacInnis, C. W. Park, & J. R. Priester (Eds.), *Handbook of Brand Relationships*. Armonk, NY: M.E. Sharpe.

Park, J. K., & Yang, S. (2006). The Moderating Role of Consumer Trust and Experiences: Value Driven Usage of Mobile Technology. *International Journal of Mobile Marketing, 1*(2), 24–32.

Paul, L. G. (2008). *How to avoid mistakes during ERP upgrades*. Retrieved from http://searchmanufacturingerp.techtarget.com/news/1325046/How-to-avoid-mistakes-during-ERP-upgrades

Paul, L. G. (2009). *ERP upgrade planning best practices demystified*. Retrieved from http://searchmanufacturingerp.techtarget.com/news/1345398/ERP-upgrade-planning-best-practices-demystified

Paul, A. (n.d.). Nigerian University System Management Portal (NUSMAP). *User Guide. Academic Press.*

Paul, A. K., & Anantharaman, R. N. (2004). Influence of HRM practices on organizational commitment: A study among software professionals in India. *Human Resource Development Quarterly, 15*(1), 77–88. doi:10.1002/hrdq.1088

Pearlson, K. E., & Saunders, C. S. (2013). *Managing and Using Information Systems – A Strategic Approach*. Hoboken, NJ: John Wiley & Sons.

Penrose, E. T. (1995). *The Theory of the Growth of the Firm* (3rd ed.). Oxford University Press. doi:10.1093/0198289774.001.0001

Pepitone, J. (2012). SOPA Explained: What It Is and Why It Matters. *CNN Money*. Retrieved November 28, 2017, from http://money.cnn.com/2012/01/17/technology/sopa_explained/index.htm

Peppard, J., & Ward, J. (2016). *The strategic management of information systems: Building a digital strategy*. John Wiley & Sons.

Pesonen, H.-L., & Horn, S. (2014). Evaluating the climate SWOT as a tool for defining climate strategies for business. *Journal of Cleaner Production*, *64*, 562–571. doi:10.1016/j.jclepro.2013.10.013

Peter, J., Paul, J., Olson, C., & Grunert, K. G. (1999). *Consumer Behaviour and Marketing Strategy* (European Edition). London: McGraw Hill.

Peters, T. (1987). *Thriving on Chaos*. New York: Alfred A. Knopf.

Phau, I., & Kong, C. L. (2001). Brand Personality and Consumer Self Expression: Single or Dual Carriageway? *Journal of Brand Management*, *8*(6), 428–444. doi:10.1057/palgrave.bm.2540042

Plummer, J. T. (1984). How Personality Makes a Difference. *Journal of Advertising Research*, *24*(6), 27–31.

Pojasek, R. B. (2007). A framework for business sustainability. *Environmental Quality Management*, *17*(2), 81–88. doi:10.1002/tqem.20168

Ponemon Institute. (2017). *Cost of Data Breach Study*. Available at www.ibm.com/security/data-breach/index.html

Posey, C., Raja, U., Crossler, R. E., & Burns, A. J. (2017). Taking stock of organisations' protection of privacy: Categorising and assessing threats to personally identifiable information in the USA. *European Journal of Information Systems*, 1–20.

Postman, N. (1998, March). *Five Things We Need to Know About Technological Change*. Address to New Tech '98 Conference, Denver, CO.

Quang, L., Bio, L., Shurong, H., & Amei, C. (2012). Design and Exploitation of Integrated Management System in University Laboratories. *Proceedings of the 2nd International Conference on Consumer Electronics, Communications and Networks*, 962 – 965.

Quinton, S. (2013). The Community Brand Paradigm: A Response to Brand Management's Bilemma in the Digital Era. *Journal of Marketing Management*, *29*(7-8), 7–8, 912–932. doi:10.1080/0267257X.2012.729072

RadiologyInfo.com. (2017). *Magnetic Resonance Imaging (MRI) – Body*. Retrieved July 24, 2017, from https://www.radiologyinfo.org/en/info.cfm?pg=bodymr

Rahim, M. M., Shanks, G., & Johnston, R. B. (2011). A Cross Industry Comparison of Inter-Organisational Systems Implementation Activities. *Journal of Electronic Commerce Research*, *11*(2), 215–243. doi:10.100710660-010-9074-9

Rao, H., Davis, F. G., & Ward, A. (2000). Embeddedness, Social Identity and Mobility: Why Firms Leave the NASDAQ and Join the New York Stock Exchange. *Administrative Science Quarterly*, *45*(2), 268–292. doi:10.2307/2667072

Raphael, T. (2014). The Pros and Cons of Texting for Talent. *ERE*. Retrieved July 29, 2017, from https://www.eremedia.com/ere/the-pros-and-cons-of-texting-for-talent/

Reed, A. I. I. (2002). Social Identity as a Useful Perspective for Self-Concept Based Consumer Research. *Journal of Psychology and Marketing*, *19*(3), 235–266. doi:10.1002/mar.10011

Reicheld, F. (1996). *The Loyalty Effect: The Hidden Force behind Growth, Profits, and Lasting Value*. Boston: Harvard Business School Press.

Reilly, C. (2015, May 31). *Data breach sees Woolworths gift cards leaked in email bungle*. Retrieved November 17, 2017, from https://www.cnet.com/au/news/data-breach-sees-woolworths-gift-cards-leaked-in-email-bungle/

Rezvani, A., Dong, L., & Khosravi, P. (2017). Promoting the Continuing Usage of Strategic Information Systems: The Role of Supervisory Leadership in the Successful Implementation Of Enterprise Systems. *International Journal of Information Management*, *37*(5), 417–430. doi:10.1016/j.ijinfomgt.2017.04.008

Richards, C. (1996). Agile manufacturing: beyond lean. *Production & Inventory Management*, 60-4.

Richardson, R. (2011). *2010/2011 Computer Crime and Security Survey*. Retrieved from http://gatton.uky.edu/FACULTY/PAYNE/ACC324/CSISurvey2010.pdf

Richardson, N. (2016). Review of Soft Systems Methodology in Action. *Philosophy of Management*, *15*(3), 1–4. doi:10.100740926-015-0023-5

Richins, M. L. (1994). Valuing Things: The Public and Private Meanings of Possessions. *The Journal of Consumer Research*, *21*(10), 504–521. doi:10.1086/209414

Robert, H., Isabell, S., Kiess, O., Ingo, B., Sacha, M., & Bradley, L. (2016). *IT Service Management for DevOps*. Retrieved from IBM: https://www.ibm.com/developerworks/community/files/form/anonymous/api/library/42529e82-173a- 4f45-805b-93d9eb35ffa6/document/19b71c8c-1675-4727-a3ab-b259ba1d49e6/ media/ITSM%20Reference%20Architecture%20-%20DevOps%20-%20Whitepaper.pdf

Robinson, S. L., & Bennett, R. J. (1995). A Typology of Deviant Workplace Behaviors: A Multidimensional Scaling Study. *Academy of Management Journal*, *38*(2), 555–572. doi:10.2307/256693

Robischon, N. (2017, February 13). Why Amazon Is The World's Most Innovative Company Of 2017. *Fast Company*.

Roos, I. (1999). Switching processes in customer relationships. *Journal of Service Research*, *2*(1), 376–393. doi:10.1177/109467059921006

Roselius, T. (1971). Consumer Rankings of Risk Reduction Method. *Journal of Marketing*, *35*(1), 55–61. doi:10.2307/1250565

Rotman, D. (2013). How Technology Is Destroying Jobs. *MIT Technology Review*. Retrieved August 1, 2017, from https://www.technologyreview.com/s/515926/how-technology-is-destroying-jobs/

Ruth, J. A. (2001). Promoting a Brand's Emotion Benefits: The Influence of Emotion Categorization Processes on Consumer Evaluations. *Journal of Consumer Psychology*, *11*(2), 99–113. doi:10.1207/S15327663JCP1102_03

Sambhanthan, A., & Potdar, V. (2016a). Business sustainability frameworks a survey. In *2016 IEEE/ACIS 14th International Conference on Software Engineering Research, Management and Applications, SERA 2016* (pp. 171–177). IEEE. 10.1109/SERA.2016.7516143

Sambhanthan, A., & Potdar, V. (2016c). Waste management strategies for Software Development companies: An explorative text analysis of business sustainability reports. In *2016 IEEE 14th International Conference on Software Engineering Research, Management and Applications (SERA)* (pp. 179–184). IEEE. 10.1109/SERA.2016.7516144

Sambhanthan, A., & Potdar, V. (2017). A Study of the Parameters Impacting Sustainability in Information Technology Organizations. *International Journal of Knowledge Based Organizations*. Retrieved from https://www.igi-global.com/article/a-study-of-the-parameters-impacting-sustainability-in-information-technology-organizations/182275

Sambhanthan, A., & Potdar, V. (2015). Green Business Practices for Software Development Companies. *International Journal of Enterprise Information Systems*, *11*(3), 13–26. doi:10.4018/IJEIS.2015070102

Sambhanthan, A., & Potdar, V. (2016b). Organisations' Responsibilities towards Corporate Sustinability. *International Journal of Strategic Information Technology and Applications*, *7*(2), 44–58. doi:10.4018/IJSITA.2016040104

Sambhanthan, A., Potdar, V., & Chang, E. (2017). *Business Sustainability Conceptualization*. Springer International Publishing; doi:10.1007/978-3-319-51472-7_1

Samuelson, P. (2012). Can Online Piracy Be Stopped By Law? *Communications of the ACM*, *55*(7), 25–27. doi:10.1145/2209249.2209260

Sarikaya. (2002). Asimetrik bilgi çerçevesinde müzayedeler. Cumhuriyet Üniversitesi İktisadi ve İdari Bilimler Fakültesi Dergisi, 3(2).

Sathish, M., Kumar, K. S., Naveen, K. J., & Jeevanantham, V. (2011). A Study on Consumer Switching Behaviour in Cellular Service Provider: A Study with reference to Chennai. *Far East Journal of Psychology and Business*, *2*(2), 72.

Schwartz, A. (2015). *The 5 Most Common Unethical Behaviors in the Workplace*. Retrieved July 28, 2017, from https://www.bizjournals.com/philadelphia/blog/guest-comment/2015/01/most-common-unethical-behaviors-in-the.html

Security Analysis on China Campus Network and Construction on Network Security System. (2011, November). *Journal of Convergence Information Technology*, *6*(11). doi:10.4156/jcit.vol6.issue11.19

Seddon, P. B., Calvert, C., & Yang, S. (2010). A Multi-Project Model of Key Factors Affecting Organizational Benefits from Enterprise Systems. *Management Information Systems Quarterly*, *34*(2), 305–328. doi:10.2307/20721429

Sedera, D., Lokuge, S., Grover, V., Sarker, S., & Sarker, S. (2016). Innovating with Enterprise Systems and Digital Platforms: A Contingent Resource-based Theory View. *Information & Management*, *53*(3), 366–379. doi:10.1016/j.im.2016.01.001

Seiders, K., & Tigert, D. J. (1997). Impact of Market Entry and Competitive Structure on Store Switching/Store Loyalty. *International Review of Retail, Distribution and Consumer Research*, *7*(3), 227–247. doi:10.1080/095939697343003

Şenalp. (n.d.). Dünden bugüne Kurumsal İktisat. Retrieved from https://www.academia.edu/3340855/_2007_D ünden_Bugüne_Kurumsal_iktisat_Eyüp_özveren_der._Kurumsal_i ktisat_imge_Yayınevi_s._45-93

Serova, E. (2013). The Role of Agent Based Modelling in the Design of Management Decision Processes. *The Electronic Journal Information Systems Evaluation, 16*(1), 71-80. Available online at www.ejise.com

Sethi, A. S., & Hnatyshyn, V. Y. (2013). *The Practical OPNET Users Guide for Computer Network Simulation*. Boca Raton, FL: CRS Press.

Shang, S., & Seddon, P. B. (2003). A Comprehensive Framework for Classifying the Benefits of ERP Systems. In G. Shanks, P. B. Seddon, & L. P. Willcocks (Eds.), *Second-Wave Enterprise Resource Planning Systems: Implementing for Effectiveness* (pp. 74–101). Cambridge, UK: Cambridge University Press. doi:10.1017/CBO9780511815072.004

Shankar, V., Smith, A. K., & Rangaswamy, A. (2003). Customer Satisfaction and Loyalty in Online and Offline Environments. *International Journal of Research in Marketing*, *20*(2), 153–175. doi:10.1016/S0167-8116(03)00016-8

Shapiro, L. M. (2010). *Severe Market Dissruption on 6th May, 2010: Congressional Testimony*. Collingdale, PA: Diane Publishing Co.

Sherif, C. W., & Sherif, M. (1967). *Attitude, Ego-involvement, and Change*. Westport, CT: Green Wood Press.

Sheth, J. N., Newman, B. I., & Gross, B. L. (1991). Why We Buy What We Buy: A Theory of Consumption Values. *Journal of Business Research*, *22*(2), 159–170. doi:10.1016/0148-2963(91)90050-8

Shimp, T. A., & Madden, T. J. (1988). Consumer-Object Relations: A Conceptual Framework Based Analogously on Sternberg's Triangular Theory of Love. *Advances in Consumer Research. Association for Consumer Research (U. S.)*, *15*(1), 163–168.

Shrivastava, P. (1995). The role of corporations in achieving ecological sustainability. *Academy of Management Review*, *20*(4), 936–960. doi:10.5465/AMR.1995.9512280026

Silva Molina, L. F. (2005). How to Identify and Measure the Level of Alignment between IT and Business Governance. *Proceedings of the PICMET*.

Sirgy, J. M. (1982). Self-Concept in Consumer Behaviour: A Critical Review. *The Journal of Consumer Research*, *9*(12), 287–300. doi:10.1086/208924

Sirgy, M. J., Grewal, D., & Mangleburg, T. (2000). Retail Environment, Self-Congruity, and Retail Patronage: An Integrative Model and a Research Agenda. *Journal of Business Research*, *49*(2), 127–138. doi:10.1016/S0148-2963(99)00009-0

Slawsby, A., Leibovitch, A. M., & Giusto, R. (2003). *Worldwide Mobile Phone Forecast and Analysis, 2003-2007*. IDC Report, No. 29586.

Sloot, L. M., Verhoef, P. C., & Franses, P. H. (2005). The Impact of Brand Equity and the Hedonic Level of Products on Consumer Stock-Out Reactions. *Journal of Retailing*, *81*(1), 15–34. doi:10.1016/j.jretai.2005.01.001

Smaldone, S., Han, L., Shankar, P., & Iftode, L. (2008, April). Roadspeak: enabling voice chat on roadways using vehicular social networks. In *Proceedings of the 1st Workshop on Social Network Systems* (pp. 43-48). ACM. 10.1145/1435497.1435505

Sneada, J. T., & Wright, E. (2014). E-government research in the United States. *Government Information Quarterly*, *31*(1), 129–136. doi:10.1016/j.giq.2013.07.005

Solomon, M. R. (1983). The Role of Products as Social Stimuli: A Symbolic Interactionism Perspective. *The Journal of Consumer Research*, *10*(10), 319–329. doi:10.1086/208971

Somonite, T. (2012). What Facebook Knows. *Technology Review*. Retrieved from https://www.technologyreview.com/s/428150/what-facebook-knows/

Soomro, Z. A., Shah, M. H., & Ahmed, J. (2016). Information security management needs more holistic approach: A literature review. *International Journal of Information Management*, *36*(2), 215–225. doi:10.1016/j.ijinfomgt.2015.11.009

Spence. (1973). Job Market Signaling. *The Quarterly Journal of Economics*, *87*(3), 355–374. doi:10.2307/1882010

Spence. (1976a). Competition in salaries, credentials and signaling prerequisites for jobs. *Quarterly Journal of Economics, 90*, 51-74.

Spence. (1976b). Informational aspects of market structure: An introduction. *Quarterly Journal of Economics, 90*, 591-597.

Spence. (1978). Tacit co-ordination and imperfect information. *The Canadian Journal of Economics. Revue Canadienne d'Economique, 11*(3), 490–505. doi:10.2307/134318

Spence, M. (2002). Signaling in Retrospect and the Informational Structure of Markets. *The American Economic Review, 92*(3), 434–459. doi:10.1257/00028280260136200

Stamatović, M., & Kurij, K. (2003). Introducion to Strategic Managemet. Savez in enjera i tehni ara Srbije – Centar za razvoj, Belgrade.

Statista. (2016). *Number of smartphone users worldwide from 2014 to 2020 (in billions)*. Retrieved from https://www.statista.com/statistics/330695/number-of-smartphone-users-worldwide/

Stephens, D. O. (1999). The Globalization of Information Technology in Multinational Corporations. *The Information Management Journal, 33*(3), 66–71.

Stern, B. B., Thompson, J. C., & Arnould, E. J. (1998). Narrative Analysis of a Marketing Relationship: The Consumer's Perspective. *Journal of Psychology and Marketing, 15*(3), 195–214. doi:

Stewart, H., Stewart, H., Jürjens, J., & Jürjens, J. (2017). Information security management and the human aspect in organizations. *Information & Computer Security, 25*(5), 494–534. doi:10.1108/ICS-07-2016-0054

Stigler. (1961, June). The economics of information. *Journal of Political Economy, 69*(3), 213–225. doi:10.1086/258464

Stiglitz. (2000). The contribution of the economics of information to twentieth century economics. The Quarterly Journal of Economics, 1441–1478.

Sung, Y., & Kim, J. (2010). Effects of Brand Personality on Brand Trust and Brand Affect. *Journal of Psychology and Marketing, 27*(7), 639–661. doi:10.1002/mar.20349

Sushandoyo, D., & Magnusson, T. (2014). Strategic niche management from a business perspective: Taking cleaner vehicle technologies from prototype to series production. *Journal of Cleaner Production, 74*, 17–26. doi:10.1016/j.jclepro.2014.02.059

Swait, J., & Erdem, T. (2007). Brand Effects on Choice and Choice Set Formation under Uncertainty. *Journal of Marine Science, 26*(5), 679–697. doi:10.1287/mksc.1060.0260

Swanton, B. (2004, September 21). *Build ERP Upgrade Costs into the Business Change Programme - Not the IT Budget*. Retrieved from http://www.computerweekly.com/

Swanton, B., Samaraweera, D., & Klein, E. (2004). *Minimizing ERP Upgrade Costs Requires Synchronizing with Business Improvement Projects*. Retrieved from Boston: http://www.amrresearch.com/

Sweeney, J. C., & Soutar, G. N. (2001). Consumer Perceived Value: The Development of a Multiple Item Scale. *Journal of Retailing*, *77*(2), 203–220. doi:10.1016/S0022-4359(01)00041-0

Tajfel, H., & Turner, J. C. (1979). *The Social Identity Theory of Inter-Group Behaviour, in Psychology of Intergroup Relations*. Chicago: Nelson-Hall.

Tan, J. (2014). *Research and system implementation of mobile phone virus network detection and system implementation* (Unpublished doctoral dissertation). South China University of Technology, Guangzhou, China.

Tao, M., Shaoqian, W., Minglian, L., & Baozhu, W. (2012). The Research on Strategy of Building Campus Network Security Based on University Management. *Proceedings of the 2012 International Conference on Mechanical and Electrical Engineering*, 142 – 147. Available online at www.sciencedirect.com

Telatar. (2004). Politik İktisat Politikası. Ankara: İmaj Yayınları.

The Nigerian University Commission. (n.d.). Retrieved from www.onlinenigeria.com

Thompson, M. (2016). *Harmonised Taxonomies of Security and Resilience: A Suitable Foundation for the Security Discipline* (Doctoral dissertation). University of New South Wales, Canberra, Australia.

Thompson, N. (2012). How to Get Privacy Right. *New Yorker Magazine*. Retrieved July 28, 2017, from http://www.newyorker.com/culture/culture-desk/how-to-get-privacy-right

Thompson, D. V., Hamilton, R. W., & Rust, R. T. (2005). Feature Fatigue: When Product Capabilities become too much of a Good Thing. *JMR, Journal of Marketing Research*, *42*(4), 431–442. doi:10.1509/jmkr.2005.42.4.431

Trusson, C. R., Doherty, N. F., & Hislop, D. (2014). Knowledge sharing using IT service management tools: Conflicting discourses and incompatible practices. *Information Systems Journal*, *24*(4), 347–371. doi:10.1111/isj.12025

Tseng, S.-C., & Hung, S.-W. (2013). A framework identifying the gaps between customers' expectations and their perceptions in green products. *Journal of Cleaner Production*, *59*, 174–184. doi:10.1016/j.jclepro.2013.06.050

Tucker, P. (2014, July). How Technology Is Transforming the Future of National Security. *Defense One*, 1-8.

Uebernickel, B.-S. Z. (2006). Service-Engineering: A process model for the development of IS services. *Proceedings of the European and Mediterranean Conference on Information Systems (EMCIS)*.

Uncles, M., & Laurent, G. (1997). Editorial, Special Issue on Loyalty. *International Journal of Research in Marketing*, *14*(5), 399–404. doi:10.1016/S0167-8116(97)80224-8

Underwood, R. L., Klein, N. M., & Burke, R. R. (2001). Packaging Communication: Attentional Effects of Product Imagery. *Journal of Product and Brand Management*, *10*(7), 403–422. doi:10.1108/10610420110410531

van Bon, E. (2007). *Foundations of IT Service Management based on ITIL v3*. Van Haren Publishing.

van Grembergen, H. (2009). *COBIT as a Framework for Enterprise Governance of IT*. Boston: Springer US. doi:10.1007/978-0-387-84882-2_5

van Schaik, P., Jeske, D., Onibokun, J., Coventry, L., Jansen, J., & Kusev, P. (2017). Risk perceptions of cyber-security and precautionary behaviour. *Computers in Human Behavior*, *75*, 547–559. doi:10.1016/j.chb.2017.05.038

Van Trijp, H. C. M., Hoyer, W. D., & Inman, J. J. (1996). Why Switch? Product Category-Level Explanations for True Variety-Seeking Behaviour. *JMR, Journal of Marketing Research*, *33*(3), 281–292. doi:10.2307/3152125

Vanguard Newspaper. (2013). *NUC. Nigerian Varsities go paperless*. Retrieved from www.vanguardngr.com

Vardareri & Dursun. (2010). Asimetrik bilgi çerçevesinde 2008 küresel krizinin incelenmesi. Bilgi Ekonomisi ve Yönetim Dergisi, 5(1).

Vernadat, F. (1999). Research agenda for agile manufacturing. *International Journal of Agile*, *1*(1), 37–40.

Vinkhuyzen, O. M., & Karlsson-Vinkhuyzen, S. I. (2014). The role of moral leadership for sustainable production and consumption. *Journal of Cleaner Production*, *63*, 102–113. doi:10.1016/j.jclepro.2013.06.045

Virtusa Environment Day. (2010). Retrieved May 18, 2015, from http://www.csrwire.com/press_releases/29830--2010-Virtusa-Environment-Day

Visentin, L. (2015, May). Woolworths Leaks $1 Million of Gift Cards in Massive Data Breach Debacle. *The Sydney Morning Herald*. Retrieved from www.smh.com.au/digital-life/consumer-security/woolworths-leaks-1-million-of-gift-cards-in-massive-data-breach-debacle-20150530-ghd8wl.html

Von Hayek. (1945, September). The use of knowledge in society. *The American Economic Review*, *35*(4), 519–530.

Von Hayek. (n.d.a). Economics and knowledge. Retrieved from http://www.jstor.org/stable/2548786

Von Hayek. (n.d.b). The pretence of knowledge. Retrieved from http://about.jstor.org/terms

Vorobyov, K., Krishnan, P., & Stocks, P. (2012). A Low-Overhead, Value-Tracking Approach to Information Flow Security. *International Conference on Software Engineering and Formal Methods*, (73), 367-381. 10.1007/978-3-642-33826-7_26

Wailgum, T. (2010, November 18). *Why ERP Upgrade Fears Affect On-Premise versus SaaS Decisions.* Retrieved from http://www.cio.com/article/637874/Why_ERP_Upgrade_Fears_Affect_On_Premise_versus_SaaS_Decisions

Wang, Y., Liao, Z. & Xia, C. (2015). Discussion on the information security of smart phones. *Technology Square*, (11), 50-60.

Wang, D., Park, S., & Fesenmaier, D. R. (2012). The Role of Smartphones in Mediating the Touristic Experience. *Journal of Travel Research*, *51*(4), 371–387. doi:10.1177/0047287511426341

Wang, E. T. G., Klein, G., & Jiang, J. J. (2006). ERP Misfit: Country of Origin and Organizational Factors. *Journal of Management Information Systems*, *23*(1), 263–292. doi:10.2753/MIS0742-1222230109

Wang, E. T. G., Shih, S.-P., Jiang, J. J., & Klein, G. (2008). The Consistency among Facilitating Factors and ERP Implementation Success: A Holistic View of Fit. *Journal of Systems and Software*, *81*(9), 1609–1621. doi:10.1016/j.jss.2007.11.722

Wangen, G. (2015). The Role of Malware in Reported Cyber Espionage: A Review of the Impact and Mechanism. *Information*, *6*(2), 183–211. doi:10.3390/info6020183

Wang, P., Liu, Q., & Qi, Y. (2014). Factors influencing sustainable consumption behaviors: A survey of the rural residents in China. *Journal of Cleaner Production*, *63*, 152–165. doi:10.1016/j.jclepro.2013.05.007

Wan, J., Liu, J., Shao, Z., Vasilakos, A. V., Imran, M., & Zhou, K. (2016). Mobile crowd sensing for traffic prediction in internet of vehicles. *Sensors (Basel)*, *16*(1), 88. doi:10.339016010088 PMID:26761013

Wanke, M., Bohner, G., & Jurkowitsch, A. (1997). There Are Many Reasons to Drive a BMW: Does Imagined Ease of Argument Generation Influence Attitudes? *The Journal of Consumer Research*, *24*(9), 170–177. doi:10.1086/209502

Warkentin, M., & Willison, R. (2009). Behavioral and policy issues in information systems security: The insider threat. *European Journal of Information Systems*, *18*(2), 101–105. doi:10.1057/ejis.2009.12

Wee, T. T. T. (2004). Extending Human Personality to Brands: The Stability Factor. *Journal of Brand Management*, *11*(4), 317–330. doi:10.1057/palgrave.bm.2540176

Wei, W., Shengzhong, Y., & Hong, H. (2010). Design of Portal-Based Uniform Identity Authentication System in Campus Network. *Proceedings of the International Conference on Multimedia Communications*, 112 – 115.

Welch, E. W., Hinnant, C. C., & Moon, M. J. (2004). Linking Citizen Satisfaction with E-Government and Trust in Government. *Journal of Public Administration: Research and Theory*, *15*(3), 371–391. doi:10.1093/jopart/mui021

Welcome to NUSMAP! (n.d.). Retrieved from https://nusmap.nucdp.edu.ng/institution_login.aspx

Westbrook, R. A. (1987). Product/Consumption Based Affective Responses and Post Purchase Processes. *JMR, Journal of Marketing Research*, *24*(3), 258–270. doi:10.2307/3151636

Whittaker, Z. (2013). *Google's European Conundrum: When Does Privacy Mean Censorship?* Retrieved July 28, 2017, from https://www.cnet.com/news/googles-european-conundrum-when-does-privacy-mean-censorship/

Wilcocks, L. (2013). *Information management: The evaluation of information systems investments*. Springer Science Business Media.

Winniford, C. (2009). *Confusion in the Ranks: IT Service Management Practice and Terminology*. Academic Press.

Woodard Charles Jason. (2006). *Architectural Strategy and Design Evolution in Complex Engineered Systems*. Retrieved from http://citeseerx.ist.psu.edu/viewdoc/download?doi=10.1.1.109.3608&rep=rep1&type=pdf

Workman, M., Bommer, W. H., & Straub, D. (2008). Security lapses and the omission of information security measures: A threat control model and empirical test. *Computers in Human Behavior*, *24*(6), 2799–2816. doi:10.1016/j.chb.2008.04.005

Xie, S. (2011). Planning, Designing and Building Large-Scale Network at Campus. *Proceedings of the 3rd International Conference on Computer Research and Development*, 495 – 498.

Xing, K. (2014). *College students mobile phone: mobile market share accounted for about 70%*. Retrieved from http://news.youth.cn/gn/201404/

Xu, H., & Gong D. (2016). Research on the way, hidden danger and prevention strategy of personal information leakage. *Legal System*, (13), 176-177.

Yang, L. (2012). Campus Network Group Design Based on Cloud Computing. *Proceedings of the 7th International Conference on Computer Science and Education (ICCSE)*.

Yi, Y. (1990). A Critical Review of Consumer Satisfaction. In V. Zeithaml (Ed.), American Marketing Association (pp. 68–123). Chicago: Academic Press.

Yin, J., Gao, Y., & Xu, H. (2014). Survey and analysis of consumers' behaviour of waste mobile phone recycling in China. *Journal of Cleaner Production*, *65*, 517–525. doi:10.1016/j.jclepro.2013.10.006

Yin, R. K. (2003). *Case Study Research: Design and Methods* (3rd ed.). Thousand Oaks, CA: Sage Publications.

Yoo, B., Donthu, N., & Lee, S. (2000). An Examination of Selected Marketing Mix Elements and Brand Equity. *Journal of the Academy of Marketing Science*, *28*(2), 195–211. doi:10.1177/0092070300282002

Youssef, S. (2013). *Network Modelling and Simulation Lecture Notes*. Anglia Ruskin University. (Unpublished)

Yusuf, Y., Sarhadi, M., & Gunasekaran, A. (1999). Agile manufacturing: The drivers, concepts and attributes. *International Journal of Production Economics*, *62*(1-2), 33–43. doi:10.1016/S0925-5273(98)00219-9

Zhang, J., & Bloemer, J. M. M. (2008). The Impact of Value Congruence on Consumer-Service Brand Relationships. *Journal of Service Research*, *11*(8), 161–178. doi:10.1177/1094670508322561

Zheng, K., Zheng, Q., Chatzimisios, P., Xiang, W., & Zhou, Y. (2015). Heterogeneous vehicular networking: A survey on architecture, challenges, and solutions. *IEEE Communications Surveys and Tutorials*, *17*(4), 2377–2396. doi:10.1109/COMST.2015.2440103

Zuckerman, A. (2004). The Non-Techie CEO's Guide to Global Supply Chain Technology. *World Trade*, *18*(2), 30–34.

Zwass, V. (1998). *Foundations of Information Systems*. McGraw-Hill.

About the Contributors

Sahid Abdelkbir was born in Casablanca, Morroco, in 1983. He received the Master's degree in Network and computer sciences from the Hassan First University, Morroco in 2012. He is Ph.D. student In SIAD laboratory, ENCG, Hassan First University, since 2014. His current research interests include Agility, Information Systems, Information Systems Security, and cloud computing.

Dominic Appiah is a course coordinator at Pittsburgh University, London campus and lecturer in business and finance at the City Westminster College. He has a PhD in Marketing from Plymouth University, an MBA from the University of Wales and a Bachelor of Arts (Politics and Philosophy), from the University of Ghana. His research investigates the dynamics of consumer purchase intentions and building resistance to brand switching. Prior to joining academia, he worked at State Insurance Company, Ghana; GIA Insurance and Ghana International Bank, UK. Dominic is a fellow of the Higher Education Academy (HEA) and member of the Chartered Institute of Marketing (CIM), Chartered Institute of Insurance (CII) and the British Academy of Management (BAM).

Emmanuel W. Ayaburi is an Assistant Professor in department of Information Systems in the Robert C. Vackar College of Business & Entrepreneurship at The University of Texas Rio Grande Valley. He received his Ph.D. in Business Administration with a concentration in Information Systems from The University of Texas at San Antonio and his Master's in Business Administration from the Colorado Heights University. He holds a Bachelor of Science in Electrical Engineering KNUST in Ghana. Ayaburi's research interests include knowledge sharing, secure software design, information systems security and economics of information systems. His work has been accepted for publication at International Journal of Innovation and Technology Management. He has also published in a number of conference proceedings including International Conference on Information Systems (ICIS), Hawaii International Conference on System Sciences (HICSS) and Americas Conferences in Information Systems (AMCIS).

Mustapha Belaissaoui is a Professor of Computer Science and t at Hassan 1st Univesity, Settat, Morocco, President of the Moroccan Association of Free Software (AMP2L), and Head of the Department Management at the National School of Business and Management. He obtained his PhD in Artificial Intelligenc from Mohammed V University in Rabat. His research interests are Combinatorial Optimization, Artificial Intelligence and Information Systems. He is the author and co-author of more than 60 papers including journals, conferences, chapters, and books, which appeared in refereed specialized journals and symposia.

Talal Butt is currently working as an Assistant Professor at the American University in the Emirates. He holds a P.h.D in the domain of Internet of Things from Loughborough University, UK. Before joining the American University in the Emirates, he worked as a part of 5GIC (5G Innovation Centre), the UK Government's funded initiative at the University of Surrey to develop 5G technologies. At 5GIC, he gained experience of working in a testbed team that owned the state-of-the-art mobile testbed and successfully developed and demonstrated novel research ideas. Dr. Butt is a published author and is passionate about next generation networks and protocols.

Razi Iqbal is an Assistant Professor at the College of Computer Information Technology at the American University in the Emirates. Dr Razi earned his PhD and Master's degree in Computer Science and Engineering from Akita University in Akita, Japan. He has published several papers in the areas of Computer Science and Engineering, specifically in computer networks, wireless technologies and wearable computing. His current research areas are use of short range wireless technologies in Precision Agriculture, Transportation and Education. Prior to working at AUE, Dr Razi served as Chairman of the Department of Computer Science and IT at Lahore Leads University, Lahore, Pakistan. He has also served as Director ORIC (Office of Research, Innovation and Commercialization) at the same institute. During his tenure at Lahore Leads University his responsibilities were to administer the Computer Science and IT Department, design research policies for the university and teaching at undergraduate and graduate levels. He has also worked as a Research Scientist at Al-Khawarizmi Institute of Computer Science (KICS), University of Engineering and Technology (UET), Lahore, Pakistan.

Mounir Kehal gained a BSc in Computing and a MBA from the American International University in London, UK, a MPhil and PhD in Computing from the University of Surrey, Guildford, UK. He is currently faculty in business analytics at Higher Colleges of Technology, Dubai, UAE. Prior to which he was associate professor in MIS (and was Dean) in the College of Business Administration at American

University in the Emirates. For sometime he was Associate Professor of Business Information Systems and Director of Strategic Planning and Accreditations at École Supérieure de Commerce – Rennes School of Business (Triple Crown accredited: AACSB, AMBA, EQUIS) in Brittany, France from spring 2010 till 2014. From 2004 till 2010, he was at the International University of Monaco – IUM, as Assistant Professor of Computing Science, Information Technology, Decision Systems and Knowledge Management. Before working with IUM, Dr. Kehal worked at the University of Surrey (School of E&PS, Department of Computing, Guildford, UK); at the same time he was conducting his doctoral research degree (MPhil and PhD) from 2001 till 2005. Hence, he was a Lecturer Assistant in E-Commerce, Knowledge Management and Business Strategy Modules. His research interests include knowledge management, international accreditations, curriculum management, business schools, and information systems to name a few.

Muhammad Laminu (MIET) received his National Diploma and Bachelor of Engineering Degree from Ramat Polytechnic Maiduguri and University of Maiduguri, Nigeria in 1995 and 2008 respectively. He just graduated from Anglia Ruskin University, Chelmsford with MSc. Mobile Telecommunications. He is a lecturer in the department of Electrical and Electronic Engineering at Ramat Polytechnic and his research interests are Cross-Layer Design, Mobility Management, Ad-hoc networks, Embedded Systems, and Electronic Systems Modelling.

Taowen Le is professor and former department chair of information systems and technologies at Weber State University. He is currently chair of the Business Division of Utah Academy of Sciences, Arts, and Letters.

Yassine Maleh is a PhD of the University Hassan 1st in Morocco, since 2013. He is IT Security Analyst at the National Port Agency in Morocco. He is Member of IEEE Communications Society and European Microwave Association, the International Association of Engineers IAENG and The Machine Intelligence Research Labs. Maleh has made contributions in the fields of information security and Privacy, Internet of Things Security, Wireless and Constrained Networks Security. His research interests include Information Security and Privacy, Internet of Things, and Networks Security. He has published over than 20 papers and 2 edited books. He has served and continues to serve on the executive and technical program committees and a reviewer of numerous international conference and journals such as IEEE Sensor Journal, International Journal of Security and Privacy, International Journal of Networks Security and International Journal of Sensor Networks and Data Communications.

Celeste See-Pui Ng is currently an Associate Professor of the Department of Information Management at Yuan Ze University. Dr. Ng received her PhD in management information system from the Queensland University of Technology, Australia. Dr. Ng has published research work and articles in the Information & Management, Journal of Information Technology (JIT), Journal of Global Information Management (JGIM), Journal of Systems and Software (JSS), Journal of Software Maintenance and Evolution: Research and Practice (JSME), Information Systems Frontier (ISF), International Journal of Enterprise Information System (IJEIS), among others. Dr. Ng's research interests include social commerce, social media brand page management, big data analytics, IS/IT success, cross-cultural issues, Enterprise Resource Planning (ERP) maintenance and upgrade issues.

Wilson Ozuem is a Senior Research Fellow at the University of Gloucestershire (UK). Professor Ozuem teaches and researches communications issues in computer-mediated marketing environments (CMMEs), particularly on marketing communications and the technology of fashion. The results of his research have been published in scholarly journals and conference papers, including European Journal of Marketing, Journal of Strategic Marketing, International Journal of Market Research etc. Professor Ozuem has undertaken numerous teaching assignments and doctoral supervisory roles in various universities, including Queens University (Canada), Plymouth University, University of East London, University of the West of Scotland, Arden University, University of West London, Cardiff Metropolitan University, University of Hertfordshire, Regents University (London), University of KwaZulu-Natal (South Africa), University of Warwick. He currently teaches MSc and MBA courses in marketing communications, Internet marketing, research methodology, and marketing management. Professor Wilson is a visiting professor at the University of Albania. He is a Senior Fellow of Higher Education Academy (SFHEA) and the Chartered Institute of Marketing (FCIM) and has worked as a marketing consultant for several companies and organizations. He received his BA in Business from the University of Portsmouth, Postgraduate Diploma from the University of the Arts (London), MA Marketing Communications from University of West London, MBA from London Metropolitan University, MEd (Educational Leadership and Management) from Open University (UK), Doctorate from Anglia Ruskin University and Postgraduate Degree in Educational Research from University of Cambridge.

Arunasalam Sambhanthan is a researcher in Information Systems and Business Sustainability with a verifiable track record of publications in peer reviewed journals, conferences and book chapters. Currently reading for a PhD at Curtin University,

Perth, Western Australia working on the area of software business sustainability funded by the prestigious Curtin Strategic International Research Scholarship.

Sufian Yousef is the creator and Director Telecommunication Engineering Research Group (TERG) at Anglia Ruskin University Chelmsford, UK since 2003. He is well known for his outstanding Academic Leadership in teaching and research in the fields of IT and Telecommunication Engineering with over 32 years lecturing and course development experience in Jordan Telecommunication College and Anglia Ruskin University. He has won the award of Royal Academy of Engineering for sabbatical to Marconi Research Centre in Great Baddow to carry out military research on ATM.

Babagana Zulum was born in August,1969 in Mafa local Government area of Borno State. After his elementary and secondary education, he went to Ramat Polytechnic, Maiduguri, where he obtained a National Diploma in Irrigation Engineering in 1988. From there, he proceeded to the University of Maiduguri to Study Agricultural Engineering between 1990 and 1994. Afterwards, he had his mandatory service year in Katsina State. Not satisfied with the thirst for knowledge, he still went ahead to obtain a masters degree in Soil and water Engineering from the university of Ibadan from 1997 to 1998. He came back to Maiduguri to his Alma-Mata to undertake a doctoral degree which was successfully completed in 2009 in Agric and Environmental Engineering. All along, he has been serving his state in various capacities as a technical officer up to the rank of a principal water engineer with Borno State Unified Local Government. In the year 2000 he took up an appointment with the University of Maiduguri as an assistant lecturer in the department of Agric Engineering, he went through the ranks to become a Senior Lecturer in 2008. During these years, he was at one time or the other in positions of responsibility, such as the siwes coordinator of his department from 2000 to 2006, Acting head of department, Agric Engineering from 2008 to 2009, Deputy Dean, Faculty of Engineering in 2010 and an Acting Dean of the same faculty in 2011 up to the time he assumed duty as the Rector of this Ramat polytechnic, Maiduguri. He has been a consultant to a lot of National and International bodies namely; World Bank, ARID, International Water Management Institute, Nigerian National Fadama III Project, just to mention few among others. He has over 30 publications both in National and International journals and attended several conferences both locally and internationally. Prof. Baba Gana Umara mni is a member of the prestigious national Institute for Policy and Strategic Studies (NIPPS).

Index

I

L

M

N

O

P

Q

S

www.ingramcontent.com/pod-product-compliance
Lightning Source LLC
LaVergne TN
LVHW080557300926
849162LV00005B/971